The Home Office Computing HANDBOOK

Editorial assistance for chapter 14 provided by AT&T

The Home Office Computing HANDBOOK

Provided exclusively to AT&T Home Business Resources customers by AT&T and the editors of *Home Office Computing*

Edited by
David Langendoen & Dan Costa

Published by Windcrest, an imprint of McGraw-Hill, Inc.
The name "Windcrest" is a registered trademark of McGraw-Hill, Inc.

This book is printed on recycled, acid-free paper containing a minimum of 50% total recycled fiber with 10% postconsumer de-inked fiber.

3 4 5 6 7 8 9 10 11 MAL/MAL 9 9 8 7 6 5 4

Library of Congress Cataloging-in-Publication Data

The home office computing handbook / by Home office computing; edited by
David Langendoen and Dan Costa.
p. cm.
Includes index.
ISBN 0-8306-4577-2
1. Home-based businesses—Data processing. 2. Small business--Data processing. 3. Microcomputers—Purchasing—Handbooks, manuals, etc. 4. Electronics office machines—Purchasing—Handbooks, manuals, etc. I. Langendoen, David. II. Costa, Dan. III. Home office computing.
HF5548.2.H5927 1993
658'.041—dc20 93-43605
CIP

Acquisitions editor: Brad J. Schepp
Editorial team: Joanne Slike, Executive Editor
Susan W. Kagey, Managing Editor
Susan J. Bonthron, Editor
Production team: Katherine G. Brown, Director
Ollie Harmon, Coding
Rose McFarland, Layout
Nancy K. Mickley, Proofreading
Joann Woy, Indexer
Design team: Jaclyn J. Boone, Designer
Brian Allison, Associate Designer
Cover design: Lori E. Schlosser

HOC1
0300194

Contents

Acknowledgments ix

Introduction xi

1 Office setup & design 1
Suggested office sites 1
Not recommended 2
Power supply 2
Bright ideas for better lighting 3
Designing your home office 4
Home office design solutions 5
Organizing your home office 6
Resources 8

2 Health & ergonomics 9
Staying healthy 9
Ergonomic furniture and supplies 10
Resources 13

3 Where to buy 15
Retail stores 15
Other sources 16
Resources 18

4 Buying computers 19
Desktop computers 19
Notebook computers 22
In general 24
Resources 24

5 Buying monitors 27
Overview 27
Size 27
Color 27
Video cards 27
Gray-scale monitors 28
Dot pitch 28
Refresh rate 28
Controls 28
Resources 28

6 Buying printers 29
Types of printers 29
Buying laser printers 30
Upgrading your laser 32
Resources 34

7 Buying phones & communications equipment 35
Telephones 35
Answering machines 35
Pagers 36
Cellular phones 36
Resources 39

8 Buying faxes, modems, & fax/modems 41
Fax machines 41
Modems 43
Fax/modems 45
Resources 45

9 Buying storage devices 47
Tape drives 47
Removable cartridge drives 49
CD-ROM drives 49
Getting the most from your hard drive 50
Resources 51

10 Buying copiers 53
Evaluating your needs 53
What to look for 53
Resources 54

11 Buying scanners 55
Types of scanners 55
Scanner options 55
Software 56
Resources 56

12 Preventing computer catastrophes 57
Minimize data loss 57
Preventative maintenance 58
Viruses 59
Power problems 60
Basic maintenance 61
"Acts of God" 62
Resources 63

13 Mobile computing 65
On the road 65
Power management 66
Remote access 67
Protecting your portable 67
Resources 68

14 Communications 69
Phone options and services 69
Three types of voice mail 69
Distinctive rings 70
Call-routing devices 70
Call waiting 70
Other services 71
Long distance 71
Small-office networks 72
Resources 73

15 Online services 75
Guide to online services 75
CompuServe 76
Helpful services and forums for home businesses 76
America Online 77
Prodigy 79
GEnie 80
Delphi 80
Task comparison 80
Internet 83
Finding information online 84
Resources 86

16 Information & time management 89
Personal information managers/contact managers 89
Electronic databases 90
Features to look for 91
File management 93
Software resources 95

17 Finance 97
Build a better business plan 97
Electronic bookkeeping and accounting 98
Steps in setting up a checkbook 99
Steps in setting up a double-entry bookkeeping system 100
Spreadsheets 101
Electronic investing 105
Resources 106
Accounting software 106

18 Taxes 109
Tax-preparation software 109
Deducting your home office and equipment 111
Other considerations 112
Resources 113

19 Sales & marketing 115
Follow-up for business prospects 116
Taking to the airwaves 117
Resources 119

20 Basic desktop publishing 121
Hardware and software 121
Using type 123
Type tips 124
DTP design tips 125
Templates 127
Clip art 127
Creating overheads 128
Laser printer creativity boosters 129
Professional printing 130
Preparing mechanicals 131
Resources 132
Illustration/paint/image-editing software 133

Appendices

A Software reviews 135

B Design makeover 159

C A sample online session 165

D Putting your business on tape with multimedia 173

Glossary 177

Index 183

Acknowledgments

THIS BOOK DRAWS ON THE COLLECTIVE expertise of all *Home Office Computing* writers and editors. Special thanks to Jack Nimersheim, Henry Beechhold, and Kay Yarborough Nelson for their expertise on technology; Steve Morgenstern for his desktop publishing insights; Stephen L. Nelson and Linda Stern for their contributions on finance and accounting; Donna Partow for her marketing ideas; Rosalind Resnick for her knowledge of the online world; and Steve Forbis for his coverage of communications. Thank you also to Charles Pappas for his excellent research work.

David Langendoen and Dan Costa deserve the biggest mention. They worked nights, holidays, and weekends editing, organizing, and writing. Their unflagging energy and depth of knowledge were critical to the book's completion.

In turn, David would like to thank Hanna, who has given him many great gifts, one of which was her much-needed support and love during this project.

— Nick Sullivan
Senior Editor
Home Office Computing

Introduction

HOME OFFICE COMPUTING IS A MAGAZINE dedicated to the small and home-based business owner. Over the past 10 years we've helped readers run their companies more effectively, productively, and profitably with the help of technology.

The Home Office Computing Handbook is a compilation of our knowledge and expertise. It is written for the small businessperson who wants to take full advantage of today's technology without breaking the bank. We'll show you how to become a more effective marketer, increase sales, manage your finances, gather information, and present a professional image. In short, we'll help you decide what equipment your business needs and show you hundreds of powerful business applications and ideas for it.

The first thirteen chapters are primarily about hardware—what kinds of computers and peripherals you need and how to shop for them. It also covers setting up your home office, how to make use of your equipment when traveling, and how to practice "healthy computing"—for both you and your computer.

Putting your technology to work is the focus of the next seven chapters. With ideas covering the major aspects of any business—sales, marketing, finance, taxes, communications, information acquisition/management—we'll show you how to integrate technology seamlessly into your operations.

Appendix A presents software reviews covering many of the top products available. By reading them you will learn what questions you should ask about a given product and how to evaluate it. Additionally we provide a listing of great software that retails for under $100—proof that you can build a solid library inexpensively.

Finally, appendices B through D show clear, real-life examples of some of the applications we discuss in the second section, including a desktop publishing makeover and a sample session on an online service.

At the end of each chapter we provide a listing of resources—books, software, companies mentioned in the chapter—that can provide further information. Use this book as an ongoing resource and reference—some topics might not pertain to you now, but when you decide it's finally time to take that step, we'll tell you how. Best of luck in your continuing endeavors.

—The Editors of *Home Office Computing*

Office setup & design

THERE ARE THREE IMPORTANT WORDS IN REAL estate: location, location, location. These three words carry equal weight when applied to home offices. Other concerns run the gamat from office size to wiring. We'll give you a rundown of these issues and everything in between.

Designing your home office is next. Where should the desk go? How far should you sit from your monitor? Why does your office seem so small and what can you do about it?

When the furniture moves in, the paperwork is not far behind. If you don't organize your home office quickly, you're liable to drown in a riptide of forms and invoices. Below you'll find an array of tips for designing an attractive, functional office and keeping it clean.

Suggested office sites

When trying to find a good to place to put your home office, you should ask yourself several important questions. Here are some of the most important ones:

- Will distractions be kept to a minimum?
- Is the space comfortable year round?
- Is the ambient temperature and humidity computer friendly?
- Is there sufficient lighting?
- Is the electrical wiring sufficient to support your needs?
- How difficult would it be to run a phone line into the space?
- Is there room to display samples of your work?
- Is there room for everything you need (desk, file cabinet, computer, printer and so on)?
- Is there enough storage space?
- Can you meet clients comfortably in this space?
- Is there a way to keep clients from seeing the rest of your home?

The spare room

The best home-office option is to dedicate a spare or unused room as your home office. This guarantees you have your own work space; you can just close the door and begin working. You can tell your children, and maybe even your mate, to keep out of that space because it is reserved for business. A dedicated office space is also the most professional place to meet with clients.

Dedicating one room exclusively for business is also the only way to ensure you can take a home-office deduction. (See chapter 18 for information on deductions.)

The basement

When planning a home office many people overlook the basement. With a little work most basements can be turned into well-lit, comfortable, and secluded offices. Of course, if you like to work near windows or have a damp and musty basement, it would be best to keep your office upstairs.

If you plan on using a computer in your basement, make sure you invest in a dehumidifier. Otherwise the natural dampness in the room could damage delicate circuits.

The attic

In most homes, attics are large, dry, and underused spaces, making them an ideal site for a home office. While the ceiling height might be restrictive, the separation and abundance of space might be worth the loss of headroom. However, the temperature might make your office a bit close. You will need to get an air conditioner to protect both your computer and your comfort.

The converted garage

Although remodeling a garage can be a lot of work, the end result can be worth it. If you go the converted garage route, make sure you install a separate business entrance. This is both more convenient and more professional. At the end of your toils, you will have a secluded, spacious, dedicated office. Unfortunately, you will have to find another place to park the car.

Not recommended

The guest bedroom

The guest bedroom provides the secluded comfort of a spare room, but it has a number of problems. First of all, when guests come over things get cramped. Also, if it is like most guest rooms, it has a space-consuming bed that will be a constant obstacle. However, if this is the only location available, look into a hide-away bed.

Your bedroom

The bedroom office also has more problems than benefits. First of all, you can't close the door on your work in the bedroom-office. You are secluded from the rest of the house, but not necessarily from your mate. (How can you tell your husband or wife to stay out of their own bedroom?) It's also usually not a good idea to meet with clients in your bedroom. If your bedroom is like most, you will be short of storage space and have to store files in another room.

Living, dining, and family rooms

Areas designated for family use tend to be high traffic and generally noisy places, neither of which are conducive to getting work done. Obviously if you live alone, these hazards become negligible.

The kitchen

Between interruptions, distractions, and the refrigerator you might be able to get some work done in the kitchen. But you will still have to worry about protecting your hardware, either with plastic coverings or, even better, a roll-top-desk-type covering. Spills, drops, and other accidents are inevitable in a kitchen. You will also have to keep your computer disks away from the microwave and refrigerator magnets. With so many accidents waiting to happen, we suggest avoiding the kitchen office.

Power supply

When choosing a home-office location, people often overlook the quality of the power supply. Electricity is the lifeblood of your home office—your computer, answering machine, copier, and other equipment all rely on the electricity, and you rely on the equipment. When your office equipment fails, your business fails; data is lost, schedules are missed, and invoices aren't mailed.

Electricity is the lifeblood of your home office.

Not knowing your home office's electrical capacity and requirements is a gamble. An inadequate and overburdened electrical system can cause downtime, damage equipment, impede work, and, in the worst case, result in an electrical fire. The slow and fragmented way home-office equipment and furnishings are accumulated often masks the buildup of high electrical loads that can be troublesome or dangerous if they remain unknown.

Only a test

Without the help of an electrician and special equipment, it is hard to know whether normal home-office operations are going to overload your electrical circuit. Generally not all equipment is drawing maximum power at the same time. You can tell whether your circuit might be nearing its capacity, though, with a simple experiment. Turn on all the equipment you normally use and have it perform its normal functions—leave the copier copying, the printer printing, and the lights lighting. Then go to the home-office circuit breaker and listen to whether the breaker is making a buzzing sound or see if it is warm to the touch. Either sign indicates the breaker is near its capacity.

To more accurately calculate the maximum electrical power requirements of your home office, locate the power-rating label affixed on every piece of electrically powered equipment in your office and total the watts or amperes. For incandescent lighting, read the wattage rating on the bulbs, and for fluorescent, read the label on the fixture. Convert all power requirements to amperes by dividing the number of watts by 110. (Amperes make a more convenient measure because circuit breakers are rated in amperes.) Next, compare your calculated amperes to the circuit breaker rating marked on the front or side of the circuit breaker handle at the electrical panel. The more your potential load exceeds the circuit breaker's rating, the greater the possibility for overloading the circuit, and the more care you must take to control the load.

Power management tips

- *Copiers.* Office copiers are usually the single biggest home-office electrical load. If you have a very big copier, we recommend putting it on its own circuit with its own breaker.
- *Extension cords.* Use round, three-conductor cords of at least 12-gauge wire. The common cheap, flat, two-wire extension cords are often undersized and are

too easily damaged by pets and furniture.

- *Surge suppressors*. To increase the number of outlets in your home office use a ganged surge suppressor with its own circuit breaker. These are metal or plastic boxes containing a gang of four or six electrical outlets connected to the box's own circuit breaker. The box is plugged into a wall outlet with its own heavy-duty extension cord, then equipment is plugged into the box, and the house circuit is protected by the outlet's breaker instead of the main panel's breaker.
- *Independent circuits*. If you are remodeling or involved in new construction we recommend installing two independent circuits, with one dedicated to sensitive equipment. Doing this at the stud stage of construction will cost only about $75. Doing the same thing later will cost at least $400 or $500.

For more on managing your power supply, see chapter 12, "Preventing computer catastrophes."

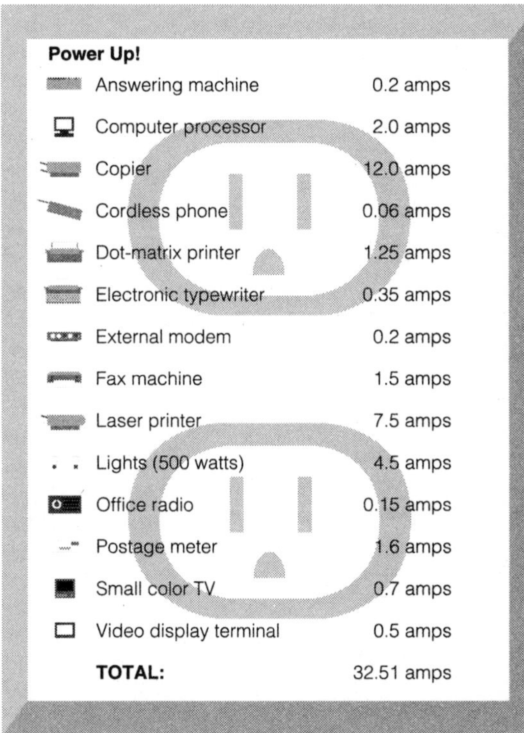

Power Up!

Answering machine	0.2 amps
Computer processor	2.0 amps
Copier	12.0 amps
Cordless phone	0.06 amps
Dot-matrix printer	1.25 amps
Electronic typewriter	0.35 amps
External modem	0.2 amps
Fax machine	1.5 amps
Laser printer	7.5 amps
Lights (500 watts)	4.5 amps
Office radio	0.15 amps
Postage meter	1.6 amps
Small color TV	0.7 amps
Video display terminal	0.5 amps
TOTAL:	32.51 amps

1-1 *Add it up! Make sure your equipment doesn't exceed the rating of your circuit breaker.*

A functionally sound home office should maximize your productivity, comfort, and convenience.

Bright ideas for better lighting

When it comes to lighting their offices, many people are in the dark and don't know it. Constant straining to see—even when you don't realize you're doing it—can lead to eyestrain, headaches, irritability, and lowered efficiency. When choosing a location, a generous supply of natural lighting is a big plus. If you're working out of the basement, you will have to pay special attention to ensuring an adequate supply of light. Following are some ideas to help you evaluate and improve your own office-lighting situation.

Enough light?

A home office should have enough light so the occupant can work without straining to see. Two types of lighting are necessary: ambient light (a blend of natural light and artificial light, usually provided by a ceiling fixture), and task lighting (provided by lamps at each work area).

Ambient lighting has two purposes: to enable you to see better and to minimize eyestrain, which is created when you look from a bright surface, such as a computer monitor, to a dark one, such as an unlit wall. The constant opening and closing of the pupils creates the strain. And eyestrain can lead to the other maladies mentioned above.

The average office should have two to four watts of ambient light per square foot, but a room with dark paneled or painted walls will require more. A 10' × 10' room would need two 100 watt bulbs to provide minimally acceptable ambient light (200 watts per 100 square feet = 2 watts per square foot).

Task lighting

Ambient light is normally not enough to work by. Task lights over work areas are necessary to provide a comfortable level of light. Many kinds are available; often stores have lighting designers who can give you advice.

When you set up task lights, make sure they don't create glare on your monitor or on any other reflective surface. Avoid placing your monitor with its back to a window; the frame of natural light you see when facing a screen set up this way also taxes your eyes. If the best location for your computer is against a windowed wall, you can eliminate glare by installing blinds or curtains (if you choose blinds, buy ones with a matte surface to prevent reflection).

Fluorescents, incandescents, and halogens

If you choose fluorescent fixtures, we suggest the warm white type; cool white fluorescents give a room all the ambiance of a police station. All incandescent bulbs provide warm light. Note that an 18-watt fluorescent tube is the equivalent of a 75-watt incandescent fixture. Fluorescents provide more light for fewer watts and less money.

Halogens are another cost-effective way to fill a room with warm ambient light. Put a standing halogen light in a room with light walls and a white ceiling and you have instant daylight.

Designing your home office

One overriding principle guides all good office designs: function. A functionally sound home office should maximize your productivity, comfort, and convenience. Everything else is secondary.

Though no two home offices are identical, most conform to one of four standard layouts: the strip, the L-shape, the galley, or the U-shape. You should be able to use some version of these layouts in your office design, but you might have to improvise. Just remember, good layouts keep everything you need within an arm's reach.

Strip

The most basic and least functional layout, the strip is simply a straight-line sequence of components. The surface might be a long kitchenlike counter or a combination of furniture pieces. The surface needs to be pretty long if you have several components and require a great deal of storage space. With the strip layout there will almost always be components out of your reach.

L-shape

The L-shape gives an added dimension to the strip. The extra leg can be used as a computer stand, alternate work surface, or storage space. L-shapes are more popular home-office designs than strips because they fit nicely into otherwise useless corner space and provide more privacy.

Galley

By placing two strip arrangements back-to-back, you create a galley-type layout. This is the layout of choice for most executives; the chair is placed between the desk and the computer (which is on a surface behind the desk). This way you can just swivel your chair to switch from computing to taking phone calls. This layout also keeps your computer and printer from consuming valuable desk space.

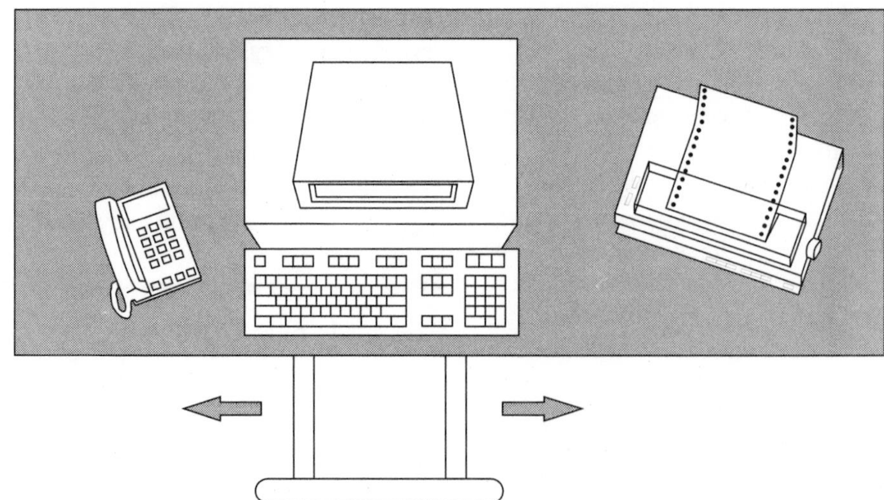

1-2A *The strip is the most basic office design, but it's the least desirable if you have a lot of equipment.*

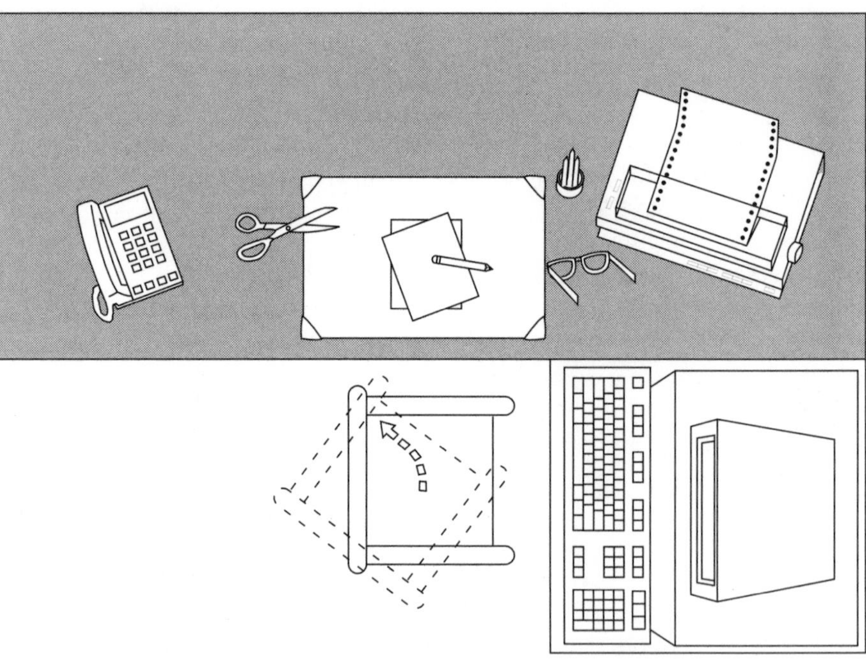

1-2B *Ls are common home-office designs, because they make good use of wasted corner space and provide desk space for a printer or other equipment.*

U-shape

The U-shape surrounds you with three work surfaces, keeping everything you need at your fingertips. Although similar to both the L and the galley, the U design makes you feel as though you were sitting in your own private control center, which is exactly what you're doing. The only disadvantage to this layout is that it requires a lot of space.

Noise is the number one cause of stress and distraction in the workplace.

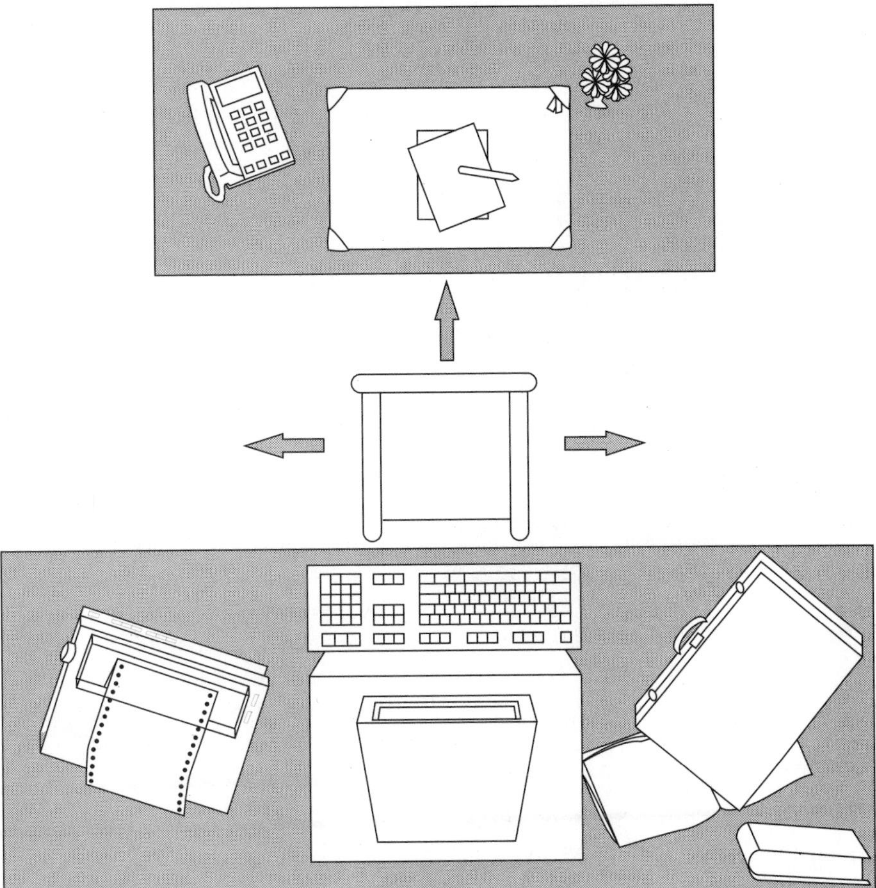

1-2C The galley—basically two strips with a chair in between—is common in executive offices. The computer usually sits on one desk, while the other is used for phone calls and manual work.

> *If you have one pile of paper on your desk, it's one more than you need.*

Furniture arrangement tips

- *Wait before you build.* The best way to customize your office is to build your own work surfaces. This way you can set the heights and widths that you are most comfortable with. However, try your office out first with the most versatile and adjustable furniture you can find. Study your work habits and then correct any annoyances when you do build in.
- *Face the wall.* Whatever you have been told, you can put your desk facing the wall. It opens up the room and gives ample space for shelves or decorations. Of course, if you use your office to meet with clients, it would be better to face outward.
- *Plan for drawer space.* When planning your office layout, account for the space needed to open a filing cabinet. A vertical file usually requires about 24". A lateral cabinet needs about a foot.
- *Avoid useless furniture.* A home office is often the first place that extra furniture gets stored. Beware of coffee tables, night stands, bookshelves, reclining chairs, and kitchen tables that are too nice to throw away, but don't seem to belong in any other room. They don't belong in your office either. As a general rule, if it has no business purpose, it has no place in your office.
- *Be flexible.* When shopping for furniture, remember three words: versatile, adjustable, and modular. You can't go wrong.

Avoiding monitor glare

- Don't place the monitor in front of or opposite a window. By keeping your monitor at right angles to your windows you will minimize glare.
- When you set up task lights make sure they don't create glare on your monitor.
- Keep ceiling fixtures slightly behind you. The further the light is behind you the more likely it is to reflect on your screen.
- Buy an anti-glare screen.
- Make sure you have curtains or blinds to keep out the sunlight while you're computing.
- Use a small mirror to choose the best spot for your computer. Hold the mirror in the place and at the angle where your monitor will be. If your lights are reflected in the mirror, they'll be reflected on the screen, so you will need to consider another location.

Home office design solutions

Even the ideal location in your home might not make for an ideal office. Fortunately there are ways to compensate for most deficiencies without spending a fortune.

Low ceiling

Some offices have ceilings that can part your hair. This is particularly true in basements, where ceilings are lower than the standard eight feet.

One way to "raise" ceilings is with decorative wall coverings. A striped or vertical-patterned covering will

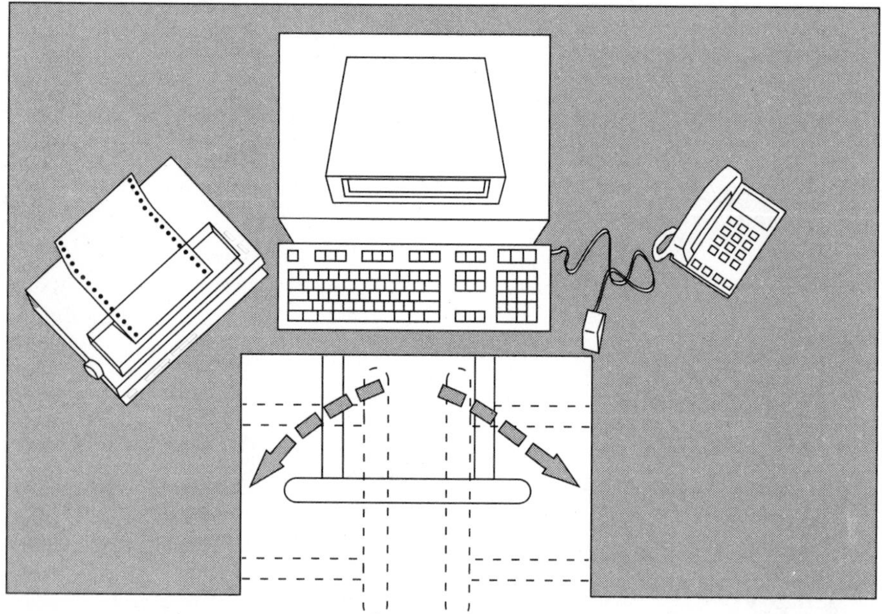

1-2D *The* U *design—think of it as an* L *with a short extension or a galley with a connecting piece—gives you the convenience and easy access of both.*

make walls look higher. Painting a ceiling a lighter color than the walls will raise the ceiling. The best color: dead-flat white. It makes the ceilings disappear.

High ceiling

Most of us would like a sky-high cathedral ceiling. If you don't, try putting a decorative border along the top edges of the wall. Border strips are available in an array of patterns and will make your office a little cozier. There are also a couple of ways you can use paint to lower your ceiling. You can use a medium-to-dark paint on all your walls and ceilings, or you can just use a darker color on the ceiling. Many people prefer the former because it looks more natural.

If such cosmetic solutions are not enough, you can install a drop ceiling, which rests on a metal grid and can be adjusted to any height you wish. This solves noise and insulation problems and hides pipes, wires and damaged ceilings.

Undersized room

If your office is too small, light-colored wall coverings with larger open patterns will make it look bigger. Paint in pale colors can create breathing room in a small space. Mirrors also help expand a room. Any kind of mirror will do, although plate mirrors work best. Plate mirrors can be cut to any size and installed anywhere with mirror glue.

Oversized room

To create a more intimate feeling in a large room, paint the walls a dark color. Border strips can also be used at the wall/ceiling juncture or around the middle of the wall. Consider painting the lower half of the room and wallpapering the top.

Narrow room

Some offices seem more like hallways than rooms. To remedy this, paint the walls at each end—the short walls—with a darker, warmer color than you used for the long walls.

Irregular walls

If a chimney or wall section juts into a room, camouflage it by painting or wallpapering with the same covering as the rest of the room. You can also hide an alcove by turning it into storage space. Fill it with shelves for storing books or office supplies. Installing shelves is a great way to hide many structural quirks.

Noise control

Noise is the number one cause of stress and distraction in the workplace. While home offices tend to be a little quieter than corporate offices, there are still plenty of distractions. If noise is a problem for you, there are a number of design solutions to ease the din.

- Carpet your floors (the thicker the better).
- Weatherstrip your doors and windows.
- Purchase double-glazed windows.
- Use room dividers or screens.
- Install solid core doors (most doors are hollow).
- Cover walls with fabric or cork.
- Place lined, floor-length draperies over your windows.
- Buy heavily padded furniture.
- Glue acoustical tile or other sound-absorbent material to the ceiling.
- Drywall or panel over your existing walls with thick insulation between the studs of the new wall.

Organizing your home office

You've selected your office. You've designed your office. Now you are going to use it. It is time to think through how you are going to keep it from looking like an entry in *Home Office Computing*'s Most Disorganized Home Office Contest.

Filing options

Whatever kind of business you run, chances are you generate a lot of paper. The paperless office never came to be. If anything, technology—copy machines, laser printers, and fax machines—has increased the number of paper documents handled by businesses. The best tool for managing clutter is still the filing cabinet. While this might seem straightforward, you do have some options.

Vertical filing cabinets

Reliable and secure, these traditional standbys come with either two or four drawers. These cabinets will protect your files from almost any hazard. Many have locks for greater security. Check the depth of the drawers to make sure it meets your needs. Make sure you get a quality product with well-attached handles and a sturdy frame.

Lateral filing cabinets

These cabinets hold files sideways. This takes up more room horizontally, but gives the cabinet less depth. Files are generally easier to access and can hold more. You can also use the top of the cabinet as a secondary work surface.

Open-front cabinets

If filing and retrieval are a major part of your business you might want to consider an Open Front Cabinet. Often seen in medical offices, these files allow you to easily read the label on each folder. The minus is they require special folders; hanging folders won't work.

Open file carts

These mobile cabinets are most often used for work in progress. However, if your filing needs are limited or you need to make space in your office, an open file cart might do the job. Unfortunately, the contents of the cart are visible to anyone who walks by.

Open file crates

These crates can store files either laterally or vertically. If you want the crate open-end-up, then use hanging files that hook over the edges. For open-end-out, use accordion files to hold your papers.

The cardboard box

Lightweight, but not very secure. The best thing the cardboard box has going for it is the price.

Organization tips

- *Don't pile paper*. Horizontal piles of papers waste valuable surface space and are an inefficient storage method. No one has enough space to create single topic piles. That's what vertical files are for. If you have one pile of paper on your desk, it's one more than you need.
- *The lap drawer*. This drawer should be used only for the items you use most often: pens, paper clips, rubber bands, stamps, white out, and so on. Unfortunately this is usually the messiest drawer in your office. Invest in a drawer organizer; it's the only way to keep track of all these small but vital office supplies. Consider using a silverware tray to subdivide your lap drawer. It will look funny, but it works.
- *Adding bins and shelves*. Stacking bins work better than stacking trays because they hold more and can sit on the floor rather than taking up desk space. Make sure you label each bin and use it only for its dedicated purpose.
- *Paper handling*. There are three types of papers in most home offices: current, reference, and historical. Paper for current projects should be readily available. Reference papers—articles from magazines, inactive client files, and other information—are used less often and should be stored in a file cabinet. Historical papers kept for legal and tax reasons can be archived outside the office.
- *Alternative desk*. Instead of buying a desk, try putting a board across the top of two filing cabinets. After all, all you really need is the working surface. Although a little more work, it lets you better adjust the height of the desk and saves you a great deal of money. If you use your office to meet with clients you might need to buy a desk in order to maintain your professional image.
- *When pressed for space, build up*. Try to maximize your vertical space. A computer cart, for instance, stores your computer and printer vertically, saving valuable working surface space.

Office supplies

What exactly do you need to run an office? In a traditional office setting, everything you needed to work efficiently could be found in the supply closet (although finding someone with the key could be difficult). In stocking your own office it's easy to overlook essentials. To prevent this, we have assembled some lists of the basic office supplies any business needs.

One-time purchases:
- *Accordion files*
- *Business card holder*
- *Calculator*
- *Calendar*
- *Check endorsement stamp*
- *Computer disk holders*
- *Daily planner (or desk calendar)*
- *Date stamp*
- *Drawer dividers (or trays)*
- *Electric pencil sharpener*
- *Hanging file frames*
- *Letter opener*
- *Paper cutter*
- *Petty cash box*
- *Postal scale (consider leasing)*
- *Ruler*
- *Scissors*
- *Stamp holder*
- *Stamp moistener (unless you like the taste)*
- *Stapler*
- *Staple remover*
- *Surge protector*
- *Tape dispenser*
- *Three-hole punch*
- *Three-ring binders*
- *Vertical file holder*
- *Wastebasket*

Repeat purchases:
- *Address labels*
- *Adhesive note pads*
- *Business cards (yours)*
- *Cellophane tape*
- *Clear computer labels*
- *Copy paper*
- *Dust-off spray (for cleaning electronic equipment)*
- *Eraser*
- *Fax paper*
- *Glue sticks*

- *Hanging file folders (plus clear plastic inserts)*
- *Highlighter markers*
- *Interior file folders*
- *Labels for file folders*
- *Laser-printer paper*
- *Legal pads*
- *Mailing labels*
- *Manila envelopes (9"×12" and 10"×13")*
- *Note-size stationery (imprinted paper and envelopes)*
- *Overnight delivery packaging supplies*
- *Paper clips*
- *Pencils*
- *Petty cash receipt book*
- *Printer ink or toner*
- *Rubber bands*
- *Stamps*
- *Staples*
- *Stationery (imprinted letterhead, plain second sheets, imprinted envelopes)*

Resources

Books and publications

Country Bound! by Marilyn and Tom Ross, 1993, Communication Creativity, Buena Vista, CO; $19.95; (719) 395-8659, (800) 331-8355.

This guide is filled with tips, insights, and resources for anyone looking to leave the frenzied city for the relative peace of the country.

Getting Organized: The Easy Way to Put Your Life in Order, by Stephanie Winston, 1991, Warner Books, New York, NY; $10.95; (212) 522-7200.

Healthy Computing: Risks & Remedies Every Computer User Needs to Know, by Dr. Ronald Harwin and Colin Haynes, 1992, AMACOM, New York, NY; $17.95; (800) 538-4761.

Home Lighting Handbook, by General Electric Corp, P.O. Box 94988, Cleveland, OH; $5.95; (800) 626-2000, (502) 423-7710.

Organizing Your Home for Success, by Lisa Kanarek, 1993, Plume, Bergenfield, NJ; $10; (201) 387-0600, (800) 526-0275.

Sunset Books, by various authors, 1986–1992, Sunset Publishing Co., Menlo Park, CA; (415) 321-3600.

Titles include: *Sunset Complete Home Storage*, *Sunset Home Remodeling*, and a series of books on home storage spaces ($8 to $17).

What to Buy for Business, What to Buy, Inc., Rye, NY; $112/10 issues, $21/single issue; (800) 247-2185, (914) 925-2566.

Office services

The Headquarters Companies, 120 Montgomery St., Suite 1040, San Francisco, CA 94104; (800) 227-3004, (800) 950-3004.

Conference facilities, mail and phone receiving, computer services in most major urban areas.

Mailboxes Etc., 6060 Cornerstone Court West, San Diego, CA 92121; (800) 949-6660 (call for nearest location).

Shipping, receiving, and business communications services.

Moore Business Forms, P.O. Box 20, Wheeling, IL 60090; (800) 323-6230 (catalog orders); (800) 472-2552 (telesales); (708) 615-6000 (headquarters).

Supply a variety of forms useful for a small business.

Retail suppliers

Filing cabinets

Esselte Pendaflex Corporation, 71 Clinton Rd., Garden City, NY 11530; (800) 645-6051.

Fire King International, 900 Park Place, New Albany, IN 47150; (800) 457-2424.

Hon Company, P.O. Box 769, Muscatine, IA 52761-0599; (800) 553-9686.

Sentry Group, 900 Linden Ave., Rochester, NY 14625; (716) 381-4900.

Venture Horizon Corp., 3463 State St., Suite 262, Santa Barbara, CA 93101; (805)-563-2030.

Computer furniture

Grolen, Inc., 1100 E. Hector St., Conshohocken, PA 19428; (215) 825-7213.

O'Sullivan Industries, Inc., 1900 Gulf St., Lamar, MO 64759-1899; (417) 682-3322.

Ring King Visables, Inc., P.O. Box 599, 2210 Second Ave., Muscatine, IA 52761-0599; (319) 263-8144.

Trendlines, Inc., 9912 Governor Lane Blvd., RR3 Box 100, Williamsport, MD 21795; (301) 223-8900.

Office Depot. Check your local yellow pages for a location near you.

This office superstore sells office supplies and equipment. Most locations have a special home-office section.

Reliable Home Office, P.O. Box 1501, Ottawa, IL 61350-9916; (800) 827-1081; (312) 666-1800.

Equipment and furniture for the home office.

Catalogues

Caddylack, 510 Fillmore Ave., Tonawanda, NY; (800) 523-8060.

Crutchfield Personal Office Catalog, 1 Crutchfield Park, Charlottesville, VA 22906; (800) 521-4050.

Illustrated catalog of computers, peripherals, office equipment, and supplies. Crutchfield also services the equipment it sells.

Hello Direct, 140 Great Oaks Blvd., San Jose, CA 95119-1347; (800) 444-3556.

Hold Everything, Mail Order Department, 100 North Point St., San Francisco, CA 94133-7807; (800) 421-2264.

Reliable Home Office Catalog, P.O. Box 1501, Ottawa, IL 61350-9916; (800) 735-4000.

Health & ergonomics

THE DANGERS OF THE COMPUTER AGE—including radiation and repetitive stress injuries—have received a lot of press. These are important concerns. Fortunately, however, staying healthy is easy if you develop good habits and take the right precautions.

Part of healthy computing is choosing ergonomic furniture and supplies. We examine what to look for and tell you what to put on your shopping list.

Staying healthy

For the most part, your equipment doesn't hurt you, bad habits do. Unfortunately since personal computers are a relatively new arrival in the office environment, most people don't know what good habits are. Below we separate the do's from the don'ts and alert you to any hazards your equipment does pose.

Healthy habits

Ergonomics is the science of comfort, convenience, and function. It refers to how you relate to the task and machinery in front of you. It has as much to do with habits as it does with equipment. Since cumulative trauma disorders (CTDs) arise from repetition, try to avoid getting into a rut—vary your activities. While you can't always vary your tasks, you can vary your positions. Follow these suggestions to prevent serious computer related injuries:

- If your fingers are above your wrists when typing, you're headed for pain. Lower the keyboard or raise your chair.
- Try putting a small cushion behind the small of your back to help maintain good posture.
- Set an alarm clock and take a walk every hour. Researchers recommend at least a 10-minute break every hour.
- Create and use macros. By taking the time to set up macros you can save hundreds of keystrokes a day. It will save you time and be good for your health too.
- Using your mouse to input saves keystrokes and can head off injury. However, make sure you are using your mouse properly. Your mouse should be at keyboard height and easily within reach. Although slightly more expensive, get a curved-top mouse. Although continual mouse use can lead to cramping it is generally safer than keyboard operations.
- Beware of neutral positions. Anything that requires static exertion can lead to problems. Stretch your fingers, wriggle your toes, and tilt your head from side to side. The object is to relieve tension by not staying put.
- Although having everything at your finger tips is nice, try elevating your printer or other peripheral equipment to a higher shelf. This way you need to stand up from your chair to service it. It seems self-defeating, but it keeps you moving and healthy.
- Your monitor should be about 20 degrees below your line of sight and should be positioned between 13 and 18 inches from your eyes. As a rule of thumb, you should have to sit up very straight to see over it.
- Avoid stress. Most researchers identify stress as a major factor contributing to workplace health problems, including CTDs.
- Keep off your elbows. If you lean on your elbows all the time, you isolate hand and wrist movements and create unnatural postures in which the shoulders are held up and the head leans forward.

- Keep your feet on the floor, with most of your weight on your buttocks.
- The fastest way to refresh your body, relax your eyes, and increase your oxygen is yawning. A similar effect can be achieved by exhaling fully every half hour.
- Periodically let your arms fall to your sides and shake out your wrists. This promotes blood flow and relieves tension.
- For painful joints, alternate hot and cold baths. Start with five minutes of heat, then seven to eight minutes of cold. Repeat this three to five times ending with 12 to 15 minutes of cold. These contrast baths increase the circulation of blood to the affected region and promote the healing process.
- Resting your wrists on the desk or your arms on the chair is unhealthy because it isolates and weakens mechanical function. When you rest your wrist, you inevitably prevent your fingers from having the proper movement coordination linking them to the rest of your body. Any hand or finger motion should involve your arms, shoulders, and upper back. We were designed to perform as an integrated machine with numerous interdependent parts. The muscles that operate your fingers are located in your forearm. By resting the wrist and working it in isolation you add stress to this function.

Radiation from your monitor

There are scores of rumors about the harmful effects of video terminal radiation. Claims have been made that very low-level frequencies (VLFs) and extremely low-level frequencies (ELFs) cause everything from cancer to cataracts. While there is little hard evidence to support these claims, there is one thing we know. ELFs do affect human tissue, both for better and for worse.

Currently ELFs are used to treat bone fractures and speed the healing process. On the other hand, some ELFs disrupt certain cellular functions and promote the growth of cancerous cells.

Is your monitor safe? No one really knows because ELFs aren't regulated in the United States.

Should you be concerned? Not terribly. But since even a little radiation can't be good, you should take some simple preventative measures.

Look for MPR II

The Swedes have the toughest monitor emission standard in the world, the MPR II. If safety is your first concern when buying a monitor, look for the MPR II standard. This standard regulates a variety of monitor emissions, including:

- X-radiation
- Static electrical fields
- Low frequency electrical fields
- Low frequency magnetic fields

Many monitors conform to the first standard, MPR I. But MPR I only covers alternating magnetic fields. If you're very concerned about safety, make sure your monitor conforms to the more comprehensive MPR II standard.

Sit back

The fields generated by your monitor do not extend far. By simply putting some space between you and your monitor you can dramatically reduce your exposure. As a general rule, you should not be able to touch your screen when sitting correctly at your keyboard. This will also do wonders for your posture and physical comfort.

Watch your back

The back and sides of your monitor emit higher levels of radiation than the front. As a result colleagues and family members often get a higher dose than the user of any particular station. Again, while the risk is not that high, we recommend rearranging your office design to minimize exposure.

Check behind walls

Electrical and magnetic fields easily pass through walls, so if the baby's crib is flush up against the wall in the room next to your computer you might want to move one of them. You can't block the fields, but you can keep away from them.

Radiation protection

Low-radiation screens reduce electrical emissions coming from the screen itself. Computer Covers Unlimited sells a variety of VU-TEK I optical devices.

A good chair might go unnoticed and unappreciated, but a bad one will plague your every working hour.

Ergonomic furniture and supplies

Comfort and productivity go hand in hand when it comes to furniture, so you should make sure your office supplies are ergonomically sound. Poor ergonomics can cause CTDs, which include such common ailments as tennis elbow and writer's cramp, and can progress to debilitating conditions such as carpal tunnel syndrome (CTS). These and other related problems are generally caused by the accumulated effects of continuous repetitive motions.

Selecting a chair

If, after sitting in your chair for 20 minutes, you find yourself changing positions a lot, your body is sending you a warning signal. A good chair might go unnoticed and unappreciated, but a bad one will plague your every working hour. Here are some guidelines to help you find the former:

- Backrests and seat that move independently.
- Downward curving (or short) armrests so the chair can pull close to work surfaces.
- Lumbar support for the lower back.
- Lumbar support for legs that allows for free movement.
- Stain- and fire-resistant upholstery.
- A supporting, but not restrictive chair back.
- Adjustable knee-tilt mechanisms.
- Adjustable tilt tension.
- Pneumatic or mechanical seat height adjustment.
- A five-prong, stable, but space-saving, base.

The primary obstacle to clear viewing is reflected light.

The Sensor I chair, manufactured by Steelcase, and the Equa chair, manufactured by Herman Miller, are well-constructed general-purpose swivel chairs with adjustable height and tilt, armrests, and reinforced lower-back support.

***2-1** A good chair is crucial for ongoing comfort. This Sensor desk chair by Steelcase provides solid support for the back and arms.*

Armrests

Armrests are important for people who compute for long periods of time, because they can relieve tension by supporting the forearms. However, for the most part they are a matter of personal preference. They make chairs more comfortable but also add several inches to the width and can make it too tall to fit under a desk. Look for short armrests that slope downward in the front. This way they support your elbows but don't bang into the desk all day.

A good covering material is self-skinning foam, the same molded resilient vinyl used to cover automobile steering wheels. It is friendly to the elbows, its color is uniform throughout so scratches disappear, and it's soft enough to protect other furniture.

Avoid fabric-covered armrests. They appear comfortable but soil easily and are otherwise vulnerable. Also stay away from wood. Wood armrests find funny bones too easily.

Footrests

If your chair has no height adjustment, purchase a footrest that will elevate your feet and increase circulation. Microcomputer Accessories sells an adjustable FootEase footrest. BackSaver Products makes the Foot Mate. Many ergonomists recommend using a footrest regardless of whether or not you can adjust your chair.

Kneeling chairs

In the early eighties, a new type of chair appeared on the scene: the forward tilting chair. The theory is if you sit with your thighs sloped downwards from the pelvis, the open angle between your back and legs tips your pelvis forward thus maintaining the natural curvature (or lordosis) of your lower back. These perches are surprisingly comfortable, but many people find it useful mainly as a task-intensive chair. As a general purpose office chair the forward tilt chair lacks something (namely a back).

Seats and backs

The best filling is molded polyurethane foam, preferably a progressive density type. Although it is sometimes hard to distinguish from slab foam, which is fabricated in large pieces, molded foam is more dense and compact. If you can press into the seat with your hand and feel the padding bottom out rapidly against the seat structure, chances are it's cheap, soft slab foam. In fairness, we should mention that a slab-foam seat applied over rubber webbing or similar resilient decking material is a close second in terms of comfort and quality.

For seat and back coverings, nothing beats leather in comfort or durability. Leather is tough, resilient, and pleasant to the touch. It breathes, yet protects the filling from UV light and oxidation. It also allows clothing to slide easily across the chair. Unfortunately, good leather can double the price of a chair. But remember leather gets better with age: a rare quality that might be worth paying for.

Setting up your desktop

Work surfaces are ordinarily 29 to 30 inches in height, which is about one inch too high for a task such as writing. Most people will find a desktop of 28 to 28.5 inches more to their liking. The keyboard should be placed on a lower surface so that your wrists are straight and your forearms are parallel to the floor. This translates into a keyboard height of about 23 to 25 inches. ScanCo's MacTable has a split surface that allows you to adjust the angle of both the keyboard and the monitor.

2-2 Placing the keyboard at a lower height is an excellent idea. Many desks come with this feature, like the Mac Table by ScanCo.

2-3 The Apple Adjustable Keyboard splits apart to provide more comfortable hand positioning. Apple Computer/John Greenleigh

If you're new to typing, or don't mind relearning, look into the DVORAK keyboard configuration. The DVORAK configuration places the most used keys in easy reach, making it more functional and ergonomically sound than the standard layout. The standard QWERTY keyboard layout was originally designed to slow down fast typists who might jam a mechanical typewriter. You can either buy a special DVORAK keyboard or use software to reconfigure a standard keyboard. You will also need to buy a special keyboard cover to rename your keys.

It looks like the next generation of keyboard design will include split or adjustable keyboards. The idea is to avoid strain by letting the user adjust the keyboard according to how his or her arms approach it. Does it work? We found it to be much more comfortable.

Keyboard-support devices fall into two categories: stationary keyboard supports, which attach underneath the desk and pull out like a drawer, or articulating keyboard supports, which attach to the desktop and can be raised, lowered, swiveled, and tilted. Microcomputer Accessories offers a Super Underdesk keyboard drawer. Steelcase sells a Details articulating keyboard support.

While you'll do just fine with a mouse, trackballs are more ergonomically sound because they allow your hand to rest in one position. However, they are slightly more difficult to use.

The wrist rest is essential in preventing CTDs. It helps your wrists support your arms and, hence, allows the arm and shoulder muscles to relax. Microcomputer Accessories makes the Keyboard Platform, which also adjusts the angle of the keyboard.

Articulating monitor stands elevate the screen and help free up desk space. Stationary monitor stands are more common and less expensive. Some of these incorporate slide-out keyboard trays, accessory compartments, and swivel/tilt features.

The primary obstacle to clear viewing is reflected light. For polarized glass models, Computer Covers Unlimited offers Champ Polar Filter Shields. Most antiglare filters can absorb up to 99 percent of reflected light. The glass variety accomplishes this with optical coatings. The metal-mesh type is less expensive but might also be unsuitable for some people since the mesh itself can obstruct viewing.

When choosing a copy stand, the only important consideration is that your document be placed within the same arc of vision as the monitor and keyboard.

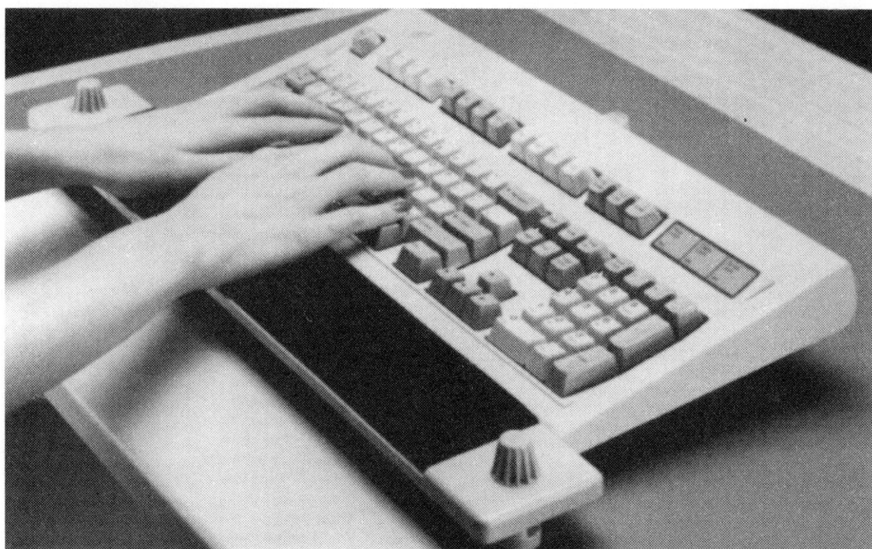

2-4 *A keyboard platform keeps your wrists and hands in an ergonomically correct position.* Microcomputer Accessories

Resources

Companies mentioned in the chapter

BackSaver Products
(800) 251-2225

Computer Covers Unlimited
(619) 277-0622

Herman Miller
(616) 772-3300

MicroComputer Accessories
(800) 876-6447

ScanCo
(800) 722-6263

Steelcase
(800) 227-2960

Books and publications

Getting Organized: The Easy Way to Put Your Life in Order, by Stephanie Winston, 1991, Warner Books, New York, NY; $10.95; (212) 522-7200.

Healthy Computing: Risks & Remedies Every Computer User Needs to Know, by Dr. Ronald Harwin and Colin Haynes, 1992, AMACOM, New York, NY; $17.95; (800) 538-4761.

Where to buy

WHERE YOU BUY YOUR COMPUTER AND equipment has an enormous impact on the price you pay and the service you get. As computers and related equipment are treated more like commodities (like microwave ovens or CD players) than specialty purchases, shoppers are relying on superstores and mail order to fulfill their orders.

What does the first-time computer shopper do? Read as much as possible and try to find a store with salespeople who will spend time evaluating your needs. Some form of retail store is the best bet. More experienced shoppers, however, should turn to other sources to get the best prices. Mail order and direct sales, for instance, offer great value for the knowledgeable customer.

Retail stores

The main advantage of purchasing your equipment from a retail store is that you can test drive it before you buy. Most people feel more comfortable dealing with salespeople they've met face-to-face and having a place to go if they have any problems. While traditional computer stores still account for a lot of sales, computer and office superstores are rapidly becoming the dominant force with their low prices, large name brand inventories, and easy accessibility.

Traditional computer stores

The first category includes any place that sells brand-name computers—IBM, Macintosh, Compaq, etc.—out of the store front. Included in this category are chain stores or franchises such as Computerland. In addition to these familiar names, most major cities have independent stores that sell brand-name merchandise but are not connected to any national organization.

Advantages:

- Salespeople are well-trained and knowledgeable.
- Service and warranties are among the best, and you know who you are dealing with.

Drawbacks

- Prices are relatively high.
- Fierce competition with superstores and mail order vendors have forced many out of business.

Local vendors

These small single-outlet stores specialize in generic IBM-compatible clones. The store assembles the computers on-site using components from a variety of sources.

Advantages

- Low prices—you aren't paying for a brand name.
- You can often have a computer built precisely to your specifications.

Drawbacks

- You can't be sure of the quality of the machine—make sure you get references before purchasing.
- Is the store going to be there tomorrow?

Superstores

Superstores are expanding into all major markets. There are two basic types of superstores: those that sell only computers, like CompUSA; and those that sell all kinds of office products, such as Bizmart. In many ways superstores provide the same advantages to computer buyers that home-improvement centers, like Home Office Depot, provide home-repair persons.

Advantages

- Low prices.
- Large inventories and wide selection.
- Many stores now have special home office sections.

Drawbacks

Average level of salesperson knowledge doesn't rival that of traditional computer stores.

Other sources

Stores aren't the only place to find your computer equipment. For the experienced user, the market for used computers can supply some great deals—but considering the ongoing price wars, buying used is rarely much cheaper than buying new, and it carries increased risks.

An increasingly popular choice, especially for people with some computer experience, is buying direct: Just call a number and have equipment mailed to you. There are several advantages to this, including unbeatable prices, but to be a savvy mail order shopper you need to know several things.

Secondhand sources (used equipment)

Secondhand sources don't usually offer any support or warranties, but you can get a good price (and usually a pile of software and accessories thrown in as well). We don't recommend buying a used computer as your primary computer, but they can be good secondary units dedicated to specific purposes—handling your voice mail, for example. Check out some of these secondhand sources:

- Classified ads (including those on online services)
- User groups
- Auctions
- Computer swaps
- Computer brokers

Secondhand buying tips

- Among the choices listed above we recommend buying from a user group. You won't get any guarantees, but you will have access to technical support.
- Another good choice is going through a national computer broker. Some brokers will evaluate the machine, clean it, and make sure it is in working order before passing it on to the buyer.
- With secondhand computers the important consideration is not the age, it's the mileage. Look at the computer's appearance. How well was it cleaned? How much maintenance was done on it? Did the former user have a habit of taking off the top and trying to figure out what's wrong?
- Don't bother buying secondhand peripherals. Hard disk drives and modems are priced affordably and come with warranties.

An increasingly popular choice is buying direct.

Direct sales (mail order)

Buying a mail order computer is as easy as making a toll-free call. Indicate what you want, and have your credit card number ready. Your computer or component could be in your hands the next day.

There are two basic kinds of direct sales firms: those that sell their name-brand exclusively (Dell, Gateway 2000, and a growing number of companies that formerly used only traditional channels like IBM and Compaq), and those that sell several brands. Brand-name vendors can't beat the prices of clearinghouse vendors, but they are generally more dependable and offer very good service.

Advantages

- Price. The direct sales industry has been booming for a reason—mail order firms offer the best prices. And you usually don't have to pay sales tax.
- Variety. Retail stores are limited by available shelf space; even superstores must limit their inventories somewhat. But direct sales vendors can stock huge warehouses with every part and component you could possibly want.
- Finding what you want when you want it. Rather than calling around to retail stores in your area to ask if they have a particular component, you can call a single toll-free number. Since direct sales vendors are staffed on weekends and in the evenings, you're not limited to business hours.
- Technical support. With a name-brand dealer you'll work with a well-trained staff that can troubleshoot problems in your system. These folks know more than what's on sale and how to run the cash register.
- Parts and labor. Many vendors offer a parts, labor, and onsite service warranty. Whether you need a part sent overnight or a visit from a technician, these firms deliver. Many vendors will try to charge you extra for one- or two-year warranties, but you can often talk the salesperson into including it in the price of your computer.

Smart shopping

The vast majority of mail order firms are completely legitimate enterprises. But some will sell you a defective monitor and charge you the return shipping costs to boot. To protect yourself from the disreputable minority of direct sales vendors, follow these tips:

- Get it in writing. If it's not in writing, it didn't happen. Verbal agreements are of little or no value to you. Have the details of your agreement with the sales rep mailed or faxed to you before handing over your credit card number.

- Haggle. If you don't like the quoted price, make a counter offer. If you don't get the price you need, shop around. The market is very competitive and sales reps have a good deal of discretion. So play hardball—don't ask if they can give you a discount, say "I'll take it for X dollars." Some vendors, especially the brand-name ones, can't drop the price much, but they can often throw in an extended warranty or extra peripherals. Remember, another vendor is just a phone call away, and you can always call back later.
- Get names. Most of the time the sales rep will be your only human contact with the company, so make sure you get his or her full name. This makes both the rep and the company accountable.
- Charge it. When ordering by mail, always pay by credit card. While most mail order stores are reputable and efficient, credit cards provide you with some insurance. If something goes wrong with your order you can protest the payment if you file within a reasonable amount of time—usually 60 days from the date of posting. Using a credit card also gets your order processed faster. Many credit card companies offer to double the manufacturer's warranty.
- Avoid surcharges. You should never have to pay a surcharge for using a credit card—granted, vendors up their prices a little to cover the costs of accepting credit cards, but you shouldn't pay anything above the advertised price. This comes up most often when using an American Express card, which charges vendors a higher percentage of revenues. Most vendors handle this by not accepting American Express. But some will charge up to 3.5% extra. In most states this is illegal, and you can force them to accept your card with no surcharge. To find out if this is illegal in the state you want to order from, call American Express at the number on the back of your card.

Make sure technical support is the responsibility of the vendor, not the manufacturer.

- Request preassembly. Find a firm that preassembles and pretests your system for problems. Call the technical support department to confirm this if the advertisement you order from is unclear. While this service might cost a little more, it can save you a lot of time.
- Ask for volume discounts. Whatever your company's size, ask your sales rep about volume discounts. Some companies call more than one item volume, others offer discounts if your total order exceeds a fixed amount of dollars. If cash flow is no problem, try consolidating your orders to take advantage of these discounts.
- Look for full mailing addresses. If all that is offered is a P.O. box, find another company.
- Check for longevity. One sign of longevity is an extensive advertising history. If you subscribe to a magazine in which the vendor advertises, check back issues to see how long it has been advertising.
- Check delivery time. If a vendor does not offer overnight service and takes more than 10 days for delivery, chances are you are going through a middle man. There are two disadvantages to doing this: Your components take longer to get to you and you have to pay for the markup.

Evaluating service

- Accessibility. There are two people you're going to want to talk to: sales reps and technical support staff. In most companies the former are much easier to contact than the latter. Almost all vendors offer an 800 number for sales, but what about technical support? Before choosing a mail order company, call the support line a few times to find out the average waiting time.
- Responsibility. You're purchasing expensive, complex equipment that might require a bit of tinkering. If you're ordering from a vendor that offers several brands, make sure technical support is the responsibility of the vendor, not the manufacturer. Don't assume anything. Make your sales rep mail or fax you the details of the vendor's technical support policy.
- Cost. You can find free, lifetime support services if you shop around. Don't be suckered into paying a premium for technical support. If your sales rep pitches premiums, play ball somewhere else.

Returning merchandise

- Warranties. You want a warranty of at least one year with any hardware purchase. A no-questions-asked, 30-day, money-back guarantee should also be part of your purchase price. The longer the warranty the better, but don't pay extra.

- Restocking fees. Think "money-back-guarantee" means you get your money back, guaranteed? Think again. By charging consumers for restocking returned merchandise, merchants can keep up to 20 percent of your money. Don't do business with companies that charge restocking fees.
- RMA numbers. Never return merchandise to a vendor without first getting a Return Merchandise Authorization (RMA) number from customer service. This way if your component gets lost in the system, it's the vendor's responsibility.
- Call the cops. While cautious buying should protect you from the Fagans of the computer industry, sometimes you can do everything right and still get ripped off. Should this happen to you, try calling the following organizations. You might get your money back.
  - The Postal Inspection Service. You can locate the postal inspector in your seller's area by contacting your local postmaster or postal inspector. The post office has a mediation service for settling disputes.
  - Better Business Bureau. To find out the address and phone number of the bureau in the seller's area, contact the Council for Better Business Bureaus, 1515 Wilson Boulevard, Arlington, VA 22209.
  - Direct Marketing Association. The DMA is the trade association of the mail-order business. It provides self-policing of the industry and can be contacted at 6 East 42nd Street, New York, NY 10017, (212) 768-7277.

Resources

Direct manufacturers

Compaq DirectPlus
(800) 345-1518, (800) 888-5858.

Dell
(800) 289-3355, (512) 338-4400.

Gateway 2000
(800) 846-2000, (605) 232-2000.

IBM PC Direct
(800) 426-2968, (919) 517-2496.

Direct resellers

Midwest Micro
(800) 682-7248

PCs Compleat
(800) 669-4727, (508) 480-8500

Computer brokers

United Computer Exchange
(800) 755-3033

User groups

Boston Computer Society
(617) 252-0600.

Not just limited to Boston, this association boasts members in 50 countries.

Buying computers

AS A PROSPECTIVE COMPUTER BUYER, YOU'LL face a daunting range of computer systems and configurations. Fortunately, all the competition in the computer market has translated into significantly lower prices for ever more powerful equipment.

There are two major classes of personal computers: desktop and notebook. Within each class you must decide what kind of system you want: 1) an IBM PC or compatible (the PC); or 2) the Apple Macintosh (the Mac). PCs are usually considered better for number crunching and Macs are generally favored by desktop publishers and designers. These traditional delineations are fading, however, as powerful software for every business function is now available for both systems.

Desktop computers

The personal desktop computer has made its way into offices across the country, but few people actually understand how it works. In a corporate environment there are usually computer experts who buy equipment and troubleshoot problems as they arise. When you run a small business you're on your own.

In this section we'll show you what to look for in a computer system and go over the advantages and disadvantages of each. If you're unfamiliar with computer terminology, first take a look at the short glossary provided in the sidebar.

Glossary

Microprocessor—The brain of every computer, this chip determines how fast your computer runs. Each kind of chip has several levels of speed. This is measured by the chip's clock speed. The higher the number (expressed in megahertz or MHz), the faster the computer.

RAM (Random Access Memory)—Computer memory used to run programs (expressed in megabytes, or MB). With enough RAM you are often able to keep several programs open at once and switch between them (called multitasking). RAM size also affects computer's speed.

Hard disk drive—A storage device that stores programs and files. Hard drive capacity is also expressed in megabytes. It is an established fact that you can never have too much storage space. Hard disk drive speed, called access time and measured in milliseconds (ms), is important. In many cases a computer can only work as fast as the hard drive can feed it information. 28ms is the slowest acceptable speed. A speed somewhere between 12ms and 18ms will ensure good performance. Most hard drives are internal, meaning that they are contained inside your computer's case. You can buy external hard drives later to add more storage space.

Expansion slots—Places where you attach special cards *that perform a variety of functions. Common uses include internal modems and cards that accelerate the computer's speed.*

Operating system—The software that controls how a computer functions. For PCs, MS-DOS and Windows are the major choices. All new Macs run System 7.x (currently 7.1, with 7.5 being released as of this writing).

The best operating systems are GUIs (graphical user interfaces). These allow you to tell the computer what to do by pointing at pictures, or icons, and selecting commands from preset menus. System 7.x and Windows are GUIs.

The PC

Microprocessor: The majority of today's PCs are built around two chips: the 80486 and the faster Pentium. The 486 has a few variations, the 486SX, the 486DX, the 486DX2, and the 486DX4, in order of speed. The DX4 is only slightly slower than the Pentium and costs slightly less. The Pentium comes in different flavors as well, with the P60 and P90 being the most common. What does all this mean for you? You can find a machine that exactly fits the level of power and performance you need. Here are some guidelines:

- Basic use (word processing, simple accounting): 486DX running at 33 MHz. While you could get away with an SX chip, we don't recommend it because the day will come when you need the extra power.
- Average use (some graphic work, spreadsheets, databases): 486DX2 (66 MHz) will be sufficient. A Pentium P60 is desirable if it fits your budget. While a DX4 is also a good machine, the Pentium offers more for very little additional money.
- Intensive use (heavy graphic use, huge spreadsheets): A Pentium P60 is a great choice and a P90 will make your work fly.

4-1 *IBM PCs and compatibles offer great performance for the price. They also have the advantage of a vast selection of available software. The machines pictured are made by Compaq (left) and IBM (right).*

RAM: While you can get by with 4MB, 8MB is the current optimal amount. Looking ahead, 16MB will be the standard.

Hard disk drive: PC software and operating systems are insatiable when it comes to consuming disk space. A 105MB hard drive is not going to last long. A 230MB drive won't seem claustrophobic, at least for a little while (until you or your kid loads up the latest game that takes up 27MB) If you can afford a 500MB drive, it's worth the extra investment.

Expansion slots: Some machines come with eight expansion slots, which is probably more than you need. Computers designed to take up less desk space will have fewer slots—but don't settle for less than four. We talk about what to put in these expansion slots later in this chapter.

Operating system: All PCs currently come with DOS (version 6.0 is the latest). While DOS has some good features, it is not a GUI and you have to learn an assortment of commands to control the computer. There are programs to help you navigate through, but they don't rival Microsoft Windows in ease of use, which is your alternative.

The best operating systems are GUIs.

Windows (version 3.1 is the latest) also comes standard on most PCs. Overall, Windows is a good operating system, but it is not as "clean" or logical as the Mac's (see below) because it piggybacks on DOS and retains some of DOS's clunkiness. Microsoft plans to release Windows95 in the middle of 1995, which promises to be a major improvement, addressing Windows 3.1's limitations.

IBM's OS/2 is another choice. OS/2 is more powerful than Windows and gets high marks from the people who use it. Unfortunately, it doesn't have many users, so not much software is being developed for OS/2. A computer without software is nothing more than a fancy doorstop.

Advantages of PCs

- Cutthroat competition has translated into attractive prices. You can get a good computer with monitor for under $2000.
- Great software selection for computers running DOS and Windows.
- About 80 percent of the computers in use are PCs, making it easy to share data with others.

Drawbacks of PCs

- While PC manufacturers and software developers have been striving to achieve the "friendliness" that marks the Macintosh, they fall short. While it certainly is easier to get a PC up and running than it used to be, there are still plenty of things that make little apparent sense. As a businessperson, you probably don't want to spend time messing with your AUTOEXEC.BAT (even if you know what it is) or memory configurations. You'll be able to do most things without trouble, but you will encounter your share of bewildering problems.
- Peripherals are harder to install and don't work as intuitively as they do with the Mac.

The Macintosh

Microprocessor: Apple sells two lines of Macintoshes, each based on a different processor. The Quadra line is built around the 68040 (roughly equivalent to the 486 in terms of speed); all previous Macs and software were originally designed around the 68000 line of processors. Apple has also introduced the PowerMac, which uses the new PowerPC chip. The PowerPC is significantly faster than the 040, and in many applications, it outdoes the Pentium.

4-2 Apple's best-selling Macintosh computers provide good power for the money. Look for a Macintosh powered by the 68040 or the faster Power PC chip.
Apple Computer/John Greenleigh

The drawback is that previous software is incompatible with the PowerPC, which is not as bad as it sounds: The PowerPC can emulate the 040 and run that software at 040 speeds. Also, new software is rapidly being released that takes full advantage of the PowerPC in its "native mode."

Apple is betting the bank on this chip. The 040 will be phased out slowly, although software support will be around for many years to come. For basic or even average use, a Quadra is an excellent buy—prices have fallen in the wake of the PowerMac introduction. For intensive use or long-term power, consider any one of the PowerMacs.

RAM: You will need a bare minimum of 4MB. 8MB is desirable.

Hard disk drive: Most Macs come with at least a 250MB hard drive, which will be sufficient for most needs. The Macintosh operating system and Macintosh programs are more efficient in their design and generally take up less hard drive space than their PC counterparts, which means you can probably get by without 500MB.

Expansion slots: Macs, almost invariably, will have enough expansion slots for your needs.

Operating system: The Macintosh operating system is the best one available for any computer talked about in this book. It is what makes the Macintosh so "friendly" and easy to use.

Operationally, the latest PC or Macintosh notebook computer can do everything their desktop siblings can.

Advantages of Macintoshes

- Easy to set up—"plug-and-play."
- Problems you encounter are usually resolvable without having to call tech support.
- As easy and intuitive to use as any computer has gotten thus far.
- Upgrading and adding peripherals doesn't require a degree in computer science. Things will work the first time around.
- Built-in multitasking (given enough RAM).
- Built-in networking.
- Can read PC disks with additional software.

Drawbacks of Macintoshes

- Macs cost more than similarly powered PCs. Apple, however, has been steadily slashing prices to gain market share and the price gap is narrowing.
- The Macintosh has less software available. You should be able to find everything you need, but you will have fewer options in some software categories.
- The PC is more widely accepted and used, meaning you will be compatible with fewer people. There is plenty of translation software available, but this is not a perfect solution. If, however, you are starting a graphics or desktop publishing business the reverse is true—the Mac is the standard.

Upgrading the PC

Microprocessor

If you currently have a computer with an 80286 or 8086 chip, it's time to move on. There are, unfortunately, limited upgrading opportunities for these machines. While you can probably keep getting by, you are losing the opportunities that the newest software and higher speeds provide.

With a 386 or better, you probably have some options. Many manufacturers provide upgrades to more powerful chips, but not all. If you are buying a new machine, make sure you have the option to upgrade.

Some chips come with a math coprocessor, which greatly speeds up any kind of number crunching. Not sure if you have one? Call the manufacturer, who will also be able to tell you how to upgrade. Do you need one? A spreadsheet junkie without one is losing a lot of time. For word processing and the like, you'll never notice the difference.

Memory

It is easy to order RAM upgrades from the manufacturer or an outside vendor. It is fairly easy to install too—a good vendor will provide a "how-to" guide for no additional cost. If you are the type that gets nervous about opening up your PC, hire a consultant or repair person to show you how to go about it.

If you need more storage space, your best bet is to purchase an external hard drive or a removable cartridge drive (see chapter 9 for more information). To save yourself money in the long run, spring for a huge drive (400+ MB) when you first buy your computer, and you might never need to upgrade.

DOS 6.0 has a built-in disk doubling function, which compresses files when you are not using them and expands them when you want to access them. There are also several software programs that will accomplish the same thing and provide more features. While these programs do allow you to pack significantly more information on a disk drive, they can slow down your machine.

Expansion cards

PCs have very poor built-in sound capabilities, so many buyers add a sound card and speakers. You don't need stereo sound to type a memo but it does add significantly to any after-hour use of the machine (especially if you have kids). Sound cards are fairly inexpensive. A more practical card is an internal fax/modem (see chapter 8 for the details).

If you long for a giant monitor, you'll need additional video support in the form of a card. Monitor manufacturers also sell the necessary cards. Accelerated video cards dramatically increase the speed with which your monitor draws images—a big plus for desktop publishers and designers (see chapter 5 for more information).

Upgrading the Mac

Microprocessor

While you can't upgrade the actual processor (except to add a math coprocessor) in most cases, there are countless accelerator boards you can plug into an expansion slot (see *Expansion Cards* below).

Memory

The best way to order memory for the Mac is via mail-order. There are many vendors, and you can find them by perusing any magazine for Mac owners. Most Mac RAM chips work with any machine, but some Macs require a certain speed level—make sure you specify what kind of Mac you have when you order. Installation is very easy in most cases (some compact Macs with built-in monitor require special tools, and installation is best done by a professional).

Upgrading your hard drive is the same as with the PC—an external hard drive or removable cartridge drive is the way to go. There are also several compression software packages available.

Expansion cards

Macs have excellent built-in sound, and it will be the rare user who needs to upgrade.

Like the PC, larger monitors require video cards to display a full spectrum of colors. If you're willing to spend the money on a large monitor, you should invest in an accelerated video card as well.

There are a host of manufacturers that make accelerator cards (as opposed to accelerated video cards) for the Mac that dramatically boost processing speed. You can add a card to most mid-level Macs that will let them rival their high-end siblings.

> *We guarantee that there already is a machine at a reasonable price perfect for your needs.*

Notebook computers

There are different kinds of portables: laptops, notebooks, sub-notebooks, handbooks (from largest to smallest). The most common kind of portable is the notebook, which we discuss later.

4-3 *Weighing in at under seven pounds, Apple PowerBooks are excellent notebook computers.*
Apple Computer

Generally, what is true of a notebook is true of the other kinds of portables.

When shopping for a notebook computer, look at the same components that you would with a desktop unit: processor, RAM, hard drive, etc.

Desktop vs. notebook comparison

Operationally, the latest PC or Macintosh notebook computer can do everything their desktop siblings can; and they can do it anywhere. However, there is a price for portability. Compared with desktop systems most notebooks suffer some common flaws:

- Smaller keyboards. While a smaller keyboard is an inevitable consequence of miniaturization, poor keyboard design is not. Try to find a portable with a keyboard layout similar to the desktop keyboard you're used to. Some notebook models, for instance, place the up-arrow key to the left of the right-hand Shift key. This kind of unusual keyboard configuration can be frustrating.
- Smaller screens. Not only are the screens smaller, but the image quality is rarely as good as a standard desktop monitor.
- Limited memory. Special low power RAM chips for portables cost three to five times more than the desktop variety.
- Fewer expansion slots. Most portables have one half-size slot for various peripherals, as opposed to the eight full-size slots found in most desktop computers. The PCMCIA standard for notebook expansion slots might eliminate this problem.
- Slower processors. Many portable PCs and Macs are slower than desktops because they are designed around older processors. As of this writing, there are no Pentium- or PowerPC-based notebooks.
- Price. While prices have come down significantly, portables are still priced well above comparable desktop models.

Notebook features

Due to the higher prices of notebooks, you might have to sacrifice some features in order to afford others. The basic features (processor, RAM, etc.) are still major considerations, but you'll also have to decide among the features described below.

Weight

The less you get, the more you pay. Most notebooks come in at under 7 pounds and will easily fit in a briefcase. However, if you also carry extra battery packs, a portable printer, and a pocket modem it starts to add up. For really light travel, you can look into sub-notebook or handbook size computers. The drawback is that they can't pack as much power as a true notebook.

PCMCIA

PCMCIA is a universal standard for the design of cards and expansion slots for notebook and other portable computers. Developed by the Personal Computer Memory Card International Association, a consortium of manufacturers including Apple, IBM and Toshiba, the PCMCIA standard is easy to install and configure. (PCMCIA slots do not come standard on Macintosh's PowerBook; however, you can purchase a special card that accepts PCMCIA cards.)

What does PCMCIA mean to you? It means you will be able to use any manufacturer's PCMCIA peripheral with your notebook without having to worry about compatibility. Some of the PCMCIA options now available include:

- Memory cards
- Modems
- Hard drives
- LANs

In the near future, peripherals like sound cards, SCSI, and tape back-up drives will be available. Plans are also underway to integrate the PCMCIA standard with desktop slots.

PCMCIA will be the upgrade standard of the future. Existing problems are currently being dealt with and tough competition is driving prices down. If you are buying a notebook, we recommend buying one with one or two PCMCIA slots.

Screens

While all notebook screens are small, there are still some significant quality distinctions. First of all you can choose either a color or monochrome screen. Color screens tend to be a little smaller and much more expensive than monochrome screens. Color screens also eat batteries. However nothing impresses a client more than showing them a full color chart on your notebook. Another screen consideration is active or passive matrix.

Passive matrix are the standard displays on most notebook computers. These displays are less expensive but offer less brightness, less contrast, and a slower refresh rate than active matrix LCD screens. Passive matrix displays can also be difficult to see from odd angles.

Active matrix LCDs uses a transistor—or three transistors in the case of color LCD—to drive each pixel. The brightness, contrast, and refresh rate for active matrix LCD screens is generally on a par with standard desktop monitors, but you will pay a premium for this performance.

Color solution

Rather than shell out thousands of dollars for an active matrix color screen for your portable, consider connecting a SVGA monitor to your notebook when you are at your desk. Most notebooks support external monitors. If you plan to run graphics-intensive software, such as a paint program or Windows, insist on a product that can support a high resolution SVGA screen, at least 4MB of memory, and at least 486SX chip.

Consider gray scale

The best compromise between price and quality is an active-matrix monochrome screen. Active-matrix monitors are easy to read and will provide 64 shades of gray. Though they are not color, shades of gray do a respectable job of rendering color images.

Docking stations

One of the most common complaints with notebook computers is their lack of expansion possibilities. Although some notebooks have one proprietary slot for a fax/modem or memory upgrade, notebooks rarely come with a lot of expansion slots. Enter the docking station.

In short, a docking station is a $300 to $900 desktop-computer-size box that you plug your notebook into. Along with expansion slots, the station might contain a drive bay or two and some interface ports. This allows you to add on a sound-board, CD-ROM drive, tape back-up drive or anything else you could want to add to a desktop.

With a docking system your expanded system is always ready and waiting for you when you, and your notebook, return home. Notebooks that support docking have a connecting port that fits into a receptacle on the docking station. To operate, just slide in your notebook, without the hassle of reconnecting an external monitor, printer cables, external keyboard, mouse, and serial ports each time you sit down at your desk.

A growing number of manufacturers offer companion docks for their notebooks, including Compaq and Apple.

In general

It is a truism that the longer you wait to purchase your computer, the more bang you'll get for your buck. There will always be a better computer coming next month (or next week, the way things have been going). Many people use this as an excuse for procrastinating in purchasing a computer or starting their business. Don't. We guarantee that there already is a machine at a reasonable price perfect for your needs.

Computers are less important than the software that they run. Finding programs that you like is what matters.

If you have fears about being left behind in the technological dark ages after you make your purchase, make sure that what you buy has expansion slots and is upgradable.

Resources

Major manufacturers

Apple
(800) 776-2333, (408) 996-1010.
Apple is the sole manufacturer of the Macintosh.

Compaq
(800) 231-0900, (713) 370-0670.

Dell
(800) 289-3355.
Dell Computers are primarily sold direct.

Gateway 2000
(800) 846-2000, (605) 232-2000.
Gateway 2000 computers are sold direct.

IBM
(800) 426-2968, (914) 765-1900.

Packard-Bell
818-886-4600.

Books

Computer Power for Your Small Business, by Nick Sullivan, 1993, Random House Electronic Publishing, Random House Inc., Westminster, MD; $45; (410) 848-1900, (800) 733-3000.

Takes the small-business owner from computer purchasing to telecommunications and management applications. Includes a full version of the software program Managing Your Money (MECA).

Datasources, Ziff Communications Co., 1 Park Avenue, New York, NY 10016; $365, also available in libraries; (212) 503-5398.

Biannual guide to all available software and hardware; 74,000 products and 14,000 companies, cross-indexed by company name, category, name of product. Also available on CD-ROM.

Guide to Notebook and Laptop Computers, by Bill Howard, 1992, Ziff-Davis Press, Emeryville, CA; $29.95; (800) 688-0448, (510) 601-2000.

New Life for Old PCs, by Alfred E. Poor, 1992, Business One Irwin, Homewood, IL; $32.00; (708) 798-6000.

The Macintosh Bible, edited by Arthur Naiman, 1992, Peach Pit Press, Berkeley, CA; $32; (800) 283-9444.

This 1000+ page tome is the classic guide for Macintosh owners.

Microcomputer Market Place 1993, by Steven J. Bennett and Richard Freierman, 1993, Random House Electronic Publishing, Random House Inc., Westminster, MD; $30; (410) 848-1900, (800) 733-3000.

In this comprehensive guide to computer-industry contacts you'll find tons of software/hardware companies, tradeshow sponsors, computer magazines and newsletters, TV/radio shows, online information services, CD-ROM publishers, computer leasing companies, consulting referral services, and on and on.

PCs for Dummies, by Dan Gookin and Andy Rathbone, and *Macs for Dummies*, by David Pogue, 1992, IDG Books, San Mateo, CA; $16.95; (800) 762-2974, (415) 312-0650.

Excellent books for novice computer users.

PC Magazine's 1993 Computer Buyer's Guide, by John Dvorak, 1993, Ziff-Davis Press, Emeryville, CA; $19.95; (800) 688-0448, (510) 601-2000.

A comprehensive buyer's guide for PCs and peripheral equipment.

Resource Reference Book, from the PCMCIA; $12.50; (408) 720-0107.

Contains a complete listing of products available on PCMCIA cards.

Ventana Press Computer Guides, Ventana Press, Chapel Hill, NC; (919) 942-0220.

Book topics range from PC operating systems to using desktop publishing as a marketing tool, to detailed troubleshooting for spreadsheets and word processors.

The Winn Rosch Hardware Bible 2nd Edition, by Winn Rosch, 1992, Brady publishing, New York; $34.95; (212) 373-8093, (800) 428-5331.

Your First Computer, by Alan Simpson, 1992, Sybex, Alameda, CA; $19.95; (800) 227-2346, (510) 523-8233.

Associations and agencies

Boston Computer Society, One Kendall Sq., Cambridge, MA 02139; $39/year membership; (617) 252-0600.

24,000 members in 50 countries run workshops, offer business and computer support via phone, computer bulletin boards, and 15 special-interest newsletters.

Audiotapes

60 Minutes Towards Computer Literacy, by Julian Padowicz and Donna Carter. Business Film International, Stamford, CT 06907; $9.95; (203) 968-2255.

Applicable to a vast array of systems and programs, this 76-minute tape will give you a solid education in computer terms.

Buying monitors

SHOPPING FOR A BASIC MONITOR IS EASY. Most PCs come bundled with good monitors and there are several high-quality choices for the Macintosh. Almost any color 13" or 14" screen will be affordable and reliable.

Complications arise when you need larger screens—16" and up. You might need a special video card, and monitor prices rise rapidly as you add on inches. For the price of a single 21" color display ($2000–3000), you could buy 8 to 10 13" monitors.

This chapter provides some pointers to consider when shopping for a monitor.

Overview

Any new computer you purchase will have enough built-in video support to run any 13" or 14" monitor. If you plan to use a monitor larger than 15", you need to purchase additional video support in the form of an expansion card. This is why large monitors are so expensive; these cards alone can cost more than half the price of the monitor.

When purchasing a monitor for a PC, make sure that it is VGA or, preferably, Super VGA (SVGA) compatible. These are the video standards for PC displays. Super VGA will give you increased resolution over VGA. For the Mac there is no equivalent set of standards; any Mac-compatible monitor will do the trick.

Size

Statistics show larger monitors increase workers' productivity by as much as 33 percent. Most people who have used one agree: Once you use a big screen, it's tough to go back to a standard-size monitor. However, when you are starting up a business, cash can be tight. Rather than spring thousands of dollars on a great monitor, you would be better served to get a more powerful computer and additional peripherals like a fax/modem or scanner. This kind of equipment will undoubtedly add more to your productivity than a large monitor. You can always reward yourself with a monster monitor later if your business is successful. Of course, if you are in the graphic design or desktop publishing business, purchasing a large monitor at the start might be wise.

Color

If you buy a standard size display, there is no reason not to buy color—the prices are low. Depending on the amount of built-in support or the power of a card, your monitor will be able to display a certain number of colors. These levels of color display are referred to as 8-bit, 16-bit, and 24-bit color:

- 8-bit color displays 256 colors;
- 16-bit displays thousands of colors;
- 24-bit displays millions of colors.

Most computers come with enough video support to display 8-bit color on a 13" or 14" monitor. If you want more colors or need a larger display, you will have to purchase a video card. Supporting 24-bit color on a 20" monitor is an expensive proposition. If you are happy with 8-bit color on a large display, you can save a lot of money.

Video cards

When shopping for video cards, there are three key questions you should ask yourself and the salesperson:

- Is it compatible with the monitor you want? Most monitor manufacturers also make cards for their systems, but you might find a bargain from a compatible third party source.
- What level of color will it give for the size display you want?

- Is the card accelerated? Accelerated video cards will dramatically speed up how quickly your screen draws images or scrolls through a document.

Gray-scale monitors

If you know you'll be frustrated with a smaller monitor, a large gray-scale display is an excellent compromise—color is an unnecessary luxury for many business applications. These monitors will cost less than half as much as their color counterparts. There are a few gray-scale monitors for the PC, but they are much more prevalent for the Mac.

Dot pitch

Dot pitch refers to the diagonal distance between two dots of the same color. It helps determine the monitor's overall clarity. The standard dot pitch is .28mm, and this distance (or less) will be sufficient for your needs.

Refresh rate

A monitor's refresh rate measures how quickly the monitor renews the screen to reflect changes in the image. To avoid screen flicker, get a monitor with a refresh rate of at least 60 hertz. However, if you are particularly sensitive to the flickering of fluorescent lights, even a 60 hertz monitor might give you headaches. Flicker-sensitive users should buy a monitor with higher refresh rates.

Controls

Ideally, large monitors should have controls for:

- Brightness
- Contrast
- Horizontal position
- Vertical position
- Height or vertical size
- Width or horizontal size
- Degaussing

A degauss button de-magnetizes your monitor if its image has become distorted due to proximity to magnetic fields. Most smaller monitors only offer brightness and contrast controls.

Resources

Major manufacturers of monitors and video cards

Apple
(800)-776-2333, (408) 996-1010

NEC
(800) 388-8888, (708) 860-9500

Radius
(408) 434-1010

RasterOps
(800) 729-2656, (408) 562-4200

Sony
(800) 352-7669, (408) 434-6644

SuperMac
(408) 541-6100, (800) 334-3005

ViewSonic
(800) 888-8583, (909) 869-7976

Buying printers

YOU ARE WHAT YOU PRINT. THE OUTPUT FROM your printer is often the first thing that a prospective client sees from your business. What type of printer should you get? For most businesses, buying a laser printer is the clear choice, especially in light of plunging prices. In this chapter we'll highlight the important features and also give you a guide to upgrading your laser, if you own an older model or purchase a used machine.

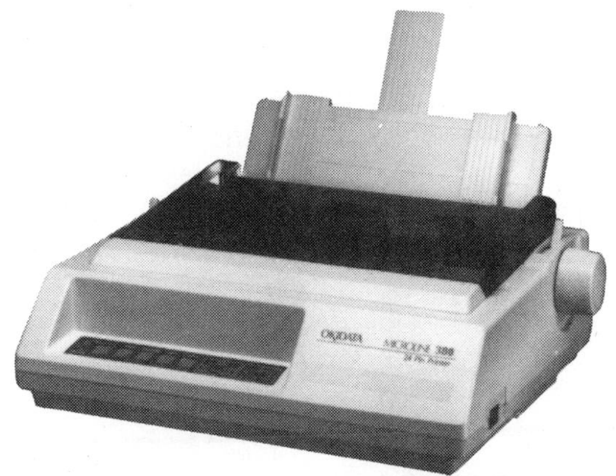

6-1 Dot-matrix printers are best suited for printing continuous-feed labels and multipart forms. For the best quality, look for a model with a 24-pin print head. Okidata

Types of printers

There are three major printer types currently on the market suitable for small business use: dot matrix, inkjet, and laser printers. Laser printers offer the best performance; inkjets provide decent performance for the budget-conscious; dot matrix printers are the only choice if you need to print multiform documents.

Dot-matrix

These printers work much like a traditional typewriter. Some form of hammer or pin drives ink from a ribbon onto the page. Dot-matrix printers are relatively inexpensive and are the only printers capable of creating multiform documents because they use an impact printing method. However print quality is poor, relative to a laser, and they are very noisy when printing.

Although the price of a dot-matrix printer might be tempting, if you care about your documents' appearance, resist the temptation. The need to print multiform documents is the only good reason to purchase one—and even then you should have a second printer for other uses.

Inkjet

Inkjet printers spray tiny drops of ink onto the page to form letters. This might seem like an imprecise way to print, but inkjet resolution is on a par with many laser printers. Since they don't use an impact printing method they are quieter than dot-matrix printers. What's more, inkjet printers cost about half as much as a midrange laser printer.

Inkjets are rapidly becoming the mobile printing standard. Apple, Epson and Hewlett-Packard all offer battery-operated inkjet printers that accept letter size paper.

Inkjets also offer affordable color printing. Since the ink is still liquid when it hits the paper, colors can be mixed together to create intermediary hues. For color printing on a budget, nothing beats inkjets.

On the down side all inkjets are slow and there is no such thing as a PostScript inkjet printer (more on PostScript later). However, if price and quality text printing are your primary concerns, an inkjet will deliver both.

Laser printers

Unless you love the sizzling sound of a dot-matrix printer or need to print multiform documents, you've run out of excuses for not adding a laser printer to your home office: prices have fallen to the basement. Today, you can pick up a four-,

6-2 Inkjet printers provide resolutions rivaling laser printers, but when it comes to speed, font variety, and graphics capability, they fall short of lasers. Apple Computer/John Greenleigh

6-3 Providing fast, professional-looking output, laser printers are the best choice for almost all businesses. Panasonic

five-, or six-ppm (page per minute) laser for under $1000—sometimes for as little as $700.

Laser quality is the professional standard. The 300-dpi (dots-per-inch) resolution, which is the lowest resolution a laser printer delivers, puts dot-matrix printers to shame. Even slow laser printers are faster than inkjet and dot-matrix printers. Laser printers also excel at printing different fonts and graphics (although we should mention printing on envelopes can be frustrating).

Choosing a laser printer is a complicated and potentially confusing undertaking.

For producing formal correspondence, newsletters, business cards, or almost anything else, a low-cost laser will do the job well. However, if you're planning to produce camera-ready work for high-quality production printing (600 dpi) or you need to produce at a faster speed (8 ppm) be prepared to spend more than $1000.

Buying laser printers

The following section lists some features you should consider when shopping for a laser printer.

Paper trays

The multipurpose paper trays that come standard on most printers allow you to stockpile the paper size of your choice: executive, letter, or legal. Look for a feeder that holds paper, envelopes, and labels. From our experience, however, printing on envelopes is an aggravating process. A typewriter, if you still have one, is the easiest way to print on envelopes.

Memory

Most printers come with 1MB of RAM, but you'll probably want to get at least 2MB. Look to 4MB if you will be doing graphics-intensive work. If you get a printer with a higher resolution, you will need even more memory.

Resolution

The standard laser printer resolution is 300 dots per inch. At this resolution you will get crisp text and solid blacks. For anyone but a professional designer, this is a good choice. (See chapter 20 for more information on higher resolutions.)

Speed

The most commonly used indicator of a printer's performance is its page-per-minute (ppm) rating, which measures the number of text pages it can output in a minute. Personal laser printers usually print between four and eight ppm. As a general rule, the lower a printer's ppm rating, the less you can expect to pay for it.

This measurement reflects the optimum speed of the print engine (the collective name for a printer's photosensitive drum, developing cylinder, transfer corona, and toner-disbursement system). Even under ideal conditions the ppm rating only tells half the tale. The true speed of a laser printer depends both on the ability of your applications to handle printing and on the design of the printer's controller card, a special circuit board that processes the commands from your computer.

Increasing the amount of RAM installed in a laser printer improves its performance.

To increase actual print speed, many manufacturers now use RISC (reduced-instruction-set-computing) chips on their controller cards. Even those companies that still rely on CISC (conventional-instruction-set-computing) technology are beginning to favor 16-MHz chips over the older and slower 10-MHz versions.

For simple text documents, a printer's ppm rating is a good indicator of its actual performance. But a more efficient controller card will noticeably reduce the time required to print graphics. If you print graphics-intensive documents, it's worth your while to check a printer's specifications to determine what kind of chips it uses. A good rule of thumb where performance is concerned: RISC over CISC, and the more MHz the better.

Disposable engines

When buying a laser printer you need to consider what you'll pay for consumables—the print engine's toner cartridge, drum, and other components. These need to be replaced regularly. How often you need to do this and how complicated the process is depends on the print engine's design.

An all-in-one print engine (Canon is one manufacturer) is by far the most convenient way to go. But be prepared to pay for this convenience. A single-engine printer's cost per page for consumables, which can be calculated by dividing the cost of the engine by the approximate number of pages it will print before needing to be replaced, works out to somewhere around three cents per page. It might sound low, but this is on the high side compared to modular engines.

Modular engines

A more frugal, if less convenient, alternative is to buy a laser printer whose print engine consists of two or even three individual components. Less expensive components are replaced more frequently. Obviously, figuring out the per-page consumable costs for an engine with multiple parts requires more work.

Adding to the economic appeal of multiple-part engines is the fact that their toner cartridges are easily refurbished. Cartridges can be refilled and reused at a fraction of what it would cost to replace them. Other components can also be recycled, although this might lower the print quality over time. You might also factor in the potential ecological advantages of recycling these items rather than shoving them under the metaphorical carpet of your local landfill. Still, it's hard to argue with the plug-and-play convenience of a one-piece print engine.

Invest the effort before you buy

Clearly, choosing a laser printer is a complicated and potentially confusing undertaking. All we can say is that the return on your effort will justify this quest. No matter what business you're in, you're competing for attention. A laser printer might not turn you into a graphic designer or a best-selling writer, but it's the first step to looking good on paper.

Page description languages

Part of choosing a laser printer is choosing a page description language, or PDL. Put simply, a PDL coordinates the way your printer manages the almost 8.5 million individual dots that can comprise an 8.5-by-11-inch page printed at a resolution of 300 dots per inch. Two page-description languages currently dominate the market: Hewlett-Packard's Printer Control Language (PCL) and Adobe Systems' PostScript.

PCL

The prevailing HP standard is Level 5 PCL. It does a good job handling text and is speedy. The downside is that it is not PostScript, which is still the standard. You will do well with PCL unless you start getting into graphics-intensive work, in which case you should upgrade to PostScript.

PostScript

Unlike HP's Level 5 PCL, PostScript has been around since 1985. The PostScript standard is device-independent, meaning that the same file can be printed on virtually any PostScript-compatible printer. The PostScript language assumes responsibility for generating printouts at the maximum resolution (dpi) available on a given printer, so it "knows" if you are printing to a 300-dpi printer or a 2400-dpi imagesetter and prints at the respective resolution. Because of this, PostScript has become the de facto standard of professional typesetters that accept both Macintosh and MS-DOS files. If you take your work to a service bureau for final output, PostScript is the logical choice.

On the negative side, PostScript printers are still pricey compared to PCL printers. List prices for even relatively inexpensive models hover around the $2000 mark, with street prices ranging anywhere from $1200 to $1600. Of course, only a couple of years ago prices for PostScript printers started at around $3300.

PostScript printers also tend to be slower than their HP-compatible counterparts. It's not unusual to wait 5 minutes or more for a PostScript printer to print a single page containing multiple fonts and graphics. But in fairness, that page is almost guaranteed to be stunning.

The rule

All right, so which one is best for you? Is there a quick-and-dirty rule that will help you choose between these two popular standards? To some extent, yes. If your documents contain a limited number of typefaces, an HP or compatible printer will suffice. Conversely, if you need visual panache, PostScript is the way to go. PostScript is also the better choice if you print oversized spreadsheets, which a PostScript printer can scale to a manageable size.

When it comes to picking a page-description language, your first choice need not necessarily be your final one. Many HP-compatible printers, including Hewlett-Packard's own LaserJet II, III, and IV series, can be upgraded to PostScript compatibility with additional memory and a special Adobe PostScript or compatible cartridge or controller card.

Upgrading your laser

If you already use a laser printer, you know how clear, crisp, printed documents provide professionalism to your business correspondence—which, in turn, increases your chances at success.

However, buying a new printer is only the first step. We found a variety of products designed to complement a laser printer. Some of these products will improve your printer's speed and resolution, while others turn a plain PCL printer into a PostScript powerhouse. A few can even transform a laser printer into a plain-paper fax machine.

Soft fonts gobble up significant amounts of disk space, so pick and choose carefully.

Adding memory boosts printing speed

One of the easiest and most practical ways to upgrade a laser printer is to increase its memory. Unlike a dot-matrix printer, which prints a document one line at a time, the contents of an entire page are transferred to a laser printer before the print process starts. Increasing the amount of RAM installed in a laser printer improves its performance in two ways.

First, it allows a page to contain more information. A minimum of 1MB of RAM is required to print, for example, a complex graphic image at 300 dots per inch. Document pages that contain both text and graphics need approximately the same amount of RAM. Try to print an elaborate page without enough memory and, in most cases, the printer either won't print or will give you only part of your page. An error message will inform you that a memory shortage has occurred.

The second way additional printer RAM helps is by allowing the printer to "stack" pages in memory as it prints. While one page is being printed, your computer can begin transferring the contents of the next page into the printer's memory. This speeds up the printing of longer documents and lets you get back to work.

How much memory should your printer have?

We recommend a starting point of 2MB for a 300-dpi laser printer. Beyond this, the higher the better. What kind of memory you'll need and how much it will cost depend on the type of printer you own. Check your printer's manual for information on what type of memory you need and how to order it.

If you own one of the more popular laser printers, you might be able to purchase additional RAM from a source other than its manufacturer. Numerous companies, for example, sell RAM boards for the various HP LaserJet models. Because third-party boards tend to cost less than the manufacturer's own expansion RAM, this option can save you money.

A second memory option—the buffer

Many of the advantages associated with increasing a printer's RAM—namely, additional speed and printing capabilities—can also be realized by adding a printer buffer to your system. Instead of being installed within the printer, however, a printer buffer is a stand-alone unit.

6-4 A printer buffer provides additional memory for laser printers. Using a printer buffer is the best way to upgrade memory if you have more than one printer because they can all take advantage of the buffer.

Choosing a printer buffer is most logical for someone who has more than one printer. By making additional RAM available to both printers, a printer buffer speeds up work to both. A buffer can also connect two or more computers to a single printer. Some even allow you to pick and choose between computer and printer configurations.

Share your printer among computers

If you own a PC

There are other ways to make a printer do double-duty if you have more than one computer. One of these is extremely low-tech: Simply pick up an A/B switch at your local Radio Shack or other electronics store (about $30). The switch won't increase printer memory, but it will allow you to connect your printer to two computers, and with a flick of a switch, the unit will direct your printout accordingly.

A second, more costly and complicated method is to install a printer-sharing card in the printer. The advantage to this approach is that the card contains the necessary circuitry to manage incoming print jobs without requiring you to cross the room to flip a switch. For example, Western Telematic's PSC-6 installs in an HP LaserJet and can accept input from up to six computers. You pay more for this convenience.

If you own a Mac

In an all-Macintosh environment, printer sharing is somewhat simpler: The hardware and operating system have a built-in networking system (AppleTalk) to hook multiple computers to a single printer.

If you have both Macs and PCs, there are many printers on the market that can accept data from either machine and even switch modes automatically.

Fonts

All laser printers come with some fonts installed—a font is a version of a particular typeface (Times is a typeface, Times Bold Italic is a font). These fonts, though, are fairly basic. It might not be long before you are itching for something with more style—a couple of well-chosen typefaces can go a long way to adding a professional feel to your work (see chapter 20 for tips on type selection). The options you have in expanding your type library depend on the type of computer you have.

If you own a PC

Most printers designed for the PC have at least one expansion slot that can be used to add font or memory cartridges. Font cartridges provide the fastest and easiest way to increase the number of fonts available for your documents. Slipping a SuperSet+, by Computer Peripherals, into the cartridge slot on an HP LaserJet or compatible printer, for example, places 425 fonts at your fingertips for a mere $299. If your needs aren't this elaborate, the company's ActionSet! cartridge includes 102 fonts, for an even more affordable $149.

If your laser printer doesn't have a cartridge slot—or if a cartridge option doesn't entice you—look into font software, otherwise known as soft fonts or downloadable fonts. Soft fonts are stored on your computer's hard drive and downloaded to the printer when used. Be warned: Soft fonts gobble up significant amounts of disk space, so pick and choose carefully.

Two companies with a long history of success in the software-based font market are Adobe Systems and Bitstream. Adobe Systems offers more then 300 packages, for both Macs and PCs, which include from one to 10 typefaces per package. Bitstream recently released a whopping 1100-font library in PC format—unfortunately, it costs almost $10,000. Bitstream sells four-font sets culled from this library. The company also offers special bundled packages, which contain three or more four-font packs.

If you own a Mac

To add fonts to your Mac you have to purchase font software, as noted above. Before you start buying new font packages, we recommend getting font management software, like Fifth Generation System's Suitcase. This does a better job of keeping your fonts organized than the Mac's built-in font handling.

The only option roughly comparable to a plug-in cartridge is to purchase an external hard drive and attach it to your printer. You can then store your font software there and never have to download it to your printer. Unless you have hundreds of fonts this is not an economical solution.

Postpurchase PostScript

To add PostScript capabilities to a PCL printer, just purchase either a PostScript cartridge or a special controller card. The cartridge approach, if you've got a free slot, is the more convenient of the two. Just pop a PostScript cartridge into your printer's cartridge slot and you're ready to go—except, of course, for the necessary step of reconfiguring your software to use a PostScript printer.

Hewlett-Packard sells PostScript cartridges for its popular line of LaserJet printers. The HP LaserJet PostScript Cartridge Plus, which supports Level 2 PostScript printing (the most recent version of PostScript) on the LaserJet III family of printers, lists for $695. LaserJet II owners should look for the older, Level 1 PostScript cartridge, which retails for $495.

In addition to supporting the newer, Level 2 PostScript standard, the Plus version allows you to switch between PCL and PostScript either from within an application or using the printer's front-panel controls. To accomplish the same thing with the older model, you have to insert or remove the cartridge and then restart your printer.

PostScript on a card

Another way to endow your PCL printer with flashy PostScript capabilities is with a special controller card. LaserMaster Corporation makes an especially attractive trio of these: the WinJet 300, WinJet 800, and WinJet 1200.

The 300 and 800 WinJet models work with HP LaserJet II and III or Canon LBP-4 printers; the 1200 model is designed for HP's LaserJet 4. All are designed to run within Windows and support a variety of print features: PostScript emulation, background printing, font management for PostScript Level 1 and Windows' True Type fonts, and the ability to print multiple pages as thumbnail sketches, among others. The 800 and 1200 also provide so-called TurboRes output, which increases the printer's normal output to 800- and 1200-dpi resolutions, respectively. That's just shy of true typeset quality. After seeing the WinJet 800's output on an HP LaserJet IIP, we can tell you it's stunning. The 1200's effect on a LaserJet 4 is equally impressive.

As if these features aren't enough, the WinJet cards greatly speed up printing, one of Windows' greatest shortcomings. PostScript documents that take up to four minutes to print directly from Windows start churning out of the printer in less than a minute with the WinJet running in PostScript mode.

Another offering in this same category is the PrintSprint 600 by Myriad Enterprises. It splits the difference between a standard LaserJet and the LaserJet/WinJet combination by providing 600-dpi printing in PCL or PostScript mode. Myriad offers four PrintSprint models. PrintSprint 600/2 and PrintSprint 600/3 are designed for LaserJet II and III printers, running in PCL mode. The PrintSprint 600/2ps and PrintSprint 600/3ps controller cards double the density of documents generated in PostScript mode.

Fax, not fiction

The most obvious benefit of turning your laser printer into a fax-receiving unit is the advantage of plain-paper reception over thermal: no curling or fading. The added ability to fax directly to and from your computer generally enhances fax quality.

One elegant and inexpensive way to do this is with a FaxMe cartridge from Practical Peripherals. Inserting the FaxMe into the cartridge slot of an HP LaserJet Series II or III printer converts it into a plain-paper, receive-only fax machine. The printer's front-panel controls let you select one of three modes: fax-only, printer-only, or automatic switching. The same controls let you change your fax configuration from the default parameters, if necessary. The cartridge stores settings in nonvolatile RAM, so you don't have to modify them each time you turn on your printer.

NEC Technologies has pushed the printer/fax envelope even further. It includes a PostScript language facsimile option for its Silentwriter Model 95 printer that can send and receive faxes to and from a facsimile-configured Mac, PC, or stand-alone fax machine. The biggest advantage associated with NEC's use of the PostScript standard is that it handles virtually any document, regardless of the resolution, print technology, or color compatibility of the sending or receiving device.

What's next?

Devices are on the market that combine laser printing, scanning, fax capabilities, and traditional copying in a single unit—Okidata's Doc•It line of machines is a good example. These machines are expensive at this point, but when prices drop they will be a good deal.

Resources

Books

Upgrade Your Computer Printer and Save a Bundle, by Horace W. Labadie Jr, 1993, Windcrest/McGraw-Hill, P.O. Box 40, Blue Ridge Summit, PA; $22.95; (800) 822-8138.

Troubleshooting and Repairing Computer Printers, by Stephen Bigelow, 1992, Windcrest/McGraw Hill, P.O. Box 40, Blue Ridge Summit, PA; $22.95; (800) 822-8138.

Companies mentioned in the chapter

Western Telematic
(714) 586-9950, (800) 854-7226.

Adobe Systems
(415) 961-4400, (800) 833-6687

Bitstream
(800) 522-3668, (617) 497-6222

Fifth Generation Systems
(800) 999-2735

LaserMaster Corporation
(612) 944-9330, (800) 365-4646

Myriad Enterprises
(714) 494-8165, (800) 593-8165

Practical Peripherals
(805) 497-4774, (800) 442-4774

Major manufacturers

Apple
(800)-776-2333, (408) 996-1010

Epson America
(800) 922-8911, (310) 782-0770

Hewlett-Packard
(800) 752-0900, (408) 246-4300

Kodak
(800) 344-0006

Lexmark
(800) 426-2468

NEC Technologies
(800) 388-8888, (508) 264-8000

Okidata
(800) 654-3282

Panasonic
(800) 742-8086

QMS
(800) 523-2696

Star Microtronics
(800) 447-4700

Buying phones & communications equipment

In Building Your Array of Office equipment, buying a new phone is probably not high on your priority list. At some point a more full-featured phone might be a good investment, but for most businesses the special services offered by the phone company should be more than sufficient (see chapter 14 for more details on communications services). This is not to say you can't upgrade your communications system yourself. You can choose from a variety of communications equipment to enhance the power of your current phone. For the mobile professional, cellular phones offer constant communication at an affordable price.

Telephones

Telephone headsets

If your business requires constant use of the telephone, pick up a telephone headset. Headsets free your hands for faster data entry and save your neck the strain of pinching the receiver between your chin and shoulder. When buying a telephone headset make sure it is lightweight and fully adjustable.

Electric phone jacks

Need another phone jack in your home office? Instead of paying for the phone company to come into your home and install another jack, look into buying an electric phone extension. When you plug one of these devices into an electrical wall outlet, every outlet becomes a potential phone jack.

Electronic phone jacks give you the convenience of having an extension in every room of your home or office without the cost. You can find electronic jacks at most electronic stores. These jacks work with any phone, fax, or modem.

Cordless freedom

Cordless phones give you mobility and flexibility, and great transmission quality too.

When buying a cordless phone follow these buying tips.

- To avoid static and other interference, get a powerful phone—a 900 MHz model will give you great transmission around the house, and good transmission up to half a mile away.
- Good cordless phones should have at least ten secured channels to limit your chances of interference.
- Speaker phones and a special paging function that helps locate a misplaced handset are also useful features.

Answering machines

The answering machine is the most common phone peripheral. Although all answering machines will take your callers' messages, numerous other options are available as well.

- Digital. Digital machines dispense with the traditional answering machine tape by digitally recording messages—making for improved recording quality and easier accessing of messages. Digital machines have a finite memory (usually 15–20 minutes) with which to record messages.
- Toll-saver. If your answering machine has a toll-saver feature, the number of rings you hear when you call in for messages will let you know whether there are any.
- Time and date stamping. This feature, as you might expect, records the time and date of each message so you can better track your calls.
- VOX or *voice-activated* setting. This lets callers leave long messages without being cut off.

- Ring selection. This lets you set the number of rings the machine will allow before answering the phone.
- Pager. When the pager feature is activated, the answering machine will call you at a preselected phone number anytime someone leaves a message.
- The ability to answer two lines.
- Security codes.

Pagers

Beepers are big. Currently, almost 20 million people are packing electronic pagers—and 53,000 more sign up everyday. Long gone are the days when pagers were for drug dealers and doctors only. Today, pagers present an inexpensive, user-friendly way to keep yourself in the loop.

Pager technology is relatively simple. When a caller dials your number, a radio transmitter, managed by your paging service, sends a signal designed for your pager. When the pager receives that signal it beeps or vibrates and displays the number of the person that called you.

Alphanumeric pagers allow you to receive short text messages. The caller talks to an operator who enters the data into the pager network.

There are many providers of paging services and countless pricing scenarios depending on the range of service (local, regional, or national) and messaging sophistication (numeric or alphanumeric). Your local phone company is a good place to start your search. And, of course, talk with your friends who already use a paging service.

Cellular phones

With the advent of affordable cellular technology, home business owners can talk to clients from their cars—even from another city. And cellular technology guarantees you can be reached quickly in an emergency—even if you are a thousand miles away.

How it works

Each transmission area is called a *cell*, and by adding computer control to the system, a cellular phone moving from one cell to the next can automatically switch from the previous cell to the next one, allowing calls to continue without interruption.

Pagers present an inexpensive, user-friendly way to keep yourself in the loop.

The FCC has divided the country into 305 metropolitan service areas and 428 rural service areas. Two carriers, one of which is usually a local phone company, are allowed to operate in each area—to create some kind of competition.

Cellular options

Choosing the right phone is mostly a matter of deciding how much weight you want to carry rather than how much money you want to spend: As usual, the less weight, the more money. Bulky phones mean low prices and probable backaches. But keep in mind that bulky phones transmit at a higher wattage, giving them greater range.

At present, you will find three active rungs in the cellular-phone evolutionary ladder: car phones, transportables, and hand-helds. Hand-helds have become the standard for most mobile professionals.

Car phones

Cellular was once synonymous with car phone. The demand for communications while on the road was, and still is, obvious. The technology is relatively simple. Size and weight are not a consideration, and neither is power—a car's electrical system can easily power a device that consumes no more electricity than a taillight. A bulky radio transceiver unit can be bolted into the trunk, leaving only the handset in the passenger compartment.

Transportables

Transportables come either as bag phones, in which the components are arranged in a soft vinyl or leather case with a strap, or in hard packs, into which all the components snap to create a relatively sleek unit that can be slipped into a briefcase.

Transportables are dirt-cheap, work well, and, at three to five pounds, are light enough to take to a job site. But they're still not convenient enough to take everywhere.

Hand-helds

Larger hand-helds fit into a purse, a bag, or a coat pocket. The smallest, latest, lightest units are more the size and weight of a scientific calculator and fit into a pants pocket.

Hand-helds generally come with rechargeable battery packs that clip on to form the back of the phone. This allows battery packs of different sizes and energy capacities to be used with the same phone. Some smaller packs might allow 30 minutes of conversation on a charge or seven hours of standby operation; larger packs can triple those figures.

Even the largest battery for a hand-held is a lot smaller than the battery of a transportable, yet both last about the same amount of time. This is partly because circuitry in the hand-held is more efficient, but mostly because the hand-held requires less transmission power. While the hand-held units' lack of power might seem to give transportables an advantage, most urban and suburban areas are always in range of a hand-held, even from inside a car.

Many hand-helds can be used with car power boosters that provide the reception and broadcasting power of a transportable or car phone. This way you can have both the convenience of a handheld and the power of a car phone.

Bundling

The street price of cellular phones usually falls far below the manufacturer's suggested retail price. A provider will give dealers subsidies of $300 or more for each phone sold with that provider's service, since customers who sign up with one provider are apt to remain forever. Although illegal in California and North Carolina, this practice, called bundling, is still done nationwide on a wink-and-nod basis.

In the rest of the country bundling is legitimate, and places legal obligations on you to stay with the subsidizing carrier for a certain amount of time: three months, six months, even a year. Before buying a phone, you should ask your service carriers what their rates are and whether they offer special features that you might find valuable, like voice mail.

Many hand-helds can be used with car power boosters that provide the power of a transportable or car phone.

The bottom line

Which phone to get? Here are the real considerations:

- Size: The smaller, the better.
- Comfort: Does the phone fit your hand and face? Are the buttons easy to operate?
- Sound quality: In most places you can test a phone while shopping, even if it is not activated, by dialing any number. You'll get a recording from the service carrier giving you a free sign-up number. If you call that number, you can determine whether the operator can hear you clearly.
- Special considerations: Can the phone be used with a car power booster, i.e., a cigarette lighter? Can it be used with the modem of a notebook computer?
- Durability: Does the phone look like it could be dropped on the sidewalk without breaking? Many phones come with cases that should increase their survival potential. Is there a service contract available that covers dropping the phone? Otherwise, you should ask yourself, "Do I feel lucky?"

Using cellular phones

Cellular phones operate a little differently than do traditional phones and will require you to make minor adjustments in the way you work. To save you some frustration, we have listed some user tips below.

- Make sure the phone is on. Don't laugh, years of picking up the phone and hearing a dial tone are hard to forget.
- After dialing a number or when the phone rings, press the Send button to complete the connection.
- When the call is over, press the End button to disconnect.
- If you make a mistake while dialing, turn the phone off, then on, and start over, or use the Clear button.
- On some phones it's not good enough to press a Power button to turn the phone on and off. You must press it and hold it down before the phone decides you really mean it.
- Because of the high per-minute cost, make your calls shorter and more to the point.
- When driving use the mobile phone's speaker function instead of the handset. It's safer, and in many states it's the law.
- Although some mobile phones work off the car's battery, carry a spare fully charged phone battery in case the signal starts fading.
- Routinely announce to secretaries you are calling from a cellular phone and you will be put on hold less frequently.

Cellular problems

Despite the numerous benefits of cellular phones there are some notable problems and limitations. First of all, the signals are easily intercepted. Anyone with a sophisticated radio frequency scanner can eavesdrop on your conversations. Even accidental interceptions are not uncommon. Revealing sensitive or confidential information over a cellular phone line can be risky.

Another problem is that in many rural areas and small towns cellular service is simply not available. No transmitter, no service. Also, in high density areas where many cellular phones are being used at the same time, you might have trouble getting a dial tone.

Cellspeak definitions

The forces of evil require that every worthwhile new technology be strangled by a profusion of buzzwords, jargon, abbreviations, and acronyms, mostly referring to "functions," calculated to frighten and confuse normal, decent people. The following is a glossary of cellular functions:

Alphanumeric memory—*This means that you can type in someone's name to go along with the numbers you have stored in the memory. Except that there are 26 letters in the alphabet and only eight buttons on the phone with letters on them, which means you'll have to search for Q and Z someplace else. To enter the letter C, say, you have to press the 2-ABC key three times, but not too slowly because if you wait too long,* *the phone assumes you are finished and moves on to the next letter. This is obviously clumsy, so some phones have a bunch of pretyped words already punched in, which you can access via an arcane set of key presses. On one phone, one of the pretyped words is Home—ready and waiting for people who can't remember their own phone number.*

Call timer*—This keeps track of the total time the phone has been used so you can argue with your service provider when the bill comes. Except, of course, by the time you get the bill, the total in the phone's call timer includes calls made after the closing date.*

Dropped call*—When you lose your connection with a caller you have "dropped" the caller, but generally no one holds this against you.*

DTMF*—Stands for Dual Tone Multi-Frequency. Now do you understand? No? Would you believe all this means is "touch tone"?*

Dual mode*—This reflects a combination of analog and digital technologies. Cellular carriers are in the process of adopting digital technology that will increase the number of conversations that can be handled within each cell by a factor of 3, 8, or perhaps even 20, depending on the technology used. Dual-mode phones will operate the old way or the new way, depending on what's available. At this point, if your local carrier is not implementing one of the new systems, it does not make sense to pay more for a dual-mode phone, since there are several competing new systems and it is hard to say which will be the predominant one in the future. On the other hand, if your local carrier is using one of the new technologies, and the price of the phone is competitive with standard models, go for it.*

Electronic lock*—Prevents the phone from being used without your knowledge. Of questionable value for pocket phones, unless you have a lot of trouble with pickpockets. Of course, if you have a habit of leaving your pocket phone on your desk or in restaurant bathrooms, this might be a lifesaver.*

FCN*—Short for Function. This is the key to all your new phone's "special" functions that you'll probably never use—press it and a menu of options becomes available.*

Hands-free operation*—This means speakerphone, and is supposed to be a boon while using the phone in the car. Speakerphones barely work in nice quiet offices, so the chances that you will find this arrangement satisfactory in the car are slim, to say the least. Nonetheless, some states require hands-free operation in cars. Using features like hands-free (auto) answering and voice-activated dialing, you could keep both hands on the wheel at all times, but you'll have to be careful what you say lest you accidentally trigger your phone to dial Mozambique.*

NAM*—Numeric Assignment Module. This is where the phone's own phone number is stored. NAM is usually used in terms like Dual-NAM or Multi-NAM and means that the phone can have more than one "home" system. This is only for people who spend a lot of time in different cities, for whom it might be cheaper to deal with numerous local carriers than to pay the extra charges that generally apply when you are using the phone outside of the range of your home system (see Roaming).*

Roaming*—Using your phone outside the range of your home system. Extra charges generally apply, and the arrangements can get complicated. If you plan to do a lot of this, check carefully with each of the two carriers that operate in your area to find out what arrangements are available and which will be best for you. In the future, roaming arrangements are expected to improve, perhaps to the point where there will be no extra charges or hassles.*

Scratch pad*—Here's the idea: The person you are talking to mentions someone's phone number. Instead of just jotting the number down (while driving with your knee), you're supposed to interrupt your conversation, take the phone away from your face, engage the scratch-pad feature, type in the number just mentioned, and take the phone back and forth from your face while you check to make sure you got the number right. Meanwhile, the person who is trying to talk to you will hear touch tones blaring from the receiver. Not to worry, you can turn the tones off if you press, say, the Function key, then the number 5 and the plus or minus key. Meanwhile, turning off the phone or, on some models, touching almost any key will erase the scratch pad. Oops!*

SND*—Short for Send. Almost everyone in the cellular business agrees that the savings in space is worth rendering one of the shorter words in the English language incomprehensible. Perhaps they are trying to obscure the paradox that this is often also the button you press to receive a call. It's a wonder they didn't abbreviate End as ND.*

Standby time, talk time*—This is the amount of time a phone's battery will last while waiting for a call (standby) or placing a call (talk). Note that these are either/or figures. If a battery lasts eight hours standby and one hour talk, after four hours of standing by you will have only a half hour of talk left, and vice-versa. Moral: It's good to have an extra battery if possible.*

Thirty-, 100-, or 200-number memory*—This is the same feature found on a lot of home phones and is based on the idea that it is somehow easier to remember that on this particular phone your friend John's number is, say, 61 instead of the usual 7- or 10-digit number that works with every other phone on the planet. It's not easier. Some of the phones in our sample devote the last few pages of the instruction manual to a "speed-dial* *memory index" where you can record what phone number and what individual or institution you have assigned to each of 100 codes.*

Resources

Manufacturers

Phones and answering machines

AT&T
(800) 222-3111

Panasonic Co.
(201) 348-9090

Cobra Electronics
(800) 262-7222

Code-A-Phone Corp.
(503) 655-8940

Electric phone jacks

Phone Technologies
(800) 437-0101

Pager and messaging services

Ericksson GE Communications
(201) 265-6600

Motorola, EMBARC
Advanced Messaging
(800) 362-2724

SkyTel
(800) 456-3333 ext. 0124

Cellular phones

Mitsubishi
(708) 298-9223

Motorola
(800) 331-6456

Murata
(214) 403-3300

Buying faxes, modems, & fax/modems

WHEN IT COMES TO SPEED, TRANSMITTING data electronically beats the Post Office and Federal Express hands down. Sometimes it even costs less. Clearly, these devices are major time savers, but they have other advantages as well. Creative faxing can be a powerful marketing tool. With a modem, you can tap into the wealth of information contained online. Fax and modem technology has also made it possible for business associates to spread out geographically. You can send a report to your partner in another city, who can annotate it and send it back—allowing for same-day distribution to six of your clients.

In this chapter we discuss what to look for in fax machines and modems. We also weigh costs and benefits of integrated fax/modems.

Fax machines

If you run a business, you need a fax, if only because people assume you have one. But besides being a mark of professionalism, they offer incredible convenience and will make you more productive. Before shopping, outline your needs. A graphic designer might need a different fax from a publicist or a contractor.

Whatever you do, get a Group 3 machine with a big document feeder and automatic paper cutting. Everything else is a matter of taste and budget.

Compatibility

Fax, modem, and fax/modem technology standards are set by the International Consultative Committee on Telegraphy and Telephony (CCITT). It's a kind of Miss Manners for telecommunications. Over the years they have set many standards, but Group 3 currently dominates the market and you shouldn't consider buying anything else.

A Group 3 fax machine scans information and then digitally encodes the image. Although all Group 3 machines meet some minimum standards and can communicate with each other, they are not all the same. Transmission rates vary from 2400 baud to 9600 and 14,400 bauds.

Group 3 fax machines support two kinds of resolution: regular and fine. Fine mode has twice the resolution of regular, but is also significantly

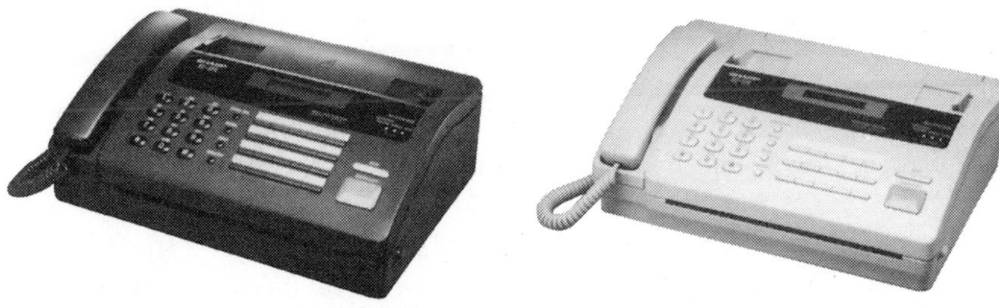

8-1 *A stand-alone fax machine is a must for any business, if for no other reason than that everyone will assume you have one.* Sharp

8-2 *Many manufacturers are making multifunction machines, like this fax/inkjet printer. Some are going all out and combining laser printers, copiers, scanners, and fax machines in one compact unit. While still expensive, they promise to one day be competitively priced.* Ricoh

slower. Only use fine mode for documents containing small type or important illustrations.

Transmission time

Transmission rates have come a long way since the old Group 1 faxes would take six minutes to send a single page. Still, fax speed is important—it saves you telephone charges and keeps your feet from getting sore waiting for your 15-page document to be sent. Two factors go into transmission speed: fax speed and the resolution of the document being sent.

Sending your document out on a 9600 baud fax doesn't ensure a fast transmission time. If you're communicating with a 2400 baud fax, the slower fax sets the pace. However, the technology keeps getting faster so buying a higher speed today will pay off in the long run.

As we mentioned above, the higher the resolution of a document the longer it will take to send. However, some features can speed up transmission time. Some faxes compress data, so that only the most important information is sent over the line. Other machines offer white space skipping, in which areas of the document that contain no image are scanned very quickly, also cutting transmission time. Unfortunately in order to use these features the fax you are sending to must have the same transmission time compression features or the normal standard will automatically be used.

Paper options

Fax machines print out on either thermal or regular bond paper. Thermal paper is coated with a colorless ink that turns black when heated, forming an image on the page. Most bond paper faxes use the same printing method as a photocopy machine, with similar results. Each method has its strong points, as shown below.

Thermal advantages:

- The machine is less expensive.
- Requires no toner or drum.
- Low maintenance cost, no moving parts.
- Can record long documents.

Bond paper advantages:

- The paper is less expensive.
- Professional appearance.
- Files easily (thermal paper curls).
- Won't turn black if left in the sun.
- Single sheet convenience, no need to cut the document off the roll.

Paper capacity

The paper capacity of a regular bond paper fax is fairly straightforward: you fill the tray as you would a copier. However, thermal paper is a little trickier. Thermal paper comes in three sizes: 30, 50, and 100 meter rolls. In general, you can expect to get 3 standard pages per meter of thermal paper. Keep in mind, not all rolls fit all machines.

Fax paper, bond or thermal, goes pretty quickly. Unless your paper supply will be closely monitored, choose the higher capacity fax.

Document size

Almost all faxes can transmit documents from 5 inches to 8.5 inches wide. Check the size of your fax scanner's nonprinting margins; just because the page fits in doesn't mean it will all be printed. Only faxes that use thermal paper can receive documents with a page size that is longer than 11 inches.

Document feeders

Unless you are a very patient person or plan to send only one-page faxes, you must have a document feeder. Document feeders usually hold a maximum of 5, 10 or 30 sheets of paper. Document feeders are essential for delayed and timed transmission faxing. Get this feature.

Automatic paper cutter

Cutting up a multipage thermal paper document can be monotonous and generally annoying. Make sure an automatic paper cutter is included (fortunately, it almost always is).

Copier option

Faxes can also be used as a low quantity, low quality photocopier. However, faxes make very slow copiers. Expect to wait 30 seconds or more for your copy. Fax paper is also more expensive than regular bond paper. The best use of this feature is to preview your fax's appearance before transmission.

If you don't have a dedicated fax line, it makes sense to have an automatic voice/data switch on your fax machine.

Phone options

- Built-in dial. Most fax machines allow you to dial through the machine, saving you the trouble of hooking up a telephone to the same jack.
- One-touch dialing. This feature works the same way it does on any telephone with memory storage. Just hit the digit designated for a number and the machine does the rest. Just make sure the machine can hold enough digits to meet your requirements. Some long distance companies require more than the standard 11 digits for U.S. calls and international calls can exceed 14 digits.
- Automatic redial. This tells your fax to continue dialing a number at periodic intervals until it gets through.

- Alternate number dialing. This works like automatic redial, but with more than one number.

Automatic voice/data switch

If you don't have a dedicated fax line, it makes sense to have an automatic voice/data switch on your fax machine. This allows the fax machine to determine whether the caller is a person or another machine. If the caller is a person the phone would ring and connect to an answering machine if unanswered. A fax would be accepted without ringing the phone. When choosing this feature, make sure it is compatible with your telephone system by calling manufacturers and your local telephone company. Voice/data switches sold separately might cost less than integrated units.

Automatic fallback

The same line noise that interferes with your phone conversations can cause problems with high-speed fax transmissions. The faster your transmission rate the more likely transmission errors will occur. To counter this many fax machines have an automatic fallback feature.

With automatic fallback, your fax machine will detect errors as they occur and then drop the transmission rate down to a level where no errors occur. If there are errors when the document is sent at 14,400 bps, the fallback feature will drop it down to 9600 bps for a cleaner transmission.

Transmit terminal identification

This feature stamps each page with your fax number, date and time of transmission, and page number. Some fax machines allow you to place a customized message—like the name of your company—on every page as well. This should be used in addition to a regular cover sheet with the standard information.

Broadcast transmission

This feature allows you to transmit a document to a number of different destinations without refeeding the document or dialing each number individually. Just press a few buttons and fax your document out to the world. However, make sure you have the permission of the recipients—it is illegal to broadcast fax without this permission.

In order to broadcast fax your machine must have some form of internal memory in which to store both the document to be faxed and the list of numbers to be faxed to. Obviously the more memory you have, the larger the document you can fax, and the more numbers you can fax to. (See chapter 14 for more information.)

Polling

Suppose your regional salespeople fax you their sales reports at the end of every day. Rather than have all ten of them compete to get through to you, you can use the polling feature to request the information from them, one at a time. Put simply, polling lets you request information rather than send it. Of course the person you are requesting information from must be expecting your call with the information already loaded and its own polling feature activated. What's more the sender has little control over who requests the information, so polling should not be used for sensitive information. This said, if you regularly need general information from the same sources, polling can save you some trouble.

Delayed and timer transmission

You can cut down on the costs of faxing by taking advantage of lower night-time rates. With a delayed or time-set transmission you can save up to 50 percent on the cost of a transmission. It's no harder than programming your VCR (let your kids do it) and the potential for savings is much greater. Timed transmissions require either a sheet feeder or internal memory.

Contrast control

This fairly self-explanatory feature can be particularly useful if you regularly send multicolored documents. Ideally you will also have a copier feature so you can preview how your document will look.

Halftone transmission

With halftone transmission capability your fax can record and reproduce the many shades of gray that compose most photographs and many graphics. While this feature does not require that the receiving machine also have half-tone capability, you are limited by the sensitivity of the receiver's machine. Fax machines are rated by the number of shades of gray they can send—usually 8, 16, or 64.

Modems

Modems send and receive data over telephone lines. They allow you to communicate with other computers, exchanging information or even running their applications. More importantly, they are your ticket to online services (see chapter 15 for details about online services).

Modems are your ticket to online services.

The following section outlines what to look for when shopping for a modem.

Transmission speed

Modem speed is measured in "bits per second" or bps—the higher the better. This is because the faster the modem,

8-3 An external modem is easy to install and provides instant access to the online world. Look for a modem that is Hayes-compatible (almost all are) and has a speed of 9600 bps or better. ©1993, Hayes Microcomputer Products, Inc.

the less time and money you will spend while online. If you've decided to trade up from a 1200- or 2400-bps modem—or if you're buying your first modem—there are two things to know:

- Get a 14,400-bps modem, rather than a 9600-bps modem. The so-called 14.4 modems sell for not much more than 9600-bps modems. If you seldom transfer files and just use your modem for electronic mail, a 1200- or 2400-bps modem should suffice.
- If you buy a new modem, buy a fax/modem. You will pay little more for the fax capability. Even if you already own a stand-alone fax machine, the ability to send faxes straight from your computer—without printing out and feeding a fax machine—is a huge plus. In addition, it's easy to create distribution lists for broadcasting faxes with fax/modem software.

Internal vs. external

Internal modems are cards that you plug into your computer's expansion slots. External modems are independent units that you simply attach to the back of your computer. We generally recommend external modems, because they are easier to set up and you can see the lights that indicate exactly what the modem is doing at any given time. Internal modems are most useful for people with notebook computers.

Modem manners

The most daunting thing about modems is the confusing array of specifications and protocols. Don't worry: Most modems include everything you need—you should just double check. Here's what to look for:

- The standard Hayes AT command set (which is to modems what MS-DOS is to PCs).
- The International CCITT V.32 and V.42 standards.

For a few dollars more, you can buy a fax/modem device, instead of a plain modem.

CCITT

The International Consultative Committee on Telegraphy and Telephony (CCITT), is responsible for defining, among other things, how modems should behave in various situations.

There are several CCITT standards to look for when buying a 14,400-bps modem. The first is V.32bis, which governs the modem's operation at speeds from 4800 to 14,400 bps. This not only ensures compatibility with other modems operating at lower speeds, but is essential to proper operation at the newer 14,400-bps rate.

You will also want the V.42 standard, which is responsible for error control. With the V.42 standard, accurate data transmission is guaranteed, even over the noisiest phone line.

For the highest possible speed, the V.42bis data-compression standard should also be included. This protocol is capable of compacting information into one-fourth its original size, resulting in one-fourth the time normally required to transmit your file. Put another way, the basic connect speed—whether 2400, 9600, or 14,400 bits per second—is multiplied by a factor of four. Using V.42bis, two 14,400-bps modems can communicate at an effective rate of 57,600 bps, at least under ideal conditions.

A caveat

These standards can be confusing, because manufacturers and retailers bombard us all with numbers—and in the process can trick us into thinking we are buying something more powerful than it really is. There is an important distinction between a modem's basic connect speed, and the effective rate of transfer when information is compressed. Look at the actual speed of the modem's "data pump," not just the theoretical maximum using compression. Don't be fooled by ads offering to sell you a "9600 (V.42bis) baud modem with 9600 send/rec fax" at a rock-bottom price. A 2400-bps modem with V.42bis data-compression capability for an effective data-transfer rate of 9600-bps—is not the same as a 9600-bps modem. Let the buyer beware.

Weakest link

Remember that for any action, there must be an equal but opposite reaction. Any compression scheme requires the same type of decompression at the other end, and a 14,400-bps modem connected to a standard 2400-bps modem will still transfer data only at 2400 bps. Your new 14,400-bps, V.42bis modem can achieve that warp-speed 57,600 bps rate only if there is a 14,400-bps, V.42bis modem on the other end. The same is true of fax transmission. A 14,400-bps fax modem won't get your document to its destination any more quickly if the receiving machine runs at 9600 bps—and most still do.

Software

Software is also a consideration; some modems are sold without communications software, some with, and some include fax software. Get a modem with software—it might not always be the best, but it will get you started right away.

Pocket modems

When you are going to be on the road, a pocket modem is a lightweight way to keep in touch with your home base and business associates. Pocket modems are generally cheaper than internal notebook modems and they use their own batteries, thus extending the life of your computer's power supply. Plus, you can also share your pocket modem between your desktop and notebook computer (if you don't need a modem for each machine).

8-4 Less expensive than internal modems, pocket modems make an excellent choice for communicating on the road. Practical Peripherals

When buying a pocket modem consider the following features:

- Size and weight. When buying a portable modem size and weight are important considerations. Make sure you consider the bulk of a modem's support devices, such as an external power supply, data cable or extra battery, when comparing products.
- Power management. Look for nickel-cadmium or alkaline type batteries for easy replacement. They should have enough power to support at least an hour of non-stop use.
- Ease of use. Proprietary adapters can be complicated. You had best stick to the 9-pin female RS-232 connectors that fit standard serial ports. If you plan to use your modem with a desktop off-site, you should carry a 9-to-25-pin adapter.
- Operation ready. Buy a modem with a default configuration already installed. If you can get a basic communication or fax program with the right default configuration at the same time, all the better. This way you can just plug it in and go.
- Portable fax modems. For a few dollars more, you can buy a fax/modem device, instead of a plain modem. A small fax modem lets you send and receive a fax from your portable computer. A portable fax/modem device more than pays for itself on those few occasions when you absolutely must send a fax and then discover your hotel will charge you $5 to $8 per page.

Fax/modems

There is no reason to buy a standard modem instead of a fax/modem. A fax/modem gives you most of the features of a fax for only a few dollars more. But it can't fully replace a stand-alone fax—a fax/modem can only send electronic documents created on a computer. You can't fax an interesting newspaper article to an associate, unless you retype the whole thing or use a scanner to create an electronic file. Another drawback to a fax/modem is that files you receive are in electronic format and have to be printed out—ideally on a laser printer. On the other hand, it's much easier to broadcast fax via a fax/modem, and transmission quality is better because it does not need to be scanned by the sending machine.

Given the limitations of a fax/modem, you will still need a stand-alone fax. But a fax/modem will serve as an excellent complement, and will be a great tool when you can use it.

If you have a stand-alone fax, you can save a little money by buying a send-only fax/modem that cannot receive faxes. If you don't have a stand-alone, make sure you have both send and receive capabilities.

Software

Software is a key element for a fax/modem. If the software that comes with yours is cumbersome, don't give up. There are many fax software packages available that are very well designed.

Resources

Major manufacturers

Fax machines

Brother International
(800) 284-4329

Hewlett-Packard
(800) 752-0900

Muratec
(214) 403-3300

Okidata
(800) 654-3282

Panasonic
(800) 742-8086

Ricoh
(201) 882-2000

Sharp
(800) 732-8221

Xerox
(800) 832-6979

Modems

Advanced Microcomputer Systems Inc.
(800) 972-3733, (305) 539-9005

Computer Peripherals Inc.
(800) 854-7600

Hayes Microcomputer Products Inc.
(404) 441-1617

Practical Peripherals
(800) 442-4774

US Robotics
(800) 342-5877

Books and publications

Dvorak's Guide to PC Telecommunications, Second Edition, by John Dvorak, Osborne/McGraw-Hill, Berkeley, CA; $39.95; (800) 227-0900, (510) 549-6600.

The Complete Modem Reference, by Gilbert Held, 1991: (2nd edition in June '94), John Wiley & Sons, New York; $28.95; (212) 850-6000.

Guide To Modem Communications, by Les Freed and Frank Dorfler Jr.; 1992, Ziff-Davis Press, Emeryville, CA; $29.95; (800) 688-0448, (510) 601-2000.

Buying storage devices

THE HARD DRIVE THAT COMES WITH YOUR computer will be your primary storage device. It is likely, however, that you will want to back it up regularly or that you will plain outgrow it (you can never have too much hard drive space). Tape drives are the ideal backup device. Removable cartridge drives provide both backup capability and extra storage capacity. CD-ROM drives can't be used for backing up—you can only read data that was put on them at the time of manufacturing. But CD-ROM drives give you access to the immense volume of information that is published on CDs.

In the end, of course, you're still going to want to get the most from your hard drive. We'll show you how.

Tape drives

If you've never backed up your computer's hard-disk drive, you might not fully appreciate the convenience and ease of a tape-backup system. Worse, you're playing digital Russian roulette—one crash could instantly wipe out your data. That's why practically all computer experts (including us) recommend periodically copying all of the data from the hard-disk drive to some other medium, so that in the event of catastrophe, you can recover everything that was stored since the last backup.

The question is, what do you copy to? For many people, the answer is floppy disks. But today's hard drives commonly store 40, 60, 80, or 120MB of data, while a floppy disk holds only 1.44MB at best. That could mean filling up more than 80 disks. Data compression can cut that number down somewhat, but you still must mindlessly switch floppies for an hour or more.

Rather than performing the tedious disk-swapping ritual, consider backing up to a data cartridge tape (also called a data cassette), one of which can typically hold the entire contents of your hard-disk drive.

The capacity advantage

Standard tape-drive data cartridges hold up to 250MB of compressed data. Generally priced between $30 and $80, standard cartridges cost less than hard-disk drives with comparable storage capacity, and the data is readily removed and replaced just by changing cartridges. Tape drives themselves range from $250 to $900.

With all these advantages, you might wonder why we use hard-disk drives at all—why not use data cassettes instead? Because they're slow at accessing information. Tape systems store information in sequence, like songs on an audio cassette: If you want to hear the fifth song, you must play or fast-forward through the first four songs. The same is true when backing up a data cartridge: If you want to load the fifth file, you must fast-forward through the earlier ones. Disk drives, on the other hand, are like CD players in that they offer quick access to any point on the disk.

Thus, tape-drive systems are most appropriate when you need to store and recall large chunks of information in one big block, such as the entire contents of a hard-disk drive or a large directory or folder. In addition to performing backup operations, tape systems can be useful for multimedia, video, and animation applications, where a single project might occupy an entire hard-disk drive. You can load each project's files to the hard-disk drive from a data cartridge when you're working on the project, and then store the files back on a cartridge to free up space on your hard-disk drive.

The software

All tape systems include software designed to copy the entire contents of a hard-disk drive onto a data cartridge. You should also look for a program that lets you:

- Store only data that is new or has changed since the last backup. Always doing a complete backup wastes your time.
- Restore the drive's contents, just in case your hard drive crashes.
- Select directories or individual files to back up or restore.
- Compare files on the backup cartridge with files on the hard disk to see if there are any differences.

Most software will set your computer to automatically perform a backup at a specified time each day or week, but such features can be problematic. You must remember to leave the computer on, and the programs that execute this function can cause conflicts with other programs. Instead, you might find it more convenient to invoke the backup program yourself at a specified time.

Buying a backup system

The first step in buying a backup system is figuring out how much information you need to back up. Then buy a system that can store more.

If you have a 60MB hard-disk drive, you will need a tape drive that uses data cartridges that can hold at least 60MB of data. To give yourself room to grow, you might want to buy a system with an extra 20MB or so. Tapes are also usually upwardly compatible, so your new 60MB tape drive will be able to read your old 40MB cartridges.

Next, you must choose a tape drive based on the physical size of its data cartridges, depending on your space limitations and personal preference. Commonly referred to as *mini* or *standard* cartridges, the 2000 series cartridges store between 10MB and 250MB (using compression). Then there's the larger 6000 series, which store between 45MB and 1.35 gigabytes (using compression). Within these series, more specific numbers (2080, 2120, 2165) refer to storage capacities, while prefixes (DC, QD, KC, or MC) designate the manufacturers.

Just as floppy disks have shrunk over the years (from 8 inches to 5.25 inches to 3.5 inches), so have data cartridges. But, it's safe to assume that the mini cartridge will become the industry standard.

Cartridge formats

Once you've settled on a size and bought your tape drive, you'll need to buy cartridges that match the drive's format. Cartridges are either QIC (pronounced "quick"), a term that refers to the former industry standard, or non-QIC. Then there's the factory format. Don't worry if it's all Greek to you: The names of the format types are based on the Greek alphabet—Kappamat, Thetamat, Rhomat, Ximat, Numat, Deltamat, Alphamat, Gammamat, and Phimat. The cartridge format your tape drive requires (QIC or non-QIC, Ximat or Phimat) has no relation to its performance—just follow the specification in your tape drive's manual.

It's safe to assume that the mini data cartridge will become the industry standard.

You can purchase either blank or preformatted data cartridges for your drive. Most drives come supplied with a preformatted cartridge, and every drive's software includes a format command. Buying preformatted cartridges can save you 30 minutes to two hours in formatting time, but you must be careful to get the format that matches your drive. Also, manufacturers charge a premium for preformatted cartridges.

Backup speed

Most drives offer a choice of compressing to minimize either the space used up on the tape, or the time it takes to perform the backup. The amount of time it takes to back up a hard-disk drive varies, depending on the speed of your microprocessor and disk drive, the amount of data, and the type of compression (optimizing space or time) that you choose. Even on a minimize-time compression setting don't expect more than three or four megabytes per minute, depending on what kind of information you are backing up.

In or out?

Before buying a tape drive, you must decide where you want it to be: inside or outside of your computer. If you're concerned about backing up only one computer's hard drive, internal installation offers the neatest appearance and the least clutter. But you'll need to open the computer, make connections, and possibly install an additional controller card.

Buying an external model, however, doesn't mean you'll get away without opening your computer. Most external models require you to install a special internal interface card. Although some do allow easy external connection to the computer's parallel or serial port.

Also available are more advanced interface cards, which offer *hardware data compression*. This method operates faster than regular software compression but achieves the same compression ratios. Installation of these cards might require you to set interrupts, direct-memory-address (DMA) codes, and other technical parameters. The advanced interface cards are most often designated by the fastest transfer rate that is theoretically possible, such as "4.7MB per minute." However, actual performance varies with the type of computer and the type of data.

Removable cartridge drives

Tape backup drives are the best archiving tools available, but they can't be used as everyday storage devices. That's where removable cartridge drives step in. These drives, which resemble a giant floppy disk drive, offer good archiving capacity as well as everyday usability. You initially buy a drive and a single large disk, called a cartridge. Additional cartridges are inexpensive (under $100) given their storage capacity. And since there are only two major standards, Syquest and Bernoulli, it is a relatively easy way to exchange large amounts of information with other people.

Standards

Syquest-based systems are the most prevalent drives in the Macintosh world. Syquest is the only manufacturer, but they sell their machines to other companies that then slap on their brand name. Despite the proliferation of names, the Syquest name is almost always included in ads.

Syquest drives come in three versions—one that supports 44MB cartridges, one that uses 88MB cartridges, and a 105MB version. Larger capacity drives can read data off smaller cartridges, but can't always write data to them. Syquest's are available for the PC, but the Bernoulli drive (manufactured by Iomega) is more common.

Bernoulli drives are technologically superior—the cartridges are harder to damage. They come in 45MB, 90MB, and 150MB versions. If you have a PC, this is the way to go. While available for Macs, Bernoullis should only be chosen over Syquest if you know you won't need to exchange data with other Macs.

CD-ROM drives

While not good for backup, CDs are a great storage medium. A CD-ROM can hold up to 680MB of read-only data. *Read-only* means that you can't add to or change its contents, but you can copy the contents to your hard drive and make alterations there. To read this data you need a CD-ROM player, which is like an industrial-strength audio CD player. With speakers attached, you can also listen to audio CDs on a CD-ROM player.

Speed

CD-ROM players are getting faster by the year, but they still pale beside hard-disk access times. A fast hard disk can access information in about 12 milliseconds; the fastest CD-ROM drives take 200 ms, but the generation of CD-ROM drives still in common use rates at about 375 ms and higher. Some increase in performance can be found in the new *multispin* technology, pioneered by NEC and since adopted by other manufacturers. In some circumstances, this increases the data transfer rate from 150K per second to 300K per second.

The simplest way for a PC user to get good CD-ROM performance is to purchase a multimedia upgrade kit.

Buying a CD-ROM drive

Unless you want to mix and match components of your own choosing, the simplest way for a PC user to get good CD-ROM performance is to purchase a multimedia upgrade kit. This includes a CD-ROM drive, sound board, and necessary software (except Video for Windows). Buying a CD-ROM drive for a Mac is simpler—buy a drive with a good access time and plug it in.

Here are some things to look for when buying a CD-ROM drive:

- MPC. One way to be sure the drive you are buying for your PC isn't a dog is to purchase a system that bears the MPC (Multimedia PC) logo. This indicates that the components meet certain basic standards for multimedia use and will ensure you get a drive with a data transfer rate of 150K per second or higher. All Macs with built-in CD-ROM drives meet these standards (although they won't have the MPC logo).
- Extended Architecture (XA) drives. These drives do a better job at integrating audio and computer data, and are PhotoCD compatible. PhotoCD drives allow you to put 35mm photos on a CD-ROM and view and edit them on your computer. Any XA drive will be MPC compatible. The new MPCII standard, which was being formulated as of this writing, includes XA.
- Multisession drives. These let you add more photos to a disc that isn't full. Such features are still in their infancy, but they are likely to become standard before too long.
- Audio. Any CD-ROM you buy should have an audio jack. You might not think you need it, but there was a time when you didn't need a CD-ROM drive either.
- Cache. You will want at least a 64K cache to speed up the system.

Installing a CD-ROM

On the Macintosh, installing an external CD-ROM drive is as simple as attaching the device to the Mac's built-in SCSI (small computer system interface) port and installing some driver software. On the PC, you'll need to install a board (some audio boards have built-in SCSI support). For an internal drive, you'll need a vacant drive bay. You can, of course, buy Macs and PCs that have CD-ROM drives built in. The CD-ROM drives used in current Macs are top-quality performers, but those in PCs are of mixed quality.

Getting the most from your hard drive

You can always buy a second hard drive to increase your storage capacity. We recommend two alternatives before you consider this option.

- Get a removable cartridge drive instead. If you outgrew your first drive, there is a good chance you'll outgrow the next one. New cartridges are much less expensive than comparatively sized hard drives.
- Make the most of your current hard drive.

In the following section we describe some tricks and techniques to get the most from your hard drive.

The amazing data-doublers

Like prospectors in the California Gold Rush, files quickly stake a claim to unused disk space. When this happens, that 200MB hard drive you thought would take years to fill seems inadequate within months.

A disk-compression utility can double the amount of information your hard disk can hold. To understand how disk-compression utilities work, imagine your hard disk as a five-pound bag of potatoes and your data as 10 pounds of potatoes. Certainly, 10 pounds of just-harvested potatoes won't fit into a bag designed to hold half that many. But what if you mashed those potatoes before trying to stuff them into the bag? Well, then they just might fit.

Symbolically speaking, this is how an on-the-fly disk compression utility, such as Stacker from Stac Electronics or AddStor Inc.'s SuperStore Pro, works. It mashes files before they're written to a disk. It also unmashes these compressed files, automatically, whenever they're called back into memory.

The downside of compression

Unfortunately, there is a downside to using compression software. First of all the compression utilities often slow data retrieval and overall hard drive performance. Manufacturers are working to correct this flaw, but the problem will persist for a while. Unless you absolutely need a lightning fast computer, you will find the extra storage space worth the inconvenience. If speed is an issue, instead of automatically compressing all your files, you can get software that lets you choose only to compress rarely used files. This won't double your capacity, but it can save several megabytes.

Exotic methods for optimizing a hard-disk drive are all well and good, but don't overlook the basics.

Data safety is another concern. Some people—particularly DoubleSpace users—have reported losing data stored on a compressed disk. This often occurs when someone doesn't understand all the steps required to set up and remove a compressed file. Thus, you should be sure to read all instructions carefully before adding disk compression to your system.

Fragmented files

When your computer stores a file it sometimes splits the file into several small sections, called *noncontiguous clusters*. Fragmented files slow system performance.

Think of a contiguous file as resembling the grooves in a phonograph record. When you place a phonograph needle on a record, it travels along this groove smoothly, in a continuous line. A contiguous file resembles that record groove. All of the sectors it occupies physically follow each other on a disk. When you access a contiguous file, the heads of your disk drive advance smoothly and quickly from one sector to the next, reading data in an orderly fashion.

Now visualize a different image: playing the game of jacks. The object is to scatter a group of jacks on the ground, then, in each successive round, retrieve one piece more than you did the last time until you've collected all the jacks. Sectors in a noncontiguous file are as scattered over the different areas of a hard disk as jacks are when strewn about the ground in the first move of the game. To access a noncontiguous file, the heads of a disk drive pick up bits of data, following the same kind of nonlinear pattern your hand does when you attempt to collect the jacks that have strayed in various directions.

A disk drive has no trouble finding all the data in a noncontiguous file, but the gyrations it must go through are time consuming. Whenever possible, your operating system attempts to store files in contiguous sectors. But as files are added to and deleted from a disk, finding enough contiguous sectors to hold a file becomes difficult.

Defragging

Defragmenting puts each file's cluster next to another, which improves system performance. Several utilities on the market defragment noncontiguous files. On the DOS side, you might want to check out The Norton Utilities or PC Tools for DOS. Along with defragmentation, The Norton Utilities provides a wealth of disk- and file-management utilities. PC Tools adds a desktop module to its selection of disk-management utilities. Windows users might want to investigate the Norton Desktop for Windows or Central Point's PC Tools for Windows. Mac users can place all their digital ducks in a row with Symantec's Norton Utilities for the Macintosh and Central Point Software's MacTools.

A new Defrag command available in DOS 6.0 is actually a licensed version of SpeedDisk, Norton's defragmentation utility. Both DOS's Defrag and Norton's SpeedDisk add the ability to optimize drives compressed with DoubleSpace.

Cache as cache can

A disk cache speeds performance by retaining the data you've most recently accessed in fast RAM, anticipating that this is the data you are most likely to need next. Disk caches can also hold data in memory and wait for a relatively idle period to write that data to the hard disk, so that it is less likely to disrupt other activities.

You can buy a caching controller card for your hard disk, but in many instances a software cache can do the job just as effectively. The Norton Utilities and the DOS version of PC Tools each include a disk-cache utility to speed things up under both DOS and Windows. Power Pak is another popular DOS package that offers a disk cache as part of its suite of performance-enhancing utilities. All three of these programs were recently upgraded to fully support DOS 6.0. Power Pak also supports disk caching for CD-ROM drives, as does Symantec's Norton SpeedCache Plus utility. (Like The Norton Utilities, SpeedCache Plus optimizes performance for both DOS and Windows environments.)

Disk caching is another feature some PC users can access at no additional cost. Microsoft includes a disk-cache utility, SmartDrive, with Windows 3.1 and DOS.

On Macs running System 7, a minimum 32K cache for every 1MB of RAM is automatically set aside, though you can increase cache size through the supplied Memory control panel.

Buffers

Exotic methods for optimizing a hard-disk drive are all well and good, but don't overlook the basics. With DOS and Windows systems, this involves special storage areas set up in memory called disk buffers. A well-tuned BUFFERS statement included in your CONFIG.SYS file can improve disk performance. Mac devotees needn't worry about fine-tuning such things—the operating system handles that automatically.

DOS uses disk buffers to temporarily hold data moving to and from a disk. Each time an application asks for specific data, DOS checks to see whether it is stored in a disk buffer as the result of a prior request. If DOS discovers the requested information there, it passes the data immediately to the application. This eliminates the need to perform an additional disk read.

In the BUFFERS statement, you can specify that a specific number of disk buffers be created in memory each time you start your PC. The default value is 15 buffers, each of which holds approximately 532 bytes of data. Barring special circumstances, you'll want to change that to 20 buffers. The main exception to this rule is if you use an application that requires more, a fact that will be stated somewhere within its documentation. Often when this is the case, the application will modify the BUFFERS statement automatically upon installation.

Resources

Major manufacturers

Tape-backup drives

Conner Electronics, An Archive Company
(407) 263-3500, (800) 821-8782

Microsolutions Computer Products
(815) 756-3411

Colorado Memory Systems
(800) 346-9881

Valitek
(413) 549-2700

Removable cartridge drives

Iomega (Bernoulli)
(801) 778-1000, (800) 456-5522

Syquest, various resellers

CD-ROM drives

NEC Technologies (PC, Mac)
(708) 860-9500

Mirror Technologies (Mac)
(800) 654-5294

Software

Stacker for Windows and DOS, Stac Electronics
(619) 431-7474

Stacker for Macintosh, Stac Electronics
(619) 431-7474

SuperStore Pro, AddStor Inc.
(415) 688-0470

AutoDoubler, Fifth Generation Systems
(504) 291-7221

The Norton Utilities, Symantec Corp.
(800) 441-7234

PC Tools for DOS, Central Point Software Inc.
(800) 445-4208

MacTools, Central Point Software Inc.
(800) 445-4208

Power Pak, PC-Kwik
(503) 644-5644

Buying copiers

ONCE YOU HAVE A DESKTOP COPIER AT YOUR fingertips, you'll wonder how you ever found the time to trek to the local copy shop. But given the cost and the must-have status of other equipment, a copier is still a luxury for most start-up businesses. After your business is up and running, however, you should reevaluate your needs. You can find plenty of good, economical models with the features you need.

Evaluating your needs

Will a copier save you money? Add up the following costs on a monthly basis:

Costs associated with not having a copier

- Money spent at the copy shop.
- Time spent at, and going to, the copy shop. (How much would you have earned by working instead?)

Costs associated with having a copier

- Cost of the machine (figure monthly cost based on copier's estimated life span). The cost is partially offset by tax savings that you will realize by writing off or depreciating the machine.
- Cost of consumables (toner, etc.).
- Cost of service contract.

For example, if you make 300 copies per month at the copy shop at 8¢ each and it takes you 1 hour to do so at a cost of $30/hour, then your total cost for a month is $54. Of course, only $24 is actual cash outlay. If you bought a $1000 copier that will last 5 years and the cost of consumables (toner, service, etc.) is 4¢ per copy then your total cost for the same 300 copies is about $29.

In the example above, the copier is a good buy. If cash flow is a critical issue, you may want to delay the purchase, but still plan on getting one. Don't take your time for granted, even if it is "free" time.

This is a pretty simple model, but you can add in other factors, such as tax savings for equipment write-offs or depreciation, to make it more realistic.

What to look for

It's unlikely you'll be in the market for a full-featured, heavy-duty office copier that will perform minor miracles at the touch of a button (and costs more than you gross in a year). Chances are you need an inexpensive personal copier with a few features to make your life easier. However, a personal copier isn't designed to make 1000 copies at a time—if you have this kind of need you should consider leasing a more powerful machine.

The following section provides an overview of what to look for in a personal copier.

10-1 *A copier, though expensive, is a great convenience. When selecting a copier, look for a large paper tray and variable reduction and enlargement capabilities.* Ricoh

Moving or stationary copying

Typically low-end machines feature a system in which the top of the copier moves back and forth to make copies. Although there is no quality difference between moving platen and stationary copiers, space can be an issue. If your office layout is tight, consider the extra space a moving copier consumes before buying one.

Duty cycle

Monthly duty cycles, or recommended copies per month on a desktop copier, can range from 800 to 3500 copies per month. Make sure your machine suits your needs; otherwise you may end up spending a lot of money replacing toner cartridges and drums.

Reduction and enlargement

This is an extremely handy feature, especially if you do any desktop publishing. We strongly recommend it. Many personal copiers only offer preset enlargement and reduction amounts. While this is better than nothing, being able to input variable amounts is far superior.

Automatic document feeder

While this is a rare feature on desktop copiers, if you do many multi-page documents, an automatic document feeder makes life a lot easier. Leaving a stack of papers to be copied in the feeder spares you from the tedium of feeding each sheet manually. Remember, you're buying a copier primarily for its convenience, not to babysit it.

Paper sizes

Do you need your copier to handle legal or tabloid size paper? Copiers that offer flexibility in paper size obviously cost more, but if this is a feature your business requires, the expense will be worthwhile.

Photo mode

The photo mode feature, generally only available on more expensive machines, enables you to make quality copies of photographs. This is a great feature for a designer or desktop publisher.

Consumables cost

How much does it cost to replace the toner and other consumables? How long do these replacements last?

Service

Service and warranties vary dramatically. Some manufacturers offer only 90 days, others provide three years of on-site service. On-site service is important—even personal copiers weigh in at 50+ pounds and you aren't going to want to ship it.

Resources

Major manufacturers

Canon
(516) 488-6700, (800) 828-4040

Mita
(201) 808-8444

Panasonic
(800) 742-8086

Ricoh
(201) 882-2000

Sharp
(800) 237-4277, (201) 529-8200

Xerox
(716) 423-5078, (800) 832-6979

Buying scanners

SCANNERS, WHICH READ TEXT AND GRAPHICS from paper and convert them to electronic form, are not a critical piece of equipment like a fax or a printer. But the ability to electronically capture and manipulate any image or text is extremely helpful on occasion. With the exception of designers, desktop publishers, and researchers, however, we recommend getting a scanner only after you have a full complement of other tools.

Types of scanners

Flatbed scanners

A flatbed scanner looks and works much like a photocopier does. You place the hard copy on top of a flat sheet of glass and the light sensitive bar moves beneath it. Instead of printing out a copy, the scanner stores the image as a computer file.

Flatbed scanners scan the entire page at once, whether it's a standard 8.5×11-inch page or legal size. Because the light-sensitive bar does the scanning and the page is held in place, there is little chance of image distortion.

Flatbed scanners are big, usually about 12 inches wide and 18 inches long. The resulting footprint on your desktop can be prohibitively large.

If optical character recognition will be a primary duty of your scanner, a flat bed scanner is the way to go. Pages can be accurately and quickly scanned. You can purchase document feeders for multipage scans.

Although flatbed scanners cost about three times more ($800–$1200) than hand-held scanners with similar scanning ability, they are the best choice for precision scanning.

Hand-held scanners

Hand-helds suffer all sorts of quality disadvantages when compared to flatbeds, but they are much less expensive.

The biggest difficulty in using a hand-held scanner is keeping your hand steady while scanning. Scanning is a delicate process. Shakes and tremors can dramatically distort the scanned image. Also, most hand-held scanners are only four inches wide, limiting the size of scanned image to the same size. Although some scanners come with software that lets you stitch together a scan (such as two halves of a magazine page) it can be a slip-shod process.

Despite these disadvantages the quality of a hand-held scanner can rival that of a flatbed if you have a steady hand. It can also be tucked away in a drawer when you're done.

Scanner options

There are three levels of scanning: black and white, gray-scale, and color. Hand-held scanners are either black and white or gray-scale, while flatbeds are either gray-scale or color. The best overall scanner for the money is a gray-scale flat-bed scanner that can also work in black and white (to efficiently capture text and line art).

Black-and-white scanners

As you might suspect, black-and-white scanners record images with black-and-white dots. This kind of scanner is more than adequate for scanning text or line art, which are exclusively black and white to begin with.

To reproduce grays, the black-and-white scanner must simulate the grays with a combination of black-and-white dots. This works okay, but should not be relied upon for fine or detailed work.

Gray-scale scanners

Gray-scale scanners are far more flexible when it comes to scanning continuous tone images. If you want to capture a photograph, a gray-scale scanner is the way to go.

These scanners digitize the gray-scale by assigning a number for every shade of gray. The current standard can scan 256 shades of gray. In contrast, a standard 300-dpi laser printer can produce only 16 shades.

Many laser printer manufacturers are addressing this discrepancy in resolution by adding special technology that does an adequate job of reproducing scanned photos (Apple's PhotoGrade, for example). Without such features, you will need to output your scans with high-end imagesetting equipment at a service bureau (this costs $5–$10 per page).

Color scanning

Color scanners work much like the gray-scale scanners, except by digitizing different colors. While color scanning technology is quite advanced—a 24-bit scanner can distinguish between 16 million colors—it is difficult to get good quality reproductions without very expensive equipment. Color scans also consume an inordinate amount of hard drive space. Therefore we recommend color scanners only for design professionals.

Resolution

The amount of detail a scanner can pick up is clearly important. The higher the resolution, the better the scan. However, after a certain point, extra resolution means little because your laser printer won't be able to reproduce it. The trick is knowing that scanning resolution cannot be equated with laser printer resolution—a 300-dpi scan is far more resolution than a 300-dpi printer can handle. In fact a 90-dpi scan is more than adequate. Higher resolutions are only helpful if you want to enlarge the image without distortion, or you plan to have it printed out on a high-end printer.

Software

Optical character recognition (OCR)

OCR software has improved dramatically in recent years and does a respectable job of scanning in pretyped documents (don't expect it to make sense of your handwriting) and converting it into a text file you can edit in your word processor. The accuracy of OCR is in the 95% range, which means you should expect 2–3 errors per page. However, this still compares favorably with typing in the original yourself.

Image-editing software

Many scanners (especially flatbed scanners) come bundled with image-editing software that lets you manipulate your scanned images—erasing portions, adding type, adjusting the contrast, etc. Simple editing can easily correct most flaws in the original, and having this ability adds great value to your scanner.

Resources

Scanner manufacturers

Apple
(800)-776-2333, (408) 996-1010

Caere Corp.
(800) 535-7226

The Complete PC
(408) 434-0145, (800) 229-1753

Epson America
(310), 782-0770 (800) 922-8911

Hewlett-Packard
(408), 246-4300 (800) 752-0900

Logitech
(510) 795-8500, (800) 231-7717

Marstek
(714) 453-0110

Mouse Systems
(510) 656-1117

Books

The Hand Scanner Handbook, (Mac and PC versions) by David Busch, 1993, Business One Irwin, Homewood, IL; $29; (708) 798-6000

The Practical Guide to Scanning by UMAX, UMAX, Santa Clara, CA 95054; Free; (408) 982-0771, (800) 562-0311

The Scanner Book: A complete guide to the use and application of desktop scanners, by Stephen Beale and James Cavuoto, 1989, Micro Publishing Press, Torrance, CA; $22.95; (310) 371-5787

Preventing computer catastrophes

A GUY IN A CHEAP SUIT AND SLICKED-BACK hair sidles up to your desk and pats the top of your monitor with a menacing smile. "Nice little computer you got here," he says. "Wouldn't want to see anything happen to it, would we?"

Granted, threats to the well-being of your computer system generally don't make themselves known quite so dramatically. The lurking perils that plague computers are usually invisible to the naked eye. You can't see problems with your electrical system, or sectors on your hard disk being corrupted, or viruses waiting to wreak havoc. But the threats are real, and so is your need for protection.

While there are some amazing programs to protect your data, most prevention comes down to good computing habits. Here are several ways to minimize data loss, perform basic maintenance and prepare yourself for "acts of God."

Minimize data loss

Unless you are truly blessed, you are going to lose valuable computer data—it might be as minor as closing a file without saving or as disastrous as your hard drive giving up the ghost. The trick is keeping the number of times these things happen to a minimum. The three ways to do this are:

- Save your files early and often.
- Back up files with reasonable diligence so that you can recover lost data.
- Keep your computer and disks healthy so that you don't lose data in the first place.

Saving

Regularly saving your work in progress is the easiest precaution you can take, and will prevent the 85 percent of data loss problems caused by computer crashes while you're working. (The preceding and subsequent percentages are not scientifically determined but based on our experiences.) Get in the habit of saving every time you pause to think, step away from your computer, or write a new paragraph. This is the second best computing habit you can have (the best is not placing full cups of coffee on your machine).

Starting off right

When you first start a new file, save it even before you begin working. This gets the file naming process out of the way and lets you save future changes with a keystroke.

Backing up

Backing up your data will prevent 10% of your problems—everything from overwriting a file to having your computer take a direct hit from your kid's Supersoaker. Everyone will tell you to back up everything every week (if not every day) and this is good advice. Unfortunately, backing up all data regularly is a feat that most people (including some of our editors) will never accomplish—it is a time-consuming process unless you make an additional equipment investment. If you can't make this investment or never remember to back up anyway, concentrate instead on saving your most critical files frequently. This takes only a few minutes and a handful of floppy disks.

Some important backup tips are described in the following section.

Backup applications

In addition to the master disks from the publisher, keep backup disks of your critical software applications—you only need to do this once and it doesn't take much time. Store them in a secure place, separate from the master disks (a refrigerator magnet is unlikely to infiltrate both storage areas).

Two copies

As with your applications, keep two copies of your most essential files. You probably won't update them both every time, but if you alternate which disk you back up onto you'll always have a second backup that is almost up-to-date.

Compress it

File-compression software can dramatically cut down on the number of disks you need for backup. Rather than simply coping megabytes of files to a set of floppies, use programs like the shareware version of StuffIt (Aladdin) to create compressed-file archives. Similar compressions can be achieved on a PC with ARC or ZIP file formats (ZIP is available as shareware or as part of XTree Gold or XTree for Windows). In each case, it is simple enough either to decompress the entire archive or extract files one at a time, and the restored files are identical to the originals.

Software solution

If you deal with a large number of changing data files, you can automate file backup by using backup software. Backup software is available from many publishers, either sold as standalone programs—such as FastBack Plus—or bundled with utility packages such as PC Tools, MacTools, or Norton Utilities. All backup software works basically the same way, tracking which files on your hard drive have changed since the last time you created a backup set and asking you whether or not to save a backup copy of these files. Most backup utilities also take care of file compression automatically.

The fact that a backup program can handle the bookkeeping chores involved in maintaining a multiple-disk set of backup files is a considerable benefit. Need to transfer mass quantities of data to a new hard drive? Use programs like Norton Backup, select the files you want and create backup floppy disks. Then install Norton backup on your new drive and restore your data on a new disk. Other backup software to consider includes FastBack Plus (from Fifth Generation Systems), DiskFit Pro (Dantz Development), and Redux (Microseeds).

Tape backup

If your business relies on large numbers of computer files that change frequently, a tape-drive backup unit is a reasonable investment and makes the backup process a breeze. The basic advantage of tape backup over floppy disks is capacity. A QIC (quarter-inch) tape-backup cartridge can hold up to 250MB (using file compression), eliminating the need to hang around inserting new floppy disks as each fills up or to swap disks when restoring backed-up files. If you require this kind of volume, you'll also find tapes significantly less expensive than the number of floppies needed to provide the same storage capacity.

Cartridge drives

Another option that costs a little more, but will provide more benefits than a tape-drive backup is a removable-cartridge drive (see chapter 9 for more information). While individual cartridges only hold 44 or 88MB (depending on the drive) you don't need that many to do a full backup and they are a great way to transfer data en masse to another computer.

File recovery

File backups are essential, crucial, vital, and irreplaceable. But what if you lose a file anyway? That's when file-recovery utilities enter the scene.

Rudimentary file-recovery capabilities are built into MS-DOS and DR-DOS today, enabling you to cope with files you've intentionally but mistakenly deleted and disks you've accidentally formatted. More extensive file-recovery options are provided by programs such as Norton Utilities, PC Tools, and MacTools. For example, you might be able to retrieve part of a file even if part of it has already been overwritten. Disk-utility software can also deal with problems that corrupt disks and make your files unreadable. For maximum effectiveness, though, be sure to install the utility programs on your drive before you experience a problem. If you install the program in advance, the utility creates a reference map of your files, which will greatly enhance your chances of finding data in erased or damaged files.

For maximum effectiveness, be sure to install disk-utility programs on your drive before you experience a problem.

Computer Rx

While your personal health insurance costs might be spiraling ever upward, you can rest assured that for a minimal cost you can keep your computer humming and avoid the 4 percent of data loss problems caused by failing disks, infectious viruses, and power fluctuations. (The last 1 percent of computer data loss problems are unavoidable—things like meteor showers selectively striking your computer and all stashes of backup disks.)

Preventative maintenance

Preventative maintenance is the computer equivalent of an annual checkup—except for the computer replace *annual* with *monthly*. These checkups don't take much time and don't usually require your attendance after you start them going.

The following section outlines some important preventative maintenance tips.

Handling irregularity

Hard-drive irregularities are typically caused when your system loses power in the middle of a disk write, or when a program crashes without finishing its disk activity. A hard-drive utility will examine the file structure and disk surface, ferret out lurking inconsistencies or undetected damage, and save the endangered data whenever possible. Often a hard-disk diagnostic such as Norton Disk Doctor (part of the Norton Utilities) or SpinRite (Gibson Research) will be able not only to identify a problem but to repair it as well.

A stitch in time

Hard drives wear down over time, and disk sectors might weaken. Hard-drive diagnostics test the soundness of each sector on your drive. If a given sector is still readable but shows signs of wear, the utility can move the information to a safe sector and mark the suspect area so it won't be used again.

Advanced diagnostics

Diagnostic programs that go beyond disk-drive analysis and repair to look at the inner workings of the computer circuitry are not for technophobes, but they can be very useful if you can stomach a few technical terms. Dariana's System Sleuth for PC compatibles, for example, has several features that take the trial-and-error out of diagnosing and fixing some common computer problems. Diagnostic programs include WinSleuth and MacSleuth (also from Dariana), and Snooper (Maxa), Help! (Teknosys), MacEKG (Micromat), and Now Profile—part of the Now Utilities (Now Software)—all for the Mac.

Knowledge is money

Even if there is a problem that requires technical intervention by a professional, knowing what's wrong in advance can save you both time and money. Having mastered a diagnostic utility, you can provide detailed information to technical-support personnel over the telephone, improving the odds that you'll solve the problem without leaving your home. Even if your computer still needs a trip to the repair shop, any information you provide that helps pinpoint the source of the trouble means fewer hours spent on diagnosis and, hence, a lower repair bill.

Viruses

A virus is a program, albeit one that serves no useful purpose other than to make mischief. Some are fairly innocuous, briefly putting unwanted messages up on your computer screen or playing a silly sound. Others permanently wipe out the data on your hard-disk drive.

Virus programs attach themselves to useful applications and operating system files. That's how they move from computer to computer undetected. Some viruses take effect and begin performing their unwanted actions immediately. Others are more insidious, waiting in a dormant state until a certain condition occurs. Often this trigger is a particular date, such as Friday the 13th or a historic anniversary (Michelangelo's birthday was the trigger for one virus).

It's wise to protect your system with antiviral software.

So how does your computer become infected? By exchanging files with a computer that is already infected. This might take place through infected disks or through downloading programs from online bulletin-board services. The large, commercial services and many user groups have become very adept at spotting and eradicating viruses in files submitted for distribution, but it's still possible for a virus to slip through.

Software solution

As always, the first line of defense against viruses is to back up your data files regularly. But more than this, given the persistence of virus creators in pumping new infections into the computer mainstream, it's wise to protect your system with antiviral software. There are many excellent commercial antivirus utilities, including Symantec Antivirus for the Macintosh (SAM) and Norton Antivirus for PC compatibles, which offer fairly complete automatic protection. Another popular commercial antiviral package is Virex (DataWatch) for both PCs and Macs. Shareware antivirus utilities distributed by user groups and over online bulletin boards are often both inexpensive and effective.

Keeping up with the times

To actually identify and eradicate a virus at work, your software has to keep up with the latest strains of virus unleashed on the computing public. This requires frequent updates. Both SAM and Norton provide up-to-date virus-definition files through their company online bulletin board. If you don't have a modem, the virus-definition files can be ordered by mail for a nominal charge. These files update the programs to deal with the latest viral strains. With other antiviral software, including programs distributed as shareware, you must acquire an updated version of the entire program in order to cope with new viruses.

Don't pirate

Besides being illegal, software piracy can cause significant problems. Even if a copy is virus-free, it might be corrupted, which is, in essence, an unintentional virus that is created by data degradation. A single corrupted font can disable your entire hard drive.

Power problems

Computer viruses aren't the only destructive force that can catch you unawares; you should also be aware of electrical disturbances—otherwise your data could be destroyed before you even hear the thunder.

There are two lines of defense you can erect against power-supply problems: surge suppressors (sometimes called surge protectors) and uninterruptible power supplies (often abbreviated as UPSs).

Surge suppressors

A surge suppressor senses incoming voltage spikes and clamps down on them, keeping them from reaching and damaging your computer. You plug the surge suppressor into your wall outlet and the computer into the surge suppressor. With any luck, you then forget it exists and get on with your computing.

The more elaborate surge suppressor provides outlets to plug in many computer devices (your system unit, monitor, printer, modem, and so on) and often has individual switches for each piece of equipment. With one of these units, you don't have to use the power switch on your computer at all.

Some surge suppressors will also warn you of low-voltage situations, a valuable indicator that something is wrong in the invisible world of your electrical supply.

While surges along the electrical lines are the primary threat for most computer owners, modem and fax-machine owners have to consider another path for destructive power surges—the telephone line. Surge suppressors for telephone lines are available as stand-alone units, or built into some power line surge-suppression units. Many companies make surge suppressors; some manufacturers we recommend are Curtis, Kensington, Tandy, and Tripplite.

Lightning can be big-time trouble for a computer system. In fact, even with a surge suppressor installed and the computer turned off, a local lightning strike can travel through the power lines and turn your equipment into a paperweight. When there's a lightning storm in the immediate area, turn off the computer and pull out the plug, no matter how pressing the deadline you're facing. This is not to minimize the importance of surge-suppression hardware, but local lightning is an extreme condition, and it calls for extreme protective measures.

Torturing your computer with extreme temperatures is a good way to bring on trouble.

Uninterruptible power supplies

For the ultimate in protection you can get an uninterruptible power supply (UPS). The UPS keeps the computer running during a power outage for a period of time ranging from about five minutes to as much as an hour or more. It also sets off an alarm to let you know the computer is running on battery power. Your job is to save your current work to disk and shut down the computer before the battery power is exhausted.

You also have two types of UPS to choose from: on-line and standby. An online power device acts as an intermediary between the electrical system and the computer. While your system is running, the online UPS constantly charges the battery from the power line and feeds the computer electricity from the battery. A standby UPS, on the other hand, simply passes the wall socket's electrical current through to your computer, monitoring for any interruption. If there is a power outage, the UPS switches to battery power.

For a single computer user, a standby UPS is usually the right choice. It is significantly less expensive than the online version, yet sophisticated enough to deal with any power interruption you're likely to encounter. What's more, it's silent: Online UPS units usually emit a noticeable transformer hum that would be distracting in the quiet of your home office. Manufacturers to investigate include American Power Conversion, Best Power Technology, Emerson Computer Power, EPE/Topaz, Exide Electronics, Kensington, Panamax, Sola Electronics, and Tripplite.

Capacity is an issue when selecting a UPS, since they come in a variety of sizes suitable for anything from a single computer user to a powerful network server. And the greater the capacity, the higher the price. To choose the right UPS, you can calculate the amount of power your system draws. The problem is, some power requirements are expressed in volt-amperes (VA), some in watts (W), some in amps (A)—so you have to convert to a common standard and then match that with the product specs of the power suppressor. (To convert your power usage to amperes divide the total watts by 110.) To simplify matters, look at the available UPS product literature and packaging for a listing of typical system configurations and the recommended UPS model to meet their needs. If you don't find a close match between your system and those listed, call your computer manufacturer's technical-support department.

Basic maintenance

Physically protecting your computer is one concern—maintaining it is another. What do you do to maintain your TV and stereo? Not a whole lot. Similarly, there are only a few simple things you need to do for computer maintenance.

Don't assume your regular insurance will protect your computer.

Keyboard

- Clean your keyboard, and other equipment, with compressed air. It's quick, easy and fairly inexpensive. Commercial brands like DustOff can be bought in computer or camera stores.
- Vacuum your keyboard regularly. You can buy a dedicated mini-vac or if you are gentle, use one of the attachments on your regular household vacuum.

Mouse

When a mouse starts behaving erratically, remove the ball and blow into the cavity to clear out dust. Also examine the rollers for caked on dirt. You can scrape this away with a fingernail.

Monitor

- When cleaning your monitor, don't spray the screen directly with glass cleaner. The liquid might dribble in through the edges of the casing and make contact with the electrical components within.
- To clean properly, start by turning the monitor off, then dampen a lint-free cloth or paper towel with glass cleaner or just plain water and gently rub the screen clean. Sprays designed specifically for computer monitors work well, but generally aren't worth the extra cost. Premoistened single-use towelettes are available for wiping down monitor screens, and they do a good, streak-free cleaning job.
- Keep magnets and phones away from your monitor—they cause distortion. If your monitor does get magnetized, you can rectify the problem by pressing the "degauss" button located on the back of most monitors.
- If you walk away from your computer, leaving a static image on your monitor, it can, over time, burn the image in. While this is not a serious risk if you don't leave the same image on screen time after time, you can avoid the problem altogether with a screen saver. A screen saver is a piece of software that, after a set period of inactivity, kicks in to change the image on your monitor.

Floppy disk drive

- There's no reason to subject the magnetic heads to the abrasion of a cleaning until you actually experience trouble with the drive, in the form of an inability to read data from floppy disks reliably. If the drive seems to be failing, however, try one of the special-purpose head-cleaning disks.
- For preventative cleaning, use compressed air. Most computer repair people can fix a "broken" drive with an air canister—and charge you $50.

Printer

- Most printer manuals provide a simple step-by-step cleaning process that you should follow.
- If you print labels and transparencies, make sure they are "laser-safe" or you might end up with a goo-filled (and broken) printer.
- Refilling an expended laser printer toner cartridge is somewhat less expensive than buying a new one. You can find numerous vendors that do this by looking in the classified section of most computer magazines. Some people have had negative experiences with this—a damaged toner cartridge being the most common complaint.
- You can refresh a fading ribbon in a dot-matrix printer by spraying it with WD-40. This is not a permanent solution, but will work well enough until you can get a new ribbon.

General

- Power switches are relatively fragile. It is better to turn your equipment on and off through a surge-suppressor.
- Powering up is one of the most potentially damaging thing you can do to your equipment. If you are stepping away for a couple of hours it is better to leave everything on. Given a cool environment you can leave your equipment on indefinitely without risk of damage. The electric bill, on the other hand, is another story.
- Torturing your computer with extreme temperatures is another good way to bring on trouble. Hard drives do have a limit on temperature tolerance. If you run your system in summer, invest in an air-conditioner. A fan probably won't cut it.
- Dust covers, whether sections of old sheets or store-bought, are great protective devices. Plastic dust covers have the added advantage of repelling liquids that are inexplicably drawn to your equipment.
- True computer-protection zealots recommend banning food from

your work area entirely. It's good advice, but is another of the great feats that most of us are incapable of accomplishing. Use a side table to rest your food and drink and don't eat greasy or crumbly food while performing keyboard or mouse work.

"Acts of God"

We've covered computer-specific woes and ways to ward them off. But your computer and home office are also vulnerable to the same disasters that threaten the rest of your property: fire, theft, and natural disaster. While insurance can't prevent these events, it can minimize the economic impact. By taking some preventative steps you can also minimize the actual damage.

Insurance

You can't assume that your regular insurance will protect your computer. At the same time, don't assume it won't.

Both Allstate and State Farm, for instance, differentiated between computer equipment used for home and recreation purposes and computers used in a home business through the early 1980s, but they have since dropped the distinction. Today's standard homeowner's policy from either company includes $5000 protection for loss of computer hardware and software, and an additional $5000 in coverage is available for an extra premium.

The folks at Prudential have also changed with the times. While home-office computers are excluded from the company's standard homeowner's policy, they can be covered through an endorsement to the policy for about $25 per year. In about half the states, Prudential also offers a premier homeowner's policy with computer coverage included automatically.

Of course, not every insurance company has jumped on the home-office bandwagon. And since insurance is a complex business, regulated on a state-by-state basis and subject to local variations and underwriting restrictions, the coverage available to you will vary. Talk to insurance providers in your area to determine the availability and cost of coverage.

Another alternative to explore is SafeWare, a national insurance company that specializes in covering computers used for personal or business purposes. Founded in 1982, the company claims to insure one out of every thousand computers in the United States. Coverage is sold through regular mail, an 800 number, and CompuServe's electronic mall.

The company's ComputerOwners policy is available throughout the United States, except in New York, Pennsylvania, and Texas (they sell other policies in these states). After you pay a $50 deductible, the ComputerOwners policy provides for the full replacement cost of hardware and software lost as a result of fire, theft, power surges, vandalism, accidental damages, and natural disasters like flood and lightning (but not earthquakes). One particularly important facet of this insurance to many portable-computer owners is coverage for loss away from home, often excluded from homeowners policies.

Disaster checklist

There are a lot of things you can do to plan for a catastrophic occurrence. The list below is fairly comprehensive and common-sensical. While some of these measures might be beyond what you are willing to do, most are straightforward.

The following list of tips to protect your office against potential disaster was compiled with advice from Joshua Lichterman, president of Emergency Management Group, in Berkeley, California; Philip Jan Rothstein, of Ossining, New York; Jeff Freeman of Front Porch Computers in Chatsworth, Georgia; and Bill Petersen of State Farm Insurance in Laguna Hills, California.

- Insure your business equipment and records adequately and reevaluate annually or whenever there's a major change.
- Take out a separate business policy that covers general liability and the full replacement cost of equipment and furnishings, including computer hardware and loss of your home office. Make sure you understand whether or not "replacement" value means full replacement value, and whether operating a business from your home could void coverage.
- Document your possessions, including serial numbers, purchase dates, and prices, with receipts and detailed descriptions as proof. Periodically send an updated copy to your attorney or a relative in another state, or store it in a safe deposit box.
- Do regular backups of computer data and store them in a safe place.
- Use UL (Underwriters Laboratory)-certified transient voltage surge suppressors on your computer and other business equipment.
- Ensure that all doors and windows lock securely.
- Conceal expensive equipment so that it's not easy to see through windows.
- Clean and organize your office frequently so piles of paper won't create a fire hazard.
- Place fire extinguishers and smoke detectors strategically throughout your home. If you already have smoke detectors, consider upgrading them to smoke-heat detectors, which are more sensitive.
- Arrange furniture and equipment to guard critical items and records against leaks, floods, crashed windows, heavy vibrations, or earth tremors.
- If you have to file an insurance claim, use an independent appraiser and adjuster rather than one sent by the insurance company.

- Store copies of data backups at alternate sites or in safe deposit boxes, either of which is cheaper and more efficient than special data-loss insurance.
- Install a hard-wired security system with an audible burglar alarm.
- Ask your insurance agent to add a rider covering your most critical records, including lists of customers, prospects and suppliers, plus corporate accounting and tax records.
- Contract specialists to check your wiring, plumbing, and chimney construction, and the structural soundness of your home.
- Buy a generator as a backup power supply.
- Install a sprinkler system.
- Keep a backup heater that doesn't require electricity or natural gas.

Resources

Books and publications

Abort! Retry! Fail!, by Susan Klopfer, 1992, Alpha Books/Prentice Hall Computer Publishing, Carmel, Indiana; $12.95; (800) 428 5331

Debugging: Creative Techniques and Tools for Software Repair, by Martin Stitt, John Wiley & Sons, New York; $32.95 ($65.90 with disk); (908) 469-4400

Easy PC Maintenance and Repair by Phil Laplante, 1992, Windcrest/McGraw-Hill, Blue Ridge Summit, PA; $14.95; (717) 794-2191, (800) 822-8138

Hard Disk Survival Guide, by Mark Minasi, 1989, SYBEX Inc., Alameda, CA; $29.95; (800) 227-2346, (510) 523-8233

IBM Personal Computer Troubleshooting & Repair, by Robert C. Brenner, 1989, SAMS Publishing, Carmel, IN; $24.95; (800) 428 5331

The Computer Virus Handbook, by Richard B. Levin, 1990, Osborne/McGraw Hill, Berkeley, CA; $24.95; (800) 227-0900

RxPC: The Anti-Virus Handbook, by Janet Endrijonas, 1993, Windcrest/McGraw-Hill, Blue Ridge Summit, PA; $29.95; (717) 794-2191, (800) 822-8138

The Dead Mac Scrolls: How to Fix Hundreds of Hardware Problems Without Going Bankrupt, by Larry Pina, 1992, Peach Pit Press, Berkeley, CA; $32; (800) 283-9444

Upgrading and Maintaining & Servicing IBM PCs, by Julien Moss, 1992 Microtrend Books, Slawson Communications Inc., San Marcos, CA; $29.95; (800) 752-9766, (619) 929-1979

Software

DiskFit Pro (Mac), Dantz Development
(510) 849-0293

FastBack Plus (DOS, Mac, Windows), Fifth Generation Systems
(504) 291-7221, (800) 873-4384

Help! (Mac), Teknosys
(813) 620-3494, (800) 873-3494

MacEKG (Mac), Micromat
(415) 898-6227, (800) 829-6227

MacSleuth (Mac), Dariana
(714) 236-1391, (800) 892-9950

MacTools (Mac), Central Point Software
(503) 690-8090, (800) 964-6896

Norton Antivirus (DOS, Windows), Symantec
(408) 253-9600, (800) 441-7234

Norton Backup (DOS, Windows), Symantec
(408) 253-9600, (800) 441-7234

Norton Utilities (DOS, Mac), Symantec
(408) 253-9600, (800) 441-7234

Now Utilities (Mac), Now Software
(503) 274-2800, (800) 237-3611

PC Tools (DOS), Central Point Software
(800) 964-6896

Redux (Mac), Microseeds
(802) 879-3365, (203) 435-4995

SAM (Mac), Symantec
(408) 253-9600, (800) 441-7234

Snooper (Mac), Maxa
(818) 543-1300, (800) 788-6292

SpinRite II (DOS), Gibson Research
(714) 362-8800, (800) 736-0637

StuffIt Deluxe (Mac), Aladdin Systems
(408) 761-6200

System Sleuth Professional (DOS), Dariana
(714) 236-1391, (800) 892-9950

Virex (DOS, Mac), DataWatch
(919) 490-1277

WinSleuth Gold (Windows), Dariana
(714) 236-1391, (800) 892-9950

XTree for Windows (Windows), XTree Company
(805) 541-0604, (800) 964-2490

XTree Gold (DOS), XTree Company
(805) 541-0604, (800) 964-2490

Hardware companies

American Power Conversion
(401) 789-5735, (800) 541-8896

Best Power Technology
(608) 565-7200, (800) 356-5794

Curtis Manufacturing
(603) 532-4123, (800) 548-4900

Emerson Computer Power
(714) 457-3600, (800) 222-5877

EPE/Topaz
(714) 557-1637, (800) 523-0142

Exide Electronics
(919) 872-3020, (800) 544-0978

Kensington Microware
(415) 572-2700, (800) 535-4242

Panamax
(415) 499-3900, (800) 472-5555

Sola Electric
(708) 439-2800, (800) 289-7652

Tandy Corp.
(817) 390-3011

Tripplite
(312) 329-1777

Insurance

SafeWare
(614) 262-0559, (800) 848-3469

Mobile computing

TAKING YOUR COMPUTER ON THE ROAD IS A liberating experience. You can use time spent traveling and waiting to be productive. Late at night in your hotel you can fine-tune a presentation, write correspondence (and fax it out), or play a game if there is nothing to watch on cable. With remote access software, you can even call up your computer at home and copy a file you forgot, or run an application that you don't have with you.

However, there is a downside to traveling with your computer. The mobile computer is far more vulnerable to damage and theft—you need to take steps to protect your portable. With the proper precautions, you can minimize the risks and stay productive.

On the road

You can perform all the same functions and run all the programs on a notebook computer that you can on a full-fledged desktop unit. To maintain this level of functionality, though, you will have to plan ahead—and sometimes be downright resourceful.

Online storage

Need to save a large file, but don't have enough space on your portable hard drive? Just upload the files to your account with an online service. When you get home or have more room you can download them. This is also a good way to protect important files from damage when traveling.

Mobile modems

When using a modem in a hotel room, always ask the switchboard operator to put your call directly through without intervening. Many hotel telephone systems are designed to automatically route calls through the switchboard. This keeps you from getting a true dial tone, and making a connection. Even phones with a separate modem jack on the side suffer from switchboard routing.

Carry a long cord

Never underestimate the ability of your hotel to find the least accessible place to put the phone jack. While this may prevent accidental disconnection it can make for uncomfortable computing. The longer your cord, the better your chances of reaching the table on the other side of the room.

13-1 *A portable fax machine with a cellular phone interface makes a powerful communications tool for the mobile businessperson.* Ricoh

Mobile accessories

In the quiet comfort of an office, we take for granted the number of accessories that make computing the productive and enjoyable experience that it is. When you're on the move though, you had better pack well. Here are some often overlooked mobile office essentials:

- Printer cables
- Spare ink cartridges
- Paper
- Spare batteries
- An ac transformer/battery charger
- Instruction booklets for whatever hardware you're carrying, as well as command cards or templates for software.

- A null modem cable (absolutely indispensable if you expect to exchange data directly with another computer).
- A pair of gender changers (which connect male-to-male or female-to-female interfaces) and a 9-pin to 25-pin adapter, for computers that use the larger interfaces.
- An English or European plug adapter, if you're going abroad.

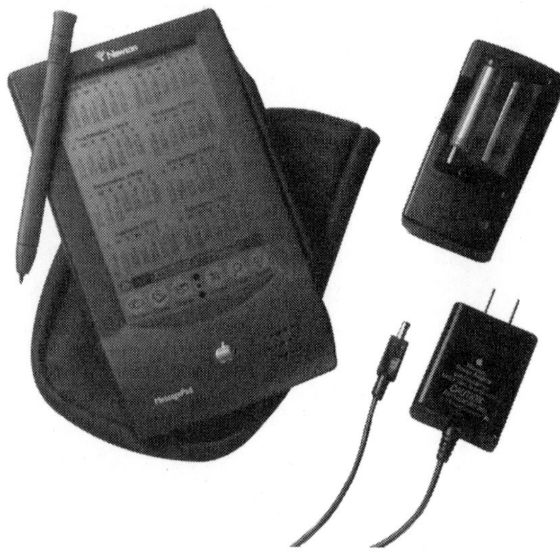

13-2 Apple's Newton MessagePad is a paperback-sized "intelligent personal assistant" cum fax/modem. If Newton's vaunted handwriting recognition lives up to its claims and additional software is developed, it could be a big hit among mobile professionals. Apple Computer

Hotwire your phone

Although fine hotels usually furnish rooms with modem-ready phones, others will have no modular jacks at all. Under these circumstances it is up to you to set up your own connection, which is not difficult if you have the right tools.

To successfully hot-wire the phone you need an RJ-11 module with four wires and attached clips, a set of clip leads, and wire snaps. You can buy these as a kit at most electronic stores. To make the connection:

- Cut off all the leads from the RJ-11 module except the red and green ones.
- Take off the telephone receiver mouthpiece and remove the voice pick-up inside.
- Attach the clip leads connected to the green and red wires to the prongs inside the mouthpiece.
- Take the phone off the hook and dial through the computer.

Power management

Portable computers sacrifice power supply for miniaturization. Depending on how you are using your computer, your battery could last as many as eight hours or as few as one. To keep your system up and running longer follow the power management tips in the following section.

Slow down

Some portables, most PowerBooks for instance, will let you run your computer at a reduced speed. Dropping down to 16 MHz from 33 MHz won't seriously affect most applications and it will dramatically extend your battery life.

Turn off your backlight

Never squint at your screen to save power, but be conservative with your brightness settings. If you can see your screen clearly without a backlight, turn it off or use the minimum brightness setting.

Deep discharges

Rechargeable nicad batteries suffer from what is called the memory effect. Say one day you drain your battery for 30 minutes and then recharge it. Suppose the next day you drain it for another 30 minutes and recharge it. After a while your battery thinks it can only be used for 30 minutes before being recharged.

To avoid this you should deep discharge your battery when it starts to run low. This is especially true when you are about to go on the road—do a deep discharge before you leave, to minimize the chances of getting caught short at the wrong time. The easiest way to deep discharge is with a special utility program (this protects you from completely discharging and damaging the battery).

Bring spares

Advertisements rarely show you spare batteries. But if you plan to use your portable for more than two hours you had better pack several fully charged spare batteries.

Stop your hard disk

You're losing power every second your hard disk is spinning, and it is spinning every second your computer is on. So stop it. Many notebooks let you set a time of non-use after which the hard drive stops spinning. While this may slow you down a little when using hard drive-active applications, if you need to conserve power it's worth it.

RAM disks

If you can spare the memory, set up a one or two megabyte RAM disk with all the applications and documents you will need. A RAM disk is created by reserving memory that might otherwise be used to run applications as a storage area. RAM disks take much less power to access than hard drives. Before shutting down, make sure you copy any files from your RAM disk onto the hard drive—otherwise they can vanish when you power down.

Remote access requires both computers to have modems, preferably fast ones, and the same remote access software.

Save to floppy

Whenever possible, save to your floppy drive rather than to your RAM disk or hard drive when mobile computing. This protects you from losing data and conserves power as well.

Remote access

With remote access software and two modems you can tap into all the files and applications on your desktop system through your portable. When on a business trip, or vacation, you only need to dial your modem to operate your computer as if you were sitting in front of it. This feature is particularly useful to computer consultants who can operate and repair a client's computer without the expense of an on-site visit.

Remote access requires both computers to have modems, preferably fast ones, and the same remote access software. Since each keystroke and every screen change is transmitted over the phone lines, a slow modem translates into a lot of lag time. You can get away with a 2400-bps modem if you plan to use only character based DOS applications. If you want to tether two Macintoshes, or run Windows on a pair of PCs, nothing less than a 9600-bps modem will suffice.

Remember, the maximum speed with which information is exchanged between two computers over a phone line is determined by the slower of the two modems involved. Buying a 9600-bps modem for your desktop will have no effect if the notebook you use to call home only supports 2400-bps communications.

Buying remote access software

Remote access software comes in two forms: computer-to-computer and computer-to-network. The former lets two stand-alone computers communicate with each other, the latter allows a stand-alone computer to access a local area network (LAN) that includes a shared modem. While some programs supply both features in a single package, most software offers only one.

See if you must purchase two copies of the software you choose. Most DOS and Windows packages contain everything you need to connect two computers. However, Timbuktu/Remote, for the Macintosh, requires a unique serialized version of the program on each system involved in the session.

Other features to consider when buying remote software include convenient file transfer, mouse support, and general communications capabilities. This last item allows a remote-access program to replace more traditional communications packages.

Protecting your portable

By taking your computer out of the protected environment of your home or office, you are placing your computer at greater risk. (No one ever dropped a desktop system getting out of a cab.) Between slips, slides, drops and theft, you stand to lose an expensive piece of equipment and get a major headache in a flash. However, you can protect your computer with a few simple precautions, as outlined below.

- Carry your portable in a plastic carrying case. Many portable computers are encased in lightweight plastic that can be easily damaged if knocked around.
- If you plan on shipping your computer, the best package is the one it came in, preferably with the same Styrofoam blocks. In lieu of that, sturdy cardboard and flannel shirts work nicely.
- Keep the cardboard inserts that came with your disk drive and use them when traveling to prevent the read/write heads from rubbing up against each other.
- The lead acid, nicad, or nickel hydride batteries in your portable have a very low internal resistance. This makes them prone to shorts. Throw your spare battery in a bag with some spare change at the bottom and you could start a fire. Keep your batteries away from any metal object that might connect the terminals.
- Tape your business card to the bottom of your computer. Cheap, easy, and not very effective, but it's better than nothing. At least it allows for the possibility of getting your computer back. A more effective approach is to etch your name, address, and Social Security number on the computer where they can't be defaced or removed. This reduces your computers re-sale value, but also deters thieves.
- Glue anchor plates, available at most computer stores, to all your portable components. These plates allow you to secure your computer to a radiator or other fixture by means of a steel cable and combination lock. This may not defeat the determined burglar, but it will thwart the casual thief from pocketing your portable.
- Keep your portable with you when you travel by plane. Nearly all portables are small enough to put in the overhead racks or beneath the seats. (Note: some airlines do not allow portables to be used during takeoffs and landings, so ask your flight attendant.)
- Register foreign made portables with U.S. Customs when leaving the country. If you can't prove the unit was purchased in the United States you could be forced to pay duty upon your return.
- It's okay to put your portable through the X-ray machine at the airport, but don't carry your notebook or floppies through the metal detector.
- When overseas don't use a Radio Shack-type transformer converter to power your computer or printer

(although you may be able to use it to charge your battery). American-made products are designed to run on 60-cycle electricity, while most of the rest of the world runs on 50-cycle. All the transformer-converter does is step down the voltage from 220V to 120V. With the wrong cycle, your computer and printer probably won't work properly, if at all, and it could damage your equipment.

- Take along a set of backup floppy disks and bootable system disk, just in case something happens to the hard disk or you accidentally overwrite a file. Carrying a repair disk, like Norton Utilities, could also save you some hassles if the problem is not too serious.
- Save irreplaceable work on both the hard drive and a single floppy disk that is stored elsewhere.
- Insure your computer. Policies are fairly affordable and will compensate you at replacement cost, minus a small deductible. (See chapter 12, which includes detailed information about preventing computer catastrophes.)

Resources

Software: Remote access

For Windows

Carbon Copy for Windows, Microcom
(617) 551-1000, (800) 822-8224.
Also available for MS-DOS

ReachOut Remote Control, Ocean Isle Software
(407) 770-4777, (800) 677-6232

Remotely Possible, Dial Avalan Technology
(508) 429-6482, (800) 441-2281

For MS-DOS

Close-Up, Norton-Lambert
(805) 964-6767

Co/Session, Triton Technologies
(908) 855-9440, (800) 322-9440

Norton PC/Anywhere, Symantec
(408) 253-9600, (800) 441-7234

For Macintosh

Timbuktu/Remote, Farallon
(510) 814-5000

Books

Office on the Go, by Kim Baker and Sunny Baker, 1993, Prentice Hall, Englewood Cliffs, NJ; $16.95

Communications

THE PHONE IS IMPORTANT FOR ANY BUSINESS. for the home-based business it is doubly so—not only is it the major link to customers and prospects, but it provides an opportunity to add credibility and professionalism. A good lineup of phone options and services will go a long way towards creating a positive image. Fortunately, AT&T has done extensive research on the work-at-home market and offers a number of programs and services designed for the home office.

Communications isn't limited to person-to-person contact. As your business grows, setting up a small-office network for your computers and equipment provides several advantages that can boost productivity.

Phone options and services

Additional phone lines

Investing in another phone line for your business should be a high priority, especially if you don't live alone. The last thing you need is your six-year-old child answering a critical business call. While there are some interim solutions (like Distinctive Ringing), you will outgrow them if your business grows.

An additional line is also recommended if you are a heavy fax or modem user—you don't want your potential customers getting endless busy signals.

Voice mail

Although most home offices still use the traditional answering machine to catch calls, voice mail is rapidly becoming the new standard. At present, more than 700,000 home offices use voice mail for the convenience, reliability and professionalism it lends their business. How is voice mail better than your answering machine?

- It provides a way to increase call volume without adding more lines.
- Many voice-mail systems can take messages from several callers simultaneously without giving a busy signal, even if you have only one line.
- You can leave detailed messages in different mailboxes for specific groups of callers. This cuts down on callbacks.
- Many voice mail services also offer sophisticated features like selective playback and retrieval, which allows users to skip through messages, save, and forward them, things you can't do with an answering machine.
- Callers can hear a complete description of your services or product, leaving a message only if they are still interested. This cuts down on dead-end callbacks.
- Clients can do business whenever it's convenient for them.
- Customers think they're doing business with a much larger firm.
- Voice mail sounds better than an answering machine.
- Voice mail service won't break down like an answering machine.

Three types of voice mail

If you decide to try out voice mail, you have several choices. You can use a service offered by your local telephone company or an outside service bureau, buy and install a voice mail board in your computer, or purchase a stand-alone system. For home-office workers, the first option is probably the simplest, most effective, and least expensive (in the short run).

Voice mail service

You pay anywhere from $5 to $20 a month for voice messaging and answering options, depending on the number of mailboxes and other options you require. Most voice mail services can answer additional calls regardless of whether you're on the phone. A beeping tone when you pick up your phone notifies you that you have a message waiting, which you can retrieve by dialing a special number. You can also pick up messages from any other touch-tone telephone.

Voice-mail board

Another option is to install a voice-mail board in your computer and attach a phone line to it. Many fax/modem boards include a voice-mail function. The voice-mail software runs in the background while you work in another program. You record a greeting, or series of greetings, and the callers' replies are stored on your disk. You receive an onscreen notification that you have a message. However, you must leave your computer on to receive messages.

The main advantage of voice-mail boards is their low cost. They start at $200. But there are several disadvantages.

- Voice processing is computer-intensive, requiring a fast computer with memory to spare. If you work at your computer throughout the day, you should probably buy a second machine to run voice mail.
- You're responsible for installation, programming, and maintenance.
- Voice-mail boards can't answer a call when your line is busy.
- You can't call in from a remote location to pick up messages.

Stand-alone systems

The final option is to purchase a complete stand-alone voice-mail system that includes its own computer. All you do is plug it into your power and phone lines, record your outgoing messages, and you're in business. However, stand-alone voice-mail systems are expensive, starting at around $3000, so they make the most sense for a business with several phone lines and workers.

Distinctive rings

Distinctive-ringing services, offered by local phone companies under different names (such as IdentaRing, RingMate, MultiRing, SignalRing, Custom Ringing, and so on), allow up to three (and sometimes four) phone numbers on a single line. Each of these numbers carries a different ring pattern (long, double ring, short-short-long, etc.) so you can determine which number was dialed to reach you. The monthly cost is about $5–$7 for each additional number on a business line, somewhat less on a residential line. (Generally, residential lines must be converted to business lines in order to add business numbers, which are listed in the Yellow Pages.)

Outside callers, of course, think that you have separate lines, since they dial different numbers for your fax, home or office. With this service you can tell immediately whether it's a business or personal call, or a fax. If call volume becomes a problem you can get a second or third line and keep the same numbers.

Installing call-routing devices is as easy as installing an answering machine.

Call-routing devices

For your fax or answering machine to distinguish between rings, you need a call-routing device. These switches automatically identify each ring cadence and direct each call to the telephone device (phone, answering machine, fax machine, fax/data modem, etc.) you have chosen. There is no manual intervention required and no reconfiguration is necessary when you leave home. There is no impact on outgoing calls.

Installing these devices is as easy as installing an answering machine. Multiport models have up to four outgoing standard modular (RJ-11) phone jacks, each labeled with its associated ring style. Simply plug your telephone equipment into the ports corresponding to the appropriate telephone numbers.

Extension phones not routed through any switch are unaffected and will receive all ringing patterns. If you put answering devices on these bypassed extensions, remember to set them to answer at a sufficient number of rings so as not to preempt the call-routing device.

Call-routing switches are comparable in purchase price to stand-alone fax switches (from $50 to $100), but you must also consider the ongoing monthly expense of the distinctive ringing service. When compared to the cost of separate phone lines, however, a distinctive-ring system will pay for itself in only a few months. Two good routers are Ring Rite+ (Call Management Products) and Ring Decipher (Command Communications).

Call waiting

You can get even more value out of your single phone line by using a call-waiting service. If you're on a personal call, you can tell by the number of clicks whether an incoming call is a business call. The only problem occurs when you're on the phone and ignore an incoming call, because the caller doesn't get an answering machine or a busy signal—the phone just rings. A voice-mail system would take a message, but wouldn't be able to distinguish between a personal, business, or fax call.

Call waiting will also mess up your online connection. If you are using your modem and someone calls you, the call-waiting feature will disrupt your connection. You can avoid this by simply turning off your call waiting before going online.

Other services

AT&T offers a variety of services to enhance your phone. Following are a list of services that are of particular value to the home office worker. Note: Not every phone company will offer every service and the names of the services vary.

- 800 service generates higher response rates from both in-state and out-of-state callers and presents a more professional image. If your business hinges on receiving telephone orders or inquiries, look into getting a toll-free 800 number.
- Caller ID has many useful applications for a home business. Besides making it easy to keep track of clients and how often they call, you can greet current customers by name, screen calls if you're busy, or build your client list.
- Three-way calling saves time and increases productivity by adding a third party to your calls.
- Call forwarding allows you to transfer calls to a number where you can be reached so you don't miss important phone calls.
- Automatic callback dials the last number that called you for up to 30 minutes.
- Repeat dialing automatically redials busy numbers and signals you when the called number is free.
- Call hold lets you put a caller on hold even if you don't have that function on your phone.
- Speed calling lets you preprogram your phone with numbers you call often.
- Enhanced fax services include a number of services to make your fax machine more productive, including a mailbox feature that holds faxes until you're ready to receive them, and a broadcast feature, which can send one or more faxes to multiple locations simultaneously.

Long distance

As you undoubtedly know, all the major long-distance carriers are eager for your business. To win you over, some companies have tried to develop innovative new services, a few of which are specially designed for the home office worker.

Special home business services

AT&T has a new program called AT&T Home Business Resources℠, which is tailored specifically for people who run businesses out of their homes. This program has a number of useful services that can make your business easier to run and more productive. Following is a list of some of these services:

AT&T TrueUSA℠ Savings With this plan you can save up to 30% on all your qualifying AT&T Long Distance calls to anywhere in the United States.

AT&T True Rewards℠ Spend a minimum of $25 on qualifying AT&T Long Distance calling and you can earn reward points good for free AT&T minutes, frequent flyer miles, and other services and items.

AT&T True Messages℠ With this service you can leave a message or send a message when you get a busy signal or nobody answers the phone. You can also catch someone overseas, or at the precise time you know they can be reached by leaving or sending a prerecorded message at the preselected time of your choice. This service can eliminate a lot of inconvenience and worry for the home business person.

AT&T TrueTies℠ 800 A good way to enhance your professional image is by getting your own toll-free 800 number. Your clients will be able to reach you at no cost to them. Toll-free 800 numbers are also of particular value if your home business depends on receiving telephone orders.

AT&T TrueChoice℠ Calling Card This card can give you the reliability of AT&T, no matter where you are, so you can take care of business from practically anywhere. The AT&T TrueChoice Calling Card is also the only card that lets you choose your own calling card number.

After looking over some of the services featured in the AT&T Home Business Resources program, you can see that AT&T is committed to the individual needs of the home business person. All AT&T telecommunications products and services have been designed to make running a business out of your home more productive and convenient.

Long distance tips

Before choosing a service, find out the best rates by checking with organizations like Consumer Reports or Telecommunications Research and Action Center. Remember to figure in any incentives the different companies offer, like frequent flier miles or sign-up bonuses. As a membership benefit, some professional associations offer discounted long distance service for a given carrier.

There are, of course, other carriers besides the Big Three. They frequently promise the customer com-

There are several innovative new services specially designed for the home office worker.

petitive rates. However, these services can be less reliable, and they generally carry certain restrictions, such as limitations on their service areas. They might require that you use a different carrier to reach small cities and towns.

If you can install an expansion card or connect cables, you can install a LAN in your home office.

Small-office networks

If your business has multiple computers, tying them together in a network is a good idea. A network allows your computers to quickly exchange data and to simultaneously send files to the same printer.

Just three or four years ago, the idea of installing a local-area network (LAN) in your home office was ridiculous. After all, you had only one, or maybe two, computers, and the popular networks were expensive and complicated. How could you possibly justify spending $1000 or more per computer to connect them, not to mention all the time and trouble to figure out how?

Networks have changed. Now, for about $200 per computer, you can connect your IBM-compatible computers for high-speed sharing of hard-disk drives, printers, CD-ROM drives, and application software. Installation and usage are a little harder than falling off a log, but nowhere near as tricky as before. You don't have to be a network expert to make it work.

What can a LAN do for you?

LANs allow several people to use the same printer simultaneously. It then sets up a print queue (a special file on whichever computer the printer is attached to) and sends the documents to the printer, one at a time.

Business travelers or telecommuters who carry a laptop can also benefit from installing a network at their business or home office—it makes it very easy to tap into your desktop units.

Finally, two people working in the same office or house can easily share files and software with each other.

Starter kits

To connect computers, you generally install LAN cards in each computer and connect them with cables. (There are some exceptions, covered shortly.) The easiest way to set up a network is to buy a complete starter kit that includes cards, cables, and software. The two biggest names in small-LAN software, called network operating systems, are LANtastic (Artisoft) and NetWare Lite (Novell). Artisoft sells starter kits with its own hardware cards and cables and the LANtastic software. Novell does not bundle hardware and software together, but other companies bundle LAN cards with Novell's NetWare Lite.

Street prices for these kits are under $500 for the first two computers. If you have more than two computers, you'll need an extra LAN card and cable for each additional one. You might want to get your feet wet by connecting only two computers, buying the hardware to connect the others later.

Ethernet cards

The cards in the starter kits are thin Ethernet (a network standard developed by Xerox, Digital, and Intel) cards. Thin refers to the thin coaxial cable that connects the computers. (An earlier standard used thicker cable and is now called, not surprisingly, thick Ethernet.)

If you want to connect more than two computers, or if you wish to buy the hardware separately, your best bet is to buy cards that are compatible with the Novell NE1000, NE2000, or NE2100 specifications. The NE2000 is usually the best choice if your computer has an 80286 or higher processor. To save money, you can use NE1000 cards in a 286 or higher computer, but you won't be able to transfer data between the processor and the card quite as fast. The NE2100 is for the IBM PS/2 Micro Channel bus. Nearly every network operating system has driver software that supports these Novell cards. Ask the dealer for cables and connectors to complete your Ethernet network.

Installation

You install LAN cards as you would any other card, except you might have to set jumpers to specify which interrupts or address ranges to use. (Artisoft is introducing "jumperless" adapters, called Node Runners.) The card's documentation should explain your choices and possible system conflicts.

The biggest problem you face is figuring out how to route the cables between your computers. If your computers aren't all in the same room, you might need professional help routing cables along floorboards or through walls. Be sure the cables are protected from foot traffic and rolling desk chairs.

Once you have the LAN cards and cables installed, you install the LAN software on each computer. You can make any computer a server, which makes its hard-disk drive and printer available for other computers to use, or a workstation, which uses a server's disk and printer but doesn't offer its own to others.

Wireless and cardless LANs

While almost all LANs use LAN cards and cables to connect computers, there are exceptions. For example, a wireless LAN does not use cables, although it does use a LAN card. A wireless LAN uses either radio signals or infrared signals to transmit data between computers. If you want to avoid the problems of running cables between awkwardly located computers, wireless LANs sound like a nice solution. However, they are much more expensive and transmit data more slowly than cabled LAN cards.

A zero-slot LAN, such as LANtastic Z (Artisoft), uses a cable, connecting either serial or parallel ports on your computer. As long as you have only two IBM-compatible computers, each has a spare parallel or serial port (you can't connect a serial to a parallel port), and you don't need to access the other computer's files at faster-than-floppy-disk speed, you're all set. Most experts don't consider this connection method to be a real LAN because it isn't fast enough and doesn't use LAN cards. However, LANtastic Z lets the two computers do everything a "real" LANtastic LAN can do, only slower. The virtue of such a zero-slot LAN is that you can connect and disconnect it quickly, should you, say, want to connect a notebook to your desktop to transfer a few files, then detach it for travel.

Another zero-slot LAN is SwiftLAN (Moses Computers), which uses adapters to connect the parallel ports (not serial ports) on two computers with standard telephone wire, and is much faster than LANtastic Z.

The bottom line: If you can install an expansion card or connect cables, you can install a LAN in your home office. A starter kit is the easiest way to begin, so you don't have to bother figuring out the compatibility of cables, adapters, and cards. Once the LAN is running, you can set up the software so any computer can access any other computer's hard disk and printer, or you can decide that only certain PCs will be allowed to access certain others.

For the Macintosh

If you own Macs, you're in luck. The Mac's operating system has built-in networking. With a little cabling (no fancy cards), you can link everything up. This system is not going to set any speed records, but it is quite sufficient for small businesses.

Resources

AT&T Home Business Resources[SM]
(800) 383-6164

AT&T Small-Business Services
(800) 222-0400

Telecommunications Research and Action Center
(202) 462-2520

Online services

THE WORDS *ONLINE* AND *UNIVERSE* ARE OFTEN seen together in the same sentence. There is good reason for this—the amount of information you can access through your modem is staggering. You can hold conversations or exchange mail with people across the globe—and the amount of time and money you can spend gives new meaning to the term "black hole."

To help you sort through this electronic universe (and save you some time and money), we've put together a guide to online services. Each of the commercial services profiled provides a mix of consumer and business information, interactive services, and e-mail communications in a format easy enough for the online novice to master. In the task comparison, we also challenged each service with common business activities, such as booking a flight, searching a database, and sending a fax.

Internet is something other than a commercial online service. We will explain what it is and how you can use it to be more productive. Finally, because it's easy to get lost in the abundance of information available online, we give you some tips for finding information online.

Guide to online services

What benefits do online services offer?

- Get free advice on everything from graphic design to business management.
- Obtain free software or shareware (if you like and use the program, you send a payment to the programmer)—utilities, clip art, fonts, games, antivirus programs, etc.
- Download copies of magazine and newspaper articles.
- Track competitors' coverage in the news.
- Send faxes without a fax machine.
- Enroll in college courses.
- Do market research from your desk.
- Find a four-star Thai restaurant in Chicago.
- Monitor the stock market.
- Get software and hardware technical support without having to wait on the telephone line.
- Establish yourself as an expert in your field. While you cannot advertise online, you can give advice. Your good name is the best marketing tool you have.
- Make travel reservations.
- Contact your representative or senator.
- List your name and company information in the Business Resource Directory, a searchable online database of businesses. Similarly you can search for other businesses yourself.
- Shop for software, hardware, and office supplies.

Costs

Many online services charge by the minute, then tack on surcharges for things like access to specialized databases, library searches, fax transmissions, and document retrievals. Some charge annual membership fees. Others offer all-you-can-eat flat fees—but charge more if you log on during business hours or access certain databases. Fortunately, a few services, most notably America Online, have significantly reduced prices.

Another potential cost is long distance charges. If you live in a midsize city, chances are calling an online service will only be a local call. Most services have hundreds of access numbers scattered around the country. However, residents of smaller cities and towns might need to use a number located in a neighboring city—resulting in additional long distance costs.

The key to minimizing your bills is to know exactly what you are trying to accomplish in any given online session. When you go food shopping, the common wisdom is not to go when you are hungry. When you go online, don't go because you're bored. When you sign up, most online services give you a few free hours to explore and find the forums and services that are of interest to you—after this, the more discipline and planning you can muster, the better.

America Online is a piece of cake to use.

CompuServe

In addition to providing access to thousands of databases and publications spanning the worlds of finance, business, and government, CompuServe offers hundreds of special-interest forums where you can leave messages, ask questions, or have live discussions on topics ranging from desktop publishing to working from home. Product support from most major hardware and software vendors is also available. The service's extensive e-mail system makes it easy to upload and download files, and to communicate with the service's one million-plus members—as well as those members on many other online services.

Weakness

Finding your way can be costly. For novices, CompuServe's extensive command structure can be difficult to navigate without a graphical front-end program like CompuServe Information Manager. CompuServe tried to take away the sting with an $8.95 all-you-can-eat-within-limits plan that offers access to basic services and e-mail services. Unfortunately, CompuServe chose not to include its popular forums in this plan.

Cost

CompuServe has two pricing plans. The basic plan is $8.95 a month for unlimited access to all basic services, with additional charges of $8 per hour ($16 at 9600 bps) for "extended services." There is also a low-user system, where you can connect for $2.50 per month plus hourly surcharges on everything at $12.80 ($22.80 for 9600 bps). Many information retrieval services also have fees for usage.

With your standard $8.95 fee you can send sixty 3-page messages free each month. For additional messages or for any messages to another service the cost is 15¢ for the first 7500 characters and 5¢ for each additional 2500 characters.

Helpful services and forums for home businesses

Services

The names in all-caps are the "go" names. To access a given forum within CompuServe you type go NAME.

BIZFILE

The BIZFILE service finds businesses by their entries in the *Yellow Pages*, and includes more than 10 million U.S. and Canadian establishments.

Business Dateline (BUSDATE)

The Business Dateline database provides the full text of articles from more than 115 regional business publications in the U.S. and Canada. Coverage includes local economic conditions, retailing, real estate, people and management, financial institutions, transportation, and electronics.

Business Database Plus (BUSDB)

Business Database Plus is a service that lets you search for and retrieve full-text articles from two complementary collections of business-oriented articles from regional, national, and international sources.

Business Demographics (BUSDEM)

Business Demographics Reports are designed to help businesses analyze their markets. The reports are based upon information from the U.S. Census Bureau, and were developed by Market Statistics.

Commerce Business Daily (COMBUS)

The Commerce Business Daily database includes the full text of U.S. Commerce Department publications listing all significant federal contracts, requests for proposals, and other data related to government contracts. The database is updated daily.

Dun's Electronic Business Directory (DYP)

The Dun's database contains directory information on more than 8.5 million businesses and professionals in the U.S. Records cover both public and private companies of all sizes and types.

Business Incorporating Guide (INC)

Provided by Corporate Agents, Inc. (CAI), the Business Incorporating Guide service is one of the largest incorporating service companies in the nation. CAI does not offer legal, accounting or financial advice. They have automated the process to the point that within 48 hours of reading this guide, you can have a legal and valid corporation for as little as $99 plus state fees! Through the Entrepreneur's Advantage Resource Network (EARN), you can give your small business the purchasing power, discounts, and benefits of Fortune 500 companies.

IQuest Business Management InfoCenter (IQBUSINESS)

IQuest gives you access to the most important databases covering information on virtually any aspect of business management, including management research, marketing studies, company ownership, mergers & acquisitions, and more.

The Business Wire (TBW)

Throughout the day The Business Wire makes available press releases, news articles, and other information from the world of business. Information on hundreds of different compa-

Prodigy's colorful interface and simple onscreen commands make the service easy to master.

nies is transmitted daily to The Business Wire's subscribers.

TRW

The reports in the TRW database include credit and business information on more than 13 million organizations. Use this database to find actual account information for more than 70 million business account relationships as reported by participating corporations. The information available in a report includes:

- Credit histories;
- Financial information and ratios;
- Key business facts such as size, ownership, products;
- UCC filings, tax liens, judgments, and bankruptcies;
- An executive summary.

The report for a specific company might not include all of this information.

Forums

Media Forum (MEDIA)

Entrepreneur's Small Business Forum (USEN)

Working from Home Forum (WORK)

Hosted by Paul and Sarah Edwards, contributing editors of *Home Office Computing*.

PR and Marketing Forum (PRSIG)

LAWSIG

This forum is devoted to the topic of law and legal matters.

NAIC (National Association of Investors Corporation)

America Online

America Online's mission is to give you the easiest and most pleasurable time online. The computing and software department is the flagship of this service, housing forums in business, communications and networking, desktop publishing, development, education, games, graphics, music, utilities, user groups, desk accessories, and more. America Online is a piece of cake to use—simply by clicking an icon, you can dash off an online message, join in a real-time chat session, or download from a choice of more than 70,000 shareware or freeware files. Running into the service's 325,000 other members with similar interests is a possibility each time you go online. America Online includes a time-efficient Download Manager that lets you select a group of files, download them all at once, and log off. Members can also exchange messages with CompuServe members through the Internet gateway.

Weakness

America Online needs more depth. While it's fun and easy to use, it does not have the range of newspaper and magazine articles and in-depth financial information that CompuServe and Prodigy do. What's more, the bulletin boards offered on the service tend to focus more on personal than professional interests, resulting in far fewer networking opportunities than exist on CompuServe.

Cost

America Online's fixed monthly fee of $9.95 includes access to all of America Online's services for five hours each month. If you use more than five hours in a given month, the rate for additional time (beyond your initial five hours) is $3.50 per hour, 24 hours a day, seven days a week.

There are no other surcharges for services such as e-mail, even on Internet mail gateway, or for software downloading.

15-1 *America Online has an easy-to-use interface. Just click on the icon for the subject area you want to access.*

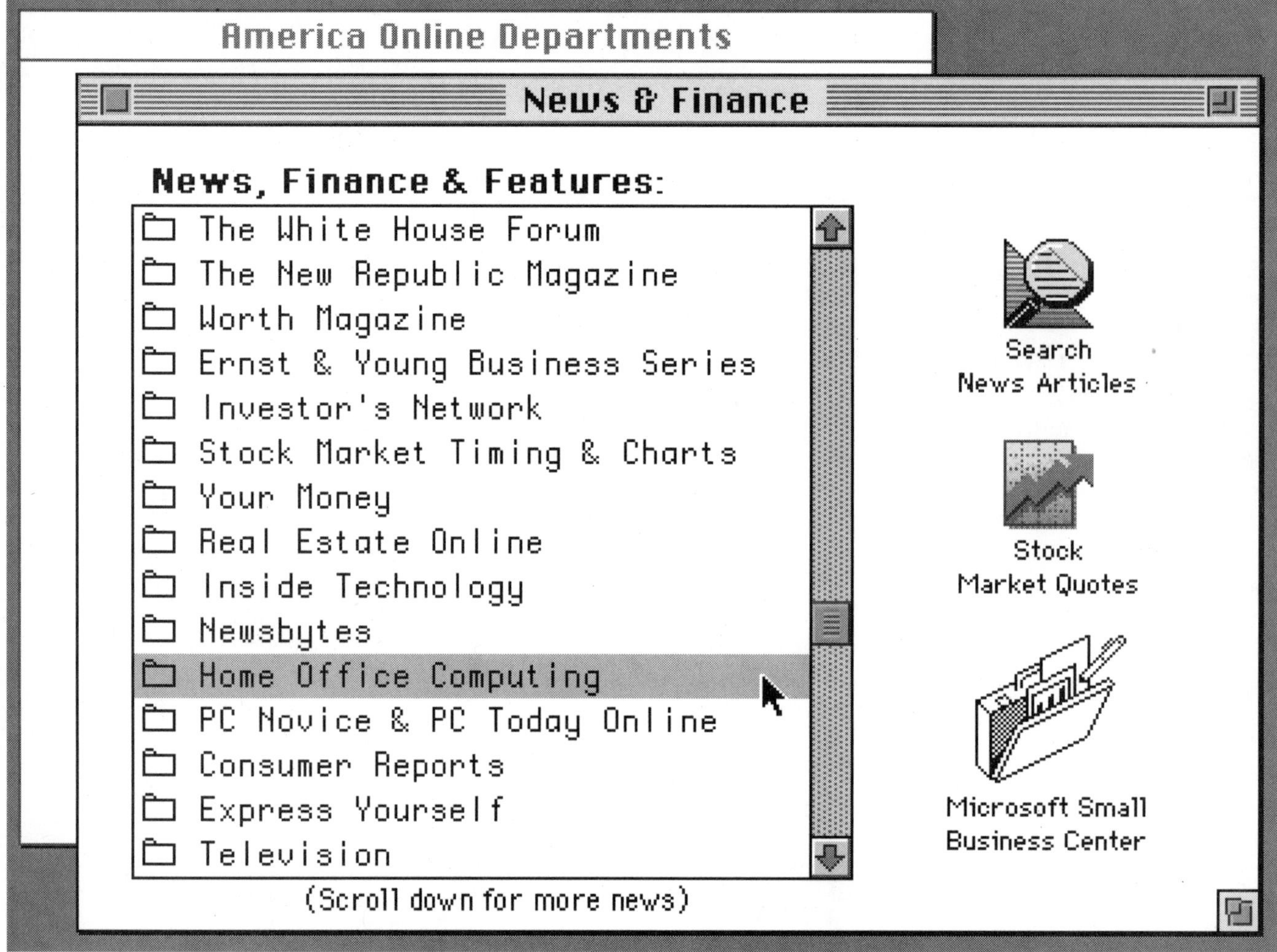

15-2 *If you go into America Online's News & Finance section, you'll find the Home Office Computing forum.*

Helpful services and forums for home businesses

Business News

Top Business news stories, with categories for market, company changes, Company finance, and Company actions.

San Jose Mercury News

The San Jose Mercury News is an online newspaper and an example of things to come. It includes a business section, like any newspaper. Click the "Networking" icon for help from other online members in establishing or building your business or career. There's a calendar of business-related events, articles about career development, and a message board for networking.

BillPay USA lets you pay bills through your computer.

You can select news by industry: Commodity, Consumer & Retail, Financial & Business, Health Care, High Tech, Transport Industry, and Other Industries.

Macintosh Business Forum

Desktop Publishing Forum

Ernst & Young Business Series

The Ernst & Young Business Series is the place to read all about starting and managing your own business from the professionals at Ernst & Young. As part of their comprehensive business services, they have created an Entrepreneurial Services Group to help entrepreneurs who are starting a new business.

Home Office Computing Magazine

Access old issues and reviews and leave questions to the editors.

Microsoft Small Business Center

The Small Business Center was created to provide a place where small business owners (or people considering starting a small business) can find information and help

Downloading a file is one of the most common uses of online services.

on a wide variety of subjects, including:

- Articles on subjects like exporting, finance, and marketing from organizations like the U.S. Small Business Administration, the U.S. Chamber of Commerce, the National Federation of Independent Businesses (NFIB), Dun & Bradstreet, Inc. Magazine, and many others.
- A list of small business seminars offered by the American Management Associations and others.
- Software templates and programs that you can download and use in your business as well as information on other software sources.
- Real time, personalized help for your small business from the Service Corps of Retired Executives. SCORE counselors are online and ready to help you with questions and issues every Wednesday night from 7-11 p.m. (EST) or leave messages for them in the message board area.

Check the Small Business Center message boards to see what other small business owners are talking about or to raise your own issues for discussion.

Investor's Network

Tax Forum

Ask your tax questions on the tax message board, download helpful tax files from the software library, and get answers from Mr. Charles Bish in the "Tax Help" room, Wednesdays at 9 p.m. EST in the People Connection forum during tax season.

Real Estate Online

This forum is designed to help people buy, sell, rent, finance and invest in real estate. This is a place to learn more about real estate, to trade ideas, to keep up with breaking information, and to debate issues.

Strategies for Business

Strategies for Business is a resource for business owners and managers. It will give you an opportunity to increase your knowledge of all phases of business management. It will also give you the chance to network with business owners, executives, and managers across the country.

The Strategies for Business software library is still under construction. However, there are already numerous text files available to meet your informational needs. Among the files already in the library or soon to be uploaded are files to help you:

- Learn to manage your time more efficiently;
- Work more productively;
- Market your products or services more successfully;
- Understand legal and tax issues;
- Be a better manager;
- Decide what kind of business to start;
- Alert you to useful new business-to-business products and services.

Prodigy

While Prodigy positions itself as a family service, providing education, entertainment, news, weather, sports, personal-finance advice, and so on, they also provide a variety of business and computing resources. Unlike other online services that charge by the minute or tack on surcharges for each specialized database, Prodigy charges a reasonable monthly fee of $14.95 for hundreds of basic services, with additional fees for Custom Choice services. Designed with the online novice in mind, Prodigy's colorful interface and simple onscreen commands make the service easy to master.

Prodigy's shopping service allows you to browse the wares of hundreds of online vendors hawking everything from computers to flowers. For serious investors, Prodigy offers Strategic Investor (available for an additional $14.95 a month), a Custom Choice that offers a wealth of information on thousands of stocks, bonds, and mutual funds without the prohibitive cost of logging onto Dow Jones News/Retrieval (DJN/R). There's a lot of free investment information as well. Prodigy claims more than 1.75 million members.

Weakness

Despite the fact that Prodigy has come a long way since its introduction in 1989, major drawbacks remain. Prodigy can be slow. There are advertisements that crawl across the bottom of most screens, dragging out the page-to-page process. Another drawback is Prodigy's limited download capabilities, a problem the service has promised to correct.

Helpful services and forums for small business

Banking Online

While limited to the participating banks, this service lets you see, print and download bank statements any time of the month. You can also transfer funds and pay bills.

BillPay USA

This service lets you pay bills through your computer and download payment information into financial software programs. It helps you keep accurate records as well.

Block on Taxes

Julian Block gives advice on keeping the government out of your pocket.

Bruss on Real Estate

Broker, attorney, and syndicated columnist Robert Bruss shares strategies for home buying and investment.

Business Headlines

Business Travel

Peter Greenberg offers tips for frequent business travelers.

Company News

Company News lists stories by company, industry, and news category.

Economy Headlines

Economic Indicators

Heady on Banking

Newsletter publisher and columnist Robert Heady helps you make the most of banking services.

Home Business

The latest tips, tricks, and secrets to running your home business from the editors of *Home Office Computing*.

Investment Digest

Syndicated Columnist Brendan Boyd offers expert advice on managing your portfolio.

Kiplinger's Personal Finance Magazine

Money Talk Bulletin Board

Money Talk is an open forum for discussing financial issues.

PCFN

The PC Financial Network lets you trade stocks and sell mutual funds from your computer.

Quote Check

Offers continually updated securities quotes.

Quote Track

Quote Track delivers the latest news and quotes on the stocks and mutual funds you follow regularly.

Strategic Investor

Offers in-depth investment information with up-to-the-minute data on stocks and mutual funds.

Software Guide

Practical hands-on reviews from the editors of *Home Office Computing* magazine.

GEnie

GEnie is a full-feature service that reminds us of a scaled-down CompuServe. Like Delphi price is one of GEnie's main attractions—as long as you log on at night and don't stray beyond its basic offerings. But GEnie offers much more for the business user than Delphi: investment and business-related bulletin boards, hardware and software support round tables, a gateway to DJN/R's wealth of financial information, and all the e-mail you can send.

> *One of the great benefits of online services is the other people who subscribe to them.*

Weakness

You can't get there from here. Though GEnie is aimed at the consumer market, its complex menu structure makes it difficult to navigate without its Aladdin front-end software. Also, it can take a while for the service to move you in and out of the basic, value, and professional service areas. GEnie doesn't offer much business information of its own, forcing users to access DJN/R at prices that, during peak hours, can approach $200 an hour.

Delphi

While not as extensive in features and forums as most of the other services reviewed here, Delphi's big plus is price—as low as $1 an hour compared to $12.80 an hour (at 2400 bps) on CompuServe. For only $3 more a month, you can tap into the Internet and exchange e-mail with users of other online services. Delphi offers a simplified command structure, foreign-language translation services, and a gateway to Latin America through its Delphi/Argentina and Delphi/Miami international services.

Weakness

Great price, but not much there. Though Delphi does offer stock quotes, commodities prices, and several stock-tip newsletters, the service doesn't have much in the way of business databases or bulletin boards, and, unless you tap into Dialog's complex and costly video text service, there are no newspaper or magazine archives to peruse. Another drawback to Delphi is its dearth of local access numbers, so long-distance charges can add up.

Task comparison

In the task comparison below, an asterisk (*) signifies the online service that performed best in each task category.

Booking a flight

Accessing flight information online is beneficial even if you don't book through the service. You can pick the flights you want, check prices, read the latest travel advisories, get deals on rental cars, find out about frequent-flyer memberships, and more. All five services utilize at least Eaasy Sabre, American Airlines online reservation system.

*CompuServe

CompuServe offers a wide variety of trip-planning options, including Eaasy Sabre, Travelshopper, and Official Airline Guides. Unlike Prodigy's graphical version of Eaasy Sabre, the one on CompuServe is text-based and much faster. Once you've signed up for the service, simply follow the menu prompts and type in your departure point, destination, and travel dates and let Eaasy Sabre do the rest. The OAG surcharge is $5 per hour.

America Online

The job was done simply with Eaasy Sabre, though characters can be a bit slow to appear on the screen.

Prodigy

Easy to do through Eaasy Sabre, though trip-planning can be painfully slow due to Prodigy's graphics-inten-

Online databases can provide you all the information of a top-notch library, without the inconvenience of paper.

sive interface. Prodigy's new Book-a-Trip option that allows online travel agents to craft model itineraries is available to novice users who find even Eaasy Sabre a little over their heads.

GEnie

Travel planning is most efficient through Eaasy Sabre, though characters can be slow to appear on the screen. GEnie also offers access to Official Airlines Guides, though it's heavily surcharged as a "professional service."

Delphi

The easy-to-use and easily accessible trip-planning options on Delphi include Eaasy Sabre, Commercial Sabre, Travelshopper, and Official Airline Guides (surcharged at $25.20 per hour).

Searching for news and articles

Up-to-the-minute news, relevant articles, and reviews are plentiful on the services we reviewed. However, the process you use to find what you want differs.

***CompuServe**

CompuServe's Newspaper Library database makes online research a snap, though costs can mount if you're not sure what you're looking for. Apart from CompuServe's standard connect-time charges, the database carries surcharges of $3 per search (for up to 10 titles), $3 per article retrieved and $1 for searches that turn up no "hits," or matching articles.

America Online

This service offers access to a number of current periodicals such as *The Washington Post* and *USA Today*, and includes some historical magazine and newspaper databases that can be searched by topic. Top news stories of the day are a click away.

Prodigy

Archived newspaper and magazine articles are not on Prodigy, but top news is provided through AP, UPI, and its own staff, as well as stories from DJN/R. You can find reviews or stories from many publications, such as *Home Office Computing* and *Consumer Reports*, although they are not searchable by topic.

GEnie

Articles are available through GEnie NewsStand, a database that includes 12 daily newspapers and 900 periodicals. Searches cost $2.50 for a group search, $4.50 for a title review (up to 10 titles), $4.50 for a full-text review and $1.25 for no-hit search.

Delphi

Searching on Delphi is difficult and costly. Since Delphi offers no newspaper databases of its own, users must tap into Dialog to do research. Accessing Dialog costs $35 an hour for Delphi subscribers, with extra fees for access to databases and articles retrieved. Though Dialog offers hundreds of databases on a myriad of topics, its command structure is notoriously complex.

Downloading a file

Downloading a file, such as a library article on how to write a business plan or the latest utility shareware, is one of the most common uses of online services. It can be as easy as choosing the file and then choosing "download" from a menu, or it could be as complicated as having to know what protocols to use for the best results.

CompuServe

Downloading is quick and easy on CompuServe, especially when it comes to retrieving library text files from the service's many bulletin boards. If you're using CompuServe Information Manager (CIM), simply select a file from a forum library by highlighting it and pressing enter; then click the "receive" button from the box that appears at the bottom of the screen, and a box will pop up with the file and directory name already listed. Without CIM, you must follow your software's rules for choosing protocols and downloading procedures.

***America Online**

Downloading is easier than on many of the other online services profiled here. Simply choose the file you want to download, name it, and choose where on disk to download it to. The Download Manager lets you choose all the files you want to download, and then takes care of the process for you.

Prodigy

Unlike most of the other online services profiled, at press time Prodigy didn't offer true downloading capabilities except in specialized areas such as Strategic Investor (financial reports), Ziffnet (shareware library), and billing information. Though users can copy any onscreen file to disk, the process is cumbersome and time-consuming. Novice users will find it far easier just to print out what they want.

GEnie

Just pick the downloading option from the online menu and the rest depends on the communications software you use. The service is free of connect-time charges during off-peak hours.

Delphi

The process is similar to CompuServe's, in which you are dependent upon your communication software's downloading functions.

Sending a fax

Even fax machines and fax/modem owners can occasionally use an online service's ability to send a fax from their computer to any fax machine, especially if they're using a local access number, and the person to whom they're faxing is an expensive long-distance call away. If you don't own a fax machine or fax/modem, then here's a way to send faxes to your clients who do. We tested this by sending faxes to a stand-alone fax on a separate phone line.

CompuServe

Faxing is as easy as uploading a file. Trouble is, the CompuServe fax took 27 minutes after transmission to print out on our fax machine, by far the slowest of any of the online services profiled. To send a fax in the United States, CompuServe charges 75 cents for the first 1000 characters plus 25 cents for each additional 1000 characters.

***America Online**

Easy, quick, and cheap. Unlike other online services that charge by the number of pages or characters transmitted, America Online charges only $2 per fax no matter how long plus an extra $2 for each additional fax address.

Prodigy

Fax service was not available at press time, though it is in the works.

GEnie

Just pick from GEnie's online mail menu. Because GEnie prices its faxes by the page times the zone rate (North America, South America, and so on) rather than by the number of characters, sending a fax on GEnie can be a better deal than on some other online services. GEnie charges 85 cents for faxes within North America, $2.50 for Europe, $3 for Asia, and higher rates for South America, Africa, and the Middle East. GEnie ranked near the bottom on our speed test, though, taking six minutes from transmission to reception.

Delphi

Quick and easy (took only two minutes from sending to reception), but expensive since Delphi faxes go through AT&T's Easylink system. In the United States, Delphi charges $1.25 for the first faxed page (about 2500 characters), plus 50 cents for each additional half-page. Overseas faxes cost more.

Support from Microsoft

We chose Microsoft because of its wide distribution of products. We thought its technical-support services would probably be represented on the online services. Note that the quality of support you receive usually depends on the software or hardware company itself, not on the online service.

***CompuServe**

Featuring four forums for Microsoft alone, this expansive service undoubtedly offers the best and broadest hardware and software support of any of the online services profiled. CompuServe's Microsoft support people generally respond to all questions within 24 hours.

America Online

It took three days to get a response from Microsoft, though, in fairness, the note was posted Friday and we received a note back on Monday. The tech-support person who responded said that Microsoft's weekend message checking is optional on America Online.

Prodigy

Support is not available from Microsoft, but there are plenty of places to post questions in the popular bulletin board section. Here, answers are posted by other members, Prodigy service experts, and *Home Office Computing* magazine.

GEnie

We got a quick reply. GEnie's Microsoft tech-support rep says it's company policy to respond to messages within a day and to try to resolve all problems within three days. However, some GEnie members complained about messages languishing for months because they had been posted in the wrong forum.

Delphi

Not available.

Getting a stock quote

Finding stock quotes online is usually quite easy. What differs between services is what you can do to stock information once you find it.

CompuServe

Getting stock quotes is easy on CompuServe, but downloading them to spreadsheets is not—until you've managed to master a complex sequence of menus and commands. Delayed quotes on stocks, options, market indexes, exchange rates, and mutual funds can be obtained at no additional charge by members who sign up for CompuServe's $8.95 flat-fee service.

America Online

It's easy enough to get stock quotes on America Online—just click "key word" and type stock—but, like most of the other online services profiled, it's impossible to download the quotes directly into a spreadsheet. On America Online, stock quotes are delayed 20 minutes.

***Prodigy**

Members can retrieve stock prices, income statements, and balance sheet information from Strategic Investor for a monthly surcharge of $14.95, and from Quote Track and Quote Check free as part of the basic service. Unlike the other online services profiled, Prodigy lets users quickly and easily download stock quotes directly to Quattro Pro, Microsoft Excel, Lotus 1-2-3, and Quicken 5.0 and 6.0. Stock quotes are available on a 15-minute delayed basis for free. Real-time quotes are accessible only through PCFN, Prodigy's online brokerage service, and only in the course of trade validations.

GEnie

When it comes to stock quotes, GEnie is the best deal in town if you can wait until the market closes. That's because, during evening and weekend hours, GEnie quotes are free as part of the $4.95-a-month basic service plan. Like most of the services profiled, there's no way to download stock quotes directly into a spreadsheet—unless you first download one of the script files available on GEnie's Investment or IBM RoundTables.

Delphi

Stock quotes cost seven cents each. Like most of the other services profiled, there's no way to download these quotes into a spreadsheet.

Searching for members with similar interests

One of the great benefits of all of these services is the other people who subscribe to them—if you can find them. You can find potential clients, others whose businesses, hobbies, and interests are similar to yours (with whom you might share a tip or two), or otherwise network.

CompuServe

Either leave a message in the appropriate forum, or search the membership directory or individual forum's listings by interest or name. A good choice is the Work from Home forum, hosted by Paul and Sarah Edwards.

*America Online

In this area, America Online is clearly the tops among the online services profiled. Members can search for kindred spirits—by real name, screen name, personal information, occupation, hobbies, and interests. You can also leave public messages in any of the business-related bulletin boards, like the one in *Home Office Computing*'s section.

Prodigy

Network with other business-minded members in the Entrepreneur section of the Careers bulletin board, in the Computer Club, and all other bulletin boards by sending public or private messages. You can search membership lists by geographic location only, not by occupation or interests.

GEnie

Done by perusing GEnie's membership directory. Search by first name, last name, e-mail address, company name, interests, city, state, and country.

Delphi

Membership directory lets you type in keywords based on personal and professional interests.

Internet

More and more people are talking about Internet. The Internet now counts more than 10 million users in 50 countries and is spreading rapidly. The number of users has been doubling in recent years.

The Internet, however, is not a commercial information service. It's a collection of more than 11,000 computer networks—including universities, libraries, museums, supercomputer centers, state and federal government institutions, and businesses—from around the globe that are linked together. Nor is it a specific entity—it's just the name that has been given to this federation of allied networks, many of which are nonprofit. Even if you don't belong to one of these organizations, you can access the Internet and exchange electronic mail and files with others on the system.

Because of its roots in the National Science Foundation, Internet is particularly valuable for scientists, academics, policy makers, market researchers, librarians, and technicians, who can keep in touch with their colleagues around the world and stay up to date on the latest developments in their fields. Nonetheless, more than half of the groups connected to the Internet are engaged in commercial activity.

Commercial-like services

Internet offers some of the same services as commercial networks: electronic mail to Internet users as well as millions of subscribers to commercial services; the ability to chat/conference with other Internet users; more than two million files and shareware programs to download; multi-player games; several thousand special-interest groups (called newsgroups) where you can post and read messages; and access to databases (such as the Library of Congress catalog records, transcripts of electronic conferences, census data, and the Department of Commerce's Economic Bulletin Board). You can download files and access many of these services for free.

Low-cost e-mail

Electronic mail is the most commonly used application on the Internet. Nearly one-third of respondents to a recent Internet survey said they carried out some kind of collaborative research or work with colleagues via electronic mail. Many people we interviewed said they used the Internet e-mail as an inexpensive alternative to overnight mail services. In fact, for many small businesses, the Internet acts as their own corporate network to transfer work in progress and to communicate via e-mail.

An Internet user can also exchange electronic mail with members of commercial services, such as America Online, Delphi, CompuServe, and MCI Mail. An Internet user with a commercial account, even on systems such as Dialog and Dow Jones News/Retrieval, can also access that system from the Internet (often at 9600 or 14,400 bps), which might cut phone costs considerably.

The downside

Wealth of information and people is one of the Internet's selling points, but it can be a drawback. With millions of megabytes of information to choose from and more than 10 million users, you can easily get lost. That's partly because of the Internet's rather unfriendly and sometimes arcane command-driven interface, in marked contrast to commercial services, which are getting more and more graphic. When sending a message from another system to the Internet, you must use the unfriendly Internet address protocol: user name@machine name. For example, the address for the NSFnet InterNIC's information service is info@internic.net. Increasingly, however, Internet sites are offering friendly navigators, which have point-and-click menus in addition to the ability to search indexed lists of resources.

How to join

Because the Internet isn't a commercial enterprise with standardized fees, you can't walk into a store and buy an Internet account. You set up an account with an organization called a Public-Access Internet Site, which is connected to the Internet, then use your own communications software to sign on. Public-Access Internet Sites are popping up in major cities around the world. Even Delphi, a major commercial online service, offers full Internet access.

Cost

Most sites charge a mere $1 an hour to access the Internet, no matter how fast your modem, although you might pay more for some selected databases. Delphi charges $3 a month in addition to its regular $10 a month (for four hours' usage) fee. If the public-access phone number isn't in your local calling range, you can expect to spend another $1 to $5 per hour in phone costs, and sometimes more for daytime usage. There are also a number of toll-free phone services, which cost as little as $20 per month, offering e-mail and selected other services.

Finding information online

Online databases can provide you all the information of a top-notch library, without the inconvenience of paper. You can access everything George Will has written in the past two years or everything that has been written about him. The diversity of information available is staggering; fortunately, all the online services will send you a database catalog. To list just a few of the topics covered:

- Complete text of articles from magazines, newspapers, and newsletters across the globe.
- References and abstracts from science, law, and medical journals.
- Financial profiles and background on millions of U.S. and Foreign companies.
- Government statistics ranging from census data to patent information.

Although all this information is available to anyone with a computer and a modem, this is not to say it's always easy to get to.

Even if you know exactly what you want and exactly where to find it, online searches can be complicated and expensive. Here are some general tips to help you successfully navigate the sea of information online.

KYA (Know Your Acronyms)

Take care to note what seemingly obscure acronyms represent; they're easy to overlook, but might represent exactly what you need. For example, if you are looking for the information about the Justice system, Dialog's NCJRS is the place to go. We recommend keeping a reference list or catalog nearby when conducting a search.

What to look for in a database

- Which files cover the popular and respected journals?
- Which files offer the most comprehensive indexing?
- How far back do they go?
- How up-to-date are they?

What's your angle?

Make sure the information you're looking for fits your specific needs. A lawyer preparing for a malpractice suit and a doctor doing research might search the same files concerning a new medical treatment, but they are looking for very different information. The lawyer wants data on court cases and complaints, while the doctor wants information from medical journals. They both might want pertinent periodicals, but clearly their individual needs are more important than the subject.

Search selectively

You can cut the costs of an online search by choosing an inexpensive, user-friendly, citation-only search environment for general searches. When you have found the citations you want, you can go to the full text database and selectively retrieve only those documents you need.

Cost

Searching databases can be expensive, very expensive. While Dow Jones News & Retrieval comes in at about $100 an hour, many services are cheaper and offer similar options. In shopping for the right database, it pays to shop around. Keep an eye out for bargains like access "happy hours" and introductory offers. However, when pricing and comparing database systems, it's important to understand all of the factors involved:

- Does the connect charge include telecommunications?
- Does the service charge extra for high-speed modems?
- How good are the abstracts? Don't let the database producer pass off the first paragraph of a story as an intelligent summary.
- Are there discounts for off-peak hours?
- How complete is the database content? Are files missing?
- Can you get information delivered to you by e-mail? How long does this take?
- How often are the systems updated?

If you are planning to do a lot of online research, invest in a high-speed modem, preferably 14,400 bps. The extra cost for the added speed will be quickly made up by the savings generated from faster downloading times.

Online comparison chart

	CompuServe	America Online	Prodigy Information Services	GEnie	Delphi
Contact information	P.O. Box 20212 Columbus, OH 43220 (800) 848-8199 (614) 457-0802	8619 Westwood Center Dr. Suite 200 Vienna, VA 22182 (800) 827-6364 (703) 448-8700	445 Hamilton Ave. White Plains, NY 10601 (800) 776-3449 (914) 993-8000	401 N. Washington St. Rockville, MD 20850 (800) 638-9636 (800) 340-4000	General Videotex 1030 Massachusetts Ave. Cambridge, MA (800) 695-4005 (617) 491-3393
Number of members	1.3 million	325,000	1.75 million	350,000	<100,000
Price	$8.95/month for unlimited use of basic services. Additional services are charged $8/hour for 1200 & 2400 bps modems and $16/hour for 9600 bps modems.	$9.95/month includes 5 hours. Additional hours at $3.50	$14.95/month for unlimited use of basic services. Additional fees for custom choices.	$8.95/month includes 4 hours. Additional hours at $3 for evenings and weekends, and $12.50 for days.	$20/month for 20 hours plus $1.80 for additional hours. Or $10/month for 4 hours plus $4 for additional hours.
Computer platforms supported	DOS, Macintosh, Windows	DOS, Macintosh, Windows	DOS, Macintosh, Windows	DOS, Macintosh, Windows	DOS, Macintosh
Modem speeds supported (bps)	1200, 2400, 9600	1200, 2400, 9600	1200, 2400, 9600	1200, 2400, 9600	1200, 2400
Number of local access numbers	2000 (local direct-dial access available from 350 U.S. cities plus several major European cities.)	700	526	Access numbers available from 600+ U.S. cities and 14 Canadian cities; also available via Datapack and Sprintnet.	800# access available.
Special interest forums	350	500+	80	100+	35 (15 computing and 20 special-interest)
Shareware/software libraries available	50,000 shareware/freeware files plus access to ZMac and ZiffNet services and thousands of nonprogram text files.	70,000+	4000 (through the ZiffNet for Prodigy Custom Choice)	150,000+	10,000+
Hardware/software vendors online	350	150+	<100	30+	20

:) Smileys

Electronic mail is a wonderful thing. However, extensive communication can be expensive. Since you are usually charged by the number of characters you send, brevity is important. Luckily, the world of online networks is filled with creative people who want shorter and more descriptive ways to communicate.

These people have developed an informal code of characters called "smileys," after the most popular one, :), the smile. See it? Try turning your head sideways. The colon dots are the eyes, and the parenthesis is the smile. There are also several commonly known abbreviations, such as "AFK" for Away From Keyboard. Many files can be found, including a desk accessory dictionary, which list hundreds of "smileys."

Smileys are a fluid and ever-changing language. Most of them are designed for personal conversations—and several have more than one meaning. We have listed some of the more popular and useful smileys below, but these are a rough guideline at best.

Smiley meaning

(:-¦K-	*Formal message*
(:<)	*Talks too much*
(@@)	*You're kidding!*
:#	*My lips are sealed (1)*
:&	*Tongue-tied*
:'(	*Crying*
:(	*Frown*
:^)	*Great! I like it!*
:)	*Smile*
:*	*Kiss*
:*)	*Drunk*
:-#	*Censored*
:-,	*"Hmmmm"*
:-/	*Skeptical*
:->	*Happy face*
:-@	*Screaming*
:-C	*Very unhappy*
:-I	*Indifferent*
:-Q	*Smoking*
:-S	*Incoherent*
:-{)	*Mustache*

<table>
<tr><td>:-|</td><td>Disgusted</td></tr>
<tr><td>:-||</td><td>Anger</td></tr>
<tr><td>:/</td><td>Chagrin</td></tr>
<tr><td>:/)</td><td>Not funny</td></tr>
<tr><td>:D</td><td>Laughing</td></tr>
<tr><td>:O</td><td>Yelling</td></tr>
<tr><td>:P</td><td>Sticking out tongue</td></tr>
<tr><td>:X</td><td>My lips are sealed (2)</td></tr>
<tr><td>:[</td><td>Pout</td></tr>
<tr><td>:_)</td><td>Nose out of joint</td></tr>
<tr><td>;)</td><td>Wink</td></tr>
<tr><td><--</td><td>Referring to self</td></tr>
<tr><td><:-(</td><td>Disappointed</td></tr>
<tr><td>> - <</td><td>Extremely angry</td></tr>
<tr><td>@:]</td><td>Baby</td></tr>
<tr><td>X-(</td><td>Just died</td></tr>
<tr><td>{}</td><td>Hugs</td></tr>
<tr><td>{{}}</td><td>Multiple hugs</td></tr>
<tr><td>|-I</td><td>Asleep</td></tr>
<tr><td>||*(</td><td>Handshake offered</td></tr>
<tr><td>||-)</td><td>Handshake expected</td></tr>
<tr><td>}:-(</td><td>Stubborn</td></tr>
</table>

BY THE WAY, ALL CAPS MEANS YOU ARE SHOUTING

Abbreviations	Meaning
LOL	*Laughing out loud*
AFK	*Away from keyboard*
BAK	*Back at keyboard*
GMTA	*Great minds think alike*
BTW	*By the way...*
BRB	*Be right back*
WB	*Welcome back*
IMHO	*In my humble opinion*
GTRM	*Going to read mail*
J/K	*Just kidding*
MorF	*Is person asking male or female?*
OIC	*Oh, I see*
Txs	*Thanks*
WU?	*What's up?*

Resources

Books & publications

Dr. Macintosh's Guide to the Online Universe, by Bob LeVitus, 1992, Addison-Wesley Publishing Co., Reading, MA; $24.95; (617) 944-3700

Dvorak's Guide to PC Telecommunications, Second Edition, by John Dvorak, 1992, Osborne/McGraw-Hill, Berkeley, CA; $39.95; (800) 227-0900, (510) 549-6600

Guide To Modem Communications, by Les Freed and Frank Dorfler Jr., 1992, Ziff-Davis Press, Emeryville, CA; $29.95; (800) 688-0448, (510) 601-2000

How to get the Most out of CompuServe, 5th Edition, by Charles Bowen and David Peyton, 1993, Bantam Computer Books, New York, NY; $25.95; (212) 354-6500

The Internet Companion, by Tracy LaQuey, 1992, Addison-Wesley Publishing Co., Reading, MA; $10.95; (617) 944-3700

OnLine Access: The Magazine That Makes Modems Work, 920 N. Franklin, Suite 203, Chicago, IL 60610; $19.80/year; (800) 366-6336, (312) 573-1700. Quarterly magazine listing bulletin boards and products

Prodigy Made Easy, Second Edition, by Pamela Kane, 1993, Osborne/McGraw-Hill, Berkeley, CA; $19.95; (800) 227-0900, (510) 549-6600

The Whole Earth Online Almanac, by Dan Ritter, 1993, Brady Publishing, New York, NY; $32.95; (212) 373-8093, (800) 428-5331

Internet resources

The InterNIC Information Services' Referral Desk (800) 444-4345, provides a list of groups that offer public access to the Internet; push 1 (registration) at the voice-mail prompt. For help finding general information or a database on the Internet, push 3 (information services).

Another way to get a list of public-access sites: Send e-mail to the Internet from another service and ask for the PDIAL list, which has information about organizations offering Internet accounts for individuals. Address your message to info-deli-server@netcom.com on the Internet and include Send PDIAL in the Subject field.

Internet Business Pages, a free service under development, provides a list of businesses on the Internet. Contact Edward Vielmetti, Msen Inc., 628 Brooks, Ann Arbor, MI 48103; (313) 998-4562.

Internet Business Journal provides ongoing information about business activity and development on the Internet; one year (six regular issues, six supplements) costs $75, small business rate; Strangelove Press, Ottawa, Ontario, Canada; (613) 747-6106. Also available in some libraries.

Desktop Internet Reference is a public-domain hypertext guide to using the Internet, which may be freely copied. Requires Windows 3.0 or higher; $10 for shipping and handling. Contact the author: John Buckman, 3520 Connecticut Ave. NW #33, Washington, DC 20008; (301) 986-0444, ext. 5841 (daytime).

For internet connections

PSI Net, Performance Systems International
(703) 620-6651

The WELL, Whole Earth 'Lectronic Link
(415) 332-4335

Information & time management

IN THE INFORMATION AGE, THE FASTER YOU can find information, the more competitive you'll be. When a client or prospect calls, you need to have information on hand or, at the very least, know where to find it.

With the right software, you can access all of your personal and professional information with a couple of quick keystrokes. There are two major kinds of information management software: personal information or contact managers, and electronic databases. We discuss the differences between them and what features to look for in each. We also show how to keep track of what's where on your hard drive by using good file management techniques.

Personal information managers/contact managers

For years, personal information software (PIM) was obscure, complicated and difficult to use. These programs did little more than eat up memory; users continued to use Roledexes, address books, and paper napkins to store personal information. Today, however, the PIM has matured into a valuable and viable tool with which to organize your business information. In essence, it is a preformatted database perfectly tailored for managing personal and contact information. While you could create a PIM yourself using a good database program, it is much easier to get started immediately with a commercial product.

A good PIM should give you quick access to all of the following:

- Appointments
- Dates
- Names
- Addresses
- Phone numbers
- Fax numbers
- Memos
- Birthdays
- Notes and other random scraps of information.

Features to look for in PIM software

- Choose a simple interface. The interface is probably the most important feature on a PIM. If it is too complicated you will just go back to post-its and paper napkins. Many interfaces resemble a loose leaf notebook making them particularly easy to use. You should also decide whether you prefer keyboard shortcuts or drag and drop commands.
- Make sure you can create more than one address book. Being able to separate your personal and business names and addresses is convenient.
- Make sure your address book lets you define your own fields, as well as sort and find as you would with an ordinary database. The more ways you can search (such as Boolean, phonetic, or free form text) the better. You should also be able to search your schedule and notepad at the same time you search your address book.
- Demand a word processor for note-taking. It won't be great, but combined with spell checking and mail merge it's an attractive package.
- Look for a PIM that automatically carries your unfinished tasks forward and that prioritizes your to-do list.
- Look for a PIM that displays both your to-do list and your schedule at the same time. This way you can plan your day between appointments and tasks to avoid conflict.
- If you will be using a PIM on both your desktop and notebook, look for an automatic reconciliation feature. This way when you come back from your road trip

you don't have to manually update your files.

- Make sure your PIM can import and export data with your favorite spreadsheet and word processor.

Contact managers

The line between a powerful PIM and a full-fledged contact manager is thin. Dedicated contact managers provide larger multifield databases, mail merge, and fancier phone options. For heavy sales and call management, a contact manager is usually worth the extra money.

Electronic databases

Personal information managers and contact managers have their limitations. They are, after all, designed to manage "personal" information. However, many small businesses must manage information for numerous purposes (inventory management, for example). If this is true for you, consider an integrated database manager that you can customize for your needs.

Any database feature that speeds data entry, automates part of the process, and ensures consistency and accuracy is worth looking for.

Types of database managers

In the old days (about six years ago), you'd commonly find only two classes of database software on the market: flat-file managers and relational databases. Today, however, most databases represent the best of both types.

Flat file

With flat files, you deal with data in one file at a time—your customer list in one place, say, and invoices in another. The one-file-at-a-time concept, while easy to understand and manipulate, makes for a lot of redundant data entry. The flat file's biggest virtue is that it can be easily set up through menus and dialog boxes. However, if flat file means access to only one database at a time, there are few true flat-file programs on the market anymore.

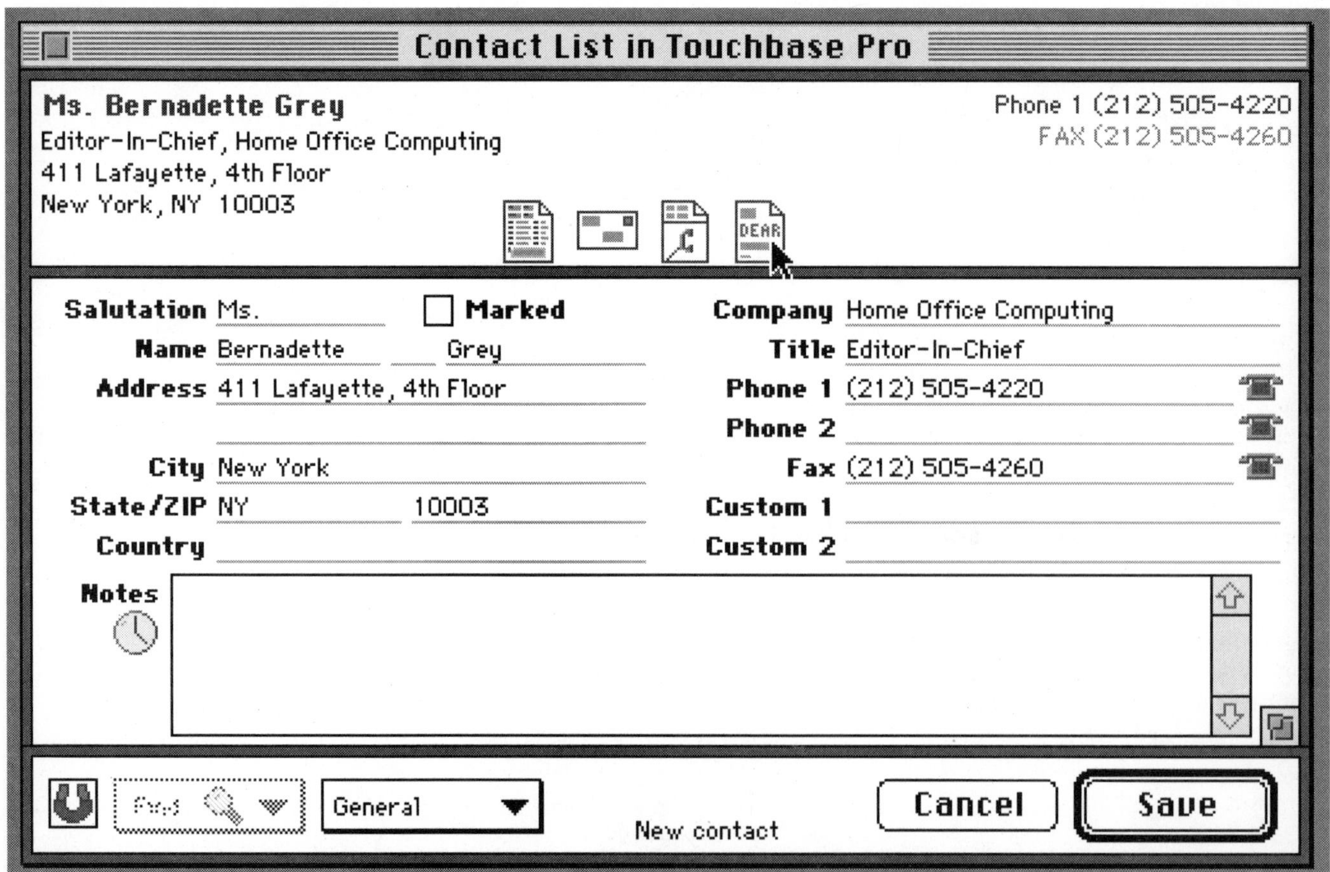

16-1 A PIM (personal information manager) like Touchbase Pro organizes contact information. Many PIMs also offer complete calendar and scheduling information. In the case of Touchbase Pro, you need its sister program, Datebook Pro.

Formulas are one of the most potentially powerful data-manipulation tools in any database manager.

Relational file

In contrast, relational file managers give you tools—typically a programming language such as dBase—to create both individual databases and linked sets of several databases that share information. That way, for instance, when filling out a bill in your invoice database, all you need to enter is the customer ID number to draw the name and address from your customer database. Clearly, relational databases have it all over their flat-file siblings when you need to manage a complex set of data. However, they can be difficult to program.

Today's database

Nearly all database managers now offer some relational capabilities and can link information from various database files. Most programs also retain the flat-file's virtue of being readily set up through menus and dialog boxes. All databases let you link files to create sophisticated systems capable of organizing your business or professional information. Through such features as menu builders, formulas, and macros, several of these programs let you create custom databases.

Features to look for

There are four basic steps in the database process:

1. Setting up—installing software and creating files.

2. Putting data in—data entry and validation, calculated fields, lookup commands, and imported data.

3. Organizing data—indexing, searching, sorting, selecting, and summarizing (grouping).

4. Getting data out—on the screen, on disk, and on paper.

None of these steps are complex. The following section outlines each step of the database process, and shows you what features to look for in a database.

Setting up

Almost all databases automate the installation procedure through batch files or a setup program. Software installation is typically only a one-time operation. Creating database files, however, is one of those jobs that can be easy or frustrating, depending on the help your software offers.

In addition to creating database files, you'll want to set up *forms*, or onscreen views of your data. These views can include one record at a time, a columnar view of several records, and a label format. Forms are also used for data entry. While several programs offer built-in forms, all give you ways to set up your own views. Here's an area where graphically based databases, those on Windows or the Mac, generally beat their text-based counterparts in ease of use. Graphical drawing tools make creating onscreen forms a straightforward job—you get what you see. However, some DOS databases also work in a graphics mode to make form creation easier.

Entering data

Typing text and numbers into a database is a vital step that is given short shrift by some programs. But that's the way many databases are gathered together, keystroke by keystroke, with all of typing's inherent potential for error. When information in your database is inaccurate, duplicated, misspelled, or missing, you're wasting time and possibly losing money. Therefore, any database feature that speeds data entry, automates part of the process, and ensures consistency and accuracy in your data is a feature worth looking for. Data-entry features fall into several categories.

Typing features

These features make entering data easier and cut down on common mistakes by:

- Automatically formatting phone numbers or Social Security numbers with parentheses and hyphens as needed—all you need to type are the digits.
- Automatically capitalizing the first letter of each word—names of people and cities, say—or correctly formatting state abbreviations with all uppercase letters.

Field limits

This style of data-entry support enhances accuracy by limiting what you can enter in any field to one or more of the following:

- Predefined pop-up lists of possible values. These let you simply choose what to enter—no memorization is required, and consistency is assured.
- Range functions. These limit which and how many characters can be entered into a field. You might use a range function; for instance, to accept numerals only, and just nine of them, to be entered into a Social Security field.
- Custom prompt screens. Remind you of possible values for given fields.

Automatic data entry

Automatic data-entry features automatically enter data for you, saving you typing time and helping you keep the data consistent. Look for:

- Default values (including auto-increment), formulas, and lookup functions. A field with a default value is a natural for a data item such as state, which you can set up with the abbreviation of the state where most of your clients

or prospects live. Auto-increment is perfect for a job such as creating invoices or bank checks, when you want them automatically numbered in the order you create them.
- A field based on a formula—which can be either a numeric or a text calculation—automatically enters data based on values in other fields. Formulas seem to bring you into the realm of programming, but no computer language is required—only a little logic. Formulas are one of the most potentially powerful data-manipulation tools in any database manager.
- Lookup functions bring relational capabilities to databases. The lookup function fills in fields based on data in another database; for example, it can draw an item description and price from your Inventory database as you enter a record in your Invoices database.

Organizing data

Once the data is in the database, you need to arrange it in ways that bring meaning to random sets of information. The main organizing features are indexing, searching, selecting, and summarizing (grouping).

Indexing

A database index is an alphabetical or numerical list of the values in a particular field that speeds up sorting by that field. You generally decide which of your fields are to be indexed, and the database manager then maintains a current index of that field as changes are made. The main disadvantage of an index is that it slows down operations when you add or alter data, since the program needs to find the correct alphabetical place in the indexed list to insert the new data. In any program, you can sort data in ascending or descending alphabetical or numerical order. Indexing not only speeds up sorts but helps speed up searches, too.

Search and select

A database search simply finds a particular record, or set of records, based on a text string or numeric value you designate.

However, searching does not isolate those records from the whole database—that's the job of the select feature. This feature lets you view just those records that have been found in the search. For example, you might want to select all the records where the City field contains New York and the Date field is later than one month ago. You'll want to look at which selection parameters a database manager offers and how it implements them.

Grouping

Another way to group connected sets of data is the summary, or grouping, feature. This tool helps you build up subtotals and other calculations from sets of data. For instance, an Invoice database might have several records for each customer. In order to find out the total orders from last year for each customer, you'd use the summary feature to group those related records.

Getting data out

Once you've entered and organized your data, you'll want to view it onscreen and print it out on paper for reports, mailings and so on.

Viewing

As mentioned earlier in the Setting Up section, forms give you different ways to view data onscreen, such as in columns (sometimes called Browse mode) or record by record. Several programs let you easily switch back and forth between those two types of views. Most programs also let you use forms for printouts in addition to onscreen views and data entry. This can be especially helpful when you need to create paper forms that will be filled in and then entered into the database—you'll want the piece of paper to match the onscreen form as closely as possible.

Printing

Finally, printed reports are often the raison d'être for your whole database operation. Whether the reports are invoices, sales summaries, or simple lists of your clients' phone numbers, the simpler they are to create, the more likely you'll get the full benefit of your database. Features to look for here are:

- Graphically based tools for creating reports. Again, Windows and Macintosh applications are often superior to DOS applications.
- The ability to use lookups and formulas in reports, for line items and totals in an invoice, for instance.
- An easy way to create mailing labels, including direct support for Avery-brand labels, by type and number.
- The ability to insert graphics into any report.

Mailings

When it comes to mailings, any database can create mail-merge files of names and addresses that will work with your word processor. In addition, a few of the programs come with a word-processing feature that works with the mail-merge files.

Phone dialing

Finally, a data-out feature worth noting is a phone dialer that will automatically dial any number through your computer's modem. This feature

By self-documenting, you'll be able to tell what a given file is for days, months, or years later.

is especially useful when you want to create a database for contact management, which requires lots of time on the phone.

File management

Keeping track of your files is an essential part of information management. Compared to paper files, electronic files are relatively easy to locate. Still, there are some hazards unique to computers: files can be deleted or overwritten, titles and contents can be forgotten and so on. In order to make sure you can find everything you need, exactly when you need it, follow these file management tips.

Name files consistently

Having hundreds of files all under the top level directory and no sub-directories is one sure sign of a computing novice. It's also maddening trying to remember the content of files. To save time, establish a set of directory and file naming conventions that will help you know where to place and retrieve your online information. Here are some suggestions:

- Establish naming conventions for all work files. A good name tells you what kind of file it is, what the client or project is, and whether it's the current version. For example, use the extension to indicate whether the file is text, the project's contact list, the proposal, and so on.
- If you create successive drafts of a file, number all but the current one. For instance, an important sales proposal might be sequentially named: Propos01.txt, Propos02.txt, and Proposal.txt. This method guarantees the file you invoke to work on is always the unnumbered one.
- Define your file-naming to indicate some mix of relative and absolute identification. This is especially important for DOS and Windows users who are limited to eight-character file names with three-character extensions. For example, use the end of the file name for per-client numbering. With this concept, your first letter to a client named Dublin might be saved as Dublin01.doc, the next letter as Dublin02.doc, and so forth. Invoices could use the file extension for instant identification. The first invoice sent to Dublin might be named as DublinIn.001, the second DublinIn.002, and so on.

This method lets you quickly pull out all correspondence, invoices, and other paperwork that relates to a particular client. DOS users can get software that gives the appearance of longer file names. Macintosh computers, on the other hand, let you use filenames up to 31 characters long. Though you won't need to be as cryptic in your naming conventions, it's still a wise idea to be consistent and informative when naming files.

Use boilerplate and comments

If you create specific text or a document repeatedly—such as your basic pitch letter, pricing, fax forms, invoices, contracts, or trip reports—create boilerplate originals, and then make copies of them as needed, which you actually edit. Put your boilerplate files in their own directory or folder; when you make a new version, save a few previous versions in an easy-to-track naming method.

To protect boilerplate files from being overwritten, use one of these three methods:

- The DOS ATTRIB command can set any file to read-only. Type ATTRIB +R filename to create such security.
- On the Macintosh, select the file in the Finder, choose "Get Info" from the File menu, and click on "Locked" to secure the file.
- When running Windows, open the File Manager, select the file, and then choose "Properties" from the File Menu; click on "Read Only" to protect the file.

If your word processor lets you embed comment lines (i.e., lines that you see within your word processor but which don't print), use this feature to self-document every possible file. Begin each file with a few comment lines containing the client or project name, date, your name, purpose of file, status for letters and invoices (such as date sent), billing codes, and so on. By self-documenting, you'll be able to tell what a given file is for days, months, or years later. (It'll also make it easier to share these files with other people.)

Research tips

There are many methods for collating data as you research in libraries or online services. Some people prefer note-cards. Some like using random scraps of paper. If your current technique works for you, then you should probably stick with it.

However, current technology has made research easier than ever. Here are some tips for sorting through the avalanche of information available:

Use card file/text retrieval software

Card-file PIM software will keep you organized; it lets you retrieve information quickly and encourages you to distill your research. The software doesn't require much memory or disk space. Use it, and you'll be ready for the serendipitous moment when you stumble across a gem.

- *For MS-DOS: Both Broderbund's MemoryMate and Micro Logic's Info Select can be used in memory-resident or nonresident modes and can search and retrieve text in any card.*
- *For Windows 3.1: Use the Windows Cardfile or Micro Logic's powerful new Info Select for Windows. Cardfile has an index line for sorting cards by keywords and can also search for text in the body of a file.*

- *For Macintosh: Mac users can configure HyperCard to their needs, using the hypertext cards and grouping them into appropriate stacks.*

Outline before you start

Organize your search before you go. Sketch what you know already by using an outliner, then use the outliner to create your own categories for research. Next, using your PIM, enter those categories as keywords in a file-index entry or the first line of text of a card. You can also use the same outline to arrange all the papers, photocopies, or other documents you will collect in file folders during your research.

Divide and distill

Research won't follow the smooth path of the final written project, so take advantage of software that lets a researcher bring up any card as soon as it's needed.

Use a single card/record (or series of appended/stacked cards) for each research subject, category, name, or date in a research project, or for each single seminar at a conference. Most cards have a size set by the software that will force the researcher to distill, to decide what is relevant.

Keep the system going as you complete whatever project you're doing. Build up the cards as you get new information. If your software has hypertext capability, use it to connect cards. If you have to find something in a hurry, you can call up cards—by keyword or by the date you did the research—with a keystroke or the click of a mouse.

Use a time-index cassette tape recorder

For years, writers and researchers have debated whether or not to use a cassette tape recorder to record interviews or lectures. The task of transcribing tapes is often a waste of time.

TV reporters and producers working on daily deadlines must find what is relevant on a videotape in minutes. In the last year or so, the technology of the professional television news camera has trickled down to the cassette recorder. Low-cost time-indexing recorders are now available from Sony and Aiwa with street prices ranging from $130 to $250.

When you hear a good quote or relevant point during an interview or lecture, note the time of day. When you play back the tape, use the time code to find those quotes you noted. Write down the time code for any other important details. Then summarize the rest of the tape with quick notes and just transcribe what you really need. (Most cassette recorders memorize hours and minutes only, but that's still an improvement on the old tape counter.)

Travel tips

If you're traveling on the cheap, or if you have to do a lot of walking, use a sturdy backpack to carry your computer. Flimsy nylon book bag backpacks don't make the grade. Extra padding for the computer can be made from small sheets of foam rubber. The backpack frees your hands for suitcases and briefcases, and most thieves dismiss backpacks.

Get a large, thick, clear, locking plastic bag, the kind camping stores sell for dried food, to hold boxes of disks, power cords, and cables. The clear bag will speed your way through security at libraries and archives (many won't let you bring the computer's carrying case into the reading room), as well as airports. Keep all the accessories in one convenient place.

On long trips, mail backup disks home at regular intervals. Take along something to clean the screen of your notebook in a library or archive, where tiny particles from old books and dust quickly build up on the screen. A well-lit screen is essential for anyone working in a dark microfilm reading room. Also, keep your battery charged. More libraries are adding power bars to carrels, and you can sometimes find a table with a plug, but don't count on it.

A good calendar program is a big help for historical and legal research as well as long-term planning—especially one versatile enough to go back before 1900.

Wrapping it up

Back at home, continue to use your card system as you find more information. Keep expanding that outline you started with, inserting new and relevant information.

With the power of outlining software, you can move material around to see what fits best. By the time you've finished the whole outline, your report, brief, or story is already half-written. Use the Export function or the Windows clipboard to move research text from a PIM card directly into your project.

CD-ROMs

CDs can hold a truly massive amount of information. Each disk can store 600MB of data. Practically speaking that's 485 double density discs or 25 encyclopedias or 600,000 type written pages or Shakespeare's complete works in both modern and Elizabethan English or . . . well you get the idea.

This data capacity make them natural choices for storing large databases—U.S. Census Data, all the business phone numbers in the United States, etc. Powerful search functions can pinpoint the information you need at the touch of a button.

You will have to invest in a CD-ROM drive to take advantage of this technology—a small price for the wealth of information it will make available. For a current list of CD-ROM titles, contact the following sources:

Bureau of Electronic Publishers (CD-ROM Sources), 141 Naw Rd., Parsippany, NJ 07054; (800) 828-7766

CD-ROM Inc., 1667 Cole Blvd., Suite 400, Golden, CO 80401; (303) 231-9373

New Media Source, 3830 Valley Centre Dr., San Diego, CA 92130; (800) 344-2621

Software resources

PIMs/contact managers

ACT! (DOS, Windows, Mac), Contact Software International
(214) 919-9500, (800) 365-0606

Info Select (Windows, DOS), Micro Logic
(201) 342-6518, (800) 342-5930

Lotus Organizer (Windows), Lotus Development Corp.
(617) 577-8500, (800) 635-6887

PackRat (Windows), Polaris Software
(619) 674-6500, (800) 722-5728

Calendar/to do software

Alarming Events (Macintosh), CE Software
(515) 224-1995, (800) 523-7638

Datebook Pro (Mac), After Hours Software
(818) 780-2220, (800) 367-8911

OnTime (Windows), Campbell Services
(313) 559-5955, (800) 345-6747

Contact list software/electronic card files

Address Book Plus (DOS, Mac), Power Up Software
(415) 345-5900, (800) 851-2917

Dynodex (Windows, Mac), Portfolio Software
(408) 252-0420

TouchBase Pro (Mac), After Hours Software
(818) 780-2220, (800) 367-8911

Standard databases

FileMaker Pro (Windows, Mac), Claris Corp.
(408) 727-8227

Panorama II (Mac), ProVue Development
(714) 892-8199, (800) 966-7878

PC-File (DOS), ButtonWare
(206) 454-0479, (800) 528-8866

File retrieval software

Golden Retriever (Windows), Above Development
(714) 851-2283, (800) 344-0116

Retrieve It! (Mac), Claris Corp.
(408) 727-8227

Finance

FINANCE IS THE HEART AND SOUL OF BUSINESS. Whether you are a freelance journalist or a supplier of designer shoelaces, money matters. Careful fiscal management can save you a bundle. Mismanagement can drive your business into the ground. How can you track your finances and run your day-to-day business affairs?

If you haven't started your business yet, the best place to begin is drafting a business plan. The research and the critical thinking it requires are worth the time it takes. And the professionalism it imparts is a vital factor in obtaining a loan. We'll tell you how to build a better business plan and what electronic tools will give you a quick jumpstart.

With your business underway, you need to address your accounting system. A personal computer and the right software puts the raw number-crunching power, and even some of the wisdom, of a trained CPA onto your desktop—if you know how to use it. We'll show you how to choose and set up the electronic bookkeeping and accounting system that's best for you.

Any successful business also requires ongoing financial planning and problem solving. Spreadsheets enable you to perform all these tasks quickly and painlessly. We'll give you a step-by-step guide on tackling some of the most common financial equations.

Amidst the daily chaos of running your own business, you need to remember your own finances. Without leaving your computer, or even picking up the phone, you can do just this through electronic investing.

Build a better business plan

A business plan is a company's blueprint for success. Business plans help you understand the market, evaluate costs, and determine your risks. They can also come in handy when looking for investors or trying to get a loan.

While creating a business plan is not difficult, it can be time consuming. Fortunately, there is an abundance of software programs that will walk you through your business plan (see the Resources section at the end of the chapter). Between sample templates, financial analysis, and canned graphics, business plan software provides everything you need to create a first class document.

Whether you use software or churn out a plan manually, you will want to make sure it includes the following information:

- Company Analysis;
- Product Analysis;
- Market Analysis;
- Strategic Plan;
- Management Profile;
- Financial Analysis;
- Executive Summary.

Company analysis

The first question your business plan must answer is: Who are you? Be sure your company analysis section contains:

- The legal name of your business;
- The owners' names;
- A brief background on each major employee;
- A short history of the business;
- A brief description of your business;
- Long-term goals and objectives.

Product analysis

Your next task is to describe in detail the product or service you intend to offer. A successful product analysis will distinguish your product from others in the market. Start with a summary paragraph that clearly and concisely describes your product or service. Then move on to:

- Product Benefits;
- Product Sourcing;

- Facilities or Location;
- Future Products.

Market analysis

Most businesses fail because they haven't done a market analysis. Market research informs you of the size of your product's market and the forces that shape it. While this can be dirty work, electronic media can help (read about sales and marketing in chapter 19). Your Market Analysis section should include:

- Industry analysis;
- List of competitors;
- Customers;
- Competitive advantages or disadvantages.

Strategic plan

What are you going to do? This section will show the reader you have devised a sound strategy based on the information presented in the first three sections. Make sure you include your expert assessment and plans for implementing the following:

- Overall marketing strategy;
- Pricing;
- Distribution;
- Sales;
- Promotion;
- Sales forecast.

Management profile

You briefly mentioned the backgrounds of the key players in your business in the Company Analysis section. Now expand upon those descriptions in the Management Profile. This assures the reader that your company is a tight, well-run ship. Make sure to include:

- Organizational structure;
- Resumes of the principal owners and management;
- List of contracted professionals;
- Personnel plan.

Financial analysis

Here's where the work on your business plan shifts from your word processor to your spreadsheet program (most business plan software includes spreadsheet functions). This section discusses where all the money will come from and how it will be used. Your financial analysis should include:

- Balance sheet;
- Income statement;
- Debt schedule;
- Pro forma, or projected, income statement;
- Pro forma, or projected, cash flow;
- Break-even analysis.

Executive summary

Even though the executive summary usually appears at the beginning of a business plan it is best to write it last, after you have researched and assimilated the other sections. This section should entice the readers and convince them your plan has merit. Keep it short—no more than two pages. The summary should include a brief synopsis of the following:

- Primary purpose of the plan (whether it is to gain financial backing or just clarify your idea);
- Definition of your idea;
- Market overview;
- Product features;
- Financial history;
- Financial requirements;
- Long-term vision.

Your computer can balance your books and pay your bills without a sharp pencil or checkbook in sight.

Electronic bookkeeping and accounting

Throw your ledger books out the window—your computer can balance your books and pay your bills without a sharp pencil or checkbook in sight. With programs available for every size business, you can have your operation totally computerized with a relatively small investment of time and money. Is electronic bookkeeping for you? Here are some points to consider before making your decision:

- If you already have someone else do your books because you don't like accounting, you are not going to like it much more on your computer. It will save you most of the time-consuming calculations, but it still requires a commitment to stay on top of it.
- If you don't mind keeping your books, but farmed out the work because of time constraints, it's worth considering. While it will still take some time, it might save enough money to justify it.
- If no one (including you) does any bookkeeping, hope you don't get audited.

Electronic bookkeeping and accounting tips

- Don't buy too much. If there's one curious thing about accounting systems, it is that they offer a tremendous amount of horsepower for very few dollars. You can buy software for $50 that can more than adequately run a $10-million company. The end result is that many people buy a far more powerful and complicated system than they actually need.
- Don't get in over your head. To use a full featured double-entry bookkeeping system you must know something about double-entry accounting. You need to understand what a debit is. You need to know what a credit is. And you need to know what trial

balances, journal entries, and general or subsidiary ledgers are. If you don't possess these skills, hire someone who does. If you want to be your own accountant take an introductory course in accounting. Otherwise even a well-documented double-entry program could be unmanageable.

- Inventory equals double-entry. If you carry inventory, you're required to use a double-entry system.
- Get a compatible system. Most bookkeeping programs will allow you to import and export data from some, but not all, popular spreadsheet, tax preparation, and personal finance software. Before buying a bookkeeping program, make sure it is compatible with your favorite financial software.

Checkbook vs. double-entry systems

Although they both perform basic bookkeeping functions there are important differences between checkbook and double-entry systems. Checkbooks offer limited features, but are far easier to use. Double-entry systems monitor every aspect of your finances, but they require thorough knowledge of accounting techniques. So which one is right for you?

A Checkbook program excels at basic bookkeeping tasks such as:

- Preparing a handful of invoices each month;
- Writing a small number of checks each month;
- Tracking your bank account balance;
- Measuring your income and expenses for tax and planning purposes;
- Grouping expenses and income by category.

If this is the extent of your bookkeeping needs, a good checkbook program should do nicely. A simple checkbook program should provide sufficient bookkeeping for the one-person service-based business.

Although more difficult to use, the double-entry-based system can handle more complex bookkeeping. For example, double-entry bookkeeping systems generate a wider variety of complex forms than a checkbook can. They track more assets and liabilities. They also precisely estimate your profits (or losses) and your financial condition using accrual-based accounting techniques. You might need this extra horsepower if your business has inventory or hires employees.

CheckFree liberates you from the tedium of bill paying.

A good double-entry system can do everything a checkbook can plus:

- Manage both your bank account and your investments in customer accounts receivable and inventories;
- Track the amount you owe suppliers, and wages you owe to employees;
- Monitor the taxes you owe to the states where you sell your product;
- Make precise estimates of profits and losses.

Full-fledged double-entry bookkeeping systems also provide preconstructed charts of accounts, or listings of assets, liability, equity, revenue, and expense accounts.

Steps in setting up a checkbook

1. List income and expense categories. The first thing you need to do is list the categories you will need for tracking income and expenses. Probably the easiest way to do this is to look at last year's tax return and make a note of each income and expense's line on the tax form (probably Schedule C) that you filled in. For example, if you only used one income category—gross income—and three expenses categories—bank service charges, office, and taxes—your category list will include those four items. Checkbook programs also let you budget by categories. So if you are someone who wants to use a formal budget and then periodically compare your actual income and expense figures to your budgeted income and expense figures you will want to include budget categories on your list. These categories might include expenses such as photocopying or utilities, and other income such as a second job or dividends.

2. Add any needed categories. All the popular checkbook programs provide predefined lists of business categories, which you then use to track income and expenses. You will, however, need to verify that the internal category list that your program provides includes all the categories you need. If the bank service charges, office expenses, and taxes don't appear on your software's existing category list, you'll need to add them. With a checkbook program like Microsoft Money, this is simply a matter of entering the commands necessary to display the "Create New Category" dialog box and then filling in a few text boxes that name and describe the category.

3. Enter the names of payees. Some programs let you enter the names and relevant information about payees. While this feature is not as comprehensive as the double-entry master file function it should allow you to store pertinent information like payees' names, addresses, and standard payments.

4. Enter the checkbook transactions. Starting from January 1 of the year you install the checkbook program, install all the transactions through the current date. (Resist the temptation to enter transactions from the date you install the software.) This way, you will have transactions for the entire year in one place, and you will be able to produce summary reports of the entire year's income and expenses. This process does not take long. Even if you have hundreds of transactions, most checkbook programs allow for quick and easy entry. For the first transaction of the year, enter the starting account balance.

5. Adjust the account balance. If needed, enter an adjusting transaction so that as of the reconciliation date, the reconciled bank-statement balance and your checkbook program's balance agree. Remember, only use an adjusting transaction if you know the reconciled balance is incorrect.

6. Start using the checkbook. Begin using the checkbook program to record transactions and print checks. As you go along, be sure to place each deposit into an income category and each withdrawal into an expense category. This allows you to summarize your business income and expenses at will. This also serves as an accurate record of your business's most valuable asset—cash.

CheckFree

Electronic checking, a service offered by CheckFree, has become a popular way to avoid the hassles of sending for printer-ready checks and still maintain the record-keeping convenience of a checkbook program. Just telecommunicate your instructions and CheckFree will pay anyone you want.

CheckFree liberates you from the tedium of bill paying. It saves time and helps you maintain a regular billing schedule. However, CheckFree is still a young company and has had its share of growing pains. Most complaints deal with the company's customer service or billing mix-ups. Although imperfect, CheckFree still offers a great deal of convenience and financial organization for the average user.

Even simple, quickly constructed spreadsheets can be great tools for working on financial tasks.

Cost

CheckFree's $9.95 monthly fee covers 20 payments. For every 10 checks after that there is a $3.50 charge. You can order the software to run CheckFree for $29.95. When you consider the money spent on postage, envelopes and checks in manual checking, CheckFree is only a few dollars more.

Software support

In many ways, CheckFree serves as its own check-writing program, tracking your balances and coding expenses, but CheckFree can be used with other software as well. The program holds your clients and other payees' names and addresses so you can pay your bills with a few keystrokes and a phone call. However, like any checkbook program, for one-time payees you must enter their name and address directly onto the on-screen check.

Steps in setting up a double-entry bookkeeping system

1. Figure out your starting trial balance. If you are going to operate a double-entry-based system, construct a starting trial balance—a list of all your assets, liabilities, equities, year-to-date revenues, year-to-date expenses, and their amounts. If you have a lot of trouble doing this, you should hire an accountant to help you get up and running or turn your accounting over to someone else.

2. Perform a system test. The first thing you do after installing double-entry bookkeeping software is make sure it works. Take half a dozen sample transactions—a customer invoice, an accounts-payable bill, an employee's check, and so forth—and make sure you can use the installed software to process each sample transaction. This keeps you from wasting hours entering data and then trying to figure what went wrong.

3. Pick an easy conversion date. Once you're certain that the accounting software you've chosen will do the things you need it to, pick a conversion date—the date you stop using your old system and start using your new one. Although, you might want to run the systems in parallel for six months to iron out any kinks. There are several basic issues to consider when picking a date:

- Don't pick a date in the middle of your company's busy season.
- Pick a conversion date that makes it easy to distinguish between transactions that fall before the date and those that fall after the date. If you chose an arbitrary date like April 23, for example, you need to be careful you don't record it twice, once in both systems.
- Finally, you should make it as easy as possible to prepare annual and monthly profit-and-loss statements, which means you will want to convert at the end of the year and/or at the end of the month.

4. Load system tables. In most double-entry-based systems you need to load a series of master files and tables that deal with system-wide issues. To do this the system might ask you to:

- Name the company for which you will be performing the bookkeeping.
- Define the fiscal year by telling your software when your

You can easily calculate how long it will take to repay a loan given a specified loan payment.

accounting year begins and ends, usually January 1st through December 31.

- Identify the conversion date.
- Set up passwords.
- Define tables of applicable sales-tax rates.

5. Load master files. Double-entry bookkeeping systems use master files to store information about customers, vendors, inventory items, and employees. In essence, master files do two things. First they store information that is used repeatedly when processing transactions related to a customer, vendor, some inventory item, or a particular employee. Second, they summarize the year-to-date transactions related to a customer, vendor inventory item, or a particular employee.

To load each of the master files, simply access the appropriate menu command for adding records to a specific file. Then fill in the blanks that appear on the window, screen, or dialog box.

6. Detail your accounts payable and accounts receivable balance. After you load the master files, you're ready to describe in detail your accounts receivable and accounts payable balances. Here's how it works in AccPac Simply Accounting:

- Once you've added at least one customer, the software modifies the Receivable Ledger dialog box so it includes two command buttons, Invoices and Payments.
- To identify a customer's current accounts-receivable balance invoice-by-invoice, select the Invoice command button.
- To record an invoice, enter the number, date and invoice amount.
- Repeat this same process for each customer's invoices. Using similar invoices you can also detail each vendor's accounts-payable balances.

7. Enter the conversion-date trial balance. After loading the necessary master files, you are ready to enter your trial date balance. As part of completing steps 4 and 5, you entered your accounts receivable, inventory, and accounts-payable balances in those respective, subsidiary ledgers. However, you also need to enter your asset, liability, and equity-account balances into the general ledger. What's more, if you are converting the new system at some time other than the beginning of the year, you need to enter all your year-to-date revenue and your year-to-date expense numbers. The one thing you need to be particularly careful about is that your general and subsidiary ledgers agree. To enter the conversion date trial balance, you construct a large, general-ledger journal entry that records the necessary account balances using the General Journal dialog box.

8. Start using the system's modules. Once you have completed step 6, you're ready to begin using the system. This is simply a matter of recording accounting transactions and if necessary, printing any associated forms such as invoices, statements, vendor checks, and payroll checks. Periodically—usually at the end of the month and again at the end of the year—you'll use the system's reporting features to summarize your business's financial condition.

Spreadsheets

Even simple, quickly constructed spreadsheets can be great tools for working on financial tasks. To help you get started, we'll describe 13 tasks such as how to figure out the monthly payment on a loan, and how to analyze sales volume vs. profits. (To perform any of these fiscal jobs, you need to be able to enter formulas that use cell references with your spreadsheet; just check your software's documentation if you're not sure how.) While we have used the two most popular spreadsheets—Microsoft Excel and Lotus 1-2-3—as examples, most of these formulas should work equally well with any other spreadsheet, such as Borland's Quattro Pro, Computer Associates' SuperCalc 5, or the one in an integrated package such as Microsoft Works.

The cost of borrowing

Borrowing money is a basic small-business task. When you apply for a loan, of course, you'll want to know what the monthly payment will be. All the popular spreadsheets include an easy-to-use function (PMT) for calculating loan payments. Suppose you're considering borrowing $10,000. Assume the bank will lend you the money at 10 percent and will let you repay the loan with monthly payments over three years.

1. Enter the annual interest rate (10 percent, or .1) in cell A1.

2. Enter the number of monthly payments (36) in cell A2.

3. Enter the loan amount (10,000) in cell A3.

4. Enter the appropriate formula into an empty cell:

1-2-3: @PMT(A3,A1/12,A2)

Excel: =PMT(A1/12,A2,A3)*–1

When you enter the formula, the spreadsheet returns the monthly loan-payment amount as $322.67.

Two notes: One, the annual interest is divided by 12 to give monthly interest so that it matches the term, which is also listed in months. Two, you can make this formula—as well as each of the following formulas—more readable by naming the input cells and then using cell names in

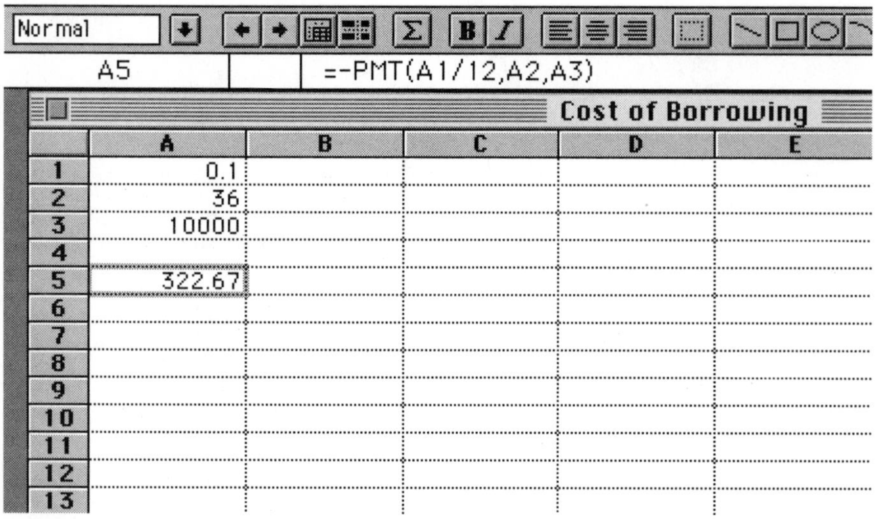

Normal

A5	=-PMT(A1/12,A2,A3)

Cost of Borrowing

	A	B	C	D	E
1	0.1				
2	36				
3	10000				
4					
5	322.67				
6					
7					
8					
9					
10					
11					
12					
13					

17-1 *Setting up the cost-of-borrowing equation using Excel.*

place of cell references. For example, if you call cell A1 Interest, cell A2 Term, and cell A3 Loan, you can enter the 1-2-3 or Excel loan-payment formula as:

1-2-3: @PMT(Loan,Interest/12,Term)

Excel: =PMT(Interest/12,Term,Loan)*–1

A business can't sustain sales growth that is faster than its capital growth.

How much do you still owe?

As you make payments on a loan, of course, a portion of the payment is credited to principal, thereby reducing the amount you owe. You can figure out how much you still owe on a loan using the present-value function (PV). To illustrate this, suppose it's been a year since you borrowed the $10,000 shown above. You've made 12 payments; you have another 24 monthly payments to go.

1. Enter the annual interest rate (10 percent, or .1) in cell A1.

2. Enter the number of payments you still have to make (24) in cell A2.

3. Enter the monthly payment (322.67, as shown above) in cell A3.

4. Enter the appropriate formula into an empty cell:

1-2-3: @PV(A3,A1/12,A2)

Excel: =PV(A1/12,A2,A3)*–1

The spreadsheet returns the value $6992.53 as the remaining loan balance after one year's worth of payments.

Build your own amortization table

You can calculate how much interest and how much principal you've paid on this $10,000 loan by combining the formulas described in the two previous task descriptions. To calculate how much interest you've paid for each period, simply calculate the loan balance using the remaining-loan-balance formula after the previous month's payment. Then multiply this amount by the annual interest rate divided by 12. For example, using the same input values described in the preceding formula tip, you could calculate the interest paid for the thirteenth month using one of the formulas shown below:

1-2-3: @PV(A3,A1/12,A2)*A1/12

Excel: =(PV(A1/12,A2,A3)*A1/12)*–1

The spreadsheet returns the number $58.27 as the interest expense for the thirteenth month.

If you want to find the principal paid in a month, calculate the interest paid during a month as just described. Then subtract this amount from the payment amount. So, if the loan-payment amount is $322.67 and you will pay $58.27 in interest for the thirteenth month, you know you will pay $264.40 in principal for that month. Furthermore, you can combine these first three formulas to calculate the loan payment, remaining balance, and principal and interest portions of a payment for any month, thereby giving you complete loan amortization, or repayment, information.

Pay back loans faster

Sometimes, a business wants to accelerate debt reduction as a way to reduce overhead and save interest charges. You can easily calculate how long it will take to repay a loan given a specified loan payment. Let's say, for example, that after the twelfth payment, when the remaining loan balance is $6992.53, as you've previously calculated, you decide you want to repay that $10,000 loan with payments of $422.67—$100 more per month than the loan agreement calls for. How long will it take to repay the loan using these new, larger payments?

1. Enter the new payment amount (422.67) in cell A1.

2. Enter the annual interest rate (10 percent, or .1) in cell A2.

3. Enter the remaining loan amount (6992.53) in cell A3.

4. Enter the appropriate formula into an empty cell:

1-2-3: -@TERM(A1,A2/12,-A3)

Excel: =NPER(A2/12,-A1,A3)

The spreadsheet returns the value 17.88, indicating that it will take roughly 18 monthly payments of $422.67 to repay the loan. In this case, the larger-than-normal loan payments mean you will pay off the loan after 18 rather than 24 months.

The secret of online market research is knowing where to look.

Calculate a loan's real rate

To pick the least expensive loan, you need to calculate the annual percentage rate, or APR. An APR counts up all the costs associated with obtaining a loan and then expresses these costs as an equivalent annual interest rate. In this way, an APR includes not only the loan's interest costs, but also all the other costs of obtaining credit—things like origination fees and closing costs. Suppose, for example, that the three-year $10,000 loan with the 36 payments of $322.67 per month also charges a $200 loan fee. Here's how to calculate the APR on such a loan using Excel:

1. Enter the total number of loan payments (36) in cell A1.

2. Enter the monthly payment amount (322.67) in cell A2.

3. Enter the loan amount (10,000) in cell A3.

4. Enter the other financing costs (200) in cell A4.

5. Then enter this formula into an empty cell:

Excel: =RATE(A1,-A2,A3-A4)*12

The spreadsheet returns .1139, indicating that with a $200 loan fee, the implied interest rate rises to 11.39 percent—up 1.39 percent from the stated 10 percent interest rate. Note: Unfortunately, calculating APRs isn't very quick or easy in Lotus 1-2-3. You have to construct a worksheet that details each of the loan's monthly cash flows and then use the Internal Rate of Return, or @IRR, function. Refer to the 1-2-3 documentation for instructions.

What's your break-even point?

Generally, you want to consider new business opportunities in light of your break-even point—the point at which you neither make nor lose money. Let's say, for example, that you're considering going into business as a computer consultant. You'll bill your time at $60 an hour, and you'll incur variable costs of $10 an hour for items such as out-of-pocket expenses and business taxes. (In a product-based business, your variable costs would also include the cost of the goods you sell.) Further suppose that you need $2000 a month just to pay for your overhead—an amount that includes both your fixed business expenses and your absolute minimum living expenses. Here's how to calculate your break-even point in units (in this case, hourly fee):

1. Enter the price of one unit of your product or service (60) in cell A1.

2. Enter the variable costs per unit (10) in cell A2.

3. Enter your fixed overhead amount (2000) in cell A3.

4. Enter this simple formula into an empty cell:

+A3/(A1-A2)

The spreadsheet returns the value 40, which indicates that you need to sell 40 hours of consulting per month to break even. In other words, if you sell 40 hours of consulting, you'll generate just enough revenue to pay your variable costs of $10 an hour plus your $2000 in fixed overhead.

The right inventory

For businesses that buy and resell goods, a handy tool for saving inventory costs is the Economic Order Quantity (EOQ) model. An EOQ model lets you find the optimal order size by considering both the cost of placing an order and the cost of the money you use to buy your inventory. Suppose, for example, that you wish to sell a total of 1000 exotic African vases by mail. You buy the vases for $25 each; it costs you $60 in overnight-international-courier charges to place each order; and to pay for the vases, you borrow money on a revolving bank-credit line that costs 12 percent annually.

1. Enter total quantity (1000) in cell A1.

2. Enter shipping costs (60) in cell A2.

3. Enter purchasing costs (25) in cell A3.

4. Enter interest rate for credit (.12) in cell A4.

5. Enter this formula into an empty cell:

+((2*A1*A2)/(A3*A4))^(1/2)

The spreadsheet returns the value 200 as the economic order quantity—the monthly order quantity that will minimize your overall costs of buying and holding inventory.

Grow your business

Ironically, many businesses fail because they're successful. At the root of these success-based failures is a simple reality: A business can't sustain sales growth that is faster than its capital growth. Fortunately, it's easy to calculate how fast a firm's capital—the difference between its assets and liabilities—can grow, because a firm's capital grows by an amount equal to the profits it leaves in the business.

Suppose that the African-vase business has $25,000 in assets and $15,000 in liabilities, resulting in a $10,000 capital balance. Further suppose that the business makes $6000 in annual profits, that half of this sum ($3000) will be distributed as dividends or capital draws to the firm's owners, and that the other half will be left in the business. Here's how to calculate the growth rate that can be sustained in sales:

1. Enter the firm's total assets (25,000) in cell A1.

2. Enter the firm's total liabilities (10,000) in cell A2.

3. Enter the profits retained in the business (3000) in cell A3.

4. Enter this simple formula into an empty cell:

+A3/(A1-A2)

The spreadsheet returns the value .3, indicating the business's sales can grow at a sustained rate equal to .3, or 30 percent. If the firm grows faster than 30 percent annually, it will need to raise outside capital—from new investors, for example—or take on additional debt by borrowing heavily from creditors.

If you're a serious investor and you can afford the high hourly rates, nothing beats the Dow Jones News & Retrieval Service.

Analyze sales increases

Even a small change in sales volume can have a dramatic effect on profits. So it's extremely useful for you to test what happens to your profits if, say, sales increase by 25 percent—or decrease by 10 percent. Suppose you're running a successful direct-mail company that grosses $100,000 a year selling high-quality children's toys. Variable costs run at $50,000 a year. (In other words, the toys you sell for $100,000 cost you $50,000.) Further suppose that your fixed costs run $40,000 a year—an amount that includes a salary for yourself plus your marketing expenses. The $10,000 remaining is the profit. Here's how to estimate how much profits will increase if sales increase by 30 percent:

1. Enter the sales-increase percentage (.3) in cell A1.

2. Enter the annual sales figure (100,000) in cell A2.

3. Enter the variable-costs figure (50,000) in cell A3.

4. Enter the fixed-costs figure (40,000) in cell A4.

5. Enter this formula into an empty cell:

+((1+A1)*(A2-A3)-A4)/(A2-A3-A4)–1

The spreadsheet returns the value 1.5, indicating that a 30 percent increase in sales will produce a whopping 150 percent increase in profits.

Test the discount waters

When you look at the effects that increased sales have on profits, it's easy to think about all sorts of ways to increase sales. For example, why not try discounting your prices? While you'll make less on each sale, of course, you'll also generate a lot more sales (you hope). If this sounds useful in your particular situation, you can test the soundness of the discounting strategy. Reconsidering the African-vase business for a moment, suppose you buy the vases for $25 apiece, sell them for $50, and want to find out how much sales must increase to pay for a 10 percent price discount.

1. Enter the current price (50) in cell A1.

2. Enter the unit cost (25) in cell A2.

3. Enter the price discount (10 percent, or .1) in cell A3.

4. Enter this formula into an empty cell:

+(A1-A2)/((A1*(1-A3))-A2)–1

The calculation yields the value .25, which indicates that your sales must increase by 25 percent just to make up for the 10 percent discount.

Plan for retirement

Within your own business, one of the things you'll want to think about is providing for your own retirement. To plan your retirement intelligently, you'll want to estimate how much you'll accumulate given your current savings and anticipated future savings. Suppose, for example, that you've been able to save $5000 in a retirement account, that you plan to save an additional $2500 annually for the next 20 years, and that you will invest in the stock market, which you believe will provide its historical average return of about 9 percent.

1. Enter your current savings (5000) in cell A1.

2. Enter your additional annual savings amount (2500) in cell A2.

3. Enter the annual return (9 percent, or .09) in cell A3.

4. Enter the number of years over which you will contribute to the retirement account and during which interest will compound (20) in cell A4.

5. Then enter the appropriate formula into an empty cell:

1-2-3: +A1*(1+A3)^A4+ @FV(A2,A3,A4)

Excel: =FV(A3,A4,A2,A1)*–1

The spreadsheet returns the value 155,922.35, which indicates that you will accumulate $155,922.35 in your retirement account by the time you stop working in 20 years.

Deal with long-term inflation

There's an important caveat about the result achieved in the preceding task description, however. Because it's likely there will be inflation over the years between now and the time you retire, a dollar at some point in the future won't have the same value as a dollar today. You can use a simple formula to convert future values to their uninflated present values. Suppose you want to uninflate the future value amount calculated in the preceding task.

1. Enter the future value amount (155,922.35) in cell A1.

2. Enter the expected annual inflation rate (such as .03) in cell A2.

3. Enter the number of years of inflation (20) in cell A3.

4. Enter this formula into an empty cell:

+A1/(1+A2)^A3

The spreadsheet returns the value 86,330.42, which indicates that $155,922.35 in the bank 20 years hence is equivalent to $86,330.42 today if inflation runs at the modest rate of 3 percent annually over the intervening years.

Retire with what you want

Another way to plan for retirement is simply to pick some future amount you want and then calculate what you need to save to accumulate that target value. Suppose, for example, that you have saved $5000 already in a retirement account, that you want $1 million by the time you retire in 30 years, and that you expect to earn 9 percent on your savings.

1. Enter your current savings (5000) in cell A1.

2. Enter the number of years you will let your interest and savings compound (30) in cell A2.

3. Enter the annual rate of return (9 percent, or .09) in cell A3.

4. Enter the target amount (1,000,000) in cell A4.

5. Enter the appropriate formula into an empty cell:

1-2-3: ((A4-A1*(1+A3)^A2)/(1+A3)^A2)*A3/(1-(1+A3)^(-A2))

Excel: =PMT(A3,A2,-A1,A4)*–1

The spreadsheet returns the value 6849.67, which indicates that you will need to save $6849.67 annually to accumulate $1 million by the time of your planned retirement in 30 years.

Electronic investing

There are a number of services and software products on the market to help the potential electronic investor. Still, choosing and then operating an investing system can be tricky. Here are some of the basics of electronic investing to keep in mind.

What kind of investor are you?

The first step in investing is deciding what kind of investments you are going to make. Stock market investors can be divided into two groups: fundamental and technical analysts.

Fundamental analysts

These investors evaluate companies based on their potential for long-term growth and their overall economic soundness. If a company's earnings are growing, but its price does not reflect that growth, a fundamental investor would buy.

How does an investor know when a company's stock price does not reflect its growth in earnings? They go online and find out. Using investment software, a fundamental analyst can search hundreds of companies for the few that meet certain criteria. A typical search might include a high earnings per share growth, steady dividend growth, and at least 50 percent institutional ownership.

Fundamental investors can get all the data they need to make informed buying decisions online. The soundness of the investment depends solely on the criteria for which the investor searches.

Technical analysts

Whereas the fundamental investor makes buying decisions based on the company's strengths, the technical analyst reacts to price movements. If a stock's price is likely to go up, a technical investor would buy without needing to know anything more about the company.

Investment software helps the technical analyst by providing up-to-the-minute price quotes and charting capabilities. Also, by allowing the investor to buy and sell himself, the software cuts out the need for a broker. Without a broker's commission many more purchases become profitable.

Screening options

There are two general kinds of screening tools: disk-based systems and online services. Although they both present the same information, they cater to different user needs.

If you plan on screening stocks frequently and for long periods of time, a disk-based system would be a wise investment. Although they require a substantial investment, disk-based systems allow you unlimited screening and could be cheaper than an online service in the long run. Keep in mind that many products have areas of specialization, whether it is active securities or smaller stocks, so choose your system based on what you expect to trade most.

For the occasional investor, the per-use charge of an online service is probably the best way to go. All major online services provide in-depth market information. Although they usually cost extra, detailed reports and news stories can be obtained through Prodigy, CompuServe, GEnie, and Dow Jones News and Retrieval. You can evaluate stocks with a dedicated software package or a spreadsheet of your own design.

Getting market information

The market information found online ranges from the factual to the fanciful. Bulletin boards post market tips but are not dependable, as disinformation and plain market ignorance are common. All of the major online services offer more reliable market monitoring as well, including 15-minute-delayed quotes, reports about general trading activity, and downloadable charts of active issues. The secret of online market research is knowing where to look.

- Want to get some inside information, legally? By tapping into the Securities and Exchange Commission's database you can find out who's trading what and for how much.

- Thinking about buying some CDs? Check out *FEDWATCH*, a weekly newsletter put out by MMS International, which attempts to predict where rates are headed. The online report can be reached on CompuServe (GO MMS).
- In the market for a mutual fund? Prodigy's Strategic Investor can help, by ranking more than 2600 funds according to performance. You can also calculate their rate of return for periods ranging from one month to ten years.
- However, if you're a serious investor looking for the highest quality market info, and you can afford the high hourly rates (as much as $200), nothing beats the Dow Jones News & Retrieval Service. It is the only service with real-time stock quotes and full text of the *Wall Street Journal*, *Barron's*, *Business and Finance Report*, and *American Demographics*.
- Want to know what the experts think? DJN/R's Investext (//INVEST) provides full-text research reports on more than 5000 U.S. and foreign companies. DJN/R's Dowquest (//DOWQUEST) database has full-text articles from the nation's best-known financial and consumer magazines.

Brokering without brokers

Online trading offers commission savings, speedy transactions, and a wider variety of profitable trades for investors who make their own trades. Still, to register your trades you need to go through a brokerage firm. All you have to do is call up and key in your trade. Brokerages that offer electronic brokering include:

- PCFN
- Charles Schwab
- E*Trade
- Quick & Reilly's QuickWay
- Fidelity's FOX service

Resources

Companies mentioned in this chapter

Lotus
(800) 343-5414

Microsoft
(800) 426-9400

Borland International
(800) 331-0877

Computer Associates
(800) 531-5236

Check Free Corp.
(800) 882-5280

Charles Schwab
(415) 627-7000, (800) 334-4455

E*Trade Securities
(800) 786-2575

Fidelity On-line Xpress (FOX)
(800) 544-0246

PCFN
(800) 825-5723

QuickWay, Quick & Reilly
(415) 326-4200, (800) 634-6214, and (800) 522-8712 (in New York)

Books and publications

The Basics of Finance: Financial Tools for Non-Financial Managers, by Bryan Milling, 1991, Sourcebooks Trade, Naperville, IL; $14.95; (708) 961-2161.

The Cash Flow Control Guide, by David H. Bangs, Jr., 1990, Upstart Publishing Company, Dover, NH; $14.95; (800) 235-8866, (603) 749-5071.

How to Write a Business Plan, by Mike McKeever, 1992, Nolo Press, Berkeley, CA; $14.00; (415) 549-1976, (800) 992-6656.

The Individual Investor's Guide to Computerized Investing, ($30 for members, includes newsletter; $60 for nonmembers). American Association of Individual Investors, 625 N. Michigan Ave., Suite 1900, Chicago, IL 60611; (312) 280-0170.

Price Waterhouse Doing Business Guides, Smaller Business Services, Washington, DC; Free; (202) 296-0800.

Small Time Operator: How to Start Your Own Business, Keep Your Books, Pay Your Taxes, and Stay Out of Trouble, by Bernard Kamoroff, 1992, Puma Publishing, Santa Maria, CA.; $14.95; (800) 255-5730.

The Wall Street Journal, Dow Jones & Company; $139/year; (800) 221-1940.

Accounting software

Checkbook systems

CashBiz (DOS, Windows), M•USA Business Systems
(800) 933-6872, (214) 386-6100.

Quicken (DOS), Intuit
(800) 624-8742, (415) 322-0573.

Managing Your Money, (Mac and DOS), MECA Software
(800) 288-6322

Microsoft Money, (Windows), Microsoft
(800) 426-9400.

Double entry systems

AccPac Simply Accounting (Windows and Mac), Computer Associates International
(800) 531-5236.

Microsoft Profit (DOS, Windows), Microsoft
(800) 426-9400.

M.Y.O.B. (Windows, Mac), Teleware
(800) 322-6962, (201) 586-2200.

Peachtree Accounting for Windows, Peachtree Software
(800) 247-3224, (404) 564-5700.

Business plan software

BizPlan Builder (DOS/Mac), Jian Software
(800) 442-7373.

Business Plan Toolkit, (DOS/Mac), Palo Alto Software
(800) 229-7526

Ronstadt's Financials (DOS), Lord Publishing
(508) 358-0033.

Success Inc. (DOS & Windows), Dynamic Pathways Co.
(714) 720-8462.

Venture (DOS/Windows), Star Software
(310) 533-1190.

First Step Review, National Business Association, Free for members, $5 for nonmembers
(800) 456-0440.

Spreadsheets

Excel for Windows, Microsoft
(206) 882-8080, (800) 426-9400.

Lotus 1-2-3 (Windows, Mac, DOS) Lotus Development Corp.
(617) 577-8500, (800) 343-5414.

Quattro Pro Windows, Borland International
(408) 438-8400, (800) 331-0877.

Investment/financial planning

Captool (DOS), Techserve Inc.
(206) 747-5598, (800) 826-8082.

Performs financial-ratio screening of stocks and includes PFROI portfolio manager.

The Equalizer (DOS), Charles Schwab
(415) 627-7000, (800) 334-4455.

More than a portfolio manager, The Equalizer is the main gateway to the online Schwab brokerage service. It accesses detailed company reports, allows what-if game playing in pretend portfolios, and is a good portfolio manager.

Investor's Accountant (DOS), Hamilton Software
(303) 795-5572, (800) 733-9607.

Portfolio maintenance and analysis, including complex after-tax calculations, asset allocations, and internal rates of return; works with downloaded prices, graphs securities, exports to spreadsheets.

Market Analyzer Plus (DOS, Mac), Dow Jones & Co. Inc.
(609) 520-4641, (800) 522-3567, (609) 452-1511.

Software downloads data from Dow Jones News Retrieval and provides technical charts of stocks, bonds, indexes, mutual funds, and options.

Mutual Fund Database (DOS), Investability Corp.
(502) 722-5700.

This database of 3800 mutual funds can be sorted and compared by objective and by before-and-after load (sales charge) performance.

Market Manager Plus (DOS, Mac), Dow Jones & Co.
(609) 520-4641, (800) 522-3567.

Monitors portfolios; links to Dow Jones News Retrieval for securities quotes and news; includes calendar for financial dates like bond maturities, dividends due, and options expirations.

PFROI (DOS), Techserve Inc.
(206) 747-5598, (800) 826-8082.

Semi-shareware that tracks investments with precision; downloads prices, records tax basis of investment using various methods; computes return on investment (ROI) for both time and dollars; generates numerous reports.

Quarterly No-Load Mutual Fund Update (DOS, Mac), American Association of Individual Investors
(312) 280-0170.

This is an annual subscription database—mailed in quarterly updates—of 600 no-load and low-load mutual funds.

Value/Screen II (DOS or Mac), Value Line Inc.
(212) 687-3965, (800) 654-0508.

Screens a database of 1600 stocks with 49 variables and creates detailed disk-based reports of individual stocks.

WealthBuilder/Smart Investor (DOS, Mac), Reality Technologies
(215) 277-7600, (800) 346-2024.

This software package develops a financial plan, keeps a portfolio, measures performance, and goes online to download quotes on stocks, bonds, mutual funds, and bank rates. It screens investments by multiple variables, offers user-set signal alarms, interfaces with PCFN, and provides tax reports. Smart Investor is also available as a separate stand-alone DOS package ($500, but it isn't available yet for the Mac).

WealthBuilder still does the financial planning, downloading, and screening, but its Mac database is considerably smaller and doesn't offer online trading or automatic investment.

Quote broadcasting services

Data Broadcasting Corp.
(415) 571-1800, (800) 367-4670.

Broadcasts real-time quotes (under a variety of fee arrangements).

QuoteMaster v1.75 (Mac), Strategic Planning Systems Inc.
(805) 522-8979, (800) 488-5898.

Software uses FM radio waves and satellites to put a real-time ticker on your computer; charts buy-and-sell indicators.

Telemet America
(703) 548-2042, (800) 368-2078.

Broadcasts real-time and delayed quotes in a variety of formats (and under a variety of fee arrangements).

Taxes

YOU ARE PROBABLY FAMILIAR WITH THE saying, "The only things you can count on are death and taxes." While we can't say that tax prep software is going to do away with taxes, it will make the drudgery more bearable.

Although paying taxes is even less fun than preparing them, we'll show you the silver lining—deducting your home office and equipment.

Tax-preparation software

Not only does tax-preparation software do your math, transfer data to the right places on the right forms, accept data from accounting programs (so you don't have to manually enter everything)—it also helps you receive your refund faster. Here's what to look for in choosing a package:

- Taxpayer interview. Basically the program asks a series of questions that guide you through the filing procedure. By walking you through the many forms and schedules the program keeps you from making mistakes and helps you maximize your deductions.
- Official IRS instructions. IRS instructions are a must; without them you might as well be doing your taxes manually.
- Forms and schedules. Most programs contain a basic 1040, deductible business expense and depreciation of rental property forms. Still, like most things, it is a good idea to check the contents before you buy.
- Counter-factual tax planning. Will you save money if you and your spouse file separately? How fast will your business grow? How much should you be giving to charity? This "what-if" function lets you organize this year's return and get a head start on next year.
- On-screen tools. Pop-up calendars, scratch pads, and calculators are handy when you don't have a pencil around. After all, the reason you're using software is to avoid all those hassles.
- Compatibility. If you use a financial planner during the year, there is no reason to re-enter all that data. Most tax-prep software will allow you to import data from a number of popular planning programs, but you should make sure yours is one of them.
- Technical support. Everyone needs technical help sooner or later. The cheapest way to get it is online (read about online services in chapter 15). However, if you're not a member of any online service you can get help via phone or fax.
- Electronic filing. Using an electronic filing service will get your claim processed much faster. If you expect a return and want it quickly, get software that lets you electronically send your claim to a third party for filing.
- Up-to-date software. Always use the most current version of tax software. Tax software is revised every year to account for the changes in the tax code. You can usually get an upgrade for a minimal fee.

Importing tax data

If you're one of the millions who use a checkbook program, you might wonder about importing information into your tax-prep program. As long as you used income and expense categories in your checkbook that match the input lines of the various tax schedules and forms, this whole process is a snap.

While the mechanics of the process are very easy, there are a couple of things to keep in mind about importing checkbook data. First, remember that you're really exporting only a couple of dozen numbers; so in many cases it's just as easy to print a report of tax categories and then manually enter, say, the 20 inputs you need.

Second, it's very likely that your checkbook program doesn't contain all the data necessary to complete your tax forms. To export W-2 information, for example, you must do more than simply record payroll checks as net deposits into your checking account. For each check, you'll need to record the Social Security and Medicare taxes, the federal withholding, and any state taxes. If you've got a mortgage, you won't be able to use the property-tax component of your mortgage payment as your property-tax deduction—which is probably what you will have recorded into your checkbook—but rather the amounts the mortgage company actually paid out of the property-tax escrow account.

Tips for using tax-prep software

1. Enter general taxpayer information. Whether you're preparing your income taxes manually or using tax-preparation software, you'll first need to identify which 1040 form you'll use: the 1040EZ form, the 1040A short form, or the regular 1040 long form. As you might guess, tax software makes most sense for those taxpayers filing the long form with its attendant supporting schedules. Once you've picked the appropriate 1040 form, filling it in is a snap. To enter things like your name, address, and filing status, you simply move the cursor to an input field and type in the appropriate chunks of text or numeric values. Any item that can be computed—such as the number of personal exemptions you'll claim—is calculated automatically.

2. Find help along the way. Most Windows and Macintosh programs provide screens that look like actual IRS forms and schedules. Most people find it easier to work with electronic forms that exactly reproduce the paper tax forms they've filled out in past years. Many of the programs also provide an interactive approach to completing the return. TurboTax, for example, provides something called Easy-Step, which guides you through the steps to complete the necessary forms and schedules. All versions of TaxCut, MacInTax, and EasyTax provide similar capabilities. People who need help deciding which forms and schedules to fill out will find these online interview features invaluable.

3. Complete supporting income schedules. As you continue with your 1040 form, you'll begin describing your various sources of income: salaries and wages, interest and dividend income, business profit or loss, and so on. In most cases, these aren't simply figures you enter onto the face of the 1040 form but totals, which get described and calculated on another schedule. For instance, a sole proprietor needs to complete the Schedule C form for business income, deductions, and profits. What's more, if a schedule requires its own supporting forms, you'll need to complete those, such as Form 8829.

4. Link Schedule C to the 1040. Home-based businesses will need to complete either the Schedule C or the abbreviated Schedule C-EZ. The tax software then carries forward information from the schedule to any other schedules or forms that use it. For example, all tax-prep programs automatically copy the bottom-line business profit figure from the Schedule C to the 1040. This linking represents one of the major benefits of tax-prep software. Here's why. If you prepare your tax return manually and find an arithmetic error on, say, your Form 8829, the error ripples through several additional forms and schedules that all have to be rectified with tedious recalculations. When you use software, however, the work of recalculating each of the linked dependent subtotals on the forms and schedules in the return happens automatically.

5. Record adjustments to gross income. If you're entitled to an adjustment in your gross income—for instance, if you're contributing to a Simplified Employee Pension (SEP) or Keogh plan—your next step is to enter these adjustments on the 1040 form. A handy feature in most of the tax-prep packages is online versions of the actual IRS instructions. As you enter an adjustment for a SEP contribution, for instance, you might want to see what the official instructions say about this matter. After you enter any adjustments, the tax software calculates your adjusted gross income. Your adjusted gross income determines the deductibility of certain itemized deductions such as medical expenses.

6. Record itemized deductions—and note them. Once you've entered information about your sources of income and your adjustments, either you accept the standard deduction amount or you enter your itemized deductions on Schedule A. One of the smarter features in just about all of the packages is attachable notes. By attaching a note to a particular line of a form or schedule, you can explain why you entered the value you did. You can also cross-reference any supporting documentation. The DOS tax pack-

Many tax-prep software programs provide an interactive approach to completing the return.

ages usually provide calculation scratch pads or pop-up calculators to figure values. This feature isn't necessary with Windows or Mac tax packages, because the operating system offers a built-in calculator. Once you enter all your deductions, the software calculates your taxable income and the actual income taxes you owe on this figure.

7. Enter tax credits or additional taxes. If you're entitled to tax credits or must pay additional taxes, you'll need to fill out more forms. For self-employed individuals, for example, there's the self-employment tax, which requires you to complete Schedule SE. Taxpayers with high incomes and lots of deductions might need to complete forms to calculate items such as the alternative minimum tax. The process for completing these forms, however, is the same as for any of the other supporting schedules or forms. You input the needed values, and then the software makes all the necessary calculations.

8. Audit the return. Most of the tax-software packages provided auditing utilities, which show a taxpayer what figures on a return appear erroneous or suspicious. While the audit capability is interesting, it's probably most useful as an error-checking tool. If you are entitled to a deduction, you should claim it regardless of whether it produces an audit warning. And if you aren't entitled to a deduction, the fact that the deduction doesn't produce an audit warning is no reason to claim it. Income-tax evasion is a crime that results in stiff penalties and, in some cases, imprisonment.

9. Print, sign, mail. The final step for most people, and the easiest one, is simply to print, sign, and then mail the return. (Remember to send your return via certified mail: It's the only evidence of mailing accepted by the IRS.) The packages we looked at all produced acceptable substitute forms and schedules with most printers, so what you produce can be mailed to the IRS. If you are going to mail a printed copy of your return, you'll need to make sure you have the final version of the software and not the early-planning or head-start version that many of the publishers provide before the end of the year.

Your home office must be your primary business office if you want to deduct it.

10. File electronically. Many packages support electronic filing. Electronic filing isn't something you do, by the way, but rather a service that many of the software publishers and many professional tax preparers provide. To take advantage of electronic filing, follow the software's instructions for saving your tax return in electronic form. Then send your electronic return to either the software publisher or a professional tax preparer who actually files your return electronically. If you go the electronic route, you still need to send the IRS some paperwork—basically a signature. So, the real advantage of electronic filing is that it accelerates any tax refund to which you're entitled.

A buyer's warning

One last point that should be made about income-tax software really amounts to a warning. Tax-preparation software is basically a calculation and forms-generation tool. So you can't use a tax software package as a substitute for tax-planning advice from an accountant or tax attorney. What's more, unless you use a package with a strong interview feature you can't use tax software as a substitute for understanding how tax preparation works.

Deducting your home office and equipment

The home office deduction

More than eight million home office workers could have legitimately taken some form of home office deduction in 1991. However, fearing an IRS audit, only four million did so. This fear costs home office workers hundreds and possibly thousands of dollars in tax savings. Should you take a home office deduction? Only your accountant knows for sure. The 1993 Supreme Court decision does make it more difficult to qualify, but millions of Americans still do.

Do you qualify?

You are allowed to deduct a percentage of your mortgage or rent and utilities from your business income so long as:

- A portion of your home is used exclusively and regularly for a trade or business.
- The home business office is your principal business location.
- You spend more than half of your business hours in the office.
- The home office is used for the convenience of your employer if you are employed by someone else.

The exclusivity test

The exclusivity test is the greatest obstacle you will face in taking a home office deduction. According to the IRS you must use your office space only for business. Dual use will not be tolerated. No leisure reading after work. No personal bill paying at your desk. No computer games. The IRS isn't Big Brother, and isn't going to have you under surveillance, but they aren't kidding about this either.

Regular use/principal business location

Exclusive use is no substitute for regular use. Your home office must be your primary business office if you want to deduct it. The Supreme Court decision applies a strict definition to the principal business test. If your primary work functions are carried on outside the home (a doctor at a hospital, a contractor, a caterer, or a salesperson, for example) and you use your home office mostly for other functions like billing and administration, the home office might no longer be deductible. Consult your accountant for detailed information.

Deductions for the home renter

Just because you don't own your own home does not mean you can't use the home office deduction. Renters are allowed to deduct a pro rated share of rent and utilities.

Think before you Inc.

Keep in mind, only sole proprietors can take the home-office deduction. One-person corporations do not qualify, so think twice before incorporating yourself.

Other considerations

Recapturing tax dollars

One reason people don't take the home office deduction is from the fear that if they do they will face a greater tax burden when they sell their home.

In fact, you can roll over any gain you make when selling an old residence into the new one. You won't have to pay capital gains until you buy a house that costs less than your old one. We suggest waiting until you are over 55 to start down-sizing as you might be able to exclude the first $125,000 of gain.

However, if you have depreciated the business portion of your home, you can't roll over the capital gain. The only way to avoid this is to move your home office out of your home while you're selling your home and don't take a home office deduction for that year. Without an active home office you can roll over to your heart's content.

Footing the bill

In order to deduct your home office you need to measure your office's square footage and calculate the percentage of your total home your office occupies. While most commonly accepted means of measuring are accepted, basic square footage is the safest way to go.

Form 8829

To take your home-office write-off use form 8829. The form feeds into the self-employed's Schedule C and will walk you through every step of your deduction. These deductions are worth more to you if you make them on your 8829:

- Renovation costs;
- A portion of the household utilities;
- Some mortgage interest;
- Depreciation on the office portion of your home that houses your office.

Keep design records

In case of an audit, keep records in the form of pictures or schematic diagrams of your office. Make sure your records include the square footage of the office.

Home expenses only

At some point, you might decide that fighting to qualify your home office is too much trouble. Battling the IRS can leave you weary, but don't give up yet. You can still deduct business expenses even though your office does not qualify. Deduct the costs of supplies, services and any other legitimate costs of doing business just as you would normally.

Deducting equipment— Section 179

You don't have to wait for your office equipment to depreciate to deduct it. Section 179 of the tax code lets small-business owners immediately deduct up to $17,500 worth of equipment annually. If you are in a 28 percent tax bracket, for example, you essentially get a 28 percent discount when buying office equipment. You can also deduct appreciation in Section 179 with Form 4562. Unfortunately, if your business lost money last year, you are barred from using 179. You can however carry them over and try to deduct them next year.

Car deductions

Keep good records of all car expenses and deduct them at the end of the year. If you have poor records, deduct your mileage at a rate of 28 cents per mile driven on business. If you can, combine business and personal trips to maximize your deduction.

What you can't deduct

- Renting to your employer. One of the most popular ways to get around the home office test was to rent your home office space to your employer. The 1986 Tax Reform Act eliminated that. Don't bother qualifying as an independent contractor and renting your space to your clients—that won't work either.
- Landscaping and lawn expenses. If you see a lot of clients at your house you might be able to make a case, but you do so at a risk.
- Investment management. You can't take a deduction for managing your stock portfolio from home. However if you are a technical stock analyst and buy and sell on a daily basis you might still qualify.
- Residential telephone service. You can't deduct part of your local telephone service bill for the first telephone in your house.

However, optional services, like call waiting, and additional lines can be deducted.

Audit statistics: The IRS and you

The sad truth is the self employed have a greater chance of being audited than traditional employees, and next year will be worse. Numbers don't lie:

- *If you reported gross receipts under $25,000 last year you had a 1 in 66 chance of being audited. In year 1993, this category is one of 2.3 million returns, and stands a 1 in 55 chance of an audit.*
- *If you reported gross Schedule C receipts of $25,000 to $100,000 you faced 1 in 50 odds of an audit in 1992. In 1993, the odds are 1 in 42.*
- *One in every 25 of the filers who claimed gross receipts in excess of $100,000 were audited in 1992. In fiscal 1993, 1 in 20 can expect to face IRS examiners.*

Audit protection

- *Use confidence-inspiring computer-generated forms.*
- *Discard the precoded IRS label (it gets you into the system faster).*
- *Avoid deductions that will look unusual.*
- *Don't cheat.*

Defining business expenses

- *Accounting fees*
- *Advertising expenses*
- *Attorney fees*
- *Automobile expenses*
- *Bad debts*
- *Bank service charges*
- *Bankruptcy*
- *Books and periodicals*
- *Business conventions*
- *Business meals (50%)*
- *Business start-up expenses*
- *Capital expenditures (Section 179)*
- *Career counseling costs*
- *Copyright costs*
- *Depreciation*
- *Education expenses*
- *E-mail services*
- *Financial counseling fees*
- *Equipment*
- *Gifts (limit $25 dollars per client per year)*
- *Insurance expenses*
- *Interest on business debt*
- *License fees*
- *Lobbying expenses*
- *Messenger services*
- *Office supplies*
- *Passport fee for a business trip*
- *Printing and copying costs*
- *Professional magazines or journals*
- *Publicity*
- *Repair and maintenance of business property*
- *Safe deposit box*
- *Social security taxes*
- *Tax software. (Although tax software is an asset that lasts longer than a year, it must be upgraded annually, so it's not unreasonable to deduct it under "Other Expenses.")*
- *Theft losses*
- *Travel expenses*

Resources

Books and publications

Commerce Clearing House, 4025 W. Peterson, Chicago, IL 60646; (312) 583-8500.

Tax reference books, analyses; most available in libraries. Call for free catalog.

Home-Office Money & Tax Guide, by Robert Wood, 1992, Probus Publishing, Chicago, IL; $21.95; (800) 776-2871, (312) 868-1100

Home-Office Tax Deductions, by Thomas Vickman, 1991, Dearborn Publishers, Chicago, IL; $19.95; (800) 621-9621, (312) 836-4400

Stand Up to the IRS, by Frederick W. Daily, Nolo Press, Berkeley, CA; (510) 549-1976, (800) 992-6656

IRS publications (free)

The publications listed in the sidebar on page 114 can be obtained at your local IRS office or by dialing (800) 829-3676 or by writing to the Internal Revenue Service, Public Services Division, 1111 Constitution Ave. NW, Washington, DC 20224.

Associations and agencies

American Institute of Certified Public Accountants, 1211 Ave. of the Americas, New York, NY 10036-8775; (800) 862-4272.

Membership estimated at 300,000; more than 75 percent of U.S. CPAs. Provides referrals, member CPA professional-status reports, other information by phone and mail.

Internal Revenue Service (IRS), Public Affairs Division, Dep't. of Treasury, 1111 Constitution Ave. NW, Washington, DC 20224. Public Affairs (202) 622-4000; Forms & Publications Hotline (800) 829-3676; General (800) 829-1040

Software

If you're preparing your own return, consider using a tax-preparation software package—many offer a full range of state and special business forms, telephone support, and last-minute updates. Using a tax program can help you organize your books throughout the year; you can even file electronically through an accountant or service bureau for faster refunds.

Andrew Tobias' TaxCut (DOS), MECA Software
(800) 288-6322, (203) 256-5999

Easy Tax (DOS), Softkey
(800) 862-7638 orders, (800) 377-6567 information

MacInTax Personal (Mac), Chipsoft
(800) 756-1040, (619) 453-5552

TurboTax Personal (DOS), TurboTax for Windows (Windows), and MacInTax Personal (Mac), Chipsoft
(800) 756-1040, (619) 453-5552

IRS publications

Title	Number
Your Rights as A Taxpayer	1
The ABC of Income Tax	2
Employer's Tax Guide (Circular E)	15
Your Federal Income Tax	17
Tax Guide For Small Business	334
Fuel Tax Credits and Refunds	378
Travel Entertainment and Gift Expenses	463
Tax Withholding and Estimated Tax	505
Excise Taxes	510
Tax Information For Selling Your Home	523
Taxable and Nontaxable Income	525
Charitable Contributions	526
Residential Rental Property	527
Miscellaneous Deductions	529
Tax Information for Homeowners	530
Self-Employment Tax	533
Depreciation	534
Business Expenses	535
Accounting Periods and Methods	538
Tax Information on Partnerships	541
Tax Information on Corporations	542
Sale and other Dispositions of Assets	544
Interest Expenses	545
Nonbusiness Disasters, Casualties, and Thefts	547
Investment Income and Expenses	550
Basis of Assets	551
Record Keeping for Individuals	552
Community Property and Federal Income Tax	555
Examination of Returns, Appeals Rights and Claims for Refund	556
Self Employed Retirement Plans	560
General Business Credit	572
Taxpayers Starting a Business	583
The Collection Process	586A
Business Use of Your Home	587
Tax Information on S Corporations	589
Individual Retirement Arrangements (IRAs)	590
Guide to Free Tax Services	910
Tax Information for Direct Sellers	911
Business Use of a Car	917
Employment Taxes for Household Employers	926
Business Reporting	937
Filing Requirements for Employee Benefit Plans	1048

Sales & marketing

THE NUMBER ONE CONCERN OF SELF-EMployed business people is sales and marketing. This comes as no surprise—no sales means no business. The good news is that with today's technology, and a little creativity, you can produce an effective marketing campaign that generates prospects and new clients. There are so many ways to market with your technology that some topics became their own chapters—desktop publishing is a prime example. There are also marketing opportunities available in online services and in using good information management techniques.

In this chapter we'll show you how to fax the word out fast, follow up business prospects, and use other people's technology when you take to the airwaves.

Fax the word out

"Reaching out and touching someone" has always been an advantage of using the phone. With a fax you can reach out and touch everyone—with a keystroke. What broadcast faxing lacks in personal touch, it makes up for in sheer call volume. Rather than having to call all your clients to announce a new service, you can fax them in a fraction of the time.

Or you can set up a fax-on-demand service so that clients and prospects can request information about your services and have it automatically faxed to them. This can be an efficient way for people to request more information after seeing one of your ads. Fax-on-demand can even be a business in itself or a profitable sideline—it's possible to charge people for information.

Broadcast faxing

Sending one fax to a list of numbers—called broadcast faxing—is similar to doing a mass mailing but has several advantages.

- It's fast. You can send out hundreds of faxes within hours, even minutes.
- It's cheap. It can cost less than the postage for a standard envelope, let alone the $6 to $16 for overnight couriers.
- It's easy. Once your lists and messages are on file, just push the send button and relax.

Caveat

There is only one real problem with broadcast faxing, it's illegal. As of December 20, 1992, it is illegal to send unsolicited faxes advertising a product or service. According to the FCC's Telephone Consumer Protection Act (TCPA) a person or entity may file suit to stop you from faxing as well as "for actual monetary loss from violations or receive $500 in damages for each violation (whichever is greater)."

To be on the safe side, get permission from all the people you fax to, even if they have never complained before.

Computer faxing

Faxing directly from your computer is often the most practical way to broadcast-fax. A fax-modem will, along with the accompanying software, send files from your computer to any number of distant fax machines. By faxing through your computer you can save time, avoid misfeeds, and get the maximum value for your phone time. Computer faxing also generates higher-quality documents.

Computer users who have a modem but no fax/modem may use a fax delivery service offered by an e-mail service. Unfortunately to use these services you must sometimes convert your files to plain-vanilla ASCII files, which cannot support highly stylized documents.

Service bureaus

If you need to send an avalanche of faxes, or need rapid delivery, a full-fledged service bureau may be the best option. It generally costs more to use a service bureau, but since the bureaus have hundreds of phone lines, the faxes can be distributed within minutes.

With a standard fax-on-demand setup, the caller can use any touch-tone phone and request that a document be sent to any fax machine.

Fax-on-demand

For you, fax on demand is a way of getting information about your business out, without constantly stuffing envelopes. To the caller, fax-on-demand is the simplest way to retrieve information instantly. Here's how it works.

Callers to a voice/fax system request your company's information or publication by pressing buttons on their touch-tone phone as directed by a recorded voice. Callers enter their fax number, and credit card number if you charge for the service. Then, the system automatically faxes the information to them within seconds.

Companies can use fax-on-demand systems to distribute in-depth product information, pricing sheets, technical support, subscription forms, and even newsletters—without paying anyone to stuff and mail envelopes.

The Programmer's Shop in Hingham, Massachusetts, a software catalog house, is an example of an effectively installed, cost-saving fax-on-demand application. They developed FastFaxts, which stores detailed product information for software that's described in brief in the catalog. Each product has a FastFaxts code printed near the product blurb for callers to use when they dial into the system.

The Avery Label Company uses fax-on-demand for technical support. A brochure bundled with their products tells customers to call its fax-on-demand system to retrieve instructions on how to print labels using specific printers. By giving customers information when they want it, fax-on-demand boosts Avery's high-tech profile, enhances customer loyalty, and cuts the need for technical-support staff.

"One-call" fax-on-demand

There are two basic types of fax-on-demand systems: the one-call setup and the standard setup. The one-call system is less expensive, but also less convenient. A one-call system keeps the caller on the line after he or she has made a selection and transmits the product information back to the caller's fax machine on his or her expense. The caller must call from a fax machine and is instructed to push the START button to keep the line open.

To set up a one-line system, you need an MS-DOS computer with two full-size slots and at least a 40MB hard-disk drive. You will need to have two phone lines to run this system: one for incoming calls that are answered by the voice board and another for the fax card to send out requested documents.

"Standard" fax-on-demand

With a standard fax-on-demand setup, the caller can use any touch-tone phone and request that a document be sent to any fax machine. The caller hangs up after dialing the number of the destination fax machine, and 15 to 30 seconds later the fax-on-demand system transmits the requested document. RoboFax Pro (Fax Quest) and FaxFacts (Copia International) are standard fax-on-demand systems that can take two calls at once. Each system comes with two boards and software and requires a dedicated computer.

Brooktrout Technology sells Flash-Fax 2x2, a system that houses its own microprocessors and doesn't require dedicated computers. It handles up to four lines.

On-site or off-site

Installing and programming fax-on-demand software isn't overly difficult, but that doesn't necessarily mean you should set up your own system. Many people don't want to undertake the responsibility of managing a system 24 hours a day. Also, if you expect heavy phone traffic, you'll need more than two incoming phone lines. It's often simpler to work with a service bureau for your fax-on-demand needs until you better understand the traffic you'll have.

Follow-up for business prospects

Follow-up is your critical link between garnering leads and turning prospects into new customers. Follow-ups rarely consist of a single step. More often they are a series of steps that take place over days, weeks, or even months. Each follow-up method poses tradeoffs between its benefits and your resources. To help you find the right follow-up method for your business, we have compared the costs and benefits of several strategies.

Letters

Thanks to laser printers, your letters can look as crisp as printed brochures. With word processing and mail merge, you can create semi-personalized form letters in quantity.

Pros

An individual letter is more personal than a brochure, it can address specific interests and be time effective.

Cons

Uncertainty—you don't know if the letter reached the right person, or says what he or she needs to know.

Although "Larry King Live" probably won't invite you to talk, you can still make the airwaves into an effective marketing tool.

Tips

Use in concert with phone calls for key prospects. Be sure to confirm the prospect's name and title.

Phone

Picking up the phone gives you real-time one-on-one contact.

Pros

Both interactive and flexible, a phone call lets you supply information and answer questions immediately. It can often qualify a prospect to avoid unfruitful meetings. It also serves as a form of research.

Cons

Phone calls can be costly, and can consume your most precious resource—time. Without careful scheduling, calling can interfere with your work.

Tips

Make calls instead of blind meetings. Use a prospect profile to prescreen. Follow strong calls with a letter or meeting. Try to pick good times to call, and start by asking the person if they have a few minutes to talk.

Fax

Send a message from your printer or fax machine direct to a prospect's office.

Pros

Faxes offer an instant way to get information to prospects, bypassing mailroom delays and phone-messaging systems.

Cons

Sending unsolicited faxes is illegal. Thermal faxes rarely file well. Faxes to a central machine often get lost or buried in a pile.

Tips

Get permission to fax first. Use an overnight courier for 10 pages or more—time and budget permitting. Fill out standard cover sheets while on the phone, or use computer-based fax, with software that creates a built-in cover sheet.

Electronic mail

All online services offer e-mail for computer-to-computer contact.

Pros

E-mail is fast and relatively inexpensive, and avoids phone tag. It also promotes ongoing relationships, and is a good follow-up after phone calls or meetings. For many businesses, showing that you are e-mail savvy adds to your professionalism.

Cons

Some e-mail services require you to use ASCII-only text files, without fonts styling or graphics, which flattens out your presentation. Prospects must have an e-mail account on the same service or gateway system.

Tips

Offer your prospect a choice of hard copy, fax, or e-mail. Create ASCII letterhead and a boilerplate letter to make it easy to send e-mail quickly.

Taking to the airwaves

Radio talk shows present an excellent opportunity for you to promote your home-based business, whether you market a product or serve as a consultant. It's said that there are nearly 1000 radio talk shows in America. Let's say that each requires an average of three guests per day. Why, that's about 20,000 guests per week and one million guests per year. Although "Larry King Live" probably won't invite you to talk, you can still make the airwaves into an effective marketing tool. In many markets, the demand for guests far outstrips the supply of people with an enticing message.

Anyone can book a radio appearance—especially on local stations—if you know how to go about it. Here are ten ways to help get yourself on the air.

1. Identify shows whose listeners are your audience. There are programs for sports buffs, animal lovers, political conservatives, and every other demographic group you can imagine. One helpful resource is the Annual Broadcasting Yearbook, the who's who of the radio business. It may be available at your local library, or you can order it from the publisher (see Resources at the end of this chapter for information). In addition, many major metropolitan areas publish their own publicity directories. These often provide more details on local talk shows, including air times, program format, and the names of both the host and the producer.

2. Tune in. Before you pick up the phone to book your first radio interview, invest some time listening to your targeted programs. Each show has its own style, so determine how you might fit in. It's also important to note the host's personality and philosophy. Is the host informal or formal, humorous or serious? If the host has published books, reading them is a good way to determine which angle will have the most appeal.

3. Package your message to suit the program. Once you've done some background research, you can begin to tailor your message accordingly. Develop four or five suggested program titles, each with a slightly different angle. Producers usually prefer practical subjects such as "Little-Known Places to Retire in Style" or "How to Get Debt Collectors Off Your Back." However, a controversial topic, like

"Why Doctors Don't Tell the Truth About Vitamins," can also work.

4. Contact the producer. Briefly explain how your topic will meet the audience's needs, and be sure to mention specific programs you have heard recently. Do not contact the host. The producer decides who gets booked and who doesn't. Most producers prefer you to call rather than write. When you call, the producer is screening you on the spot; some radio programs actually record these conversations for later review. So know exactly what you want to say and how you plan to say it.

5. Make the producer look good. Make certain you have a clever angle, and be the kind of lively guest who guarantees listener response. To be safe, ask your friends to call in with prearranged questions or comments. But by all means, use this idea only in a pinch and sparingly even then. Of course, don't let on that the callers are your parents or your cousin Charlie. If the show usually features a panel, identify several qualified people who can join you on air. Make sure the panel is available on short notice.

6. Follow up with a media kit. Within 24 hours after your initial contact, send complete publicity materials to the producer. The kit should include the following items:

- Cover letter. Briefly recap your conversation and emphasize that you want to help the program's listeners solve a specific problem.
- Interview topic and question list. Include an outline of your suggested program topics, with questions the interviewer may wish to ask. Believe it or not, some hosts will use your list of questions verbatim.
- Press release. Send an article or announcement on the project or product that is motivating you to seek publicity. Cite research, trends, or statistics that show why your topic will interest the talk show's listeners.
- Biography. Offer a brief overview of your career accomplishments and credentials. It should explain how and why you began your business. If you have any public-speaking experience, here is the place you should mention it.
- Quote sheet. Under a headline, such as "What People Are Saying About (you, your company, your products)," include quotes from a wide range of clients, peers, and respected authorities.
- Article reprints. If you have written or been the subject of newspaper or magazine articles, be sure to include copies. They enhance your credibility as a guest.
- Audiotape. Also send a recording of you displaying your wit and wisdom for the benefit of others. It should provide evidence that you can handle yourself well before a live audience. Most radio programs do not require an audiotape, so don't go to great lengths to create one; however, it can improve your chances, particularly for the big-name shows.

7. Place another phone call, and then another. Don't expect the producer to contact you. Take the initiative and don't give up until you get a firm yes or no. It is okay to be persistent, provided you don't become a pest. (Where you cross that line depends on your personality and the producer's patience.)

8. Make the most of your time on air. The secret to capitalizing on radio publicity is offering listeners a way to respond. If you have one, mention the 800 number of your company so listeners can call to inquire. However, some programs won't let you hawk your wares. But if you offer a free booklet that happens to have an order form for your product, everyone wins. Most hosts encourage such freebies, because listeners love them.

9. Parlay one appearance into dozens more. The first interview is always the hardest to obtain. Once you've proven your ability to perform well on the radio, it's just a matter of capitalizing on it. The power of radio happens when you are featured again and again, on a wide range of programs. Ask the producer to provide you with an audiotape of your program. Then you can market yourself to other shows as an experienced interviewee. With each show you book, the next one becomes a little easier.

Once you've proven your ability to perform well on the radio, it's just a matter of capitalizing on it.

10. Send thank-you notes. As always, a little courtesy goes a long way. Remember to mention that you are available for future interviews. If you usually work in your home office and have a flexible schedule, you should also indicate your willingness to serve as an emergency guest, in case someone cancels out at the last minute.

Marketing tips

Marketing by mail

- *Use Word Perfect as a database. Most word processor programs cannot automatically bunch data together, such as matching zip codes in a mailing list, like a database can. However, Word Perfect is quite capable of sorting records in a mail merge file. See the Select function under the Sort command.*

- *Code lists for flexibility. Every record in your mailing list should contain a code field, such as CUST for current customer, PRSP for a prospect, or RISK for a past customer who is a credit risk. Then, selecting records by the code field lets you divide your list any way you wish.*
- *Include as much information as possible on your mailing list. Extra information can only help you. Create extra fields in your database to record what your customers bought, when, why, and any pertinent demographic information. Keeping extra, unused fields may slow your searches, but it gives you room to expand your information base.*
- *Convert your database into a word-processing merge file. A perpetual problem encountered by many businesses is getting your contact list, usually kept in a database, into a word processor for merge letters. To get the information out of the database simply save it under a new name as either a comma-delimited or a tab-delimited ASCII text. Comma-delimited means the file contains a comma between each field, usually with quotation marks around the contents of the field. Tab-delimited files contain a tab-character between fields, often without quote marks. To reformat the exported data use the word processor's search and replace function to substitute the quotes and commas with the program's merge codes.*

Marketing by phone

You know the saying "You never get a second chance to make a first impression." For many people, that first impression is often made by phone.

The human voice projects an astounding range of emotions. If, when you answer the phone, you sound angry or brusque, you start things off on the wrong foot—at the very least. At worst, you may drive away a potential customer.

- *Keep it short and sweet. What should you say when you answer the phone? It's generally best to use your company's name in the greeting because it reassures callers that they have reached the correct number. But a long, complex salutation can leave callers reeling. Just as important as the message is the tone of voice. Although it sounds trite, smile when you talk to create a more upbeat phone manner.*
- *Be sincere. If you're cold calling a complete stranger chances are you don't really care how his or her day is going. People will notice insincerity and be turned off. Be polite and friendly but don't pretend you're old friends.*
- *Don't name drop. Whatever you have been told in the past, using the name of a client or prospect on the phone does not create intimacy. You don't use your friends' names in casual conversation. When a stranger uses your name it jars you. Use the prospect's name at the beginning and closing of the phone call only.*
- *Record your voice. Few people have any idea how their normal speaking voice sounds. Find out by taping your phone greetings. For about $10, you can purchase a device that attaches to the phone and a tape recorder. Turn the recorder on each time you answer the phone for one day (it's not illegal to tape phone conversations so long as the other party knows it is being recorded). When you replay the tape, listen for flaws in diction (can you easily recognize the name of your company?), speed problems (do you speak too quickly?), and tone and effect (does your voice exude enthusiasm or boredom?).*

Resources

Companies mentioned in this chapter

Fax Quest
(415) 771-0923, (800) 925-ROBO (demo)

Brooktrout Technology
(617) 449-4100, (800) 33-FLASH (demo)

Copia International
(708) 682-8898, (708) 924-3030 (demo)

WordPerfect
(800) 321-4566, (801) 225-5000

Fax-on-demand service bureaus

For a fee, these companies will store your documents and fulfill customers' fax-on-demand requests.

MarketFax
(914) 478-5904, (800) 992-TONE, ext. 666 (demo)

World Data Delivery Service
(800) 238-3337, (800) USA-FAX4 (demo)

Instant Info
(617) 523-7636 (no demo)

Dynamic Fax
(815) 398-9009, (800) 933-3661 (demo)

Books and publications

Annual Broadcasting Yearbook, Reed Reference Publishing, New Providence, NJ; $160; (800) 521-8110, (908) 464-6800.

The who's who of the radio business.

Creating Customers: An Action Plan for Maximizing Sales, Promotion and Publicity for the Small Business, by David H. Bangs, Jr., and the editors of *Common Sense*, 1992, Upstart Publishing Co., Dover, NH; $19.95; (800) 235-8866

Direct Mail Magic, by Charles Mallory, 1991, Crisp Publications, Menlo Park, CA; $8.95; (415) 323-6100, (800) 442-7477.

This pithy guide to selling by mail offers great advice.

Getting Business to Come to You, by Paul and Sarah Edwards & Laura Clampitt Douglas, 1991, Jeremy Tarcher/Putnam, Los Angeles, CA; $10.95; (800) 631-8571, (213) 935-9980.

Modular, fact-filled resource for marketing any type of product or service.

Guerrilla Marketing Attack, by Jay Levinson, 1989, Houghton-Mifflin, Boston, Ma.; $8.70; (617) 351 5000, (800) 225-3362.

Field-proven strategies by successful marketing guerrillas.

How to Get Big Results from a Small Advertising Budget, by Cynthia S. Smith, 1989, Carol Publishing Group, New York, NY 10016; $7.95; (201) 866-0490, (800) 447-2665

Marketing for the Home-Based Business, by Jeffrey Davidson, 1990, Bob Adams, Inc., Holbrook, MA; $9.95; (617) 767-8100.

How to project a high-level image and make the most of your equipment in marketing your business.

Improving Your Company Image, by Sylvia Ann Blishak, 1992, Crisp Publications, Menlo Park, CA; $8.95; (415) 323-6100, (800) 442-7477

Media Power—How Your Business Can Profit from the Media, by Peter G. Miller, 1991, Dearborn Financial Publishing, Chicago, IL; $19.95; (800) 621-9621, (312) 836-4400.

A step-by-step demonstration of how to attract media attention to your business.

On the Air: How to Get on Radio and TV Talk Shows and What to Do When You Get There, by Al Parinello, 1991, Career Press, Hawthorne, NJ; $12.95; (800) 227-3371, (201) 427-0229

Practical Market Research, by Jeffrey L. Pope, 1993, AMACOM, New York, NY; $32.95; (800) 538-4761

Sales on the Line, by Sharon Drew Morgan, 1993, Metamorphous Press, Portland, OR; $14.95; (503) 228-4972

CD-ROM discs

Advantage Plus Business Master (PC), CD-ROM Inc.
(800) 821-5245.

More than 1100 shareware programs with a business flair.

Business Yellow Pages of America (PC and Macintosh), Innotech Inc.
(416) 492-3838.

More than 200,000 American businesses on a single disc.

1990 Census Data on CD-ROM (PC), CD-ROM Inc.
(800) 821-5245.

More than 100 key variables from the 1990 census by census tract, zip code, place, county, and state.

Basic desktop publishing

FOR THE SMALL BUSINESS, DESKTOP PUBLISHING is close to the ultimate marketing tool. Used properly, it can give your business the aura of a corporation several times its size. Image isn't everything, but it can go a long way.

DTP will also aid you in your sales efforts. It can generate sales leads (customized brochures and mailings), help land an assignment (powerful presentations), and increase customer retention (newsletters).

This kind of power and flexibility does come at a cost. It will require additional investment in hardware and software. It also takes an investment of time—not only to master the software, but to train your eye to pick out good design from bad. We'll give you an introduction to using type and present some DTP design tips to get you started.

To inexpensively add some panache to your work, look to laser printer creativity boosters. If you need professional printing for your first newsletter, we'll tell you how to prepare.

Hardware and software

More than any other use you'll put your computer to, desktop publishing is equipment intensive. If you plan to undertake DTP on a regular basis, you'll need more power than you might otherwise purchase. The following section outlines important points to consider.

Mac or PC?

Here's the situation today in a nutshell: You can produce identical desktop-published output today on a Macintosh or a PC. Given the fact that the end product is indistinguishable, how do you make up your mind? Consider three factors:

- Ease of use. Macintosh is legendary for its ease of use. Without going into detail, Macintosh computers still maintain an ease-of-use advantage over PCs, even when the latter are outfitted with Windows. The commands used in Mac programs are more consistent from one program to the next, file sharing is easier, and it is generally simpler to add new peripherals (such as hard-disk drives, scanners, or CD-ROM drives) to a Macintosh.
- Software availability. A virtual dead heat. There are tons of fonts and clip art for both Windows and Mac systems, and illustration and page-layout programs are comparable, both for novices and for sophisticated users.
- Price. Once marketed as a sports car, the Macintosh line now also includes a substantial number of family sedans, at prices roughly competitive with similarly powered PCs. The operative word here, though, is *roughly*. At any point along the price/performance continuum, you are going to pay a premium for a Macintosh computer. The premium is relatively small at the low end of the line, and grows into significant money as you look at more powerful models. Simply put, while there are dozens of reputable manufacturers of 386- and 486-based computers, there's only a single supplier of Macintosh computers. In the wake of the price wars that raged throughout 1992–1993, you will still pay less for comparable speed and features if you buy an IBM-compatible.

Low-scale DTP

The requirements in terms of hardware and software vary widely within the broad desktop-publishing spectrum.

Let's start with the simplest kinds of projects. These might include product price lists; simple fliers (consisting mostly of type, with perhaps a single illustration included); or a basic all-type newsletter (set in two columns, with a decorative banner at the top of the cover and articles that run newspaper-style from one column to the next, versus jumping articles from page to page).

If you already own a computer and a laser printer, you probably don't have to spend a dime to undertake these projects. In terms of software, a good DOS—or any Windows or Macintosh—word processor will let you run type in multiple columns on a page and insert graphics. Word processors don't offer the sophisticated type controls found in dedicated page-layout programs, but they're adequate for the three projects mentioned above.

Even a low-end computer—a one-piece compact Macintosh with the screen built-in (like the Classic II or Color Classic) or a 386-based PC-compatible—can suffice at this level. Mind you, we don't recommend going out and buying a 386-based machine in today's market. However, if you already own a 386 and it's good enough for your word-processing needs, it can be good enough for basic desktop publishing.

High-end DTP

Let's crank the complexity level of our publications up a notch. Now we have a product catalog with several illustrations on each spread; or a newsletter with line art or photographs, and stories that don't follow a neat sequence; or a flier with a picture or two, a fancy headline, and a coupon with a dotted border at the bottom of the page.

Now you want page-layout software. Could you struggle by with your word processing program? Sure, but why bother, when it is faster and easier to use a dedicated page-layout program? What's more, powerful midlevel page-layout software is dirt cheap.

Mid-range software

If you walk into your local computer store and ask the guy about desktop publishing, he'll probably push you towards one of the Big Three: Aldus PageMaker, Ventura Publisher, or QuarkXPress, each of which runs about $600 to $800 at retail for either Windows or the Mac. Don't be intimidated.

PostScript gives you tremendous flexibility in selecting and sizing both type and graphics.

For $100 to $150 you can buy a midrange program that offers an extraordinary amount of power and won't take you weeks to master. For the Macintosh, look into Publish-It! Easy (Timeworks) and Aldus Personal Press. On the PC side you can find Microsoft Publisher, Publish-It!, and Express Publisher (separate versions for DOS and for Windows, from Power Up Software). These are not second-rate tools by any means, but quality programs that should meet your basic publishing needs.

Hardware essentials

Now let's talk computer hardware. Here are some points to consider:

- Serious page layouts should be done on a computer with a separate monitor, of 13 or more inches diagonal (although a 12-inch monitor will do in a pinch). A 19-inch monitor is a dream, but will run you several thousand dollars. You should settle for nothing less than Super VGA display if you have a PC.
- A 40MB hard-disk drive is okay if that's what you already own (you'll probably outgrow it fast, though), but if you're going out to buy a system now, get at least a 120MB drive. The more graphics-intensive your work is, the larger the hard disk should be. Graphics files eat space.
- 4MB of system memory is mandatory for basic work. You'll need 8MB if you get serious.
- You'll also need a mouse, an under-$100 purchase (if it isn't already bundled with the PC you're considering).

Speed

Intel's aggressive pricing for its industry-standard microprocessor line has made the gap between powerful and more powerful virtually inconsequential among PCs. Some catalogs offer 486-based machines for as little as $100 more than a fast 386. In this situation, the smart shopper spends a little extra money for a far superior machine.

If you're in the market for a Mac, you can do very well with a 68030-based machine. But Apple's pricing on 68040 computers is very attractive, and anyone looking to get into DTP is well advised to get one.

Printers matter

The make-or-break component in even the simplest desktop publishing setup is the printer. Hook up the fastest, most sophisticated computer on the market to an old 9-pin dot-matrix printer and your printed pages are going to look pretty lame. For professional-looking desktop publishing, a laser printer is essential. Actually, the term laser isn't entirely accurate, since printers that use LCDs rather than laser beams to make toner cling to paper produce equally crisp output. The key specification, though, is at least 300-dpi resolution. For simple projects, you can do without PostScript capability (more on that later), and you don't need a speed-demon printer made for multiple users in an office environment.

When only the best will do

600-dpi printers have become surprisingly affordable. A few years ago you would pay $18,000 for this resolution; some are now available for around

Many font vendors sell display faces at reasonable prices either individually or in collections.

$2000, only a few hundred dollars more than 300-dpi models. When deciding whether this is worth it, you should know that 600-dpi printers have four times the resolution of 300-dpi models, not two times as many people think (you calculate overall resolution by squaring the dpi. The 600-dpi printers have 360,000 dots per square inch versus 90,000 for 300-dpi printers). This resolution makes a significant difference when you print shades of gray, photographs, and small type.

PostScript printers

If you're going to tackle relatively sophisticated desktop-publishing projects, you will want a PostScript-equipped printer. Without going into depth on the merits of PostScript, suffice it to say that PostScript gives you tremendous flexibility in selecting and sizing both type and graphics. If you're serious about desktop publishing, you want a PostScript printer. And, like most computer hardware, prices for PostScript printers sank like a stone in 1992. Figure less than $1500 for a basic PostScript printer today, versus about $1000 for a laser printer without PostScript.

Scanners

If you own a scanner, life is good. If you also have Optical Character Recognition (OCR) software, it's even better. You can't always find the right clip art and clip art often looks like, well, clip art. With a scanner any image is yours, assuming it doesn't infringe on a copyright. With OCR you can capture typed documents in seconds.

For most DTP, a monochrome or gray-scale scanner will be sufficient—you only need color if your business is DTP. Hand-held scanners are inexpensive, and probably all you need. A flatbed scanner is easier and provides better image quality. They also usually come bundled with image-editing software, so you can manipulate your masterpieces.

Using type

Type is the most powerful element of any design. The typefaces you choose will say a lot about you and your company to those that read your material. Take time selecting what's right for you—experiment with using different type in your sales brochure and ask others what a given type says to them.

Typeface vs. font

A typeface refers to a similar set of characters regardless of their size, whereas a font is an individual typeface in a particular style and of a particular size. Therefore, Palatino would be a typeface, but Palatino 14-point-bold would be a font. Because most page-layout programs allow you to scale the size and change the style of type by hitting a few keys, many desktop publishers use the words font and typeface interchangeably (much to the annoyance of traditional printers).

Due to the scalable nature of many fonts, point size has become increasingly flexible as well, allowing for minute variations. Standard Font sizes include 9, 10, 12, 14, 18, 24, and 36 points. There are 72 points in an inch, so 36 point type is ½ inch high.

Serif vs. sans serif

A more obvious distinction between type styles is that between serif and sans-serif type. Serif type includes those little decorative brackets that close the ends of letters. Serifs are a holdover from Roman times when they were used to prevent splitting as letters were carved in stone. Sans-serif type is any type without those decorative brackets.

Serif type like Times or Palatino is generally better for setting large blocks of body type. The serifs serve to hold the line together and make the type easier to read. Sans-serif type is usually used for headlines and subheads. However if you want your text to look decidedly modern, sans-serif type is the way to go.

Text face vs. display face

Another type distinction is between text face and display face. The first group is made up of faces that are appropriate for setting lengthy blocks of text, or captions, headers, and footers—the meat-and-potatoes information in your publication. Display faces are more complicated.

What makes a typeface a display face?

- A display face is generally used in a larger point size than regular text—bigger than 14 point, let's say.

Serif Type

Sans Serif Type

20-1 *Examples of serif and sans serif type.*

- A display face is used for short, attention-grabbing text such as headlines for articles, advertisements, and fliers, publication cover lines, and posters.
- A display face is often more stylishly designed than a text face.

Text faces can be very attractive, but they can't be too ornate or they distract and become hard to read. For instance, it's a pain to read a long block of text in some outrageous art deco typeface with swirly serifs and unusual letter shapes. However, the same decorative display face might be the perfect choice for setting the name of a restaurant in a large size for a flier headline or the cover of a menu.

Clairvaux

Dolmen

MESQUITE

20-2 *Examples of display typefaces.*

Type tips

Create a mood

A font like Tiffany, with its elaborate serifs and dramatic transitions between the thick and thin strokes that make up the letters, is at once formal and festive—a good choice for garden party luncheon announcements. On the other hand, a face like Aachen makes a big, bold, heavyweight statement through its rectangular design and sheer mass. It's a good choice for the headline on a flier announcing a massive close-out sale at a hardware store, for example.

Reduce for resolution

One short cut for higher resolution is to print larger than your final copy and then reduce it with a photocopier. Just make sure you size all the information in your document, including leading, at the proper proportions. This process will work best with smaller documents, otherwise you will have to paste separate sections together on a mounting board for reproduction.

Your company logo must be graphically pleasing and consistently presented.

Aachen

Tiffany

20-3 *Different typefaces can create different moods.*

Building your font library

Many display faces will only be used on rare occasions, so you don't want to pour a lot of money into building up a collection. Happily, you don't have to. Many font vendors sell display faces at reasonable prices either individually or in collections. One unusually wide-ranging and reasonably priced type collection is offered in both Windows and Macintosh formats by FontBank. The company's PostScript display typeface collection—also available in TrueType—includes 250 fonts ranging from the elegant and restrained to the unabashedly wild, all in a library with a street price under $100.

Additional sources of fonts in quantity include some drawing programs. Finally, if you're modem-equipped and up for some online exploring, there are thousands of fonts available for downloading through private and commercial bulletin boards. Some are free for the taking, others require a shareware fee, but in either case you can try them out in your layout at no cost.

Lighten up

Adjust your toner density to a lighter setting when you want to print detailed or fine print. On most laser printers the default setting opts to print pure black rather than fine contrasts. After a few sheets have been run through on a lighter setting, you should start to pick up more detail.

Shape up

Your display typography doesn't have to adhere to horizontal left-to-right conventions. How about a layout where the headline runs diagonally across the upper left corner of the page? How about setting one or more words in an arched shape? How about giving the type perspective, by having it diminish toward a point on the horizon? Accomplishing these special effects will probably require either an object-oriented drawing program or a special-purpose type manipulation program such as TypeStyler (Broderbund, for the Mac) and MakeUp (Bitstream, for Windows). There are a few page-layout programs, however—such as Microsoft Publisher and Publish-It—that incorporate significant type-manipulation capabilities.

Add nontype elements

Your type doesn't have to sit alone and unadorned on a blank white page. Think about enclosing the display type in a shape. An ordinary rectangle? An extraordinary irregular dodecahedron filled with horizontal slashes at random angles? The shape you choose depends on the editorial context. But combining display type with a geometric shape (often called a panel) that either encloses it or complements it, draws the reader's eye to the headline and adds interesting visual elements to the page layout.

A template is a ready-to-use publication file, with spaces for you to insert text and graphics into a "prefab" layout.

Shady characters

Solid black is, well, solid. Trustworthy. Believable. But not particularly exciting.

If you're creating a color publication, the display type is a prime opportunity to liven up a page that doesn't have an illustration, or create headlines that color-complement the graphics.

Even if you're printing in black-and-white, there are plenty of gray areas worth exploring. Type reproduced in a shade of gray might not have the visual impact of hot pink or neon green, but it adds a richness and variety to the page. There is a significant caveat here, though. A 300 dot-per-inch laser printer can produce a few shades of gray, and they are relatively coarse (since the printer is really mimicking gray-scale). If you are producing a publication that will be printed commercially, let the print shop produce the shades of gray you want by applying a screen to the black original type you provide. They'll charge you a few dollars, but the results are much smoother and more precise than laser-printed grays.

DTP design tips

Any business, large or small, should strive to create a design identity—a distinctive visual presence that makes your printed materials immediately recognizable. All of your business forms and promotional material should adhere to this design standard.

How do you create a visual identity?

- Company logo. It needn't be an ornate production number—all-type logos can be simple, attractive, and effective. But whether you choose to use type alone or to add graphic elements, your company logo must be graphically pleasing and consistently presented.
- Customized ink. Your company's identity could be marked with the use of a particular colored ink—think of Kodak's bright orange or IBM's "big" blue.
- Type face. You might also want to standardize your documents using a particular typeface or set of typefaces on all of them, including business forms.

Page size

Sure, any print shop can print an 8.5-by-11-inch sheet. But is that the optimal size for your project? That will depend on a number of factors:

- The amount of information you are trying to convey. It might be more cost-effective to use a larger page rather than to add pages. Or you might be able to economize by using a smaller sheet if you don't need much room.
- The impact you are trying to achieve. When it comes to promotional pieces, bigger is often better. An oversize catalog that arrives in a big envelope will stick out among the clutter of the day's mail. A bigger page might allow you to use larger graphic images, too. On the other hand, if you're preparing a publication oriented toward ready-reference purposes (a member directory, for instance), then a smaller page size might be easier to store on a shelf or stow in a briefcase.
- Your print shop's equipment. Sometimes changing a dimension by a fraction of an inch can cut your printing costs substantially, because different sizes work better on different printing presses. The only way you'll find out if there are savings to be had is to speak with your print shop expert before you go ahead and design the job.

Your computer isn't a typewriter

For professional-looking type, there are a few basic rules:

- For emphasis, don't underline—use italics or boldface instead.
- Except for the occasional headline, don't use ALL CAPS either—it is difficult to read. If you need to, use small caps instead.
- Only put one space after a period, not two.
- Use an em-dash (—) rather than a double hyphen (--).
- Between numbers (e.g., "30–40"), use an en-dash (–) instead of a hyphen (-). Only use hyphens in phone numbers.

Boxing

Whether you're designing a newsletter or a brochure, try segregating the nitty-gritty facts from the body of the presentation. A separate box with listings, product-description details, or statistical information will offer in-depth information without disrupting the flow of your presentation. And for those who zero in on that kind of information, boxing it (perhaps with a distinctive border) makes it easier to find than burying the stats in the body text.

White space

White space is not simply a blank area you forgot to fill—it actually emphasizes useful information. A photograph of your computer learning center sitting in a rectangle bordered on all sides by text makes your product look relatively unimportant. But give that same photograph a page or even a half page of its own, bordered by a generous swath of white space, and the product suddenly commands attention.

This concept is particularly effective with mailed promotions that are casually thumbed through. Overly packed, gray-looking pages will consign your brochure to the recycling bin. However, don't try to trap white space inside your designs. "Bubbles" of white space pull apart your design and break up your elements.

Big initial caps

For catching the reader's eye and leading them into your text, nothing beats a big initial cap. Whether it rises above your text or drops down into it, an initial cap lends elegance to your layout. In fact, an initial cap is essential when your text is separated from your headline.

What kind of initial cap should you use? The safest thing to do is to choose a initial cap of the same typeface as your body type. However, feel free to experiment, as long as it looks reasonably consistent. Many stylized alphabets are available as clip art, and you can customize your own with a drawing program.

Here are some thoughts to keep in mind when positioning an initial cap:

- Drop or raised caps should generally be as large as 3 or 4 normal lines of text.
- Initial caps must be set next to the left margin.
- Adjust the space between the Initial cap and the body text. If left alone, letters like A, W, V, and Y will trap white space in your text and pull apart your design. However, if the letter is a word by itself (e.g., I or A) leave its rectangular space alone.

Keep type consistent

Whatever type you choose, maintain a degree of consistency. For example, an advertising-layout template will frequently use a large, bold typeface for the leading headline, and other typefaces from the same type family elsewhere in the ad. Perhaps the company name and phone number will be set in the same bold type in a smaller size, the company address in the nonbold version of the same face, and subheadings within the body text in the italic version of the typeface. This complementary type selection helps to hold the layout together.

Ruling line treatments

You can get an awful lot of design mileage out of relatively simple combinations of lines and boxes. Though an attractive ruling line doesn't get the attention it deserves, ruling lines can lend a layout flavor. However you decide to use ruling lines, maintain consistency throughout the piece. Is there a thin underscore beneath each caption? A combination of thin and thick lines setting off the table of contents? A ruled box around each illustration, or a drop shadow, or a shaded rectangle?

With this said about the simple beauty of ruling lines, let us add: Don't get too complicated. Too many rules, boxes, and sections break up the page and can turn your graceful layout into a Mondrian nightmare.

Being able to easily find the image you need is as important as having that image in the first place.

Design troubleshooting

Here are some suggestions for avoiding potential trouble spots:

- Fix bad breaks. Watch out for bad breaks in the text. Edit to avoid the design flaw of a single line left at the beginning or end of a column.
- Dam rivers. When there is too much white space between words, "rivers" of white space can form throughout your text. Dam these rivers up with hyphenation, editing adjustments, or by changing from a fully justified setting to ragged right.
- Inspect imports. Monitor the way your page-layout program imports your graphic files. Often the software will squash or stretch your illustration into the shape of the template's place-holder box, distorting the graphic's dimensions in the process. More likely, you'll want to either crop the illustration to fit the space or adjust that space to match the size of your graphic.

Line length

The only hard-and-fast rule for line length is that you take notice of it. Long lines can be tiring to read. Short lines are frustrating because you have to keep going to the left hand margin. To help you find a happy medium length try following these general guidelines.

- Text looks good at about 9 or 10 words per line (50–60 characters).
- The alphabet and a half (a through z plus a through m) in lowercase letters also works well.
- Lines of sans-serif type should generally be set shorter than serif lines.

Testing your pieces

Testing your promotional materials lets you know what's working and what's not. With desktop publishing technology it's easy, because producing multiple versions of a document is relatively simple. Just distribute a promotional piece with a distinct call to action, and count the number of responses it generates. Say you're planning to include a coupon in a flier. Is $1 off too little to draw attention? Would $2 off bring in just as much business as $5 off?

For a "big business" look, create your own custom multipart order forms, invoices, and so on.

The best way to find out is to create multiple versions of the flier with a tracking device built in (a coded coupon, for example), and tally up the results of a small sample. If you compile your results using a spreadsheet program, analyzing the result will be a snap. Then, when you've received feedback from the public, you'll know which offer works best and be ready to roll it out to a larger audience. This approach is standard procedure in professional direct marketing.

Templates

Template temptation

You could start your design from scratch, determining all the margin and column settings, type styles, ruling lines, text and image placement, and so on. As a time-saving alternative, you could use a prepared desktop-publishing template that poses the design question in a simpler, fill-in-the-blanks format.

A template is a ready-to-use publication file, with spaces for you to insert text and graphics into a "prefab" layout. Most page-layout programs today come with a variety of templates, and additional template files are available in several program formats, both commercially and as shareware.

Although they are no substitute for a thorough knowledge of desktop publishing, we recommend using—and creating your own—templates whenever possible.

Adjusting templates

Every template you use will need some fine tuning. The key to making these tweaks is changing the template proportionately. If you have a complex multicolumn template laid out for an 8.5-by-11-inch page, but you're printing on 8-by-10-inch paper, the easiest answer is to trim away those outside edges. Don't. Whacking away at the outside margins will guarantee that your page layout will look awful. If you like a template but have to adjust it for size, adjust each element roughly proportionally.

Why roughly? Because sometimes the mathematically correct proportional adjustment is just too picayune to be practical. For instance, you want to change an 8.5-inch-wide template with two 22-pica-wide columns, and a 2-pica space between columns, to fit on 8-inch-wide paper. (Note: There are 6 picas to the inch and 12 points to a pica. Designers think in terms of picas and points, so try to become familiar with this standard.) Mathematics would tell you to change the 2-pica space between columns to 1.882 picas, but nobody should ever have to deal with making changes of 0.118 picas except as punishment for the most flagrant design crimes. Instead, lop off 2 picas from the outside of each text column and be done with it.

Smart templates

While most template programs offer standard, fill-in-the-blanks options, others give you multiple options from which to choose. Instead of simply delivering entirely prefabricated templates, these "smart" template programs ask for your input and create templates tailored to your responses.

That's the approach taken in two innovative midrange page-layout programs: Microsoft Publisher running under Windows, and Aldus Personal Press on the Macintosh.

If you're too busy to construct entire page layouts, but want more variety than the standard template software provides, smart templates could be right for you.

Clip art

Clip art gives you a quick and inexpensive way to jazz up your documents with graphic elements. Your image options are really only limited to how long you want to spend looking for the "right" image. You'll find a list of popular clip art suppliers in the resources section of this chapter.

When acquiring clip art, pay attention to format. You will generally have two options: a low end and a high end. Most page-layout software will accept either of these formats, but the differences go beyond price. The following section provides a quick rundown of what each has to offer.

Bitmapped graphics

The low-end option represents pictures as a collection of dots with a process called bitmapping. Bitmapped images are designed to be reproduced at a given size or smaller. If you significantly enlarge a bitmapped graphic it gets very jagged or even unrecognizable.

20-4 *Clip art is an inexpensive way to add graphic pull to your work. Electronic clip art is easy to work with because you see it onscreen before you print it and, with the right tools, it can be edited to suit your needs.*

Editing the images is quite easy. Just import the image into a paint program and play with the dots.

Bitmapping is the least expensive graphics format. In fact, by searching online bulletin boards you can usually find a number of images for no charge.

There are a number of bitmapped formats, but only a few are well supported. The TIFF format (used for most scanned images) is well supported in both the PC and Mac worlds, while PCX and BMP are exclusive to the PC arena (BMP is for Windows only). The Mac uses the PICT format.

Object-oriented and PostScript drawings

PostScript and object-oriented formats are the high end option. They let you alter the size of the image without distorting its quality. These formats store the image as a whole rather than as a series of dots. With these formats the size and resolution of an image are only limited by the capacity of your output device.

There is one major limitation: PostScript artwork can only be output on PostScript printers or image-setting equipment. It will reproduce poorly, if at all, on a non-PostScript printer.

Commercial vendors

A host of vendors specialize in producing clip art packages, among them well-known players such as Image Club and T/Maker. In some cases, vendors' clip art libraries are available as small collections geared to particular themes (business, sports, education, or maps, for example); other collections are really massive image resource libraries with something for everyone. Such one-stop-shopping collections are increasingly available on CD-ROM, which can hold 600MB worth of images on one disk. Before vendors began shipping their clip art on CDs, you often had to sort through dozens of floppy disks to find the picture you needed or give up valuable megabytes of hard-disk space to store the images.

Sloppy or obviously amateur promotional materials will be counterproductive to your business.

Being able to easily find the image you need is as important as having that image in the first place. Most vendors reproduce their electronic images in an accompanying booklet, ideally with a comprehensive index that lets you look up a category or an object—flower or baseball, for example—and then directs you to all the relevant images. Some companies also provide software utilities that search the image collection based on the keywords you choose. Once the search is completed, you get a thumbnail display of the graphics for quick preview before the software actually loads them.

Online art

You can log onto CompuServe, America Online, and many private bulletin boards, to find lots of clip art files ready for downloading. These are generally shareware offerings—software you can try before you buy (usually at modest prices). But sometimes, some bulletin boards might post artwork that's just been scanned in from printed sources without permission. So if you're planning to distribute your document publicly, you might be better off buying a piece of clip art from a reputable commercial source.

Printed art

In the midst of this electronic age, you might be surprised to learn that a wide selection of paper-based clip art still exists, ripe for the scanning. The biggest name in this area is Dover Publications, with hundreds of inexpensive clip art collections in book form (sold in art supply stores or through Dover's own catalog). The traditionally sedate Dover also recently came out with its first disk-based collection (published by Bantam Books), and the company promises more to come.

Creating overheads

With desktop-publishing software and a laser printer you can create some show-stopping overheads and presentations. You can lay out your text, tables, and graphs on your computer and print directly onto a transparency with your laser printer. Make sure you print on laser transparency film (beware—other types of film might melt inside your laser printer!).

Highlight with color

A touch of color conveys a very professional image (not only because it looks great, but most people think it is very difficult to do). The simplest way to add color is to use color-tinted or bordered transparency films. There are plenty of options available (Paper Direct has a wide selection). If you want to add color in specific places, you can purchase color toner and run the transparency through your printer twice (once for black and once for the second color).

Graphic highlights

Tables, graphs, and diagrams often illuminate otherwise dry data. Overheads are a particularly effective medium for presenting graphic information. What's more, with most presentation and DTP software, creating these graphic elements is simply a matter of entering data into a template. But don't get fancy. Complex diagrams or spreadsheets become unreadable at a distance.

Line art

Properly placed line art livens up an overhead presentation. You can choose from the ample supply of clip art available or use your scanner to in-

If you'll be preparing a significant number of mechanicals, you should invest in the professional tools that make this task faster and more precise.

put any appropriate images (the logo of the company you are presenting to, for example).

Keep in mind that photographs rarely reproduce well on overheads. If you can avoid using them, do so.

Don't crowd the page

An overhead should not be a full text version of your verbal presentation. Nor is it intended to simply serve as an outline from which to give your speech. Use your overhead text to reinforce key points and ideas, not to try to explain complex issues. That's what you're there for.

Avoid fine print

Your overhead will almost certainly be seen from a distance. Even though it will be projected bigger, you should still use large type with ample spacing. In an overhead, it is better to err on the side of legibility. As a general rule of thumb, don't use type smaller than 24 point.

Bullet for impact

An overhead is no place for subtlety: bullet your key points. Bullets draw attention, define your points, and ease the reader (or viewer) through your information.

Laser printer creativity boosters

A business adage says, "Dress not for the job you have, but for the job you want." Here are some creative ways to use your laser printer, teamed with some specialty products, to "dress" your business for the jobs you want.

Business identity

- Today's selection of stationery-grade laser paper includes a variety of colors, finishes, and exotic looks such as parchment, granite, and marble. Paper preprinted with background patterns or other graphic designs can also be the basis for beautifully distinctive letterhead. We recommend papers from Paper Direct.
- Envelope printing on a laser is still largely a trial-and-error process. Until fully laser-friendly envelopes are available, clear laser labels provide an excellent alternative to direct printing. These specially designed labels, available from office supply stores, tend to "disappear" on most finishes when applied, yielding a polished look—even on colored envelopes. Try Avery Clear Laser Labels.
- Be sure to maintain a professional look on outgoing packages and oversize mailing envelopes. Large laser labels can be found in white and clear, with designer graphics. Paper Direct carries shipping labels in a unique "one-up" format for convenience when printing individual labels.
- For special announcements and other mailings, Idea Art has compiled a wide array of laser paper illustrated to suit any business occasion. For more formal business invitations or announcements, Shaffer Software offers raised-edge announcement cards, die-cut four to a page, in three colors.
- Colored light card stock, bordered papers, and translucent vellum are among the many laser-compatible choices for attractive proposal or report covers. Use solid or clear labels to customize heavier cover materials; these are available from Paper Direct and others.
- Avery manufactures several kits for producing professional-looking divider pages. These items, as well as others in the extensive line of Avery laser products, can be found at office-supply dealers. Prices vary widely.
- For a "big business" look, create your own custom multipart order forms, invoices, and so on, with carbonless paper and supplies from Laser Label Technologies.

Advertising and marketing material

- One of the most exciting and useful developments for desktop publishers is preprinted brochure paper. These sheets are now available in a variety of colors, sizes, weights, and artistic layouts. Simply type your information in the proper format, and laser-print directly onto the professionally designed stock. The result is an instant, colorful, customized brochure for your company at a fraction of what a commercial printer would charge. Paper Direct offers a wide selection.
- Letraset's brand-new Paperazzi line of premium-quality papers (available at art materials dealers) is perhaps the most beautiful and versatile available. These 20 stunning double-sided designs will help you create memorable announcements, fliers, and other promotional materials.
- For catalogs, price lists, specifications sheets, maps, and the like that will see heavy-duty service, there are durable pages that are tear-proof and moisture-repellent. Queblo Images offers a Mylar-reinforced paper for three-ring binding durability.

- Audiocassette, videocassette, diskette, and standard labels are available in a variety of sizes, colors, and adhesive types for your products or promotional media. One option is Paper Direct's full-page neon-color label stock for eye-catching stickers, or choose from Laser Label Technologies' selection.
- Perhaps your business could benefit from having small quantities of custom-printed T-shirts, caps, aprons, or other apparel, either for promotional purposes or as a uniform. BlackLightning develops and markets transfer toner for many popular laser-printer models. Simply install the cartridge, print a mirror image of your design onto plain paper and then heat-transfer to the clothing item (preferably 50 percent polyester, 50 percent cotton). There are some limitations; but, in general, this is an ingenious product with many potential applications for the small business.
- For business gifts, incentives, or premiums, personalize appropriate items with transfers or clear labels. Try transfer toner on mouse pads, tote bags, or luggage tags. Clear labels work nicely on calendars and other desk accessories. Paper Direct carries clear labels in uncut 8.5-by-11-inch sheets for convenience in customizing items of various sizes and shapes.
- For an instant display, laser-print headlines, graphs, charts, and explanatory text in large type onto drafting appliqué film, and affix it to a ready-made trifold display board. Repositionable adhesive, full-sheet formatting, and a choice of finishes make appliqué film handy for many other projects as well. The film is available from drafting supply stores or by mail from Laser Label Technologies.

General tips and tricks

- Remember that fancy paper is no substitute for good design. Sloppy or obviously amateur promotional materials will be counterproductive to your business. Take advantage of the design tips and layout examples from supplier catalogs or use software templates.
- Color toner is available for most laser printers and will enhance any kind of printed material. Contact your local cartridge remanufacturer, or BlackLightning, for availability. By printing in separate passes you can even produce a document in several colors.
- For beautiful metallic color accents, try laser films marketed under the trade names LaserColor, Desktop Color Foil, and CopyFX. The film is secured over a printed image and rerun through the printer, where the heat and pressure bond the color to laser or copier toner. Smooth-finish papers are preferred for proper application. Many people report success using this same technique with Letraset's Color Tag films as well, although this is not recommended by the manufacturer.
- Perforated laser postcards are available, but an inexpensive alternative is to print four copies onto 67-pound Vellum Bristol from an office-supply store. Cut the sheet into quarters and you will have postcards that meet post-office requirements.
- Many factors, including the type of printer and even the climate, can affect paper-printer compatibility. It is wise to test paper or other laser products before committing to large quantities. Some companies will supply free samples, while others sell sample kits for this purpose.

Professional printing

As we have discussed, DTP technology can help you construct, design, and edit just about any kind of page layout. What's next? For any kind of large scale circulation, you will be bringing your pages to a printer.

Sometimes you can just hand the print shop a page direct from the laser printer and leave it at that, and other times you might be able to hand over a computer file on disk. However, there's often more to the process. Let's look at what a print shop needs to reproduce your pages, and what you must do to provide it.

Are you camera ready?

As we said, sometimes your page layout can go right to the print shop with no additional work. All of the following must apply:

- All of the type and artwork are already in place and ready to be shot by the printer's camera.
- There are no special instructions about individual elements on the page.
- The finished page size will be the same as the laser-printed page.
- Page numbering is already included within the page layout itself, or the finished page size is small enough to let you include crop marks on the laser-printed page.
- You're not planning to hand the same output to a printer again.
- There's no client involved in approving the final output.
- The print shop has no objection to working with your unmounted materials.

If all of the above apply to your situation, then the sheets that come from your laser printer (or from the imagesetter service bureau if you've opted for high-resolution output) can be delivered as camera-ready repro to the print shop. It's camera-ready because it will be reproduced exactly as it is: The print shop uses a specialized large-format camera to take a picture of the material you provide and prints from that photographic image. It's called repro because it's used for reproduction purposes.

If any of the conditions listed above don't apply to your situation, then camera-ready repro isn't enough—you'll have to provide a camera-ready mechanical. A mechanical is a piece of white board with the elements of your page pasted precisely in their final positions. In fact, mechanicals are sometimes referred to as boards, and the process of creating them is called paste-up.

Preparing mechanicals

Board stiff

Simply mounting a complete page produced by the computer on a board makes it less susceptible to folding, tearing, crumpling, and myriad other mutilations. To protect against smudges and fingerprints, a sheet of tracing paper is often attached to the top edge of the mechanical with wide masking tape, creating an overlay called a tissue. For even more protection on a small job (a half-page ad, for instance), you might add another sheet of thin board or thick paper on top of the tissue.

The board used for mechanicals can vary widely. It must have a coated white surface, but the thickness can range from a thin, flexible board (similar to oak tag) to a thicker bristol board. You can also buy boards with blue ruling lines especially for mechanicals.

Paper

Imagesetter output is actually a photographic process as well. The type from an imagesetter won't smear, and the paper itself is coated with resin to keep adhesives from penetrating the surface. If you'll be using laser-printed pages as camera-ready proofs, consider buying a special paper that provides some of the advantages of resin-coated imagesetter output. Hammermill's Laser Plus paper works well. It has an extra-bright white color for maximum contrast and a special coating to resist adhesive damage. The best special-purpose laser paper we've seen is LaserGloss from mail-order supplier Paper Direct. LaserGloss costs roughly four times more than the Hammermill paper, but it produces exceptional results for the job.

Adhesives

You have several choices when selecting adhesives for attaching materials to the boards. Rubber cement is available in two varieties: two-coat (which must be applied to both the board and the material to be pasted down) and one-coat (just glue up the item to be attached). One-coat is harder to find but easier to use. You'll also want rubber-cement thinner, which lets you unglue a piece to reposition it, and a pick-up, which you rub around the edges of pasted-down material to pick up any extra glue that has spread out onto the board. A roller with a plastic cylinder is also helpful for ensuring a flat surface and over-all adhesion.

Spray mount in an aerosol can is another popular adhesive, though not the most environmentally sound option. It can be inconvenient to apply (the can spritzes a wide area) and tacky rather than gluey (that is, lacking permanence)—but many professionals love the stuff. One major caveat, whether you're using rubber cement or spray mount: Work in a well-ventilated area. Both glues contain chemicals whose fumes pose long-term health hazards.

If you're going to be doing a lot of mechanicals, one more possibility is wax. A traditional approach indeed, this requires a machine that melts sticks of wax and applies a thin coat to your repro. Hand-held waxers sell for as little as $50, but a truly serviceable motorized waxer will cost somewhere in the neighborhood of $300. Working with wax can be messy, but it does let you pick up and move page elements easily.

Cropping

Instead of submitting page-by-page notes describing the handling required for your print job, you can mark up the mechanical itself—on the tissue overlay—with virtually all the information the print shop needs.

Start by indicating the size of the final printed page. Mount your pages on boards that allow a few inches' margin on all sides of the "live" page area. Then use crop marks to indicate where the actual edges of the printed page fall. If your page is small enough, you'll be able to print these crop marks directly on your laser printer or imagesetter output. Some page-layout programs—such as PageMaker—can insert crop marks automatically, while others—like Publish-It!—require you to draw them by hand.

Manual cropping

You can insert crop marks manually with a ruler and a red pen by measuring the appropriate distance from the horizontal and vertical page edges and drawing a set of short lines in each of the four corners. If you'll be preparing a significant number of mechanicals, you should invest in the professional tools that make this task faster and more precise. These include a drafting table that provides a true straight edge along the vertical side and a T-square that provides a true horizontal edge when held against the side of the drafting table. You'll also want a triangle to rest against the horizontal T-square to provide a reliable vertical edge where you need it.

The drafting table is essentially a tool to provide true horizontals and verticals, which are useful not only in drawing crop marks but whenever you are inserting page elements on a mechanical. For instance, if you are placing a graph on the page, a T-square provides a true horizontal to line up against the bottom line of the graph, ensuring against crooked placement.

Mechanical communication

What other messages might you want to send to the print shop?

Pagination

Pagination isn't always obvious by looking at an individual page, and sometimes the information on the page is downright misleading (such as in the case of a page 1 that follows several pages of introductory material numbered in a separate Roman-numeral sequence). In the nonprinting margins of your mechanical, indicate the actual sequential number of each page.

This is the Acme newsletter

It is all too easy for individual pages of a mechanical to be separated from the rest of the job in a busy print shop. Each page should be identified consistently in the margins, either with your own name, your company name, or the name of the project.

Print this in a second color

To indicate which elements on your page are supposed to appear in a second color, write directly on the tracing paper tissue. Outline the type or graphic in question and write the color instructions.

Inserting graphics

Some graphic elements can be included directly on your mechanical and shot with the text—a simple graph or a line-art illustration, for example. If you plan to include photographs, though, or illustrations with solid blocks of color or gray tones, you'll want the printer to shoot the artwork separately and strip it into the final printing film. You have to indicate the illustration's exact positioning on the mechanical.

The simplest way to accomplish this is by providing a keyline—a rectangular box the size of the final illustration. You can create the keyline right in your page-layout software and print it out with the page. However, you'll have to indicate to the print shop whether you want the keyline to be printed or if it's just there for reference.

Indicating which graphic to print in a given space is another matter. If your layout is simple, you can number your graphics sequentially and write the corresponding numbers on your mechanical. If the layout has lots of graphics to be stripped in, though, or if the mechanicals must be approved by a client who wants to review it once the graphics are in place, you'll need to provide final-size graphic placeholders. If you have a scanner, you can handle this task easily by scanning in the graphic. The number of images involved might exceed your computer memory, though, and the extra printing time required to output scanned images might exceed the limits of your patience. If that's the case, or if you don't have access to a scanner, graphic placeholders can be created on a photocopier with enlargement and reduction capabilities.

No matter how you create your placeholders, be sure to clearly mark them FPO on the mechanical. FPO means "for position only" and tells the print shop that the graphic on the mechanical is just a placeholder to be replaced with the final artwork.

Resources

Companies mentioned in the chapter

Aldus
(800) 333-2538

QuarkXPress
(800) 788-7835

Ventura Software
(800) 822-8221

Power Up Software Corp.
(415) 345-5900

Microsoft
(800) 426-9400

TimeWorks
(708) 559-1300

Broderbund
(800) 521-6263

Bitstream
(800) 522-3668, (617) 497-6222

Paper Direct
(800) 272-7377

Avery
(909) 869-7711

Laser Label Technologies
(800) 882-4050

Letraset
(800) 343-8973

Queblo Images
(800) 523-9080

BlackLightning
(802) 439-6462, (800) 252-2599

FontBank
(708) 328-7370

Dover Publications
(212) 307-7521

Books and publications

Color for the Electronic Age, by Jan White, 1990, Watson-Guptill, New York, NY; $32.50; (212) 764-7300

Color Publishing on the Macintosh, by Kim and Sunny Baker, 1992, Random House Electronic Publishing, New York, NY; $45; (800) 733-3000

Desktop Publishing: Dollars and Sense, by Scott R. Anderson, 1992, Blue Heron Publishing, Hillsboro, OR; $14.95; (503) 621-3911.

Flash ($10 per year) and *Flash Compendium 1992*, BlackLightning, Riddle Pond Rd., West Topsham, VT; $12.95; (802) 439-6462, (800) 252-2599.

This newsletter of laser lore provides solutions to all sorts of printing problems and offers guidance in enhancing all your laser-printing activities.

Looking Good in Print, 2nd Edition, by Roger C. Parker, 1990, Ventana Press, Chapel Hill, NC; $23.95; (919) 942-0220, (800) 743-5369

The Makeover Book: 101 Design Solutions for Desktop Publishing, by

Roger Parker, 1989, Ventana Press, Chapel Hill, NC; $23.95; (919) 942-0220, (800) 743-5369

Newsletters from the Desktop, by Roger Parker, 1990, Ventana Press, Chapel Hill, NC; $23.95; (919) 942-0220, (800) 743-5369

No-Sweat Desktop Publishing, by Steve Morgenstern, 1992, AMACOM, New York, NY; $22.95; (800) 538-4761

The Presentation Design Book: Projecting a Good Image with Your Desktop Computer, by Margaret Y. Rabb, 1990, Ventana Press, Chapel Hill, NC; $23.95; (919) 942-0220, (800) 743-5369

Type in Use, by Alex White, 1992, TAB/McGraw-Hill, Blue Ridge Summit, PA; $34.95; (717) 794-5461

Type from the Desktop: Designing with Type and Your Computer, by Clifford Burke, 1990, Ventana Press, Chapel Hill, NC; $23.95; (919) 942-0220, (800) 743-5369

Winning Forms series by various authors, 1992, (paperback and disk). Random House Electronic Publishing, Random House Inc., Westminster, MD; $45; (410) 848-1900, (800) 733-3000.

This fabulously illustrated book and disk series, available for Word for Windows, Lotus 1-2-3, WordPerfect for DOS, and other programs, tackles one of the most time-consuming business-design tasks known to computing: form making.

Associations

National Associations of Desktop Publishers, Topsfield, MA; (508) 887-7900.

Publishes a monthly magazine, bimonthly newsletter and holds seminars (membership: $95/year).

Videotape

Design & Layout Techniques, by MacAcademy, ($49, two hours). Mac Academy, Ormond Beach, FL; (904) 677-1918, (800) 527-1914

Software page-layout programs

PageMaker (DOS, Windows, Mac), Aldus Corp.
(800) 333-2538

Microsoft Publisher (DOS/Windows), Microsoft Corp.
(800) 426-9400

Publish-It! Easy (DOS/Windows), Timeworks, Inc.
(708) 559-1300, (800) 323-7744

QuarkXPress, (Windows, Mac), Quark Inc.
(800) 788-7835

Personal Press (Mac), Silicon Beach/Aldus Corp.
(619) 695-6956

Clip art

Artbeats (DOS, Windows, Mac), Artbeats
(800) 444-9392, (503) 863-4429

ClickArt (DOS, Windows, Mac), T/Maker
(415) 962-0195, (800) 395-0195

Clip-Art Connection (Windows), Connect Software
(206) 881-8251, (800) 234-9497

Cliptures (DOS, Windows, Mac), Dream Maker Software
(303) 762-1001, (800) 876-5665

Designer's Club (DOS, Windows, Mac), Dynamic Graphics
(309) 688-8800, (800) 255-8800

DigitArt (DOS, Windows, Mac), Image Club
(403) 262-8008, (800) 661-9410

The Dover Electronic Clip Art Library, Volume 1 (DOS, Windows), Random House
(800) 726-0600

Images With Impact, (DOS, Windows, Mac), 3G Graphics
(206) 774-3518, (800) 456-0234

Masterclips (DOS, Windows), Masterclips
(305) 983-7440, (800) 292-2547

Presentation Task Force (DOS, Windows), New Vision Technologies
(613) 727-8184

ProArt, (DOS, Windows, Mac), Multi-Ad Services
(309) 692-1530, (800) 447-1950

Vector Art (DOS, Windows, Mac), Holmes & Cottrell Graphic Technologies
(813) 992-5125, (800) 597-0688

Wet-Paint (DOS, Windows, Mac), Dubl-Click
(818) 888-2068, (800) 359-9079

Illustration/paint/ image-editing software

The editing tools in illustration software, paint programs, and image-editing packages can make your average, everyday piece of clip art fit the needs of your specific project. Illustration software is the choice for editing vector-based clip art. For bitmap editing chores, a simple paint program might suffice. In fact, the Paint application shipped with Windows might be all you need for basic bitmapped editing. If you are more artistically inclined or want to perform precise, detailed image retouching on bitmap graphics, high-end image editing programs give you professional quality power tools with support for all the color your system can produce. Here are a few suggestions.

Illustration software

Adobe Illustrator (Windows, Mac), Adobe Systems
(800) 833 6687

Aldus IntelliDraw (Windows, Mac), Aldus
(206) 628-2320 (800) 333-2538

CorelDraw (Windows), Corel Inc.
(613) 728-8200, (800) 772-6735

Designer (Windows), Micrografx Inc.
(214) 234-1769, (800) 733-3729

Paint software

PC Paintbrush (DOS), ZSoft Corp.
(404) 428-0008, (800) 227-5609

MacPaint (Mac), Claris
(408) 987-7000, (800) 544-8554

Image-editing software

Adobe Photoshop (Windows, Mac), Adobe Systems
(800) 833-6687

Aldus Photostyler (Windows), Aldus
(206) 628-2320, (800) 333-2538

Picture Publisher (Windows), Micrografx Inc.
(214) 234-1769, (800) 733-3729

Software reviews

SOFTWARE IS VITAL TO ANY BUSINESS THAT uses computers—most of the ideas and solutions in this book are software derived. In this section, we provide a number of in-depth reviews that cover some of the best products available. Additionally, we give mention to 100 great programs under $100. Despite their low price, many are very powerful. If your needs are not tremendous, you might be able to substitute a $695 page-layout program with something for $75.

IN-DEPTH REVIEWS

Word processors

Microsoft Word (Macintosh, Windows)

At a glance Great, easy-to-use word processor.

Ease of use Easier to use than many other word processors with this many features, because it's simple to customize menus to show only those items you regularly use.

Documentation Clearly illustrated, step-by-step getting started manual leads naturally to complete, well-arranged user's guide.

Support You pay for the call but information is thorough.

Version reviewed 5.0, Macintosh.

System requirements 1MB Macintosh (2MB recommended, 2MB required for grammar checker, 4MB recommended for grammar checker and System 7.0) or higher; hard-disk drive; System 6.0.2 or higher.

Publisher Microsoft, One Microsoft Way, Redmond, WA 98052; (206) 882-8080.

Reviewing a new version of an extremely popular software package like Microsoft Word for the Macintosh always means addressing two sets of readers: people who have used the earlier version and are interested in upgrading, and those considering the program for the first time.

To those in the second group, we'll say up front that you really should give Word some serious consideration when choosing a full-featured word processor for your Mac. There's a good reason why Word has sold more copies than any other program in its category. At its best, Word lets you get your thoughts speedily down on the page without all the superfluous features that interfere with the basic act of writing. Then when you need ancillary power, it's easy to reach. The improvements in version 5.0 make Word a nearly complete word processing package.

Hot new features

To those of you in both groups let's see how the improvements have helped Word grow from good into excellent software. One of our favorite additions is drag-and-drop editing. Just highlight the text you need to move and drag it with the mouse to the new location—no more cutting and pasting.

Another useful feature is the more sophisticated search-and-replace function. For example, Word will now search up, down, or through your current document—not just down. More important, it now searches or replaces by character or paragraph formatting, including preset styles from the style sheet.

One feature we can imagine using often is the equally sophisticated Find File tool: It searches not only by name or date, but also by optional summary info (such as subject, author, or keywords) that can be attached to the file. As you build up collections of files with Word, this tool will make it easier to keep track of their contents. Another way Word helps you track files is by listing your four most recently opened documents on the file menu, ready to open.

Mail merge, which can be bothersome for many time-pressed business people trying to market their businesses, is greatly simplified with Word's print merge helper. This tool steps you through the merge process, with drop-down menus for inserting both field names and keywords (including complicated if-then-else statements). A classic example of the latter's usefulness is in letters to customers, where you might insert a thank you paragraph for recent payments or a please-pay-up paragraph for deadbeats.

Other additions include a built-in thesaurus and grammar checker, which are okay but a bit on the slow side; an onscreen icon ribbon for fast forming of text (bold or italic, say, and single- or double-spaced; a basic, draw-mode graphics editor for creating and inserting basic graphics, like logos or boxes; and the Symbol command, which makes inserting hard-to-remember graphics—such as the check mark (Option-v) or those Zapf Dingbats fonts—visual by letting you choose them from a chart. We also like the way you can now not only place shaded borders or boxes around paragraphs or cells but add shading as well. Word is a decent substitute for a page-layout program for many kinds of documents.

Word's module method of adding features—such as file converters, the equation editor, and grammar and spell checkers—makes it potentially easy to upgrade this version. Either Microsoft or third-party publishers could come out with new features that you simply install by dragging their files to the Word Command folder.

Getting graphic

You can continue to insert graphics through the Insert Picture menu command, or use the graphic function, which is accessible through an icon on the ribbon bar. Clicking on the icon brings up an Insert Picture Window, in which you can draw graphics to add to your document or paste graphics from the clipboard and enhance them to your liking.

Not perfect yet

As fine a word processor as Word is, it's still not perfect. For instance, why didn't Microsoft include a complete Macro language, as it did for the Windows version of the same program? However, Word's glossary does let you insert frequently used blocks of text, fully formatted, with a couple of keystrokes, which negates some macro needs. Inserting graphics (such as a company logo) is equally easy.

Finally, one more niggling complaint: Word is a memory hog as when self-configured, taking up 2MB instead of the 1MB that is suggested on the programs box.

Worth buying?

Yes, if you have a previous version of Word, upgrade—every change is an improvement. Yes to group two, as well—buy it and you will like what you get. Word delivers a blessed balance between gobs of features and great ease of use.

WordPerfect (DOS)

At a glance This impressive upgrade to an already outstanding program brings true WYSIWYG capabilities to non-Windows users. It also includes some surprising features, such as built-in spreadsheet functions, fax support, and e-mail capabilities.

Ease of use Coaches (interactive, online tutorials and help screens) walk you through unfamiliar tasks using your own data, not canned examples.

Documentation Five manuals and a quick-reference card cover all the bases. The manuals are clearly written and well indexed.

Support WordPerfect continues to offer the best customer support in the industry. The company provides toll-free support Monday through Friday, from 7:00 a.m. to 6:00 p.m. (Mountain time). After-hours support—available every day but Sunday—is not toll free, but it is still available.

Version reviewed 6.0

System requirements 420K 286 PC or higher (520K 386 or better recommended); hard-disk drive with 7MB of free disk space for minimum installation, DOS 3.1 or higher (DOS 6.0 with memory management recommended).

Publisher WordPerfect Corp., 1555 N. Technology Way, Orem, UT, 84057; (801) 225-5000, (800) 451-5151.

Let's face it, due to either financial restraints or an emotional attachment to DOS, not everyone has caught Windows fever. The trouble is, as 486-based PCs drive 386s into extinction and Windows evolves into a full-fledged operating system (Windows NT and the forthcoming Windows 4.0 will not require DOS), more and more software vendors are concentrating their efforts almost exclusively on Windows-based programs. The end result is that staying state-of-the-art with DOS applications is not an easy task—unless you happen to be a WordPerfect user.

WordPerfect 6.0 defines a new standard of excellence for DOS-based applications, offering a number of features and functions normally associated with Windows-based programs, such as sophisticated document viewing and drag-and-drop text-editing functions. The new version provides three different display options: Text, Graphics, or Page mode. Text mode resembles earlier versions of the venerable word processor, although it emulates familiar graphics-based items such as pull-down menus, command buttons, and scroll bars with text characters. The Graphics and Page modes offer many of the same advantages of a true GUI environment, such as true WYSIWYG editing and scalable fonts, without the excessive hardware demands. A practical way to take advantage of these three modes is to enter your text in Text mode, switch to Graphics mode for initial formatting, and then select Page mode (which displays headers, footers, margins, and the like) to fine-tune the overall appearance of your document prior to printing. Both Graphics and Page modes perform adequately (if somewhat sluggishly) on a 286-based PC; a 386 or higher processor is necessary to fully appreciate the program's new capabilities.

Adding it all up

WordPerfect 6.0 offers much more than word processing, including desktop publishing and file management capabilities. There's no real news in this, because quite a few programs offer similar features. What might surprise you is WordPerfect's inclusion of number-crunching capabilities via an integrated spreadsheet. The Table feature includes 98 spreadsheet functions that let you incorporate complex calculations anywhere within a document. Two other features that tend to blur the lines differentiating applications are new built-in fax capabilities and e-mail links, both of which work with any Class 1, Class 2, or CAS-compatible fax/modem. Further contributing to the Windows-like feeling of this impressive upgrade is the ability to open and work with up to nine documents concurrently, making it easy to break complex projects into more manageable components.

Walk with me

Given its robust nature, you might think that WordPerfect 6.0 would be difficult to master. In fact, the new version is actually quite easy to learn—thanks to the addition of Coaches. Coaches differ from traditional online tutorials by incorporating your own data into the lessons. If you want to learn how to apply formatting to multiple paragraphs, for example, a Coach walks you through the formatting process using a series of interactive dialog boxes. Coaches also use the current text—your text—rather than a static example file. Consequently, you produce actual documents while you learn.

Alive and kicking

Despite its impending demise, DOS is still the operating system of choice for millions of PC users. The newest WordPerfect pushes DOS to its very limits, and the electronic view is breathtaking.

—Jack Nimersheim

MacWrite Pro (Macintosh)

At a glance An old standard Macintosh word processor with a new blend of power, flexibility, and ease of use; a choice program for all but the most advanced needs.

Ease of use Excellent. The user interface is logical and uncluttered, and the addition of floating palettes makes manipulating text and graphics enjoyably fast and easy.

Documentation Superb. The tutorial and reference manuals are clearly written, profusely illustrated, and well organized. Online help is quick and clear, though not as detailed as the manual.

Support Claris provides top-notch, toll-call direct support on weekdays only, a toll-free prerecorded hint line, toll-free fax support, and active online forums on both America Online and CompuServe.

Version reviewed 1.0

System requirements 1MB Macintosh Plus or higher; hard-disk drive; System 6.0.5 or higher (2.5MB required for System 7).

Publisher Claris Corp., 5201 Patrick Henry Dr., Santa Clara, CA 95052; (408) 727-8227.

MacWrite Pro is the fourth generation of the original and deservedly popular word processor for the Macintosh. Like its predecessors, this release is intended to provide a broad spectrum of users with all the text-processing power they need and an intuitive interface that is easy to learn and use at an attractive price. I believe that Claris has succeeded admirably on all counts.

Room to spare

Despite adding more than 130 new features, MacWrite Pro runs comfortably with as little as 1MB of RAM under System 6 and 2.5MB with System 7. Owners of PowerBooks and compact Macs such as the Plus, SE, and Classic will appreciate this miserly use of memory resources. All users will enjoy significantly increased speed; no longer will implementing search and replace or global formatting options tempt you to take a coffee break.

Best of all, the added functionality has been accomplished without disturbing the simple and intuitive user interface that was such a strong point with MacWrite II. If anything, user convenience has been enhanced, with buttons to control column layout and screen magnification, floating toolbars for commonly used text, style and graphics commands, and cascading menus for advanced options.

Under the hood

Of all the changes to text-processing operations, I really appreciate the inclusion of style sheets found on most major word processors. Now you can define often-used combinations of formatting (such as outline levels, sections of resumés, scripts, and research reports), name them, and call them up from a menu instead of having to redefine the ruler or copy a previous setting each time. All occurrences of that style within a document are automatically updated. Finally, there is a floating toolbar for styles, so you can call up or change a style setting without using the menu.

Another change is the ability to break a document into several sections. Unlike simple ruler changes, each section can have radically different formats; for example, new headers and footers, different numbers of columns, a new page-numbering sequence, and even a unique title page. Because you can define a section to begin in the middle of a page, it is easy to create a single page where two or more completely different layouts are seamlessly embedded.

A third new concept added to MacWrite Pro is that of frames. Within your basic document, you can define text, table, note, or graphics frames that are independent of the document. Frames can be with or without word wrap, moved and resized freely, made fixed or floating, defined as opaque or transparent, and can use your choice of borders and fills. In combination with other formatting options, frames let MacWrite Pro function quite nicely as a medium-duty desktop-publishing program.

Little goodies

MacWrite Pro's file-translation capabilities have been extended to include Word for Windows and Microsoft Write, which makes sharing documents with Windows users as easy as saving a file. The spelling, thesaurus, and mail-merge functions are faster and easier to use. There are more color options and choices and a greatly expanded range of keyboard commands. These improvements extend the convenience and flexibility of MacWrite Pro to a truly impressive level.

The complaint department

Unfortunately, a few minor things detracted from my overall enjoyment of the program. Search-and-replace operations still require two separate confirmation steps, which slows down repetitive use of this feature considerably. The program marks files that you have worked with as open, even after they have been closed, so you must actually quit MacWrite Pro in order to copy, rename, or duplicate files. Finally, onscreen help is occasionally skimpy; we had to resort to the manual to find out how to enter invisible control characters in the search and replace dialog box.

But overall, MacWrite Pro is an impressive accomplishment. If your work involves long and highly technical documents or requires tables that are longer than one page, you might need the extra features of Microsoft Word or WordPerfect. If you work in a very tight memory environment, Write Now is slightly more memory efficient. But for the vast majority of Mac owners who fall between those two extremes, MacWrite Pro is easily an excellent choice.

—Charles Gajeway

Ami Pro (Windows)

At a glance New version of easy-to-use word processor offering Fast Format (a "paintbrush" that lets you format text with a couple of mouse clicks), customizable icons, automatic envelope printing, formidable tools for desktop publishing, and much more; its only problem is an excruciatingly slow spelling checker.

Documentation User's guide is well written and complete.

Ease of use Easier and more intuitive than any word processor I've used.

Support 24-hour technical support. Toll call, but it doesn't take long to connect with a human. Generally very helpful; support by fax also available.

Version reviewed 3.0

System requirements 2MB IBM compatible; hard-disk drive; EGA, VGA, or Hercules; mouse; Windows 3.0 or higher and DOS 3.1 or higher.

Publisher Lotus Development Corporation, Word Processing Division, 1000 Abernathy Rd. NE, Bldg. 400, Suite 1700, Atlanta, GA 30328; (404) 391-0011, (800) 831-9679.

In the Windows word-processing world, Ami Pro 3.0 comes close to being perfect. In my mind, it stands above Word for Windows and WordPerfect for Windows both in its function and in its speed. And Ami Pro is incredibly rich in features. It has all the top-of-the-line features such as graphing and drawing capabilities, a collapsible outliner, a full-featured macro language, a grammar checker and thesaurus, OLE support, and then some.

What's new?

I could take up the rest of this space just listing new features in Ami Pro 3.0. I found Fast Format the most useful. You simply format one paragraph as you like it, choose the Fast Format icon, and select the text you want to apply that same formatting to. It's faster than using style sheets, because you don't have to remember the name of a style and then use a menu to find it; just click on the Fast Format icon and go. You'll never believe how useful this is until you've used it to standardize your reports, articles, whatever.

Creating style sheets isn't that hard, either. As with Microsoft Word, you can format a paragraph as you want it, and then create a style based on that selected paragraph. To modify a style, just click the right mouse button. Combined with Fast Format, this takes almost all the pain out of formatting and styling documents.

Drag-and-drop delights

Version 3.0 also provides drag-and-drop editing: You can move and copy words, paragraphs, rows, or columns using the mouse. You can also create sets of custom icons, rearrange the SmartIcons (an included set of icons representing frequently used features) in any order, delete icons you never use, and turn the icon button bar into a floating toolbox that can be resized and positioned anywhere on the screen.

I found the custom-icon feature useful for inserting special characters, because I didn't have to reach with the mouse to click at the top of the screen. If icons get in your way, a Clean Screen feature lets you remove the icons, the title bar, the scroll bars—everything except the text—so you have a clean screen and more room to work.

Previewing saves time

There's a new Preview mode that lets you see what's in a document before you open it. In addition, you can do file management in the document viewer—print, search through files, or copy documents without retrieving them to the screen.

Also new in version 3.0 is SmartMerge, a feature that guides you through the mail-merge process. In addition, there's a front-end card-file setup for creating your own phone book and name-and-address lists. This is a vast improvement over WordPerfect for Windows' mail merge, and with the card-file interface, it's also even better than Word's mail merge.

No more address mess

The best aspect of SmartMerge is an Envelope feature, which lets you create and store different return addresses, so you can access both your home and business addresses. Avery label formats are set up and ready to use, too. Ami Pro comes with its own print manager that replaces (and enhances) the Windows Print Manager. You can continue to work while you're printing in the background. The program is also bundled with ATM (Adobe Type Manager), meaning that what you see on the screen will print more quickly and easily.

Attempting to get a share of the WordPerfect market, the new version of Ami Pro comes with not only an online tutorial but also a SwitchKit that lets you use familiar WordPerfect commands.

Good DTP functions

In general, I would also rate Ami Pro 3.0 better for desktop publishing than the other Windows word processors, because of its abundance of refined features. For example, you can do image processing, such as tweaking scanned-image files, right there in the program. Its graphics handling and capabilities are excellent.

I found Ami Pro easier to use right out of the box than any other Windows word processors I've tried. Maybe this is because I'm used to Windows, and in Ami Pro things happen in Windows-like ways. If you're considering switching from a DOS-based word-processing program, this could ease your learning curve and help you master Windows at the same time.

One small problem

Okay, even with all this great stuff I've said about Ami Pro 3.0, I have to admit the spelling checker kept it from getting a perfect rating. Although the spelling checker was upgraded along with version 3.0 to contain financial, legal, insurance, and general business terms, the spelling checker chugs along so slowly that it makes me want to scream. Worse, it stops at every hyphen, even if the hyphenated words are spelled correctly (rumor has it Lotus is aware of that bug and is working to correct it).

If you can live with the snail's-pace spelling checker until it's fixed, Ami Pro is an excellent Windows word-processing program—all things considered, the best I've seen yet.

—Kay Yarborough Nelson

Utilities

Norton desktop for DOS

At a glance Menu-driven file manager (plus a whole lot more) that brings DOS a little closer to Windows, without the excessive hardware demands.

Documentation Two full-size manuals and two supplemental booklets clearly explain the program's impressive range of features; comprehensive index makes information easy to find; context-sensitive help, organized by program command, is always a keystroke away.

Ease of use Extensive menu structure requires some effort to master, but it beats the heck out of that old DOS C: prompt.

Support Symantec offers top-notch technical support; however, the proper way to access this support is not easily found.

Version reviewed 1.0

System requirements 512K 8086 PC or higher; hard-disk drive; CGA, EGA, VGA, SVGA, Hercules; DOS 3.1 or higher.

Publisher Symantec Corp., 10201 Torre Ave., Cupertino, CA 95014; (408) 252-3570, (800) 441-7234.

Let's face it: For at least the next year, not everyone will be using Windows, the current darling of PC operating environments. Many people either lack the equipment Windows requires or, being perfectly satisfied with DOS-based programs they've used for years, perceive no logical reason to switch to all new software just to give a new look to their familiar tasks.

Even DOS diehards, however, must admit that few things in life are as ambiguous as the infamous C> system prompt. Norton Desktop for DOS (NDD) endows your PC with a Windows-like look and feel, without sacrificing the lean-and-mean performance people expect from nongraphical applications.

Maximized menu

NDD superimposes a multilevel menu structure over DOS. Select the disk option and you'll see a pull-down menu listing nearly all disk-related operations, saving you the trouble of having to remember a multitude of cryptic DOS commands. Formatting, labeling, copying; they're all there, a mouse click or keyboard command away.

Many operations don't even require accessing menu options. It's possible, for example, to display directories in cascading windows à la Windows. With this feature, you can copy or move files by simply using a mouse to drag a file name from one directory window to another. The ability to reposition and resize directory windows lets you set up a display ideally suited to the types of tasks you want to perform.

Bag of tricks

NDD offers more than mere command simplification. The package includes a cornucopia of useful tools and utilities. Its calculator, calendar, and scheduler add numeric computation and coordination to your PC capabilities. SmartCan, UnErase, and UnFormat, all terminate-and-stay-resident (TSR) utilities, help guarantee that you'll never again accidentally lose data through an ill-timed delete or format command. By automating correspondence over MCI Mail, Norton Mail puts you in touch with the outside world, while Norton

AntiVirus protects your PC from potentially destructive outside influences. As icing on the cake, Symantec throws in the popular Norton Backup program and Norton Disk Doctor, a collection of system information and file-recovery utilities culled from the company's best-selling Norton Utilities.

Just like fine wine

Although impressive straight out of the box, NDD actually increases in value over time because it can be customized to reflect your needs and work habits. Virtually every aspect of the program, from its top-level menus to its file-manager display, can be modified easily. It even offers quick access to a "naked" system prompt, for DOS diehards.

So, what sacrifices must you make for all this convenience? Surprisingly few. The core Desktop for DOS program—that is, its menu-driven file-management shell—consumes a mere 4.5K of memory. RAM requirements increase as you incorporate additional Desktop TSRs (AntiVirus, SmartCan, and so forth) into your environment, but almost every program and utility returns value in excess of its memory demands.

Simple setup

Installing NDD is a breeze. The program ships on seven 3.5-inch disks and can require up to 8MB of disk space, depending on how many and which of its modules you choose to use. Getting everything installed takes a while, but explicit instructions make the process relatively painless. If problems arise, however, don't be surprised if a support number is nowhere to be found. Here's a tip: Check out the back of the Desktop for DOS User's Manual, after the index, under Customer Support.

Once you are up and running, Symantec's typically comprehensive documentation—two full-size manuals and a pair of quick-start booklets—greatly simplifies the process of mastering the program's copious capabilities. A well-organized help system places online assistance at your fingertips. Command help is also context-sensitive. An index lets you quickly find help on general concepts and other procedures. It's all very intuitive, extremely straightforward, and can be helpful as heck when you're first learning (or need to be reminded of) all of the nuances found in this feature-laden package.

MS-DOS has been on the receiving end of some pretty bad raps down through the years. "It's obtuse," many people say. "How are you supposed to know what to do at the system prompt?" others ask. NDD eliminates these common complaints about the operating system everyone loves to hate and throws in a plethora of pleasing utilities to boot.

—**Jack Nimersheim**

XTree for Windows

At a glance Superior file and disk management utility for Windows.

Documentation Manual is clear and easy to read and use.

Ease of use Excellent; navigating the program is fun and straightforward.

Support Toll call; XTree forum available on CompuServe.

Version reviewed 1.0

System requirements 2MB 286 PC or higher; hard-disk drive; EGA, VGA, SVGA; DOS 3.3 and Windows 3.0 or higher. Cable (not included) required for file transferring from PC to PC.

Publisher XTree, 4115 Broad St., San Luis Obispo, CA 93401; (805) 541-0604, (800) 395-8733.

If you're tired of the same old Windows File Manager, or if you'd like to add more capabilities for doing file-housekeeping chores, you might be interested in XTree for Windows. It installs quickly and adds features that you don't get with Windows, such as file compression (in the popular PKZip format) and a viewer that lets you see into all sorts of different files without having to start the program that created them.

In addition, XTree for Windows comes with XTree Link, which lets you connect two PCs (including a PC and a laptop) and transfer files almost instantly. No more copying to floppies and using SneakerNet (my own feet) to take files from one of my PCs to another!

XTree is so convenient that I hardly know where to start. For example, to save connection-time charges, I often Zip the large files—long book chapters or graphics files—that I send via e-mail. With XTree, I can just drag a file to a Zip folder to compress it.

The program comes with 52 different kinds of file viewers, so I can look at virtually any file I've stored on my hard-disk drive without opening it. That saves a lot of time when trying to check which PCX file is the illustration for a particular article or review. These viewers aren't just for graphics files. You can view word-processing documents (32 different kinds; the only exception I found was VisiWord); Excel, Lotus, and Quattro Pro spreadsheets; and dBase and Paradox databases, without ever leaving XTree. You can add new viewers to XTree as programs come on the market by downloading them from an information utility such as CompuServe.

Once you've got a document in a viewer window, you can also search for a word or phrase. This is a great help for finding a letter, say, that has a mention of "Deerfield Industries" in it. You can't select a bunch of files and search through them for a word or phrase all at the same time, though. Otherwise you'd see a perfect rating for this highly versatile file manager.

—**Kay Yarborough Nelson**

PC Tools for Windows

At a glance A customizable Windows-desktop alternative with a mega collection of useful utilities; you can also view files without opening the programs that created them. Truly drag-and-drop heaven!

Ease of use Excellent and very intuitive. I hardly looked at the manual and found myself creating a custom desktop for a project right away. Extensive online help is provided as well.

Documentation Excellent; the 700-plus-page manual explains each feature in detail and is well-organized, clearly written, and easy to use when you're in a panic.

Support Exemplary phone and fax support, four bulletin boards, America Online and CompuServe forums, TTY/TDD lines for the hearing impaired, FaxBack support for documentation, and an automated voice-response system, all available to registered users 24 hours a day. You even get a Rolodex card with all of these numbers.

Version reviewed 1.0

System requirements 4MB 386 PC or higher; hard-disk drive; Hercules, CGA, EGA, VGA, SVGA; DOS 3.3 and Windows 3.1 or higher.

Publisher Central Point Software, 15220 NW Greenbrier Pkwy., Beaverton, OR 97006-5798; (503) 690-8090, (800) 964-6896.

PC Tools for Windows is a joy to use, starting with its intelligent installation program, which automatically scans your system for viruses and creates an emergency start-up floppy. Central Point Software gives you a shiny, red Emergency label for your new start-up disk, so you can find it easily if you have computer trouble. These are only a couple of the intuitive touches that make this Windows-desktop alternative and system utilities such a pleasure to use.

Goodbye program manager

The first thing you'll notice about PC Tools for Windows is that it's a lot easier to use than the Windows Program Manager and File Manager. Documents, folders, and even drives can reside directly on your desktop so they're available instantly, not buried inside a group. I keep an icon of my letterhead, a fax form, and America Online on my desktop so that I can quickly write a letter, set up a fax, or get online to check my e-mail. I put a floppy-drive icon there too, so I can quickly see what's on a disk with a mouse click.

With PC Tools for Windows, you can easily organize folders into projects. Instead of having a WordPerfect folder, for example, make a folder just for documents that relate to this week's client billing. Put a copy of WordPerfect and your spreadsheet in there, your client name and address list from your database, along with a calculator for totaling figures quickly.

Working on lots of projects at once? Instead of creating one desktop cluttered with folders, create several custom desktops, each set up for a different project, with its own custom colors, button bar, and different background so you can tell them apart at a glance. To switch from one desktop to another, just click in one of the miniature desktops in the MultiDesk window, which displays all your desktops in thumbnail view.

More drag and drop

In Windows you can drag and drop to launch an application, print a document, and copy or move a file, but PC Tools adds about 20 more drag-and-drop items! For example, you can drag a disk icon to the Anti-Virus icon to scan it for viruses, to DiskFix to repair it, or to the improved PC Tools File Manager icon to see what's on it. You can even drag and drop files to compress and expand them within PKZip. I'm still discovering new tricks for dragging and dropping in PC Tools. Here's one: Say you've copied a set of files to your C:\WP51 directory. Minimize the dialog box you used to copy the files; it will become a tiny icon. From then on, any files you drag to that icon will be copied to C:\WP51.

Little touches that count

Renaming icons works the way it should have all along: Just click on the icon and type a new name instead of filling out dialog boxes. In the File Manager, to see or select only files of a certain type, press F3 or F4 and type a name pattern. Erase files with DOD (Department of Defense) Wipe Delete so that even the most dedicated utility, including PC Tools itself, can't get them back. PC Tools will even deinstall itself.

Want more? PC Tools's Optimizer defragments your hard-disk files so they're no longer stored in bits and pieces all over the disk. This tool can run in the background, like a screen-saver, so that your disk is always being optimized. Or use the Scheduler to set up disk sweeps or anti-virus scans at certain times of the day when you're not using your computer.

DiskFix, which repairs disks, is the invaluable tool to use when you get the message "Invalid Drive Specification." (In case you've never seen that message, it's very bad; it means your File Allocation table has been lost, and you can't access your hard-disk drive.) The basic criteria for evaluating a disk recovery tool is not only how well it works but how easy it is to use when you're in a panic. Enter the emergency disk. Restart your computer with it and follow the instructions on the screen instead of nervously flipping through a 1000-page manual.

The Anti-Virus utility checks for more than 1500 viruses, including stealth viruses that masquerade as parts of a program, making them hard to track down. This feature is quite similar to DOS 6's Anti-Virus utility (Microsoft licensed theirs from Central Point), but the PC Tools version has more advanced features. The Backup utility lets you back up to tape and selectively restore backed-up files. DOS 6's Microsoft Undelete was also based on Central Point's utility, but PC Tools's version is heavier duty, letting you undelete directories, not just individual files. Then there's a macro recorder for Windows, a TSR manager, built-in file viewers, a SmartFinder utility that lets you search through the contents of files, a System Consultant that analyzes your system and recommends actions to take to improve performance, and more.

Bottom line

In terms of increasing your productivity, PC Tools is probably the best investment any Windows owner could make. The Anti-Virus, Backup, Undelete, and disk-repair utilities alone make it worth its price, and PC Tools also improves Windows' performance—and your own productivity—by making your Windows desktop much easier to use.

—Kay Yarborough Nelson

Spreadsheets

Lotus Improv for Windows

At a glance A cleverly designed spreadsheet that lets you use words for column and row names, provides easy rearrangement of data, and much more.

Ease of use Very easy to use—once you get used to its unique worksheet.

Documentation Though generally clear, the manual overcomplicates its explanation of items, categories, and groups—the three components of an Improv worksheet; the included animated "tour," however, is a friendly introduction to these new concepts.

Support 90-day unlimited toll-free support, $129 per year after that. The line was busy the first three times I called; when I finally got through, the technicians were well meaning but faltered on a couple of tough questions.

Version reviewed 2.0

System requirements 4MB 386 PC or higher; hard-disk drive; EGA, VGA, SVGA; DOS 3.3 and Windows 3.1 or higher.

Publisher Lotus Development, 55 Cambridge Pkwy., Cambridge, MA 02142; (617) 577-8500, (800) 343-5414.

Lotus Improv for Windows represents the next generation of spreadsheet. Improv uses an unusual but intelligent type of worksheet with several extremely clever enhancements.

Perhaps the most striking difference between a traditional spreadsheet such as 1-2-3 and Improv is that it lets you name your rows and columns rather than using predefined letters and numbers. What does this do to a spreadsheet? Formulas suddenly resemble English. For example, a formula that used to look like +L81+K412 now reads as Profit = Revenue – Expenses. (While other spreadsheets let you construct "plain-English" formulas once you've renamed individual cells, Improv formulas always read with words.)

Flexible data

Another interesting aspect of Improv is that the rows and columns of a spreadsheet aren't fixed. Every row or column (items, as they are called in Improv) is assigned to a category. By dragging icons representing the categories, you rearrange the data. For example, revenue data that's organized by product line can be reorganized geographically, then by customer, then by product profit, and so on.

There's also something very clever about the formulas Improv uses. With Improv, unlike traditional spreadsheets, you don't enter formulas into the cells of a worksheet. You enter them into a separate formula list, called the formula pane. Among other things, the formula pane lets you specify which cell or cells a formula should calculate and, when you click on a formula, it highlights those cells the formula was applied to. This seemingly subtle feature has a huge effect. It means that one Improv formula can do the job of dozens of cell-specific formulas in a traditional spreadsheet. As a result, Improv worksheets are physically smaller and easier to error-check.

Programming power

Another noteworthy aspect of Improv is that it includes a built-in structured programming language called Lotus Script. This is not a macro command language (the kind included with Excel and 1-2-3) but really an extended version of the popular BASIC programming language, with roughly 200 special commands added for dealing with functions specific to Improv and to Windows.

Given all this, the obvious question is this: Is Improv a better spreadsheet than 1-2-3, Quattro Pro, or Excel? Yes and no. Improv's unique worksheet is much better than its competitors'. You'll conclude this after only a few minutes of working with it. Improv's built-in programming language also makes it a serious candidate for people who use spreadsheets as platforms to build other applications. But relative to its more traditionally designed competition, Improv is hampered by a few weaknesses. Its worksheet functions—the set of shorthand formulas you use to calculate such things as loan payments—is better than 1-2-3's, but probably not as good as Quattro Pro's, and clearly not as good as Excel's. Though easier to use, Improv's charting capabilities aren't quite as good as Quattro Pro's or Excel's either. And for power-users, one other relative deficiency of Improv is that it lacks some of the esoteric modeling commands—tools for optimization modeling (such as linear and nonlinear programming), regression analysis, or what-if analysis (including solving for a target value)—that the other programs have recently included.

So, what's the verdict?

When you weigh the program's strengths and weaknesses, it's pretty clear that for most people Improv will be a superior spreadsheet. Its strengths—meaningful column and row names, general formulas, and easy data manipulation—are extremely valuable to spreadsheet users. On the downside, Improv's charting could be better, and the expanded worksheet function set might be overkill. But the same is probably true of the quantitative modeling commands that Improv is missing. After all, if you don't plan to use a spreadsheet for a complex function like linear programming, this deficiency might not matter.

—Stephen L Nelson

Quattro Pro for Windows

At a glance Third of the "big three" electronic spreadsheets; a robust and well-designed program that promises to heat up the Windows war.

Documentation Two large manuals clearly explain Quattro Pro's many features; online help in the standard Windows format makes finding information easy, even from within the program.

Ease of use Quattro Pro's Notebook metaphor makes it much easier to manage complex spreadsheets than the traditional, multiple-display window approach used by the Windows versions of both Excel and Lotus 1-2-3.

Support Borland offers comprehensive support that includes voice phone, fax, its own electronic bulletin board (BBS), and online access through several commercial information services.

Version reviewed 1.0

System requirements 4MB 386 PC or higher (5MB recommended); hard-disk drive; VGA, SVGA; Windows 3.0 and DOS 3.3 or higher.

Publisher Borland International, 1800 Green Hills Rd., P.O. Box 660001, Scotts Valley, CA 95067; (408) 438-8400, (800) 331-0877.

To paraphrase an old joke: What do you call an electronic spreadsheet that requires 4MB of RAM and 10MB of disk space to install and use? "Sir"—that is, if you're the competition (Lotus 1-2-3 or Microsoft Excel) and you're talking about the new Windows version of Borland International's Quattro Pro.

Quattro Pro provides a new twist on the old concept of working with numbers. Unlike Excel and 1-2-3 for Windows, which organize multiple spreadsheets into multiple display windows, Quattro Pro uses what Borland calls a Notebook metaphor. Individual spreadsheets in a Quattro Pro file are represented by separate tabs, running across the bottom of a stylized Notebook display. Initially marked with single letters (A, B, C, and so forth), the tabs can be assigned representative names. Quattro Pro's Notebook metaphor results in a display that's much less cluttered than either the Lotus or Excel screen and multiple spreadsheets that are much easier to access on the fly.

Despite its gargantuan size, Quattro Pro installs faster than most other Windows programs. A self-explanatory installation routine begins by copying several compressed files from the program's distribution disks to your hard disk. Each file then expands for use, after which the original files are erased.

Plenty of extras

It's not hyperbole to say that Quattro Pro for Windows is feature-laden. And most of the features are designed to make even complex procedures easy to master. Consider, for example, the program's Object Inspector menus. Pressing the right mouse button while pointing to an object onscreen brings up a menu of formatting options and other related operations. Call up the Object Inspector while you're pointing to a column heading, for instance, and the resulting menu includes options for adjusting the size of both columns and rows. This feature also allows you to customize, among other things, your overall Quattro Pro environment, a multi-spreadsheet Notebook, single spreadsheets, columns, rows, individual cells, and graphic frames.

Quattro Pro supports a wide range of Windows features. With drag-and-drop editing, for example, you can easily select and then move or copy cell ranges, Notebook pages, graphic frames, and other items, either to a different location within a single spreadsheet or onto a different Notebook page. Toolbars (horizontal and vertical rows of commonly used command buttons) are becoming increasingly popular devices in Windows applications. On Quattro Pro's toolbar, called the SpeedBar, common procedures such as Cut, Copy, Paste, cell alignment, type formatting, and the like are reduced to a single mouse click. If you don't like the default options, Quattro Pro's SpeedBar can easily be customized to contain icons that automate virtually any computing activity.

Convenient for calculations

Performing complex computations in Quattro Pro is especially easy. Start to enter or edit information in a cell, and a Function icon (@) automatically appears in the SpeedBar. Selecting this icon opens a dialog box that provides immediate access to 100 built-in mathematical and database functions: the so-called "at" functions first popularized by Lotus 1-2-3 and now a familiar tool found in almost any spreadsheet.

Creating professional-looking graphs or charts from your spreadsheet data is an equally straightforward procedure. You begin by dragging your mouse over those cells containing the data you want graphically represented. Next, click the Charting button in Quattro Pro's SpeedBar. A series of interactive dialog boxes walks you through all steps required to select one of the numerous graph types and add formatting options (legends, titles, callouts, and so on) to a graph or chart.

Presentations, too

With Quattro Pro, multiple spreadsheets and graphics can be combined into impressive slide shows. Select from a wide range of transition effects—wipes, dissolves, overlays, and more—to turn an otherwise static slide show into a dazzling presentation.

It took Borland a while to fine-tune Quattro Pro for Windows. The final release was delayed several times, for additional development. So, you wonder, was the wait worth it? In a word, yes. Excel and Lotus 1-2-3 have been in a head-to-head battle over the Windows spreadsheet market for a couple of years. Now Quattro Pro promises to heat up the competition.

—**Jack Nimersheim**

Lotus 1-2-3 for Windows

At a glance Lotus 1-2-3 for Windows, release 4, is a top-drawer spreadsheet packed with useful features. This version will appeal to any spreadsheet user, regardless of experience.

Ease of use Very good for a program of this sophistication. Lotus has completely redesigned the program's interface and menu structure, making it much more straightforward and intuitive.

Documentation The tutorial and manuals are organized, well written, and nicely illustrated. Online help is context sensitive and clear. However, Lotus skimped a bit by not providing hard-copy documentation on functions and macro commands.

Support Unlimited support via fax, automated voice, CompuServe, and the Lotus BBS. You get 90 days of direct voice support, after which you must either buy an annual contract or call a 900 number and pay as you go. Lotus's technicians are knowledgeable and polite, but you might have to endure several busy signals and long waiting periods to get through.

Version reviewed Release 4

System requirements 4MB RAM 286 PC or higher; hard-disk drive with at least 15MB free and at least a 2MB Windows swap file; EGA or better display; DOS 3.3 and Windows 3.0 or higher; mouse.

Publisher Lotus Development Corp., 55 Cambridge Pkwy., Cambridge, MA 02142; (617) 577-8500, (800) 343-5414.

The original version of Lotus 1-2-3 for Windows received a lukewarm reception when it entered the marketplace. Most people found the program sluggish and inconvenient when compared with Microsoft Excel. The latest version of 1-2-3 (release 4), however, is a complete top-to-bottom overhaul, and the results are admirable. Spreadsheet users will be delighted with all the convenience, features, speed, and overall functionality that Lotus has packed into its new Windows product.

Everyday ease of use

The improvements are noticeable as soon as you start up the program. The first new feature I noticed was that Lotus has added tabs to the top edge of its three-dimensional spreadsheets, making it easy and convenient to navigate among the various pages of your files. Previous versions of the program denoted each sheet by a letter (for example, the cell address for the fifth sheet, second column, third row, was E:B,3), but the new tabs accommodate up to 15 characters, so that keeping track of where you are and what you are doing is much more straightforward.

Other new enhancements in the basic environment abound. The status indicator at the bottom of the screen contains buttons that control number formats, named styles, fonts, and font sizes. Across the top of the worksheet is an array of SmartIcons that provide single-click access to a variety of commonly used commands (for example, save, print, draw a graph, and so on). If you can't remember what command an icon represents, just place the cursor over it, click the right mouse button, and a definition will appear across the top of the screen.

The menu structure has been revamped and streamlined from the DOS versions, but old hands set in their ways can still use keystrokes. To use the original program commands, simply press the slash key, and the 1-2-3 Classic menu opens above your worksheet.

Heavy-duty features

There are more than 120 new @ functions, many of which greatly expand 1-2-3's statistical analysis capabilities. The program's charting options now provide increased flexibility in creating mixed format charts. A new radar plot, available on the chart-type menu, compares individual data to group results.

Three new features that I found to be extremely useful for business planning and analysis are Backsolver, Solver, and Version Manager. Backsolver lets you specify a desired result for your model, then work backward to see what values are required in one or more variables to achieve that result. Solver allows you to set some basic values, specify operating constraints (for example, production capacity, working capital, and so on), and then find the best solution using the relationships in your model. Version Manager facilitates what-if analysis by letting you establish sets of values for key variables (versions) and then set up different combinations of versions into a scenario to show the effect of such versions and scenarios on worksheet formula results. This capability is extremely valuable in examining how unrelated events can impact your business.

The compatibility question

Release 4 uses a new file format, logically called WK4. A utility that converts files from other programs to the WK3 format is included, but it is decidedly less convenient than direct translation to the WK4 format. You can also open Excel files, though you cannot save your work in the Excel format. Overall compatibility between Excel and 1-2-3 files remains shaky, as a fair number of commonly used functions will not translate.

As a result of the new menu structure and changes to the macro language, macros from previous versions of 1-2-3 must also be translated. Lotus supplies a translation utility and detailed instructions on conversion, but those who rely heavily on macros can look forward to investing a fair amount of time and effort in converting macro libraries (especially if you intend to share files with 1-2-3/DOS or 1-2-3/Mac users).

The bottom line

1-2-3 for Windows, release 4, is definitely the best version of 1-2-3 that I have used—and one of the best spreadsheets around. The program has a different balance of features and performance than Excel, but it is a full-fledged equal in every respect. If integrated charts and graphics are more important to you than Excel's vector math capabilities, release 4 is for you.

—Charles Gajeway

Finance

Microsoft Profit for Windows

At a glance Windows-based, small-business accounting system with accounts receivable and invoicing, accounts payable, inventory, sales tracking, general ledger, simple payroll, and project costing features.

Ease of use Extremely easy to use, even if you're not an accountant.

Documentation User's guide is illustrated and well written.

Support Telephone (toll-free but $2/minute) and 24-hour/seven-day fax and bulletin-board support available from Great Plains Software, Profit's developer.

Version reviewed 1.0

System requirements 4MB 386 PC or higher; hard-disk drive; Hercules, EGA, VGA, SVGA; DOS 3.1 and Windows 3.1 or higher.

Publisher Microsoft Corporation, One Microsoft Way, Redmond, WA 98052; (206) 882-8080, (800) 426-9400.

Profit for Windows is Microsoft's entrée into the crowded but fragmented small-business accounting software market. The basic concept is simple: People don't have to be accountants to keep their records; in fact, to use Profit, all you need to do is fill out standard business forms—checks, invoices, purchase orders, and so on. The program uses these forms to update the business's financial records.

Optimized for Windows

Profit puts Windows's graphical-user interface (GUI) to good use. Onscreen forms closely resemble real ones. Financial records go into a file cabinet; to see a particular type of information, click the appropriate file drawer. Also, instead of using the usual accounting master file or subsidiary ledger to store customer, vendor, employer, project, and inventory information, Profit uses a simple card-file metaphor, much like a Rolodex.

Profit also exploits the GUI to report and summarize a firm's financial information. A feature called Profit Signs brings up quick, visual financial summaries—such as last month's daily cash flow and the most profitable customers and products—with a few mouse clicks.

Remarkably, Profit is even easier to use than Teleware's M.Y.O.B., last year's Editors' Pick. Sure, M.Y.O.B. provides onscreen flow charts that guide you through the accounting, but Profit does all of the accounting work for you, once you've completed the forms.

It's the real thing

Fortunately, despite its forms-based approach, Profit doesn't step away from the traditional accounting model. The program employs all the usual accounting controls and techniques—or what accountants refer to as *generally accepted accounting principles*. Profit insulates people who aren't degreed accountants from the nuts-and-bolts accounting activities and trickier accounting techniques. Note, though, that you and your accountant can still roll up your sleeves and accrue and defer amounts, make adjusting journal entries, and work with contra-asset accounts. (The program's general ledger model, which is where the actual business of accounting for debits and credits occurs, works just as an accountant like me expects it to.)

The limitations

So, is this the perfect accounting product? Well, it's awfully good and will certainly raise the standard for small-business accounting, but it's not perfect. The payroll feature is quite limited. You can use it to prepare a payroll for salaried employees or a handful of hourly employees, but Profit wasn't meant to have all the features of a stand-alone module such as DacEasy Payroll. If your business has complicated payroll-processing or a lot of hourly employees, you might opt for a more powerful solution—or see if Microsoft comes up with a payroll module for Profit.

Also note that while mature and venerable small-business accounting products such as DacEasy Accounting and Peach-tree Accounting don't provide the same ease of use as Profit, they do more. Profit, for example, doesn't provide job costing, fixed assets, or a report-writer module for producing custom reports.

Who should consider using Profit?

Microsoft Profit is meant for businesses that can't get away with a simple checkbook program, such as Microsoft Money for Windows or Quicken—businesses that, say, need to use accrual-based (rather than cash-based) accounting or closely monitor assets and liabilities beyond bank accounts and credit cards. (The checkbook programs work fine for these items.) Profit is probably best suited for the small-business person who has no desire to become an accountant. If you are a CPA, or you enjoy working with ledgers, posting journal entries, and fiddling with debits and credits, you'll probably benefit from one of the other less friendly, but more powerful, applications.

—Stephen L. Nelson

Hi, Finance! (Windows)

At a glance A financial and business calculator for the Windows environment.

Ease of use Point-and-click directness guides you through the program.

Documentation Minimalist, but not really needed; the program is self-explanatory, with full-featured on-screen help.

Support The person who wrote the program, Roger Hoover, answers, ready to inform.

Version reviewed 2.18

System requirements 2MB 386 PC or higher (4MB recommended); hard-disk drive; EGA, VGA, SVGA; DOS 3.3 and Windows 3.0 or higher.

Publisher Brightridge Solutions, 1534 Brightridge Dr., Kingsport, TN 37664; (615) 246-3337, (800) 241-7203.

You can learn a lot from working and playing with Hi, Finance! This comprehensive business and financial calculator teaches how your money grows to retirement, how loans are front-loaded with interest, how to judge whether your investments are performing as they should, and much, much more.

All this education is a sort of bonus; the real purpose of the program is that it does all of these calculations for you. Want to refinance your mortgage? Type in the amount, interest rate, and term of the loans, and Hi, Finance! will display or print out a complete payment and amortization chart.

Want to face down future tuition bills once and for all? Tell the program how much you'll need and when, and it will tell you how much to save monthly.

The program's biggest advantages come not in the financial calculators that, admittedly, many programs now offer, but in the five business utilities included. Product resellers can use Hi, Finance! to calculate optimum markups, add sales taxes, and figure out how many widgets to order for the most economic balance of inventory carrying costs and reordering expenses.

Break-even business analysis

Best of all, the program includes a break-even analysis that can push any would-be entrepreneur to confront his dreams in dollars and cents.

Want to start a newsletter? Say you have $5000 to promote it (fixed costs) and that it will cost you $7.20 a year (variable unit costs) to mail out each subscription that you sell. Plan to price the subscription at $29, and Hi, Finance! shows you—in numbers and graphs—that you will have to sell 229 subscriptions to break even. If you want to make $15,000 a year on the newsletter, you will either have to sell 900 subscriptions or raise the price to $35 and sell 750 subscriptions. Even if you never want to start a newsletter, you can learn a lot about break-even pricing just by entering hypothetical numbers into Hi, Finance!.

Try it before you buy it

Hi, Finance! is distributed as shareware, so if you can find it on a bulletin board or shareware disk, you can try it before you buy it. Pay the fee and register with Brightridge, and you will receive the 80-page manual and learn about the program's regular updates.

—Linda Stern

QuickBooks (DOS and Windows)

At a glance Simple but powerful checkbook program.

Ease of use Very easy, especially if you're already familiar with Quicken.

Documentation Good.

Support Free and unlimited support (toll call); excellent built-in support.

Version reviewed 1.0, DOS

System requirements 640K IBM compatible; hard-disk drive; CGA, EGA, VGA, SVGA, Hercules; DOS 2.1 or higher.

Publisher Intuit, P.O. Box 3014, Menlo Park, CA 94026, (415) 322-0573; (800) 624-8742.

QuickBooks is from Intuit, the same company that's been wildly successful with the popular checkbook program Quicken. In effect, QuickBooks is Intuit's attempt at better, stand-alone record keeping for small service businesses. QuickBooks, like Quicken, lets you print checks and keep a checkbook on your computer, using the familiar checkbook register setup for tracking other assets and liabilities. The big difference between the two programs is that QuickBooks generates invoices and tracks accounts receivable.

Works like Quicken

If you use Quicken, you already know QuickBooks' basic mechanics. You tag checks, as you record them, with particular expense categories. To generate an invoice, you fill out a screen that looks like an actual invoice. To record a deposit, you tag it with a particular income category or you identify which receivable it pays. That's about all there is to it.

QuickBooks provides a remarkable amount of online support. When setting up, for example, QuickBooks asks about the sort of business you're in—accounting, construction, consulting, medical, and so on. Then it creates accounts and income and expense categories tailored for your particular business.

Help with the paperwork

QuickBooks provides three basic invoice forms, suitable for almost any small business: a product invoice for businesses that sell goods, a service invoice for non-professional service businesses, and a professional invoice for businesses that print invoices on letterhead.

QuickBooks compares favorably to other super-charged checkbook programs, like M-USA's CashBiz, for example. QuickBooks gives you more flexibility in terms of invoice generation. QuickBooks' manual and online support are both good. Automatic payroll preparation, not available on QuickBooks, can be met with Intuit's comparably priced, add-on utility, QuickPay (reviewed below).

Precision problems

For some businesses, there is a serious problem with cash-based accounting, which QuickBooks and other checkbook-based programs use. Easy to understand and normally acceptable for reporting profits and losses to the Internal Revenue Service, the cash-based system is fine for small businesses with cash flow closely tied to revenues. But the imprecision of cash-based accounting is a serious weakness for businesses with cash flows related to other factors. You won't know for sure whether you're making or losing money, and if you don't know that, you probably won't be in business very long.

Another criticism I have is that Intuit is publishing comparisons of QuickBooks to more powerful packages like DacEasy and Pacioli 2000. These comparisons show that QuickBooks is much easier to use than these other, more powerful programs. But this isn't a fair comparison; QuickBooks is easier to use because it doesn't do as much.

Who needs QuickBooks?

Despite the shortcomings of cash-based accounting, QuickBooks is a good choice for any small business that can keep its financial records on a checkbook yet wants to generate invoices, too. (If you're currently a Quicken user and are preparing invoices manually, consider getting QuickBooks immediately.) On the other hand, if you've got other mission-critical accounting tasks such as fixed asset accounting, inventory, or job costing, or if your business is complex enough that positive cash flows don't necessarily equal profits, you'll be much better off with one of the full-featured accounting programs like DacEasy Accounting, Pacioli 2000, or Peachtree Complete Accounting.

QuickPay (DOS)

At a glance Add-on payroll module for Quicken and QuickBooks users, which prints payroll checks and sorts out and stores the often-complicated employee deduction information.

Documentation Illustrated user's guide is very thorough, with many example transactions.

Ease of use If you currently use Quicken, you already know most of the mechanics of QuickPay; in general, a very easy program to use.

Support Toll call. Intuit's free and unlimited support is impressive; the technicians are always very responsive and know the product well.

Version reviewed 2.0

System requirements 512K 8086 PC or higher; hard-disk drive; CGA, EGA, VGA, SVGA, Hercules; DOS 3.0 or higher; Quicken for DOS 3.0 or higher, or QuickBooks 1.0.

Publisher Intuit, 66 Willow Pl., P.O. Box 3014, Menlo Park, CA 94026; (415) 322-0573, (800) 624-8742.

If you have employees, you already know the drill: First you have to calculate the gross wages amount for the period—something that can be a lot of work if some employees are hourly, some are salaried, and you've got overtime and commissions to worry about. Then you calculate those pesky payroll taxes and withholding amounts: federal income taxes, Social Security, Medicare, and so on. Next, you calculate any other special deductions for employee benefits—and it doesn't end there, of course. You'll need to periodically remit any payroll taxes you owe or income taxes you've withheld to the federal and state government. On a quarterly basis, you'll need to file state and federal payroll tax returns. Finally, at the end of the year, you have to contend with W-2s, W-3s, and any annual payroll-tax returns.

Fortunately, however, you can make each of these payroll-preparation tasks a lot easier with payroll software. Quicken or QuickBooks users, for example, can use QuickPay, an add-on payroll utility for the popular Quicken checkbook program. To use QuickPay, you need to be running Quicken for DOS version 3.0 or higher or QuickBooks 1.0.

With QuickPay, you easily make gross wages, income tax, Social Security, and Medicare tax calculations—as well as most other payroll-tax calculations. You can effortlessly print payroll checks. With the payroll information that QuickPay collects and stores, you'll find quarterly and year-end payroll-tax return and form preparation a snap.

What's left for you?

The only significant work in using QuickPay involves describing your employees and how you'll pay them in the first place, including the number of personal exemptions they've claimed, their Social Security numbers, the day, frequency and rate of pay, and so forth. If your payroll processing is complicated, this can be quite time-consuming—not because of the program, but because of the complexities inherent in preparation.

Because QuickPay, in effect, lies on top of the Quicken (or QuickBooks) program, QuickPay uses the same basic register for recording payroll transactions. It prints checks and reports in the same way that Quicken does. In fact, if you currently use Quicken, you'll be delighted to discover that you already know most of what you need to know to deftly operate QuickPay. For these reasons, if you're using Quicken for payroll, but you find the process of manually specifying withholding amounts and payroll taxes tedious and time-consuming, you should, without question, invest in the QuickPay utility.

Closing caveat

No, QuickPay is not a substitute for payroll-tax knowledge or bookkeeping skills. In essence, it makes payroll preparation easier by making the calculations for you—not by supplying payroll-tax or bookkeeping knowledge. So, if you're having trouble preparing payroll manually, it might be that you need help with the bookkeeping or payroll taxes involved. And in that case, a fancier, more powerful tool isn't going to make things easier. You'll just create a bigger mess faster.

—Stephen L. Nelson

M.Y.O.B. (Macintosh, Windows)

At a glance Outstanding full-featured accounting program.

Ease of use Ease of use is this program's hallmark.

Documentation Good.

Support Good.

Version reviewed 3.0 (Macintosh)

System requirements 1MB Macintosh; hard-disk drive; System 6.0 or higher. Also for Windows: 5MB IBM compatible (286 or higher); hard-disk drive; VGA, SVGA; mouse; Windows 3.0 and DOS 5.0 or higher.

Publisher Teleware, 300 Roundhill Dr., Rockaway, NJ 07866; (201) 586-2200, (800) 322-6962.

Version 3 of M.Y.O.B. is the newest edition of Teleware's outstanding full-featured accounting system for the Macintosh. (IBM compatible users should note that there is also an equivalent Windows version of the M.Y.O.B. program.)

M.Y.O.B., like many other comparable, full-featured accounting systems, provides for general ledger, accounts receivable, accounts payable, and inventory accounting. The tools are solid in each of these areas. For example, inventory accounting doesn't just track on-hand unit and dollar balances; the tools also support simple manufacturing operations by simultaneously decreasing the units and dollars of raw material or component items while increasing the units and dollars of manufactured items.

M.Y.O.B. also has a checkbook feature. It can be used either in conjunction with the complete accounting package or as a stand-alone module for folks not quite ready to step up to a full-blown accounting package.

Great interface

If it were judged solely on the basis of its feature set, M.Y.O.B. wouldn't be all that remarkable. The program doesn't support such common accounting tasks as payroll, job costing, and fixed assets, which powerhouse programs like Great Plains and Insight Accounting from Peachtree do. (Note that you can tag transactions to associate them with a job or project with M.Y.O.B., but this isn't the same thing as job costing. This capability just amounts to another way to view and summarize financial data.)

So, given this, why do I think M.Y.O.B. is so great? Simple. M.Y.O.B.'s well-designed interface makes using the program much easier than using any of its competitors. This is critically important. Standard accounting packages are notoriously difficult to use because you must understand not only how the software works, but also the principles of business accounting. M.Y.O.B., on the other hand, was designed for people who aren't accountants.

Show it like it is

The data-entry windows, for instance, look like the forms they represent. The invoice data-entry screen imitates an invoice; the check form data-entry screen looks just like a check. Also, M.Y.O.B. provides command buttons arranged into flowcharts so you know exactly the order in which commands should be chosen. For this reason, you shouldn't ever have a problem determining, say, whether you should first print a sales invoice or the sales journal.

Noteworthy, too, is the fact that M.Y.O.B. fully exploits visual representation of real-life metaphors to make accounting easier. The chart of accounts screen, for example, resembles an open file drawer with file folders representing each of the major account categories: assets, liabilities, income, expenses, and so on. The command button for automatically dialing a customer's telephone number shows a picture of a telephone.

Who would benefit from M.Y.O.B.?

Those people who need full-featured accounting programs but don't understand all the nuances and subtleties of double-entry bookkeeping and accrual-based accounting. Only people who both need and can handle the extra horsepower of more complicated packages—or need features such as payroll or job costing—should look elsewhere.

Desktop publishing

CorelDraw 4 (Windows)

At a glance CorelDraw 4 rates as a near must-buy both for professional illustrators and for general business users who take on graphics chores. This latest version adds an animation module, desktop-publishing features, and many other enhancements. Painfully slow execution of some operations rates as the package's most damaging drawback.

Documentation Well written and well illustrated but sometimes terse.

Ease of use Excellent within its class, thanks partly to the program's minimalist approach to graphics tools.

Support Free through CompuServe (Corel Forum). An automated voice system and live technical support are available through a toll number, though the live support often involves long waiting periods. The Corel file-download system also is only a toll call. In addition, as indicated in the CorelDraw manual, technical support is also available for a fee from Software Support Inc.

Version reviewed 4

System requirements 4MB RAM (8MB recommended); 386- or

486-based PC; hard-disk drive; VGA or better; DOS 3.3 and Windows 3.1; mouse or digitizing tablet (including pressure-sensitive tablets).

Publisher Corel Corp., 1600 Carling Ave., Ottawa, Ontario, Canada K1Z 8R7; (613) 728-8200, (800) 772-6735.

Past versions of CorelDraw have managed with admirable success to satisfy the needs of professional illustrators as well as people who use graphics in their businesses but can't afford to spend the time learning one package for illustrating, another for image editing, and a third for charting. CorelDraw 4 succeeds in the same feat, but even more so. The collection of enhancements and new features rates as no less than remarkable—both in their magnitude and range—for anyone who needs a tool set for any design need, from a slide for a presentation to a brochure.

A two-dimensional animation module, CorelMove, tops the list of new additions, at least in terms of gee-whiz value. You can expect to hit bugs fairly often in this initial release, but the module is relatively easy to learn and use. With it, you can certainly add flair to your presentations. Corel has also enhanced its six previously existing modules. The CorelChart module, for instance, now supports all CorelDraw fills (including patterns and textures) and outlines. Corel Photo-Paint benefits from a redesigned user interface and the ability to apply impressionistic or pointillistic styles to images. Both the Photo-Paint and CorelTrace modules now support direct image scans via TWAIN compliance.

Vastly expanded prepress controls have been added across modules, at long last giving graphics professionals the capability they need to produce color separations and other high-quality output. Of course, the CorelDraw drawing module has always rated by far as the package's richest component, and a lengthy list of improvements seems to ensure that it will stay that way. Most notably, the module includes support for documents of as many as 999 pages and boasts a slew of desktop-publishing-like features. Instead of having to arrange short strings of text, for instance, you now have as many as 4000 characters in a single frame, which can be placed on the page and manipulated much as you would in a DTP program. To flow text from one frame to another, simply link the two.

Other welcome additions include the ability to define and save styles, which control the attributes of graphics or text, and templates, which define the layout of a page. The list of new features extends to support as many as 99 levels of undo, new types of lines and fills, dimensioning, and the ability to attach information to objects and maintain a database of that information. If you have a CD-ROM drive, you'll appreciate the 750 TrueType and Type 1 fonts and more than 18,000 clip art images and symbols (many of them in color) that ship on CDs.

Two drawbacks bear mention: CorelDraw 4 performs much slower than version 3 on some chores—to the point of seeming ridiculous—and the abundance of new codes seem to have introduced many new bugs. Even so, CorelDraw 4 offers powerful features, like ease of use, and such economy of price that you'd be hard-pressed to find a better deal.

—**Mitt Jones**

PhotoFinish (Windows)

At a glance Edits scanned images; paints.

Documentation Excellent tutorial and examples; good explanations.

Ease of use Easy; Windows-type intuition. But there's a lot here to learn.

Support Free and helpful; toll call; 24-hour bulletin board service available.

Version reviewed 1.0

System requirements 2MB IBM compatible; Windows 3.0 or higher; mouse or other pointing device; graphics card; EGA, VGA, SVGA, XGA with 16-bit high color or 24-bit true color card.

Publisher ZSoft, 450 Franklin Road Suite 100, Marietta, Georgia 30067; (404) 428-0008.

PhotoFinish is a powerful image-editing tool for retouching and painting images that have been scanned in or previously saved as a graphics file. It's like having an electronic darkroom on your desktop.

The program installs easily under Windows in about half an hour; most of that time is spent unpacking files. Compatible with 47 different flatbed and hand-held scanners, PhotoFinish lets you carefully control scanning operations. If your scanner is not on the provided list, you'll have to use your scanner's own supplied software to create a file, and then use Photo-Finish for advanced retouching. You can also edit images created by video capture boards and paint programs.

Format heaven

File formats that can be input include PCX, BMP, GIF, MSP, TGA, and TIF. After using the program, files can also be saved in Encapsulated PostScript (EPS) format for delivery to a service bureau, but these files cannot be read back into the program for further editing.

Supposedly, PhotoFinish lets you open up to eight different images simultaneously and cut and paste among them. But my 386SX with 4MB of RAM ran out of memory after stacking five images. The manual vaguely states that your computer should have "sufficient RAM to run Windows in the mode you want." I'd guess 2MB is the minimum. My only real complaint, which undoubtedly goes hand-in-hand with heavy-duty graphics software, is that for some operations my 25 MHz SX was painfully slow.

Special effects

PhotoFinish offers one very powerful cutting tool—a "magic wand" that attempts to outline areas that have similar colors. I say "attempts" because it takes some experience to use this properly—subtle variations can throw it off. A "color tolerance" adjustment allows you to specify the range of variation. Each time the computer analyzed the color picture with the magic wand, I had to wait about half a minute. That made the learning curve frustratingly slow.

But another powerful feature, the "color/gray map," worked quite quickly on my computer and provided endless fun. The gray map is actually a graph that correlates numbers stored in the computer file to the brightness of each pixel. Normally this graph is a 45-degree line, reflecting proportional increases. But, using the mouse, you can change the curve—even to a squiggly line if you want—and convert certain shades wherever they appear.

If an image is too washed out, for example, you can add contrast just by adjusting the map for a larger range of dark grays. For color images, you can separately program curves for red, green, and blue response. Having been a photography buff since high school, I was quite impressed. Best of all, these visual effects for black and white images could be previewed almost immediately, while color images took just a few seconds.

Save in many ways

You can readily convert among 24-bit color, 256-color palette color, and black and white in gray scale, halftone, or line-art formats, and can store files in any format (except the obscure and outdated Microsoft MSP format, which can be input only). In addition to the usual sorts of adjustments you'd expect to find for brightness, contrast, palette, and so on, advanced filter operations allow you to add picture noise (graininess), diffuse the image, create motion blur, sharpen edges, remove spots, blend images, and create mosaic distortions, among other effects.

To add interesting twists to your graphics documents, you can rotate images in 90-degree increments, or by plus-or-minus 5 degrees for minor alignment errors. Unfortunately, you can't rotate by any number of degrees you choose, or rotate text to fit at any angle—you're limited to the 90-degree increments. Of course, you can flip and invert images to your heart's content.

You can paint, too

PhotoFinish also includes the full complement of standard paint tools—spray can, paint roller, gradient paint roller, tile pattern paint roller, airbrush, curves and polygons. It has excellent brush adjustability and color replacement. For example, an eyedropper tool picks up a specific color and shade from the screen, for replication elsewhere. Some of the more exotic retouching tools include a "smudge spray can" and a "smear paintbrush."

On top of all this, a separate memory-resident utility lets you capture a screen from any Windows application and make an image file from it.

As for the manual, what it lacks in explanation it makes up for with excellent visual examples of how various effects can be used. A superb, separate tutorial guide teaches you the art of photo retouching using a woman's face that is supplied as a sample file—topics include animating her eyes, highlighting her hair, smoothing skin, and eliminating blemishes.

Overall, PhotoFinish is an excellent, advanced image-manipulation package. It's not a paint program for rank novices, but anyone who has done light desktop publishing will appreciate PhotoFinish's features. Its ability to work with numerous standard file formats makes it suitable for use with video graphics and multimedia, as well as with print media. But be forewarned: your computer should have a bit of muscle, and to use PhotoFinish to its fullest extent, your scanner should be compatible.

Database managers

FileMaker Pro (Windows, Macintosh)

At a glance New version of popular Mac database, now available for Windows; the most practical and productive database I have used. A near-perfect balance of power and ease of use.

Documentation Excellent tutorial and fine online help system; the reference manual is profusely illustrated and generally well-written, but occasionally fragmented.

Ease of use Much better than average for a database with this power; you will be up and running in a couple of hours, and tackling tough projects in short order.

Support Just about the best around, with telephone technical support augmented by toll-free fax and prerecorded answer lines, and user forums on America Online and CompuServe.

Versions reviewed 2.0 (Windows and Mac)

System requirements Windows: 2MB 286 PC (4MB 386 PC recommended); hard-disk drive; mouse; VGA, SVGA; DOS 3.1 and Windows 3.0 or higher. Macintosh: 1MB Macintosh or higher (2MB with System 7); hard-disk drive; System 6.0 or higher.

Publisher Claris Corp., 5201 Patrick Henry Dr., Santa Clara, CA 95052; (408) 727-8227, (800) 325-2747.

Really good software is deceptive. It starts out simple and intuitive, not overwhelming you with power and complexity. Then, as you attempt more and more complex tasks, the program doesn't run out of steam, but keeps on helping you do your job better.

FileMaker has been the top-selling Macintosh database program for a long time, and deservedly so. From the beginning, FileMaker has offered more power, speed, and flexibility than most form-manager programs, but with very little of the complexity associated with powerful relational software (which lets you link multiple databases with common fields). Now Claris has developed a Windows version. I was eager to start digging into both.

Platform equality

I found the Windows and Macintosh versions of FileMaker to be essentially identical. Not only are data files 100 percent compatible (as long as Mac users follow the more stodgy MS-DOS file-name conventions), but the programs look and work alike, right down to many of the keyboard command shortcuts.

I was nervous getting started, remembering past problems with various database programs. Right from the beginning, though, the process was easier with FileMaker. The program guides you through the task at hand, and never presents an overwhelming variety of choices. Often-used commands and tools are available at all times, while more complex operations are handled with cascading menus and dialog boxes. Each operating mode—browse, layout, find, and preview—has its own set of tools and menu choices, helping you focus on what you're doing instead of getting frazzled by an overstuffed menu and a cluttered toolbox.

FileMaker uses the graphic operating environment to great advantage. The layout screen works like a simple drawing program, with fields treated as variable text or graphics objects that can be freely dragged and dropped, sized, and mixed with fixed text and graphics to create strikingly attractive reports.

Fields of glory

FileMaker has two exceptionally useful kinds of fields. The repeating field extends a normal data field, allowing it to hold several different entries. Functioning like a database within a database, this capability enables you to track related items in a field separately, such as inventory on a shirt that comes in three colors, test scores by subject, or invoice payments by customer.

The lookup field compares specified fields in the current file and another FileMaker file, and retrieves data from the second file if there is a match. For example, if the customer code you enter into your invoice file matches a field in your mailing list file, lookup fields can automatically retrieve the customer's name and address. This limited but powerful relational capability lets you save time and avoid errors by concentrating key data in a single common source.

It's in the script

A new and extremely powerful feature in version 2.0 is ScriptMaker, a macro language that allows you to automate tedious or time-consuming procedures. Activating the ScriptMaker command opens an editing window, where you can choose commands from a master list, assign options, then edit and reorder your final list. A finished script can be included in the Scripts menu, assigned to a button on your layout (any screen object except a field can be turned into a button), or both. For example, I easily wrote a simple script that instructs my billing file to look up the latest prices from my inventory file, and a more complex script that selects all open invoices more than 30 days old, then prints collection letters and customer statements.

Some dislikes

While the reference manual was good, it didn't measure up to the tutorial. I frequently had to look in more than one place for an answer, and while the writing was thankfully nontechnical, it was a bit long-winded and occasionally on the fuzzy side. Claris usually does a better job.

Because I'm a Macintosh user, I love having Macintosh keystroke commands in FileMaker. Dedicated Windows users, however, will probably find them annoyingly unfamiliar. Claris should have provided standard Windows key commands as a user-selected option, like the alternate navigation keys in Excel.

Then there's the auto-save function, which is also subject to debate. Sure, it might save your neck if your system crashes, but a more likely scenario has you wishing you could erase that 15-minute mistake you just made and start over.

The worst problem, however, is that the program is sensitive to unusual file operations. The Macintosh version crashed abruptly when I inadvertently tried to use a damaged file, and the Windows version crashed the entire system when I tried to switch to the file manager after launching Windows from PC/GEOS instead of DOS. While these were unusual situations, I subtracted a half-star from FileMaker's rating because the program keeps data files open while they are in use, and such crashes could damage them beyond repair. Until Claris fixes these problems, you should try to run your computer in a normal configuration, and make sure to back up all of your important files.

The final word

All in all, FileMaker is a fast, friendly, and powerful program that will help you handle a wide range of tasks with confidence. It's the best all-around database program I have used to date, and would make a fine choice for all but the simplest or most complex needs.

Charles Gajeway

Integrated software

ClarisWorks for Windows (Windows, Macintosh)

At a glance ClarisWorks, a popular Macintosh program, finally migrates over to the PC side of the fence. The Windows version of this package offers truly integrated access to a word processor, spreadsheet, database, drawing tools, and communications.

Documentation A getting-started booklet walks you through installation and ClarisWorks for Windows's online tutorial. Comprehensive online help is always available.

Ease of use ClarisWorks for Windows complements the already familiar Windows interface by providing easy access to features across the individual components of its integrated modules. Menu options automatically change as you work in various modules.

Support Claris provides several ways to contact technical support. Direct support is not toll free, but an 800 number provides automated answers to commonly asked problems. The company also sponsors forums within several online services, including America Online and CompuServe. An 800 fax line lets you submit queries 24 hours a day, seven days a week.

Version reviewed 1.0v1 (Windows)

System requirements 2MB 386 PC or higher; hard-disk drive; DOS 3.0 or higher and Windows 3.1.

Publisher Claris Corp., 5201 Patrick Henry Dr., Santa Clara, CA 95052; (408) 727-8227.

Few terms generate as much confusion as integrated software. Too many so-called integrated packages are actually a hodgepodge of diverse program modules that, at best, share information with one another by way of complicated import/export procedures—and sometimes through activities as rudimentary as a traditional cut-and-paste approach. With the recent migration to DOS territory of ClarisWorks—long a popular choice among Macintosh owners—Windows users now have access to a truly integrated package that adds a few nuances of its own to the familiar Windows design.

ClarisWorks for Windows provides direct and immediate links among its various modules. As you create a text document, for example, selecting the appropriate icon from an onscreen toolbar lets you easily insert a new frame containing the familiar rows and columns of an empty spreadsheet. Accomplishing this doesn't require that you close one program module and open a second, as is the case with other integrated packages. Rather, a working spreadsheet integrates (there's that word again) directly into your document. Once this spreadsheet-within-a-document exists, you fill its individual cells with values, formulas, functions—anything you'd normally use when crunching numbers. It's even possible to mark specific spreadsheet cells and use their contents to create a chart, which then becomes another frame within your text document.

ClarisWorks for Windows packs a lot of power into each program module. The spreadsheet, for example, includes more than 100 built-in functions, formulas, and other features, including the ability to create 3-D charts. The word processor contains enough formatting options to double as a rudimentary desktop publisher. Charts can include titles and legends and can be flipped or rotated on demand. The program's spell checker is accessible from within any module, and a thesaurus stands ready to help you find the perfect word to communicate your thoughts.

The ClarisWorks for Windows database module is modeled after FileMaker, Claris's popular database manager, which was also recently released in a Windows version. Because the package runs under Windows, the databases aren't limited to the typically boring data entry screens found in many programs. Boxes, lines, and formatted text are only a few of the visual enhancements available to spruce up your database displays.

Claris went to great lengths to allow ClarisWorks to coexist peacefully with the rest of your software arsenal. A built-in conversion feature automatically imports files created with a number of popular word processors, spreadsheets, and database managers, including Microsoft Word, WordPerfect, Excel, Lotus 1-2-3 (the DOS version), and dBase. Supported graphic formats include PCX, TIFF, and BMP files.

Listing communications as one of ClarisWorks' features is somewhat deceptive. In fact, selecting the communications module opens Windows' own Terminal accessory—an anemic offering, at best. Should you desire a complete suite of PC applications, I suggest getting a stand-alone Windows-based communications package.

Nothing I could recommend would improve ClarisWorks' ease of use. Well-written and indexed documentation explains every program option clearly. During installation, you can elect to include an online tutorial, designed to walk you through the creation of an integrated file incorporating elements of each ClarisWorks' module.

Perhaps the best news of all is that the package fits its large array of impressive features into a mere 3MB of disk space. A single stand-alone Windows application often consumes several times this amount. ClarisWorks for Windows replaces four such applications, and it demands only minor sacrifices in the critical areas of power and performance to do so.

—Jack Nimersheim

100 GREAT PROGRAMS UNDER $100

No, money isn't everything, but who's going to argue if you can save some dough? Software potentially runs into big bucks when you're setting up or expanding your library. So we went on a search for great programs that cost less than $100.

Utilities seem to dominate the under-$100 software arena. But we also found a surprising number of business and productivity products—spreadsheets, databases, graphics programs, and so on—in this price range, including nine choice shareware and freeware packages.

Shareware and freeware are applications and utilities that usually aren't commercially available but can be found on online services and bulletin boards or sent through the mail. Freeware is free for the taking, but shareware authors ask that if you use their product, you send them the requested fee.

About the prices

Some of the products reviewed here have suggested retail prices (or list prices) of more than $100. However, nearly every computer store or mail-order company significantly reduces the cost of products to its customers, sometimes by as much as 50 percent. The software listed below is categorized by the prices that can be found through stores like Office Depot and mail-order companies like PC Zone and MacConnection.

$100 and under

PC-File (DOS), ButtonWare, (206) 454-0479, (800) 528-8866.

Choose between graphic- and text-based operation to design your database. Search and retrieve, as well as easy mail-merge management and mailing-label production, is PC-File's strong suit.

TouchBase (Mac), After Hours Software, (818) 780-2220.

This address-book database desk accessory provides rapid, multicriteria searches. Some fields are customizable, autodialing is built in, and printing layout options include a double-sided layout for address books.

FAXGrabber (Windows), Calera Recognition Systems, (408) 720-0999.

This easy-to-use optical character recognition (OCR) software converts incoming high-quality faxes into text files for editing.

Aldus Personal Press (Mac), Aldus Corp., (619) 558-6000, (800) 333-2538.

From the company that brings us one of the top desktop publishers comes the tops in midrange category. Personal Press has basic word-processing features, good half-tone and graphics controls, style-sheet support, and spot-color printouts. Template making and designing are fast with the help of the AutoCreate feature.

Freedom of Press Light (Windows), Custom Applications, (508) 667-8585, (800) 873-4367.

Freedom of Press Light lets you print PostScript-quality printouts on non-PostScript printers, and the results are impressive. The difference between the full-fledged version and Light is the number of printers supported. Adobe Type Manager output is supported, as are Type 1 fonts.

Graphic Impact (Windows), Autodesk Retail Products, (206) 487-2233, (800) 228-3601.

Designed for beginning and occasional presentation makers, Graphic Impact creates professional onscreen, overhead, and 35mm shows. The button bar, split screen, clip art, templates, and thumbnail slide sorter get you presenting almost immediately.

Procomm Plus for Windows DataStorm Technologies, (314) 443-3282.

Procomm includes sample log-in scripts for CompuServe, MCI, and others. This version's interface is customizable, and has 40 programmable "metakeys" that run a variety of macros with one click.

PICTure This (Mac), FGM Softworks, (703) 478-9881, (800) 783-7428.

PICTure This translates PC graphics files (PCX, TIFF, CompuServe GIF, and many others), Unix, Amiga ILF/ILBM, Mac EPS, and MacPaint files (among others) into PICT 1 and PICT 2 files. An ideal addition to a desktop publisher's arsenal that will help save money on color separations.

Express Publisher (DOS and Windows), PowerUp Software Corp., (415) 345-5900, (800) 851-2917.

Ideal for the beginning or occasional desktop publisher, the DOS version of Express Publisher includes excellent online design assistance. Text and graphics are easily manipulated in both versions, and numerous attractive page and document templates help get you started.

Collage Complete (DOS and Windows), Inner Media, (603) 465-3216, (800) 962-2949.

Screen captures are ideal for illustrating instructional manuals or presentations. Collage Plus captures PCX, TIFF, and BMP graphics files with one keyboard command. You can also preview your captures or edit them in a graphics application.

AccessPC (Mac), Insignia Solutions, (415) 694-7600, (800) 848-7677.

This utility lets your Macintosh Desktop mount and access DOS disks (including PC removable cartridges) as if they were Mac disks. AccessPC also lets you assign Mac Type and Creator information to a DOS file so you can open the file in a specified Mac application without having to go through Apple File Exchange.

FAXability Plus (Windows), Intel Corp. Personal Computer Enhancement Division, (800) 538-3373.

FAXability Plus gives you easy control over transmitting and receiving faxes from your PC. Sending cover sheets and faxes is as easy as printing, and most functions—such as setting up multiple phone books, or setting up how your computer tracks, sends, and receives faxes—are customizable.

QuickBooks (DOS), Intuit, (415) 852-9696, (800) 624-8742.

QuickBooks is ideal for small businesses that don't want to fuss with accounting terms and trials but need more financial-management functions than those offered by checkbook programs such as Quicken. If you can write a check and fill out invoices, QuickBooks does the rest.

BizPlan Builder (DOS, Windows, Mac), Jian Tools for Sales, (415) 941-9191.

Combined with a compatible word processor and spreadsheet, BizPlan Builder helps you create bank-ready business plans. A good chunk of the manual is dedicated to honing your goals and objectives, and streamlining management, marketing, and financial planning.

DacEasy Instant Accounting (DOS), DacEasy, (214) 250-3752, (800) 322-3279.

Flexibility is the key attraction to Instant Accounting. It's packed with modules covering general ledger, accounts receivable, accounts payable, cash management, inventory, product assembly, purchase orders, billing, budgeting, graphics, forecasting, and customizable reports.

Nolo's Partnership Maker (DOS), Nolo Press, (510) 549-1976, (800) 992-6656.

Nolo's Partnership Maker prepares legal partnership agreements for almost every state, and its 84 standard and alternative contract clauses and online legal help assist you in painlessly completing a customizable contract.

PrintCache (DOS and Windows), LaserTools Corp., (510) 420-8777, (800) 767-8004.

Do you hate waiting for your printer? PrintCache works in the background to spool your print jobs to RAM or disk, making printing almost instantaneous. In Windows, PrintCache replaces and outperforms the Print Manager.

LotusWorks (DOS), Lotus Development Corp., (617) 577-8500, (800) 343-5414.

Our favorite of the DOS integrated packages, LotusWorks proves its value with a striking spreadsheet module, near-DTP-quality word processor, graphics applications, communications module, and sophisticated flat-file database.

Lotus Organizer (Windows), Lotus Development Corp., (617) 577-8500, (800) 343-5414.

This realistic time and contact manager not only visually impresses with its colorful calendar, to-do list, address book, and memo pad but also organizes your time and contacts logically and seamlessly. Information from an appointment can, in one click, be attached to other applicable activities.

Virex (DOS and Mac), Datawatch, (919) 490-1277.

To destroy viruses and prevent them from attacking your system, Virex is an excellent, easy-to-use choice. It stands by, unnoticed, in the background until it catches any suspicious activity.

Windows Draw Plus OLE (Windows), Micrografx, (214) 234-1769, (800) 733-3729.

Complete with 2600 clip-art files, Windows Draw makes creating documents and illustrations easy and intuitive. A fine program for drawing novices to learn and grow with.

Stacker (DOS and Windows), Stac Electronics, (619) 431-7474, (800) 522-7822.

If you've run out of room on your hard-disk drive, the software-only version of Stacker can save you money by doubling your current drive's storage capacity. Once installed, you need never concern yourself with Stacker again—performance isn't noticeably affected, and suddenly you have twice as many megabytes.

Business Management Toolkit (DOS, Windows, Mac), Palo Alto Software, (503) 683-6162, (800) 229-7526.

Working with a compatible spreadsheet, Business Management Toolkit helps you develop budgets, financial strategies, and business plans. The manual guides you through each step and every tactic.

Norton Desktop for DOS Symantec Corp., (408) 253-9600, (800) 441-7234.

An intelligent graphical interface for DOS, allowing flexible file and disk management through mouse-accessible menus and keyboard shortcuts. All DOS functions are made easier by menu commands.

Norton Desktop for Windows Symantec Corp., (408) 253-9600, (800) 441-7234.

This front end for Windows improves file management by placing drive icons on the desktop and provides a customizable applications toolbox. Thrown in are backup, anti-virus, file-find, and data-repair utilities.

Norton Utilities (DOS and Mac), Symantec Corp., (408) 253-9600, (800) 441-7234.

Norton Utilities is a worthwhile investment, with valuable utilities from emergency disk and file rescue, to disk optimization and disk backup. Floppier, an included utility, lets you copy or format multiple disks; WipeInfo securely destroys data you don't want recovered, and Encrypt protects files from the curious.

Publish It! Easy (Mac), Timeworks, (708) 559-1300, (800) 535-9497.

Along with a built-in word processor (with spell checker and thesaurus) and simple database, Publish It! Easy's midlevel desktop-publishing capability is a pleasure to use. Make impressive newsletters, posters, and other promotional materials, and use its slide-show feature to create business presentations.

LapLink Pro (DOS), Traveling Software, (206) 483-8088, (800) 343-8080.

If you have to transfer files from one computer to another, LapLink Pro can make it a painless process. This software and cable package also provides disk and file management, remote program installation, text editor, subdirectory synchronization, and file compression during transfer.

XTree for Windows XTree Co., (805) 541-0604, (800) 964-2490.

Moving and managing files, directories, and disk volumes are made easy with XTree for Windows. View files from more than 50 applications, even if you don't have the programs on disk. A new feature, XTree Link, lets you copy, view, move, and manage files between two computers.

XTree Gold (DOS), XTree Co., (805) 541-0604, (800) 964-2490.

This smooth DOS disk manager and shell makes file management and manipulation quick and easy. View all disk files in a single list, rename directories, sort files by a number of variables, view files, and more. A great way to get away from the C: prompt.

$75 and under

DiskTop (Windows and Mac), CE Software, (515) 224-1995, (800) 523-7638.

If you're tired of double-clicking your way through layers of folders or directories to find your applications, DiskTop might be your answer. This desk accessory/utility launches applications and makes time-saving group copies and other moves, all from one dialog box.

QEMM-386 (DOS and Windows), Quarterdeck Office Systems, (310) 392-9851, (800) 354-3222.

Managing your PC's memory can be confusing, to say the least. If you run DOS and Windows on your multimegabyte computer, QEMM chooses the optimum configuration for your system, then automates management of lower-DOS, expanded, extended, and high-DOS memory.

CPU (Mac), Connectix, (415) 571-5100, (800) 950-5880.

This collection of 13 super utilities for Macintosh PowerBooks includes a cursor locator, battery-life management, screen saver specifically for LCD screens, programmable hot keys, and security mode to protect your computer from outsiders.

Procomm Plus (DOS), Data Storm Technologies, (314) 443-3282.

Log on to services fast with Procomm's sample log-in scripts for CompuServe, MCI, and others. The straightforward interface helps you customize your telecommunications.

WinFax Pro Windows Delrina Technology, (408) 363-2345, (800) 268-6082.

One-button faxing is an attractive proposition, but WinFax Pro has more. A favorite is the capability to include multiple faxes in a single call (saving on phone charges). AnyFax OCR, included, converts high-quality received faxes to editable word-processing files pretty reliably, and faxes can be annotated onscreen with text and drawing tools.

Adobe Type Manager (Windows and Mac), Adobe Systems, (415) 961-4400, (800) 833-6687.

This utility not only makes your type look smooth onscreen but is invaluable for those wanting to print PostScript-type fonts on QuickDraw printers such as an ImageWriter II or HP DeskWriter (for the Mac version). Windows users will also appreciate the ability to view fonts as they actually look before printing.

StuffIt Deluxe (Mac), Aladdin Systems, (408) 761-6200.

StuffIt is perhaps the most popular file-compression and archiving utility for the Macintosh, and this commercial version (it started out as shareware; the company still maintains the shareware version) proves its worth. StuffIt Deluxe compresses single or multiple files and can create self-extracting archives. Ideal for those who upload and download lots of files between computers or online services.

Automap—The Intelligent Road Atlas (DOS and Windows), Automap, (602) 873-2400, (800) 545-6626.

Automap searches its database of more than 350,000 miles of roads to give you routes to anywhere in the United States. Automap gives you specific driving instructions, including mileage and landmarks (for example, go two miles, then turn left after the Holiday Inn) to ensure you get to your destination.

Direct Access for Windows Fifth Generation Systems, (504) 291-7221, (800) 873-4384.

This automatic menuing utility groups applications into logical groups (such as word processing or utilities). Customized menus are easily created. A usage-tracking feature keeps track of how long each application is used, or how long a user has been working—good for people who bill clients by the hour.

CanOpener (Mac), Abbott Systems, (914) 747-4171, (800) 552-9157.

This interesting utility reads and displays text, MacPaint, PICT, EPS, TIFF, RIFF, and MacDraw II files even if you don't have the application that created the files. CanOpener is a practical addition for those who use a lot of different files from a variety of applications (such as graphics and text in a newsletter), but who don't have a lot of applications.

GeoWorks Desktop (DOS), GeoWorks, (510) 644-9362.

Desktop is a slick, quick, useful combination of Windows-like accessories featuring a great DOS menu, easy file management, and telecommunications. The program is a good choice for those with 8088 and 286 machines or who don't want to make the switch to Windows software.

BiPlane (Mac), Night Diamonds Software, (714) 842-2492.

If it's a basic Mac spreadsheet you need, it's a basic spreadsheet you get—and more. BiPlane includes charting capability as well as a desk-accessory version, and is an incredible value.

WinSpeed (Windows), Panacea, (603) 437-5022, (800) 729-7420.

Windows users will benefit from WinSpeed's capability to speed up your video performance as much as threefold. While it works only with specific video boards, the speed increase is a worthwhile addition.

WealthBuilder by Money Magazine (DOS and Mac), Reality Technologies, (215) 387-6055, (800) 346-2024.

If financial planning on your computer is your passion—especially if you dabble in long-term investments—WealthBuilder is an invaluable tool. Instinctive and easy to use, WealthBuilder aids in tracking your increasing riches.

Business Plan Toolkit (DOS, Windows, Mac), Palo Alto Software, (503) 683-6162, (800) 229-7526.

Business plans and forecasts are easy to create with this mix of Excel macros and templates. The well-written and well-illustrated manual helps you write business summaries, develop strategies, and create supporting charts and graphs to illustrate finances.

Correct Grammar (DOS, Windows, Mac), WordStar International, (415) 382-8000, (800) 523-3520.

If you're worried about the grammatical structure of your documents, Correct Grammar can put you at ease. This application analyzes your documents and checks for clichés, redundancies, passive sentences, and more.

SAM (Symantec AntiVirus for the Mac), Symantec Corp., (408) 253-9600, (800) 441-7234.

Fighting viruses is easy with SAM 3.5, a slickly designed virus protection and prevention utility. SAM checks for suspicious activities such as potentially dangerous code changes (even in archived or compressed files), and repairs what it can.

American Heritage Dictionary (DOS, Windows, and Mac), WordStar International, (415) 382-8000, (800) 523-3520.

Containing more than 116,000 definitions and 500,000 synonyms, WordStar's American Heritage Dictionary is tops in versatility and writing assistance. The program gives you access to spelling corrections, hyphenation tips, inflections, derivatives, word sources, and much more.

PC Paintbrush 5+ (DOS), WordStar International, (404) 428-0008, (800) 227-5609.

Here's an easy-to-use, classic graphics application that helps novices and experts alike edit graphics, imported clip art, and scanned images. More than 40 editing tools and a Windows-like interface invite experimentation with 3-D effects, filters, and more.

$50 and under

Grammatik 5 (DOS and Windows), Reference Software International, (800) 321-4566.

No grammar checker is perfect, but Grammatik gets the highest grade in our book. It's easy to use, offers insightful suggestions, and gives you grammar lessons along the way.

Dashboard (Windows), Hewlett-Packard, (408) 720-3005, (800) 554-1305.

Dashboard is a utility panel that works as a customizable, speedy Windows navigator. Click to open an application, drag and drop documents to be printed, monitor your memory usage, and instantly switch among nine virtual screens.

AutoDoubler (Mac), Fifth Generation Systems, (504) 291-7221, (800) 873-4384.

AutoDoubler transparently and quickly compresses the files on your Mac's hard-disk drive. The utility can save up to 50 percent of disk space, so it's a priceless addition to anyone with a lot of files or a small hard-disk drive. Version 2.0 includes CopyDoubler, a System 7 utility that copies files 2 to 10 times faster and empties the Trash up to 10 times faster.

WillMaker (DOS and Mac), Nolo Press, (510) 549-1976, (800) 992-6656.

Whether you are single, married, or divorced, with kids or without, a will is imperative. WillMaker offers a step-by-step process for creating a customizable, legal will for any state except Louisiana. The manual also provides an excellent introduction to estate planning.

Design Your Own Home series (DOS and Mac), Abracadata, (503) 342-3030, (800) 451-4871.

Interested in interior design, building a home, or landscaping your backyard? The Design Your Own Home series help you to do just that. Sample plans and layouts get you started even if you're not an expert.

Instant Artist (DOS), Autodesk Retail Products, (206) 489-7711, (800) 228-3601.

Not only do you become an instant artist, but you'll have instant fun with this one. Hundreds of customizable predesigned layouts—signs, banners, greeting cards, business cards, letterhead, and more—are enhanced with text effects and numerous pieces of clip art.

The Home Series (DOS), Autodesk Retail Products, (206) 487-2233, (800) 228-3601.

Design your home, kitchen, bathroom, deck, or landscape with one of these intuitive plan-drawing packages that include more than 350 predrawn symbols. Once your project is designed, The Home Series produces a handy "shopping list" of all the elements in your design.

3D Plan (DOS), Autodesk Retail Products, (206) 487-2233, (800) 228-3601.

Once you've drawn a layout plan in one of the Home Series products (also reviewed here), load it into 3D Plan to transform your flat drawing into a three-dimensional model.

Li'l Bits Font Packs (Windows), Bitstream, (617) 497-6222.

For a bit of fun in your documents, consider The Star Trek Font Pack, The Flintstones Font Pack, or the Winter Holiday Font Pack, each a set of top-notch, easy-to-download fonts.

BannerMania (DOS and Mac), Broderbund Software, (415) 382-4600, (800) 521-6263.

Here's a different kind of graphics program: BannerMania helps you design and print banners, bumper stickers, posters, T-shirt designs, and signs. The program includes 19 outline fonts for flexibility in your promotional products.

Correct Writing (DOS, Windows, Mac) WordStar International, (415) 382-8000, (800) 523-3520.

This program is a professional writing course in a box. If you want to learn the rules of writing, including punctuation, outline structure, and bibliography rules, give Correct Writing a try.

Kid Pix (DOS, Windows, Mac), Broderbund Software, (415) 382-4600, (800) 521-6263.

No, it's not just for kids! Perhaps the best Mac graphics application for nonartists. The tools make this a winner: Rubber Stamps of 80 images (frogs, trees, faces) show up wherever you click. Big blobs of paint or random fractal lines fly out of your pencil, and a bomb blows up your mistakes. Sound effects, including Spanish and English pronunciation of the alphabet and numbers as you choose them, are almost more fun than drawing.

Print Shop (Mac), Print Shop Deluxe DOS v1.2, Broderbund Software, (415) 382-4600, (800) 521-6263.

Greeting cards, banners, signs, and letterhead appear almost instantly with the help of Print Shop. Includes tons of graphics, with holiday, business, computer, food, sport, and other motifs in a variety of sizes, as well as a selection of stylish or silly borders.

After Dark (Windows and Mac), Berkeley Systems, (510) 540-5535, (800) 344-5541.

After Dark fills your screen with images and sounds while preventing screen-image burn-in. It's quite simply the most colorful and creative screen-saver application around. More After Dark adds lawn mowers, psychedelics, and more to the original flying-toaster collection. Star Trek: The Screen Saver has quickly become a favorite After Dark set.

TurboTax (DOS and Windows), ChipSoft, (619) 453-8722.

TurboTax includes more than 90 forms, worksheets, and schedules, as well as handy context-sensitive IRS instructions. EasyStep utility guides you through returns for an (almost) painless tax preparation session.

CompuServe Information Manager (DOS, Windows, Mac), CompuServe Information Service, (614) 457-8600, (800) 848-8199.

CompuServe Information Manager (CIM) is an easy-to-navigate front end for accessing the CompuServe online service. CIM sends and receives mail automatically, assists in downloading and uploading, and generally makes CompuServe less intimidating. The Windows version makes CompuServe as inviting as America Online.

Power Toolboxes (Windows), hDC Computer Corp., (206) 885-5550, (800) 365-8553.

Clicking on an icon to accomplish a task such as copying or printing can save lots of time. Power Toolboxes automatically adds customizable icon toolbars to such applications as Ami Pro, Persuasion, Excel, Word, Works, PageMaker, WordPerfect, and more, to speed up your productivity in Windows by giving you instant access to tons of functions.

Pacioli 2000 (DOS), M-USA Business Systems, (214) 386-6100, (800) 933-6872.

The eight feature-packed Windows-like modules—general ledger, accounts receivable and payable, inventory control, billing, purchasing, budgeting, and auditing—were accessible right out of the box. A great value that won't be left behind as your business grows.

Calendar Creator (DOS, Windows, and Mac), PowerUp Software Corp., (415) 345-5900, (800) 851-2917.

A calendar of nearly any format can be designed and printed with Calendar Creator. The program easily handles daily, two-day, weekly, two-week, monthly, six-week, and yearly calendars. One idea: Make and distribute custom calendars for your clients as a promotional gift.

LetterWorks (DOS and Mac), Round Lake Publishing, (203) 438-5255.

LetterWorks is a basic collection of 400 letters; Sales' 300 letters will help you get and keep clients; Legal boasts 165 customizable legal forms and agreements; Professional has 250 documents for doctors, dentists, lawyers, and CPAs.

Easy Working Address Book & Label Maker (DOS), Spinnaker Software Corp., (617) 494-1200, (800) 826-0706.

You want labels? Want to print out an address book? Address Book & Label Maker is the best DOS deal around, with impressive data management and a bonus of 16 Bitstream typefaces.

Easy Working Spreadsheet for Windows Spinnaker Software Corp., (617) 494-1200, (800) 826-0706.

Easy Working Spreadsheet for Windows has many of the features of Lotus 1-2-3 and Excel except for database functions, macro capability, color charts, and a several-hundred-dollar price tag. The toolbar lets you access functions easily. Borders and shades add pizzazz to your printouts and presentations.

Easy Working Presentation Maker (DOS), Spinnaker Software Corp., (617) 494-1200, (800) 826-0706.

You can run this back-to-basics presentation creator from a floppy. While it's not meant for high-flash, big-business presentations, Presentation Maker is fine for the occasional user. A seven-color palette breathes some life into standard charts and graphs.

FaxMania (DOS, Windows, and Mac), T/Maker Co., (415) 962-0195.

Do you send faxes to prospective clients and the media? FaxMania is a collection of 80 customizable fax cover sheets for business, personal, and just plain fun faxes.

Amaze Daily Planner (Windows and Mac), Delrina, (206) 820-7007.

This Far Side or Cathy cartoon-a-day onscreen calendar series is a flexible time-management system that offers numerous calendar-printing options with weekly, monthly, and daily layouts. The daily dose of humor or Trivial Pursuit challenges is a boon to any working day.

Homebuying & Refinancing Pro (DOS), Byers Software, (713) 859-7302.

If you want to buy a home, refinance, or professionally prepare loan and payment reports, Homebuying & Refinancing is for you. It also helps in preparing your loan agreement, and in deciding how much to consider for a down payment.

Quicken (DOS, Windows and Mac), Intuit, (415) 852-9696, (800) 624-8742.

Perhaps the most popular personal finance program of all time, Quicken continues to smoothly track income and expenses, analyze finances, and print checks. Quicken just keeps getting better.

Managing Your Money (DOS and Mac), MECA Software, (203) 256-5000, (800) 288-6322.

This personal financial package puts you in control of your budget, manages your checkbook and investments, helps to determine how much insurance you need, and aids in tax estimation. MYM also helps you with financial planning and analyzing.

CalendarMaker (Windows and Mac), CE Software, (515) 224-1995, (800) 523-7638.

As its name implies, CalendarMaker makes calendars. While layout selection is limited, calendars are attractive and easily customizable. Holiday and event icons add visual interest to your creations. Version 4.0 for the Mac will be available when you read this.

Shareware

A few notes on shareware: Shareware is usually free to use for a short period of time—you try it out for a few days to see if you like it, and pay the author if you choose to continue using it. If you use it, please pay for it. Some authors ask only for a postcard or other memorabilia; some request payment from $5 to more than our limit of $100.

These entrepreneurial individuals (like you) are trusting you to fulfill your obligation of payment. Many of the authors can be reached through online services and support registered users just like the commercial biggies—and often integrate your suggestions and send you upgrade notices or the upgrades themselves. If you decide to send for freeware rather than downloading it, send a blank, formatted disk and a self-addressed stamped envelope to the author (addresses are listed in the shareware/freeware section when available).

Time Is Money (DOS), Custom Data Solution, 248 Woodlake Dr., Maitland, FL 32751, (407) 767-9278.

Ideal for consultants and other businesses that bill by the hour, this reliable time and expense billing program also automates the filling of invoices. Time Is Money also prints statements and tracks your receivables.

PKZip (DOS), PKWare, 9025 North Deerwood Dr., Brown Deer, WI 53223, (414) 354-8699.

PKZip is a combination compression/decompression package for shrinking files to fit on floppies or for shortening modem transmission time. One DOS command compresses; one decompresses. PKZip is, perhaps, the most popular compression utility on the DOS platform. OS/2 version is also available.

As-Easy-As (DOS), Paris Karahelios, TRIUS, (508) 794-9377, (800) 468-7487.

This shareware spreadsheet is worth every nickel: It's fully mouse-compatible, lets you combine text and graphics on the same page, supports PIC graphics, and has 12 professional graph formats—and more than enough features to satisfy any spreadsheet aficionado.

Paint Shop Pro (Windows), JASC, 110901 Red Circle Dr., Suite 340, Minnetonka, MN 55343, (612) 930-9171.

This slick graphics conversion and manipulation program gives you control over bitmapped images (such as scans or screen captures) in GIF, PCX, TIFF, and 11 other graphics formats in up to 24-bit color. Flip, rotate, resize, convert to gray scale, brighten, and otherwise spiff up your images for desktop publishing and presentations.

WinEdit (Windows), Wilson WindowWare, (206) 938-1743, (800) 762-8383.

WinEdit is a flexible ASCII file editor. While originally designed for programming, it is great for basic, day-to-day word processing.

WinGRAB (Windows), ZPAY Payroll Systems, (813) 866-8233, (800) 468-4188.

This application "grabs" addresses from your letters and prints them on envelopes. It also prints bar codes on dot matrix and laser printers (including PostScript), and comes with macros to work more efficiently with Word, WordPerfect, and Ami Pro for Windows.

Disinfectant (Mac) (freeware; available on online services, or send a self-addressed stamped envelope and a blank floppy disk), John Norstad, Academic Computing, Northwestern U., 2129 Sheridan Rd., Evanston, IL 60208.

Known as one of the best Mac virus-detection products available, Disinfectant scans your disks, gets rid of viruses, and repairs files. The utility silently keeps watch over your hard-disk drive for intruders. The intricate Help file includes detailed information on each known virus.

Design makeover

by Steve Morgenstern

DEBORAH EVANS CRAWFORD STARTED HER mail-order catalog based on a need she experienced in her day-to-day life. She had worked both in golf-course maintenance for many years and on her own small farm and consistently found it difficult to outfit herself for comfort and safety.

"I would be spraying chemicals, and I could not find a pair of gloves that fit on my hands properly or a pair of boots that would protect my feet from the chemicals. I had an argument with my supplier about why there weren't any products to ensure the safety of women spraying chemicals, and he said there weren't that many women involved in this business. I told him there would never be many women working in this business if they all died from chemical exposure."

The perceived need for high-quality women's work gear led to the birth of WorkAbles for Women, the direct-mail business Evans Crawford founded in 1986. "I found a work glove at a local welding-supply store, and I was ecstatic," she recalls. "These were the first work gloves that ever fit my hands. And I started thinking—boy, this would be a good first product for a catalog."

With that glove and some money from an income-tax refund check as a starting point, Evans Crawford set off to launch her company. She read everything she could get her hands on about direct mail, took some courses, and did a mail survey of women working in nontraditional jobs to find out what kinds of products they really wanted. Today she sends out 20,000 catalogs twice a year, and says her business is growing by an average of 50 percent annually.

Making a good catalog better

When the idea of a desktop-publishing makeover came up, Evans Crawford's business immediately sprang to mind. She sends out a few other mailing pieces, but the business lives or dies with the catalog. While the current catalog has a lot going for it, there are several areas where some design tweaking could produce a much stronger presentation.

The existing catalog conveys the personal touch that makes WorkAbles for Women so distinctive. Much of that personality comes across in the copy, which Evans Crawford writes herself, with editorial assistance from her mother and her husband. The catalog is then laid out in PageMaker on a Macintosh by a local print shop, which also does the typesetting.

One of the tricky aspects of redesigning this catalog is the large amount of copy involved. The words make you realize that you're ordering products from an honest-to-goodness human being who cares about what she sells (an impression reinforced rather dramatically when Evans Crawford answers the phone to take your order). However, to keep printing and postage costs as low as possible, there are only 16 pages in a small size, so the pages tend to get crammed full.

When I offered to take a crack at creating a new format for the publication, my first inclination, frankly, was to cheat like a bandit and spend Evans Crawford's money lavishly. Make the pages larger to provide more white space and room for graphic flourishes. Add full-color photographs, instead of the two colors currently used. Ultimately, though, I decided to play by the rules: same page size, roughly the same illustrations, about the same amount of copy, and no big, beautiful color pictures. In fact, the limits I faced in creating a better catalog for the same basic cost is just the kind of restraint that desktop publishers often come up against—whether they're working for others or on their own projects.

WorkAble Women Don't Get the Blues!

Deborah,

Just wanted to write a quick note to rave about the safety sunglasses! I used them all summer. I am working on a penthouse roof, fitting for a welder between two huge cooling towers. All that sun and heat and galvanized metal and my eyes stayed cool as a cucumber and never misread the rule or level!

The service you provide is invaluable. As a woman who has been in the trades 8 years I can testify how tough it was outfitting myself safely.

Thanks again,

Keyosha, Journeywoman Plumber, Lansing, MI

Dear Ms Crawford,

We are producers of pure maple syrup and will be using your mittens, gloves, sock liners, and even stickers in our production of maple syrup. We have worn "WorkAbles" before and appreciate your woman owned business.

Best regards,

Lisa Nathanson, Janet Woods
Hurry Hill Pure Maple Syrup
Edinboro, PA

10

Dear Deborah,

Thanks for the boots, I received them in time to go back to work after a six-week recuperation from a work-related injury. I love them. Just knowing you cre out there with the rest of us doing it a day at a time is really reassuring. I enjoyed talking with you. Keep up the good work and good luck with your business. Hope to see you at the Tradeswoman Conference next year.

Sincerely, Christina Herzog, Chicago, IL

Deborah,

Please send one, right hand small WorkAble glove. I am thoroughly delighted with your gloves and my partner refuses to take your Dunham boots off. Thanks for taking care of us!

Patti Kauffman, Bradenton, FL

Deborah,

I did take the trip to Scotland and was sure glad to have the right equipment. The soil on the island is all bog, peat bog... mushy, wet, and cold. I wore the wool socks, boots and work gloves with pleasure! They also took advantage of having 22 hours a day of daylight, so we worked long hours and needed good "protection from the elements." Anyway, what I'm happiest about is that a company like yours exists for women's needs.

Denise Heller
Manhattan Beach, CA

Thanks Deb!

I really enjoy talking with you, you sound like a wonderful woman! Thanks for bringing nice things available to women who are sick of shopping in men's departments! You're great!

Cindy Caldwell, Salt Lake City, UT

B-1 BEFORE *The existing catalog basically comes without a cover. While curiosity might get you to flip it open, I'll easily trade that "Gee, what's in that black box?" level of interest for a cover that clearly identifies the catalog, communicating something about WorkAbles for Women's identity and generating excitement among the readers.*

B-2 AFTER *Here's one of my ideas for a new catalog cover. I knew two of the elements I wanted on the cover: a bold type treatment of the company name and WorkAbles for Women's attractive logo. I also wanted to clearly identify the target audience—hence, the cover line FOR THE WORKING WOMAN. Evans Crawford wanted to see some people on the cover, so I used her existing cover photograph and came up with this revision.*

Initial analysis

- For a publication with such a friendly writing style, the catalog has a gray, intimidating look. This is at least in part because of the lack of white space. White space, logically enough, consists of the blank areas on the page that give your eye a rest and help focus the reader's attention on the picture or text. As Evans Crawford freely admits, "I fill up every inch." The trick here is to balance minor cuts in copy length (I figure 10 to 15 percent of the original can be sliced through judicious editing) with a space-saving layout.
- The existing catalog essentially has no cover. When you sort through the arriving mail, you reach this 16-page publication and ask, "What the heck is this?" While curiosity may get you to flip it open, I'll gladly trade that "Gee, what's in the black box?" level of interest for a cover that clearly identifies the catalog and generates some excitement in the target audience.
- WorkAbles for Women has a well-designed logo that reads *WOMAN POWERED*. I like the logo a lot, and so does Evans Crawford's market: T-shirts and other apparel sporting the logo are among her best-selling items. In the redesign, I wanted to exploit that strength.
- The photographs used are not strictly A-quality. Ideally, I would go out with a professional photographer and reshoot them from scratch. At the same time, I'd love to change paper stock so the pictures would reproduce more crisply. Evans Crawford has been using an uncoated matte stock that isn't very photo-friendly, but she's currently considering a change. Without assuming either better photographs or better paper, though, I have to look for a design solution that gives those pictures more visual presence on the page.
- The existing catalog doesn't lead the reader through the publication effectively. The page elements sort of lie there. There's no visual movement across the page or from spread to spread. Your eye just drifts off in all directions. We need to cure that in the makeover.

What's in it for you?

By looking over the three before-and-after page layouts, you can probably find ways to enhance your own page designs. The changes I've suggested are more practical than artistic, but I don't want to undervalue the artistic element of design. Sometimes the sheer inventiveness and graphic oomph of a layout will not only grab a reader's attention but will also convey a dramatic visual impression at the same time.

For most desktop-publishing projects, though, design is a meat-and-potatoes business of producing clear, easy-to-read, attractive, and professional-looking communication. That fundamental level of design expertise can be yours by applying a little common sense and following simple concepts like the ones guiding this makeover.

Second spread

The first page (inside of the front cover) is Evans Crawford's chance to introduce herself to her potential customers. That's very important, yet the page looks dull in the original. There's nothing that says "Start reading here," and the lengthy, uninterrupted copy says, "Don't start reading at all—it's a chore."

The second page is also crucial. It's the first merchandise offer the catalog recipient encounters. That's why I moved the gloves up to this spot. Evans Crawford says gloves are her best-selling item, and I want to lead with products that have sales strength and proven interest on the part of her customers.

While the company name, address, and phone number are included on every spread, they don't constitute much of a call to action. I want to make ordering as easy and spontaneous as possible, no matter where you are in the catalog.

Original spread

1. It's important to have the company address available in the catalog, but it doesn't have to appear on every page. Also, there is no mention of the toll-free 800 number here, hence no strong call to action.

2. I feel the Evans Crawford-plus-horse picture is weak both as a visual element and as a means of communicating what the catalog's about.

3. The copy here is basically one long block that seems to go on forever, with no easy point of entry and a high "why bother?" factor. That's partly a design problem and partly editorial. Instead of cramming information about every special offer onto one page, the information can be distributed onto other spreads in boxed text blocks.

4. These headlines don't anchor the pages well at the top, nor do they add much to the sales presentation of the products.

Makeover spread

5. I added a headline to provide easier entry into the page visually, and to give the reader a quick idea of what the page is about.

6. The typefaces in the existing catalog are acceptable but dull. I switched the body type to Adobe Caslon, one of my favorites, adding some personality to the text and retaining a high charac-

As I read my mail, I am constantly impressed by the marvelous things women are doing these days! I am working hard to keep up with your needs by providing quality products that solve the problems women have in their daily lives. So look over my catalog, try my products, and **see for yourself why WorkAble Women don't get the blues!**

For example, many women that work outside are having problems with small skin cancers that are associated with overexposure to the sun. This appears to be an increasing problem with the breakdown in the ozone layer. In response, I am now carrying the NEW! Super-Shader, made by the same woman owned company that brought us the popular Ultimate Cap.

Active women who enjoy the outdoors have been writing to me for years about the difficulties they encounter relieving themselves outside when no facilities are available. See the **very discreet solution** a woman entrepreneur came up with that combines concealed comfort with exceptional fabrics and fit.

BEFORE

Th[illegible] m[illegible]er [illegible] I [illegible] req[illegible]sts for [illegible]d wou[illegible] li[illegible] to ca[illegible]y. [illegible]fortun[illegible]ly, the [illegible]spons[illegible] fr[illegible] ma[illegible]actur[illegible] is tha[illegible] [illegible]rke[illegible] is t[illegible] s[illegible] produce them. If you know of any small, **preferably women owned**, clothing producers that would understand our needs better, please let me know about them. Also, please continue to keep me aware of what your needs are or any new ideas for products for today's hardworking women.

Sincerely,

Deborah

Deborah

P.S. In celebration of all the wonderful things you do with my products, I am holding the **First Ever WorkAble Woman Photo** contest. Send me a photo of you using one (or more) of my products, along with a quick note describing what you are doing. You could win a **$100 WorkAble gift certificate** AND have your picture featured on the cover of my next catalog. So start snapping today! All entries must be in by **August 30, 1992.**

P.P.S. Because of its popularity last year, I am bringing back the **FREE OshKosh Bandanna offer** for orders over $50, received by September 30, 1992. See order form for details.

For those who may be new to WorkAbles for Women, a brief "herstory". I started this company in 1986, being totally fed up with the lack of clothing and equipment available for active women. I sent a survey to thousands of other hardworking women asking about their needs. What a list! The survey input helped me to provide all of the products you'll see on these pages.

To protect our jobs, all WorkAble products are made here in the United States.

Dear Deborah,

Bobbye's 2nd pair of boots arrived last evening and they fit perfectly. She's de-lighted! She wore them to work today. Thanks so much for the ease and friendliness in taking care of this exchange!

Gini Edwards, Cincinnati, OH

WorkAbles for Women is not associated in any way with Womanswork, Strong Women Building a Gentle World®, of Maine.

2 **WorkAbles for Women, Oak Valley, Clinton, PA 15026-0214 · 412-899-3555**

PLAY IT SAFE IN THE SUN

The **NEW Ultimate Super Shader** and the popular Ultimate Cap are designed for women who are concerned about the damaging effects of the sun. **Both are Union made in the US** by a woman owned company and **GUARANTEED FOR A LIFETIME!**

NEW! Ultimate Super Shader: For those women who prefer a round hat, the Ultimate Super Shader's extra width gives added protection against the sun's damaging rays. Natural white 100% cotton material is water repellant and mildew resistant. Washable with solid brass ventilation grommets.

Slip knot chin cord keeps the hat on in the gustiest winds. Revolutionary Hydrofil™ sweatband absorbs perspiration, to keep your head dry and comfortable.

USS Ultimate Super Shader
Natural **WHITE** **$33**

Contrasting color braids dress up hat for a jauntier look.

UHB Hat braid: Choose **NAVY** and white, **RED** and white or all **WHITE** **$2.50**

Measure loosely around the head above the brow at the widest part

Head size:	21-1/2"	21-7/8"	22-1/4"	22-5/8"	23"	23-1/2"	23-7/8"	24-1/4"
Hat Size:	7	7-1/8	7-1/4	7-3/8	7-1/2	7-5/8	7-3/4	7-7/8
Hat size:	Small		Medium		Large		X-Large	

The popular Ultimate Cap returns just in time for sunny days in a new lighter Supplex nylon, as well as the classic white cotton duck. Extra long and wide bill for sun protection also floats so you won't lose it in a sudden dunking! The unique **"key wester" back unsnaps for rain and sun protection**, or wear it up as a traditional cap. Both cotton and nylon caps are washable, rain repellant, mildew resistant and feature British brass snaps and grommets that are rust proof. Adjustable chin cord so the cap won't blow off.

UC Ultimate Cap: Choose WHITE cotton or **BLUE** Supplex **$27**

All WorkAbles for Women Products MADE IN THE USA

WorkAbles for Women, Oak Valley, Clinton, PA 15026-0214 · 412-899-3555 3

YOU'RE MY KIND OF PEOPLE...

Lorem ipsum dolor sit amet, consectetuer adipiscing elit, sed diam nonummy nibh euismod tincidunt ut laoreet dolore magna aliquam erat volutpat. Ut wisi enim

ad minim veniam, quis nostrud exerci tation ullamcorper suscipit lobortis nisl ut aliquip ex ea commodo consequat. Duis autem vel eum iriure dolor in hendrerit in vulputate velit esse molestie consequat, vel illum dolore eu feugiat nulla facilisis at vero eros

et accumsan et iusto odio dignissim qui blandit praesent luptatum zzril delenit augue duis dolore te feugait nulla facilisi. Lorem ipsum dolor sit amet, consectetuer adipiscing elit, sed diam nonummy nibh euismod tincidunt ut

laoreet dolore magna aliquam erat volutpat. Ut wisi enim ad minim veniam, quis nostrud exerci tation ullamcorper suscipit lobortis nisl ut aliquip ex ea commodo consequat.

Duis autem vel eum iriure dolor in hendrerit in vulputate velit esse molestie consequat, vel illum dolore eu feugiat nulla facilisis at vero eros et accumsan et iusto odio dignissim qui blandit praesent

luptatum zzril delenit augue duis dolore te feugait nulla facilisi. Nam liber tempor cum soluta nobis eleifend option congue nihil imperdiet doming id quod mazim placerat

Deborah

A Brief Her-Story Lesson

autem vel eum iriure dolor in hendrerit in vulputate velit esse molestie consequat, vel illum dolore eu feugiat nulla facilisis at vero eros et accumsan et iusto odio dignissim qui blandit praesent luptatum zzril delenit augue duis dolore te feugait nulla facilisi. Lorem ipsum dolor sit amet, consectetuer adipiscing elit, sed diam nonumautem vel eum iriure dolor in hendrerit in vulputate velit esse molestie consequat, vel illum

TO ORDER CALL 800-862-9317

OR USE THE ORDER FORM ON PAGE 15

GLOVES

All WorkAble gloves are fully guaranteed for ONE FULL YEAR (what other glove company can make that claim?)! They are washable, and can easily be waterproofed with a good silicon spray. You can also get just one glove, right or left for ½ the pair cost.

Workhorse WorkAble
ad minim veniam, quis nostrud exerci tation ullamcorper suscipit lobortis nisl ut aliquip ex ea commodo consequat. Duis autem vel eum iriure dolor in hendrerit in vulputate velit esse molestie consequat, vel illum dolore eu feugiat blandit praesent luptatum zzril delenit augue duis dolore te feugait nulla facilisi. Lorem ipsum dolor sit amet, consectetuer adipiscing elit, sed diam
EWG Workhorse WorkAble Glove
Sizes: Small (7), Regular (8), Large (9)
Price: $19.50 per pair

> *I've liked everything I've ordered from you. I could do brain surgery in the elkskin gloves — no interference with dexterity. Plase send another pair at once, for a friend who is threatening to steal mine.*
> *Dr. N.J Lindsey, Overland Park, KS*

Winter WorkAble
laoreet dolore magna aliquam erat volutpat. Ut wisi enim ad minim veniam, quis nostrud exerci tation ullamcorper suscipit lobortis nisl utoreet dolore magna aliquam erat volutpat. Ut wisi enim ad minim veniam, quis nostrud exe aliquip ex ea commodo consequat.Duis autem vel eum iriure dolor in hendrerit in vulputate velit esse molestieUt wisi enim ad minim veniam, quis nostrud exerci tation
WW1 Winter WorkAble Glove
Sizes: Small (7), Regular (8)
Price: $17 per pair

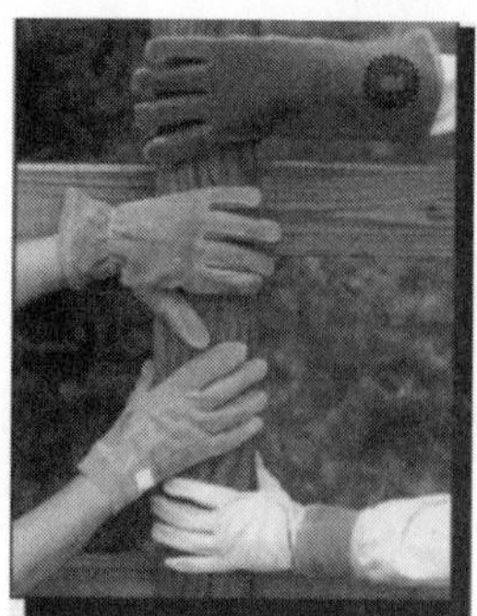

Consectetuer adipiscing elit, sed diam nonummy nibh euismod tincidunt ut laoreet dolore magna aliquam erat

WorkAble Glove
consequat, vel illum dolore eu feugiat nulla facilisis at vero eros et accumsan et iusto odio dignissim qui blandit praesent luptatum zzril delenit augue duis dolore te feugait nulla facilisi. congue nihil imperdiet doming id quod mazim placerat facer possim assum.
WG1 WorkAble Glove
Sizes: Small (7), Regular
Price: $11 per pair
Order 3 Pair and Save!
WG3 3 pair @ $10.50 per pair

AFTER

Eelskin Glove
Lorem ipsum dolor sit amet, consectetuer adipiscing elit, sed diam nonummy nibh euismod tincidunt ut laoreet dolore magna aliquam erat volutpat. Ut wisi enim ad minim veniam, quis nostrud exerci tation ullamcorper suscipit lobortis nisl ut aliquip
EEG Elkskin Glove
Size: Regular (8) Price: $17.50 per pair

-3-

ter count per inch. The headlines and section headings are set in the same sans serif type used on the cover, in a regular bold weight.

7. I substituted this hardworking-woman publicity photo from the company files for the horse shot. Here Evans Crawford is gesturing, looking happy and ready for work—a major improvement.

8. A black drop shadow? The oldest trick in the book, maybe, but it works to pop these pictures off the page.

9. The company history deserves prominent placement, and the page needs to be broken up into digestible pieces. Hence this full-width text block. Of course, the text itself doesn't run full-width—I kept it to a readable length by indenting the left side and wrapping the right around the logo.

10. I want readers to know how to order wherever they flip open the catalog. Hence this bold block of copy, repeated on every spread. And since 800-number ordering has high-impulse-purchase immediacy, we'll feature that and mention the other ways to order.

11. To create a visual flow from top to bottom of each page, and to identify at a glance what's being offered on a given page, I've added these ruling-line-and-type-box treatments consistently through the catalog.

12. This short, easy-to-read bold copy block provides strong selling points for all the products on the page.

13. Ganging up all four products in a single shot may be an effective way to save space in a tight catalog, but if I were art-directing the photo shoot I'd try to have more glove and less fence post and background.

14. I've kept the headings for each product plain and simple, and standardized each listing so it begins with

Deborah Evans Crawford

a boldface head, proceeds with normal-weight body type, and ends with a boldface product description.

15. Evans Crawford rightly calls the unsolicited testimonials she receives "marvelous." One way to show them off is to indent the copy and use great big quotation marks (from the Zapf Dingbat typeface) to catch the reader's attention.

16. The caption is set in the italic version of the body type. Notice the thin black rule below the caption, separating it from the product listing below.

Third spread

The products aren't showcased as effectively as possible in the original layout. There are lots of text lines set so wide they seem to go on forever, and two money-saving offers that are nearly invisible to the naked eye.

Original spread

17. Those of you with toddlers in the house hum along: "One of these things is not like the others, one of these things doesn't belong." Why have one boot with a background while the other three are silhouetted? Because the other three are manufacturer's photos, while the knee boot is a home-grown shot. It really doesn't require that much work to silhouette the fourth photo, and the more professional-looking result is worth the effort.

Also, look at all four boots. Where are they going? Back where the reader already came from, instead of onward into the rest of the catalog. You always want to make sure people's faces are pointing toward the copy or on to the next page when you create a layout: The same goes for other photos that clearly convey direction, like this phalanx of boots.

18. Much of the copy is set too wide for easy readability. Ironically, these powerful product testimonials are the worst offenders.

Makeover spread

19. The first key step is to impose a strict column arrangement throughout the catalog. Body copy is set no more than one column wide; display type (such as ordering info) and rules can be full width.

20. The testimonials make ideal captions here. Visually, their italic setting gives a nice contrast and texture to the mass of text on the page, and they are

RAVES FOR OUR KNEE BOOTS

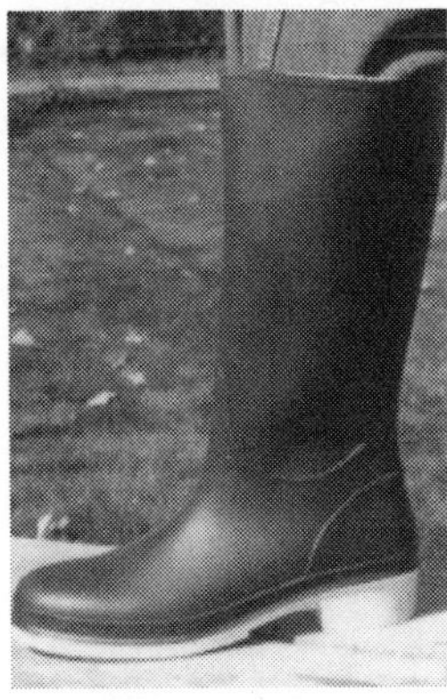

Dear Deborah,

I got my all weather knee boots this week, and can hardly wait to use them, they fit! With a size 10 it is so hard to find a comfortable boot, but these fit the bill! Here are some names and addresses of others who might be interested in your products!

Thanks, M. Flint Suter, Hampton, IA

My customers rave about the Tingley knee boots for many reasons. They are comfortable, resistant to just about any chemical (even manure), and provide good traction in slippery conditions. Add in the fact that they are guaranteed not to leak or crack, their amazing good looks and you have an unbeatable combination. Designed to be worn without shoes, they have a high quality, removable cushion innersole. Get them dirty, just hose them off. Navy blue upper and white chevron sole. A great bargain at $29.

Women's shoe size 5, 6, 7, 8, 9, 10
TKN Tingley Knee Boot $29

Dear WorkAbles for Women,

Thank you for replacing my gloves so quickly. I really like working with small businesses because they seem to be more committed to customer service!!!

My husband ordered me a pair of Rainbow boots and we are both so impressed by the price and quality. I really enjoy my boots – It's hard to find women's work boots that really hold up to any heavy work.

Thanks for offering your products. Keep it up!

Myrhh Shaw, Solvang, CA

CLOSE OUT SAVINGS

The Dunham Boot Company has unfortunately decided to discontinue their Rainbow Boot. So act quickly and take advantage of this opportunity to order this light work/sport boot now at a reduced price. Made of lightly brushed suede leather with Thinsulate® to keep you warm in winter and cool in summer. Soft Cambrelle® lining wicks perspiration away from the feet. Other quality features include silver D-rings for [illegible]

Women's Sizes 5-[illegible], [illegible], 6-[illegible]2, [illegible] 7-1/2, 8, 8-1/2, 9, 10 Medium width.

#DRB Rainbow Boot Regular Price $56 Close-out price $52.
Indicate **1st and 2nd color choice** of BLUE or GRAY.

8 **WorkAbles for Women, Oak Valley, Clinton, PA 15026-0214 • 412-899-3555**

EXTRAORDINARY BOOTS FOR EXTRAORDINARY WOMEN

WORKABLE BOOT – A true classic, the WorkAble Boot has been used and loved by women in all occupations. This six inch high boot provides plenty of support and doesn't bind around the heavier part of the calf, as some eight inch boots do. The Tan Nubuck leather is **soaked for days in silicone waterproofing**, and all the seams are triple stitched and then sealed with latex to guarantee a dry foot. For extra warmth this boot is insulated with 400 Thinsulate™ (twice as much as other boots), and then is additionally lined with Cambrelle™ to wick moisture away from your foot. The dual density sole is **20% stronger than traditional soles** and also is oil resistant. Extremely lightweight, it features a fiberglass shank for great support.

You may notice an emphasis on feet in my catalog, and this is because it has been so hard in the past for women to find good, long lasting footwear. **These boots won't let you down** and are now available in **MEDIUM** and **WIDE** widths and a **steel toe model** for safety.

Woman's size 5-1/2, 6, 6-1/2, 7, 7-1/2, 8, 8-1/2, 9, 9-1/2, 10

DWB	**Tan Leather Women's Work Boot**	**Medium and Wide Widths**	**$95**
DST	**Tan Steel Toe Women's Work Boot**	**Medium Width**	**$99**
DBB	**Black Leather Boot (postal approved)**	**Special order**	**$95**

Deborah,

I ordered my Dunham work boots from you a year ago. That should be a long enough time to test them. YES, they are still going strong. I am an aircraft mechanic who previously went through boots in 6 months, if I could find a pair to fit me at all. The boots required almost no break-in time and your ad is absolutely right, your feet do go "aah" when you put them on. They are very comfortable and durable. Thank you very, very much for finding a way to help women like us. *Carol McKechnie, Millersville, MD*

ULTIMATE BOOT – This boot is the state of the art in technological breakthroughs in comfort and durability. The sole was designed for **extremely long wear**, and the chevron cleats and wedge sole provide plenty of traction. The fiberglass shank is twice as strong as steel and doesn't transmit the cold. Incredibly lightweight, **these boots weigh only about a pound a piece** and that makes an amazing difference at the end of a hard day.

The finely tanned, water resistant golden leather has been "tumbled" and worked so there is a very short break in period. Inside is a full, **fitted Gore-Tex™ "bootie"**, the miracle fabric which permits your foot to breathe, but absolutely, positively won't let water in. **(Guaranteed).**

To keep you warm, this new boot is **ALSO lined with Thinsulate**, and the inner lining is Cambrelle to keep perspiration away from your feet. A total of **FOUR layers to keep you warm and dry!** Seven inches high, the top inch of the boot is padded leather for NO chafing.

The leather tongue is fully sewn all the way up and **ALL the seams are triple stitched** and sealed on the inside to keep out any water. Brass speed rings for faster lacing and long life laces. If you have been searching for the **finest made, most comfortable women's boot available**, this is it!

Women's size 5-1/2, 6, 6-1/2, 7, 7-1/2, 8, 8-1/2, 9, 10 Medium Width
DGB Tan Women's Gore-Tex Boot $150 Summer Special $139

WorkAbles for Women, Oak Valley, Clinton, PA 15026-0214 • 412-899-3555 9

highly likely to be read as they hug the photos to which they relate.

21. I've brought the two sale items on the page up to the top of the spread. There's no need to use blaring headlines or starbursts from your weekly supermarket flier. Simple placement on the page, the combination of boldface and capitalization, and the use of a second color are more than adequate to proclaim, "Here's something you don't want to miss!"

22. There are a few items in the catalog that can't be found anywhere else. That's an incredibly strong marketing statement that's never mentioned in the original version. Here I've created a simple design element—the logo combined with centered boldface sans serif type—to be used every time an item is a WorkAbles for Women exclusive.

23. Two of these photographs have been flopped left-to-right so they now face forward, leading the eye into the copy (the knee boot in the upper left) and onto the next page (the Ultimate boot at the bottom of the third column).

BOOTS

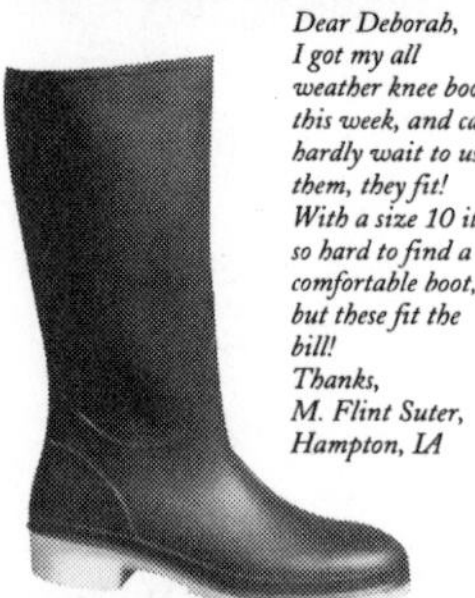
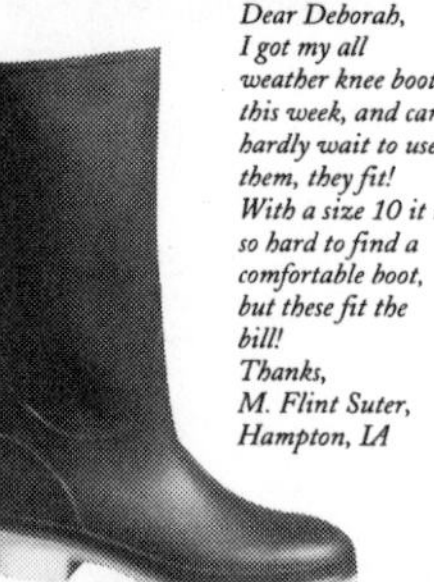

*Dear Deborah,
I got my all weather knee boots this week, and can hardly wait to use them, they fit! With a size 10 it is so hard to find a comfortable boot, but these fit the bill!
Thanks,
M. Flint Suter,
Hampton, IA*

Tingley Knee Boot
ad minim veniam, quis nostrud exerci tation ullamcorper suscipit lobortis nisl ut aliquip ex ea commodo consequat. Duis autem vel eum iriure dolor in hendrerit in vulputate velit esse molestie consequat, laoreet dolore magna aliquam erat volutpat. Ut wisi enim ad minim veniam, quis nostrud exerci tation ullamcorper suscipit lobortis nisl utoreet dolvel illum dolore eu feugiat blandit praesent luptatum zzril delenit augue duis dolore te feugait nulla facilisi. Lorem ipsum dolor sit amet, consectetuer adipiscing elit, sed diam
TKN Tingley Knee Boot
Sizes: Women's 5, 6, 7, 8, 9, 10
Price: $29 per pair

CLOSE OUT SAVINGS
Rainbow Boot
laoreet dolore magna aliquam erat volutpat. Ut wisi enim ad minim veniam, quis nostrud exerci tation ullamcorper suscipit lobortis nisl utoreet dolore magna aliquam erat volutpat. Ut wisi enim ad minim veniam, quis nostrud exe aliquip ex ea commodo consequat.Duis autem vel eum iriure dolor in hendrerit in vulputate velit esse molestieconsequat, vel illum dolore eu feugiat nulla facilisis at vero eros et accumsan et iusto odio dignissim qui blandit praesent luptatum zzril delenit augue duis dolore teUt wisi enim ad minim veniam, quis nostrud exerci tation
DRB Rainbow Boot
Sizes: Women's 5, 5½ , 6, 6½, 7, 7½, 8, 8½, 9, 10, Medium Width
Regular Price: $56 per pair
CLOSE OUT PRICE: $52

*Dear Deborah,
My husband ordered me a pair of Rainbow boots and we are both so impressed by the price and quality. I really enjoy my boots — it's hard to find women's boots that really hold up to any heavy work.
Thanks for offering your products.
Keep it up!
Myrhh Shaw
Solvang, CA*

TO ORDER CALL 800-862-9317

OR USE THE ORDER FORM ON PAGE 15

SUMMER
SPECIAL
The Ultimate Boot

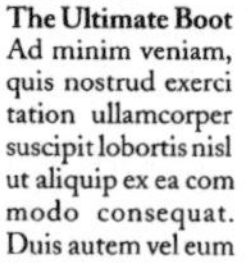

A WorkAbles for Women Exclusive

Ad minim veniam, quis nostrud exerci tation ullamcorper suscipit lobortis nisl ut aliquip ex ea com modo consequat. Duis autem vel eum iriure dolor in hendrerit in vulputate velit esse molestie consequat, laoreet dolore magna aliquam erat volutpat.

Ut wisi enim ad minim veniam, quis nostrud exerci tation ullamcorper suscipit lobortis nisl utoreet dolvel illum dolore eu feugiat blandit praesent luptatum dolor in hendrerit in vulputate velit esse molestie consequat, laoreet blandit praesent luptatumzzril delenit augue duis dolore te feugait nulla facilisi. Lorem ipsum dolor sit amet, consectetuer adipiscing elit,

Ut wisi enim ad minim veniam, quis nostrud exerci tation ullamcorper suscipit lobortis nisl amet, consectetuer adipiscing elit, sed diamsed diam
DGB Tan Women's Gore-Tex Boot
Sizes: Full and half sizes from 5½ to 10, Medium Width.
Regular Price: $150 per pair
SPECIAL SALE PRICE: $139

*THE ULTIMATE BOOT AT A SPECIAL SALE PRICE
Our GoreTex lined, triple-stitched Ultimate Boot ordinarily sells for $150, but order today and you pay only $139.*

*Deborah,
I ordered my Dunham work boots from you a year ago. That should be a long enough time to test them. YES, they are still going strong. I am an aircraft mechanic who previously went through boots in 6 months, if I could find a pair to [illegible]e at [illegible] required alm[illegible] brea[illegible] time. Th[illegible] are very comfor[illegible]d d[illegible]ble. Thank[illegible]ou very, very [illegible]ch fo[illegible] finding a way to help women like us.
Carol McKechnie
Millersville, MD*

AFTER

WorkAble Boot
Ad minim veniam, quis nostrud exerci tation ullamcorper suscipit lobortis nisl ut aliquip ex ea commodo consequat. Duis autem vel eum iriure dolor in hendrerit in vulputate velit esse molestie consequat, laoreet dolore magna aliquam erat volutpat. Ut wisi enim ad minim veniam, quis nostrud exerci tation ullamcorper suscipit lobortis nisl utoreet dolvel illum dolore eu feugiat blandit praesent luptatum dolor in hendrerit in vulputate velit esse molestie consequat, laoreet dolore magna aliquam erat volutpat. Ut wisi enim ad minim veniam, quis nostrud exerci tation ullamcorper suscipit lobortis illum dolore eu feugiat blandit praesent luptatumzzril delenit augue duis amet, consectetuer adipiscing elit, sed diam
Available in 3 models, each in full and half sizes from 5½ to 10.
DWB Tan Leather Women's Work Boot, Medium and Wide Widths
Price: $95
DST Tan Steel Toe Women's Work Boot, Medium Width
Price: $99
DBB Black Leather Boot (postal approved), Special Order
Price: $95

-5-

A sample online session

by Ian Fisk

YOU'VE SEEN A MILLION TESTIMONIAL COMMERCIALS on TV. "I was about to throw myself off a tall building before I discovered new Detergent X, which not only got out those unsightly chocolate fudge stains, but attracted my current wife with its clean and effervescent scent. I'm a new man."

Someone should write one for online services because they really can change the way you work. This is how mine would go:

"Two months ago I was a freelance work-at-home researcher, political consultant and desktop publisher. For information I went to the library, for political news I had to call friends in far away states, and for the latest publishing information I had to buy expensive trade journals.

"Then I started using online services. Today, I interview people quickly and easily whom I have never seen or heard, access information from my desk in minutes that would have formerly taken me hours to find, swap shop-talk with professional designers, and follow the minutiae of state campaigns from 800 miles away. I'm a new man."

This is all true. What I wouldn't say in a commercial is that I also have a credit card bill to wince at and more e-mail to answer every morning than I can possibly keep up with. Everything has its price.

But on the whole, online services have major benefits for your business. To give you an idea of what is out there, I have recorded an actual session on CompuServe, one of the major services. Most services, including CompuServe, offer graphic interfaces so you can just point-and-click without typing. This session, however, is a non-graphical session because 1) I couldn't reproduce one and 2) only the bigger services (except the InterNet) offer these, and I wanted to show you what to expect if you use any of these.

My comments are in brackets. All other text is exactly as it scrolled across my screen. Let's begin:

atdt 388-3303

[*atdt* stands for "AT (access Modem) DT (Dial-Tone)." *atdp* is access modem, dial pulse. There are a whole set of modem commands, beginning with "AT" that have become the standard. They are usually referred to as the "Hayes Command Set."]

CONNECT 2400

[Connecting at 2400 bits per second. 2400 is currently the standard for most online services, but by fall of 1994, it may well be 9600 bps or 14,400 bps.]

07DWC

[I have no idea what this means. This is often the case online, where strange characters will flash at you. As long as they don't interrupt what you're doing or expect an answer, don't worry about them.

Host Name: CIS

[CIS is CompuServe. I am accessing CompuServe through a communications software program called MicroPhone, which came with my modem. Bundled in with most modems is the software to access many of the popular online services.]

User ID: 75720,2357

[My CompuServe ID]

Password:

[This usually will not echo on the screen, in case anybody is looking over your shoulder.]

?? LOGINE - Invalid entry - try again

[One of the problems of the password not echoing—you can incorrectly type it without realizing it.]

Password:

[Got it this time.]

CompuServe Information Service
20:12 EDT Thursday 17-Jun-93
(Executive Option)
Last access: 09:14 17-Jun-93

Copyright (c) 1993
CompuServe Incorporated
All Rights Reserved

You have Electronic Mail waiting.
GO RATES for current information

[Oh, good. Mail. I love mail. So much so that I get much too much to handle. I'm not going to read it now, since I don't want my mail reproduced in this book!]

What's New This Week

1 Surcharge Eliminated for MCI Mail
2 Medical SmartSCAN Charge Waived
3 'GO Graphics' Hosts First Picnic
4 CompuServe's European Services Expand
5 Conferences in Florida Today Forum
6 First-Timers Get Free Articles
7 Play Knowledge Bowl in The Mall
8 FM MIDI Driver in MIDI/Music Forum
9 High-Speed Modem Execs in ZiffNet
(Above Articles Are Free)

10 On-line Today
11 Special Events/Contests Area (FREE)

Enter choice ![Enter]

[Most systems work with a list-prompt method—they show you a list of choices, and you are asked to make a selection. As I mentioned, several offer front-end systems that have icons and buttons for your mouse to click. America Online is the best at that. CompuServe offers CIM, GEnie offers Aladdin, and Delphi offers D-Lite. Prodigy is also a graphically based system.]

CompuServe TOP

1 Access Basic Services
2 Member Assistance (FREE)
3 Communications/Bulletin Bds.
4 News/Weather/Sports
5 Travel
6 The Electronic MALL/Shopping
7 Money Matters/Markets
8 Entertainment/Games
9 Hobbies/Lifestyles/Education
10 Reference
11 Computers/Technology
12 Business/Other Interests

Enter choice number !New

I don't recognize that command. Key H for Help !Go New

[CompuServe is a "go" based system. Most systems work on keywords—each area has a name ("Mail," "New," "Basic," "News," "Work," "Games") and you have to access it using that name or keyword. In this case I remembered seeing the word FREE flash by me on my screen in the "What's New This Week" menu (note how it had the word "NEW" next to the heading—that's the "go" word), so I wanted to check it out.]

What's New This Week NEW

1 Surcharge Eliminated for MCI Mail
2 Medical SmartSCAN Charge Waived
3 'GO Graphics' Hosts First Picnic
4 CompuServe's European Services Expand
5 Conferences in Florida Today Forum
6 First-Timers Get Free Articles
7 Play Knowledge Bowl in The Mall
8 FM MIDI Driver in MIDI/Music Forum
9 High-Speed Modem Execs in ZiffNet
(Above Articles Are Free)

10 On-line Today
11 Special Events/Contests Area (FREE)

Enter choice !6

[Yes, sure enough, #6 said "FREE" articles. Never one to pass up a bargain, I think I'll find out what that means.]

What's New This Week NEW-30

FIRST-TIMERS GET FREE ARTICLES (17-Jun-93)

In June, first-time users of Magazine Database Plus will receive the first two articles free. Magazine Database Plus provides access to the full text of more than 163,000 articles from more than 130 general-interest magazines.

You'll find articles on current events, business, science, sports, personalities, personal finance, family issues, cooking, education and more. Although CompuServe standard connect charges remain in effect, the charges for downloading or reading the first two articles you access have been eliminated.

To access Magazine Database Plus, part of CompuServe's extended services, GO MAGDB.

[Oh. Not as interesting as I had originally thought. But we're in the BASIC SERVICES area of CompuServe, which is not expensive to be in. Most services have tiered rates—a flat monthly fee for basic services (Mail, Help, Basic News), connect-time charges for advanced services (Dow-Jones quotes, games), and serious charges for some services (Database Research).]

Last page ![Enter]

Enter choice number !go work

["Work" is the working from home forum. A forum is an area set aside for discussion of and files about a certain topic, in this case working from home.]

You have left basic services

[Uh oh. Connect time charges now. Connect time charges are invariably higher in the business hours. Much higher. Luckily, it's 8:00 pm now.]

Professions WORK

One moment please . . .

Welcome to Working From Home Forum+, V. 3A(131)

[Like I said, sometimes characters flash on my screen that I just don't understand.]

Hello, Ian Fisk

[I've registered at this forum. It doesn't cost anything, it just lets them know who I am. The Forum is an area in, but distinct from, CompuServe. Just because CompuServe knows who I am doesn't mean these people do. I had to tell them.]

Last visit: 14-Jun-93 06:26:25
Forum messages: 228247 to 309227
Last message you've read: 307067

[CompuServe gets so many messages that they are deleted after being on the system for a week. That 300,000 figure is real.]

Press <CR> ![Enter]

[To prevent text from scrolling by too quickly, the communications program or CompuServe, depending on your set-up, will set breaks in the middle of the text so that only a screenful gets sent at a time. If you're Evelyn Wood, these are annoying. If you're human, they're a lifesaver.]

Working From Home Forum+ Menu

1 INSTRUCTIONS
2 MESSAGES
3 LIBRARIES (Files)
4 CONFERENCING (0 participating)
5 ANNOUNCEMENTS from sysop
6 MEMBER directory
7 OPTIONS for this forum
Enter choice !2

[Let's see if anybody has responded to my comments. Messages are different from mail in that they relate to messages I posted under specific topic areas. Messages are public—that's the point, like a giant bulletin board. Mail is private. That's the main difference. Messages can get very heated—this forum is peopled with some rational folks, but you should see the political forums . . . .]

Working From Home Forum+ Messages Menu

Message age selection = (New)

1 SELECT (Read by section and subject)
2 READ or search messages
3 CHANGE age selection
4 COMPOSE a message
5 UPLOAD a message
Enter choice !2

Working From Home Forum+ Read Menu

Read

1 (NEW) messages
2 Message NUMBER
3 WAITING messages for you (0)
Search (new) messages

4 FROM (Sender)
5 SUBJECT
6 TO (Recipient)
Enter choice !1

[I'm just reading the most recent messages, in particular the ones posted since my last visit here. Since I didn't specify, it gives me the first bulletin board, "News and General Info" to read first. What follows are actual interchanges.]

#: 308263 S1/News & General Info
14-Jun-93 14:31:15
Sb: Books on Home Work
Fm: John L. Bryant 73657,1364
To: Harvey Summers 76350,2114 (X)

Harvey,

Thanks for your message. I am archiving all the message that I receive on this subject for further reference. It is good to hear from someone who is actually really working from home. I have downloaded several of the suggested files about business ideas and several newsletters.

John

Press <CR> for next or type CHOICES !

#: 308057 S1/News & General Info
13-Jun-93 15:06:52
Sb: Books on Home Work
Fm: Renee Pearson 71062,2007
To: Laura Lee Lemmon 74740,2060 (X)

Whew! I'm glad we cleared that one up.

I too left a large company to start my own home-based business. I've read the Edwards/Douglas book along with almost anything else I can find on small business marketing. It's been tough but I wouldn't go back to corporate America for anything.

Good luck!

Renee

Press <CR> for next or type CHOICES !

[That last one didn't seem to follow the topic of the previous message. Even though Forums try to sort messages by topic, sometimes people talk back and forth on top of other people.]

#: 308672 S1/News & General Info
16-Jun-93 01:36:20
Sb: HOW YOU USE COMPUSERVE??
Fm: James A Magnant 76400,2070
To: Doug Allen 75020,3071 (X)

Doug—

50 percent or better is good enough. TapCIS took a while for me to get going, but that's another thread . . . .

FWIW, your FWIW was very informative. Thanks.

Jim M.

[See where James uses the term "Thread?" A thread is a series of connected messages on the same topic. People follow message threads, and are thus assured of sticking to at least something similar to what first drew them into this line of comments. Other services, like America Online, post folders and ask people to keep within the topic of the folder. I generally find the thread method works better. After all, you don't have a lot of time, and you want to read about what you are interested in.]

[FWIW? What does that mean? Because time is money, people use abbreviations a lot. James is obviously a big CIS user. FWIW means For What It's Worth]

Press <CR> for next or type CHOICES !

#: 308418 S1/News & General Info
15-Jun-93 04:52:28
Sb: #help! Personnel forum?
Fm: Paul & Sarah Edwards 76703,242
To: Horace Mitchell (UK) 100136,2412 (X)
Horace, we have tried a section here for trainers because a substantial share of this industry is made of home-based consultants. Perhaps we should broaden the topic to call it "human resource consultants" to capture the interest of the many specialties embraced in the HR field. Our emphasis here is on the self-employed or otherwise home-based for a field.

I am interested in your reaction to this forum as a locus of activity and those of other people in the HR field reading these messages. — Paul

There is 1 Reply.

Press <CR> for next or type
CHOICES !

[Hey look—Famous people! Paul and Sarah Edwards actually manage this forum, as well as writing books on working from home. The people who run these forums are experts in the field, and will respond to direct questions or interject themselves into interesting threads.]

#: 308512 S1/News & General Info
15-Jun-93 13:57:52
Sb: #308418-#help! Personnel forum?
Fm: Gregory Clark 72242,727
To: Paul & Sarah Edwards 76703,242 (X)

Paul—I sort of jumped in here as your reply to Horace is of great interest to me too. I don't know a lot about HR, per se, except that's where I used to go to get my health insurance forms when I was with "The Firm". But I think maybe there are two areas—Human Resources and maybe another one called Training and Education (and/or Development; although I think the meaning of this T&D term will change too). I'm sure my opinion is not new, but I think we are facing a complete re-training of America over the next ten years. It's an area that I have a great deal of interest in perusing also. Having been a consultant for years and the one aspect which I live for is the "teaching" element. While I still have to do the fieldwork, analysis and preparation of lengthy reports (in order to get paid), I feel like I've entered the next dimension when I take it in front of a crowded room and start "teaching". I feel silly asking, but do people make a career out of "just speaking"? I've hesitated asking but when I ask myself "What do I really like doing and what am I good at, that's what comes up. Any thoughts?"—GC

There is 1 Reply.

[This means somebody replied directly to this message.]

Press <CR> for next or type
CHOICES !

[Choices would bring out to a menu of options for dealing with the Forum.]

#: 308692 S1/News & General Info
16-Jun-93 04:13:39
Sb: #308512-#help! Personnel forum?
Fm: Paul & Sarah Edwards 76703,242
To: Gregory Clark 72242,727 (X)

People sure do make a career out of "just speaking." First, there are professional speakers. While probably no more than 200 earn more than $100,000 a year speaking, thousands of people supplement their incomes being paid to speak. The primary professional association for speakers is the National Speakers Association, 3877 North Seventh Street, Ste. 350, Phoenix, AZ 85014, 602-265-1001. Sarah and I used to belong and can tell you the training the organization offers is worthwhile and membership in the local chapter, of which there's a strong one in the LA area, can be helpful.

Then there are professional trainers and seminar leaders. The number of people earning six figure incomes in these fields is likely in the thousands. Unlike speaking, one is more apt to be full-time at this. The primary professional association is the American Society for Training and Development. If you're interested in contacting ASTD, I'll provide you with their address and phone information. It's also in our book "Best Home Businesses for the 90's". So, Gregory, you can make all or at least part of your income doing what you like to do—standing in front of a room of people and "talking." — Paul

There is 1 Reply.

[Note that Paul plugged his book. As the SYSOP (Forum Manager) he's allowed to do that. Generally, however, commercial activity is discouraged on all of the networks—the idea is to bring people together. The one exception is where, as in this case, commercial activity relates directly to questions asked of a vendor. Software manufacturers are online, and you can ask them questions about their products. They can answer, but they can't send you junk mail. Prodigy has online advertisements, and they're very annoying.]

Press <CR> for next or type
CHOICES !choices

Working From Home Forum+ Read Action Menu

1 REPLY with same subject
2 COMPOSE with new subject
3 REREAD this message
4 NEXT reply
5 NEXT SUBJECT
6 READ reply

Enter choice ! [Enter]

[Remember, Enter moves me back one menu towards the top. Think of Ask/Prompt menus as a tree. The further down you go, the more branches/possibilities. To get back to the top, you return to the single entry point.]

#: 308866 S1/News & General Info
16-Jun-93 17:37:23
Sb: #308692-#help! Personnel forum?
Fm: Gregory Clark 72242,727
To: Paul & Sarah Edwards 76703,242 (X)

What an encouraging reply to my "speaking request"! I am absolutely amazed and the tremendous amount of useful information I'm receiving from going through this forum.

I'll contact the National Speakers Association and follow-up with seeing how to get involved in the LA chapter. The training route sounds most appealing since I am expanding this "mid-life career question" (although I don't think I'm at the mid- point yet), from "What do you like to do?" to "What do you like to do and what will provide the greatest service to others?" I would certainly like to contact the ASTD so if you have a number and/or address, that would be helpful. I've been noting a lot of references to your book since joining the forum a couple of weeks ago and will be picking up a copy this week. Can't wait, actually. Thanks again.—GC

There are 2 Replies.

[Please note—this is not an ad for Paul and Sarah Edwards. These messages are real—you can look them up yourself.]

Press <CR> for next or type
CHOICES !top

Working From Home Forum+ Menu

1 INSTRUCTIONS
2 MESSAGES
3 LIBRARIES (Files)
4 CONFERENCING (0 participating)
5 ANNOUNCEMENTS from sysop
6 MEMBER directory
7 OPTIONS for this forum

Enter choice !top

[Top is going to the top of the Tree. It returns you to whence you came—Basic Services.]

Exiting at 17-Jun-93 20:15:29

Thank you for visiting Working From Home Forum

You have entered basic services

CompuServe TOP

1 Access Basic Services
2 Member Assistance (FREE)
3 Communications/Bulletin Bds.
4 News/Weather/Sports
5 Travel
6 The Electronic MALL/Shopping
7 Money Matters/Markets
8 Entertainment/Games
9 Hobbies/Lifestyles/Education
10 Reference
11 Computers/Technology
12 Business/Other Interests

[I'm a political consultant. I need to know the latest news. Yesterday, Bill Clinton nominated a new Supreme Court justice. I knew about it before the evening news reported it, because I read it online.]

Enter choice number !4

News/Weather/Sports NEWS

BASIC NEWS SERVICES

1 Associated Press On-line
2 Weather
3 UK News/Sports
4 On-line Today Daily Edition

EXTENDED NEWS SERVICES

5 Executive News Service ($)
6 NewsGrid US/World News +
7 Sports
8 Newspaper Library
9 Florida Today Forum +
10 Global Crises Forum +
11 The Business Wire +

[The "+" signs mean there is a connect time charge in addition to the flat rate. The "$" sign means there are extra charges for specific services you ask the Executive News Service to do.]

Enter choice or <CR> for more !1

One moment please . . .

AP On-line

Associated Press On-line
Associated Press Videotex News Service

Copyright 1993, Associated Press
All Rights Reserved

The information contained in the AP On-line news report may not be published, broadcast or otherwise redistributed without the prior written authority of the Associated Press.

[Yeah. This isn't re-broadcasting a baseball game. This is the real world. Online news services cannot be reused commercially.]

Press <CR> for more !

AP On-line

1 Latest News-Updated Hourly
2 Weather
3 Sports
4 National
5 Washington
6 World
7 Political
8 Entertainment
9 Business News
10 Wall Street
11 Dow Jones Average
12 Feature News/Today in History
13 Science & Health

Enter choice !7

That choice is temporarily empty !
[News]

News/Weather/Sports NEWS

[One of the annoying things about ask-prompt, is that when you draw a blank, as in above, you have to go back to the previous menu. In graphical interfaces, like America On-Line, CIM, Aladdin, D-Lite, or Prodigy, it's the windows format. You just click the icon you want.]

BASIC NEWS SERVICES

1 Associated Press On-line
2 Weather
3 UK News/Sports
4 On-line Today Daily Edition

EXTENDED NEWS SERVICES

5 Executive News Service ($)
6 NewsGrid US/World News +
7 Sports
8 Newspaper Library
9 Florida Today Forum +
10 Global Crises Forum +
11 The Business Wire +

Enter choice or <CR> for more !1

AP On-line

Associated Press On-line
Associated Press Videotex News Service

Copyright 1993, Associated Press
All Rights Reserved

The information contained in the AP On-line news report may not be published, broadcast or otherwise redistributed without the prior written authority of the Associated Press.

Press <CR> for more !

AP On-line

1 Latest News-Updated Hourly
2 Weather
3 Sports
4 National
5 Washington
6 World
7 Political
8 Entertainment
9 Business News
10 Wall Street
11 Dow Jones Average
12 Feature News/Today in History
13 Science & Health

Enter choice !5

AP On-line

3 Sen., 1st Lady Talked Medicare
4 Panel OKs Black History Museum
5 Poll: Press Rough On Clinton
6 Coverage Of Clinton Criticized
7 Young Gun Trafficker Testifies
8 Home Workers Not Goof Offs
9 Home Workers Not Goof Offs
0 House Passes Foreign Aid Plan

[Look, more stories on people like us! Usually this news is what you'll see in the morning papers. It's not till you get to the Internet that you get the real inside scoop.]

Enter choice or <CR> for more !8

AP Online

AP 06/17 18:07 EDT V0744

WASHINGTON (AP) — People who work at home are no more likely to goof off than people who go to an office every day, and they actually smoke, drink and take drugs less, according to a government report released Thursday.

The Small Business Administration report looked at growing trends toward home-based businesses and "telecommuting," or doing office work at home during normal business hours.

A home office, complete with computer, printer, telephone and fax costs about $5000. Thus, Americans are increasingly expected to start home-based businesses or work from home, according to Joanne Pratt, a management consultant who prepared the report for the SBA.

"One of the things this research has done is dispelled a lot of myths about why people can't work at home," Pratt told a briefing Thursday.

For example, they are no more likely than others to have children at home, according to the report, "Myths and Realities of Working at Home."

And employees do not care for their children on telecommuting days. Work patterns among telecommuters and nontelecommuters are very similar. On average, men spend just over an hour and women just under an hour on lunch, coffee breaks and relaxing during the work day, Pratt found.

Telecommuters also have positive attitudes toward their work and do not feel

Press <CR> for more !

AP Online

isolated from their peers, the report found. It said they work an average of six to eight hours a week at home.

The report did not measure productivity, but Pratt said her research has found that telecommuters are about 20 percent more productive. She said 33 percent of the work force spends some time telecommuting.

Home-based businesses also are growing, not only because of technological advances but as a result of layoffs and an increasing use of outside contractors by businesses, Pratt said.

The number of home-based businesses grew from 3.6 million in 1985 to more than 5.6 million in 1991, according to the report.

Pratt's study found differences between home-based businesses run by men and by women. Women in their 20s are less likely to have a home-based business than

Press <CR> for more !

AP Online

those over 30, she found. For men, the decision to own a home-based business bears no relation to age. White people are more likely to have home-based businesses than nonwhites. Women running businesses from home work fewer hours than men, according to the report. However, they also work the equivalent of three business days a week on household tasks, not including child care. Women in their 20s report greater job satisfaction than men of the same age even though the women earn considerably less, the study found. Women in their 30s and 40s make about the same amount of money from home-based jobs as in other sectors of the work force, according to the report.

The report was based on the Bureau of Labor Statistics' National Longitudinal Study, including 1988 surveys of men and women ages 23–30; women ages 34–44; and

Press <CR> for more !

[If these ever really annoy you, there's a way on most systems to take them out. And again, these news reports are real.]

AP Online

a 1989 survey of women ages 52–66.

Last page !

AP Online

3 Sen., 1st Lady Talked Medicare
4 Panel OKs Black History Museum
5 Poll: Press Rough On Clinton
6 Coverage Of Clinton Criticized
7 Young Gun Trafficker Testifies
8 Home Workers Not Goof Offs
9 Home Workers Not Goof Offs
0 House Passes Foreign Aid Plan

Enter choice or <CR> for more !!bye

[That's all for now. Bye, Exit, or Quit are the three words that will likely free you from your service and disconnect the modem.]

Thank you for using CompuServe!

Off at 20:17 EDT 17-Jun-93
Connect time = 0:05

So that's what it's like to be online. If I wanted to, I could have added comments to the forum on home businesses, or sent mail directly to some of the people in the discussion.

There are four basic uses for a network—electronic mail, accessing databases, downloading files, and participating and learning from Forums.

You'll notice that I keep fretting about getting too much mail. It's very easy to stop by in a forum or two, leave messages to everything you see, like "I agree" or "No, I disagree." Don't—it clogs up the message board. All postings should be substantiative. Similarly, because sending e-mail is so convenient, you might soon find yourself sending out dozens of quick notes and receiving dozens of answers that require a thoughtful response. That is what I mean by too much mail.

Accessing databases is the prime capability of online systems, albeit the most expensive one. Anything you want to know is online somewhere. The Library of Congress has significant chunks of its files online. Roger Ebert's Movie Reviews are online. Numerous magazines, including *Home Office Computing* are available online. Not that they are easy to read that way, but they are easy to store. No need for bookshelves, dust cloths, or trips to the library. If you need an article from a major (or an obscure) journal, just look it up online, download only the file you need, and you're all set. Market research is easy to do this way. Thinking of opening a store in Ghana?

Check the state department files. Want to know the oil production for Saudi Arabia last year? It's there. It's just finding it that's difficult.

Downloading files is the activity that should be most useful (thousands of free files! only charge is phone time!) but must be handled right. Sure, there are files of all kinds available for your downloading for no extra charge on the networks, but downloading takes time. A lot of time. This is what really runs up your phone bill. If you need a file for your business, best to find out what it is by asking people on the network, and buying it, then downloading a copy. In most cases. Know what you want before you go hunting for it.

Despite the numerous books on the commercial services, and a spate of books now being published on the Internet, it's still hard to understand online services without using them. Luckily, many companies now have free trials, most notably GEnie, America On-Line, and Delphi. But for your home business, the ability to send messages to many people cheaply (e-mail), access information quickly (Databases), find experts in a field or discuss a topic of interest (Forums), or download computer files (Downloading) can be invaluable if you know what you want to do with the information. After a couple of trial runs, you'll probably be writing your own testimonials . . . .

Putting your business on tape with multimedia

by Philip Bishop

MEDIA ARE WAYS OF COMMUNICATING. IN THE computer world this includes text and numbers, graphics, sound, animation, and video. By bringing together two or more of these methods, multimedia is created.

"Multimedia" is one of the big buzzwords in the computer industry. It's projected to be a multi-billion dollar industry—a critical technology for interactive TV, movie special effects, and even your business.

Fortunately, there are some practical applications for multimedia in the here and now. With a relatively modest investment of time and money, it is well within your power to produce a multimedia promotional videotape for your home-based business— containing pictures, text, music, and narration. I'll show you, step by step, just how to do it. Once you have created one, who knows, perhaps you'll want to create tapes for others.

Production work, however, requires additional hardware and software. Ideally, you should have a multimedia-ready PC, designated by the MPC logo. Otherwise, you can easily purchase a multimedia upgrade kit. On the Macintosh front, a machine with a built-in CD-ROM drive is your best bet—but you can always buy an external drive.

To create a promotional videotape you will need a video adapter board, a Hi-8 or S-VHS VCR, presentation software, and QuickTime for the Macintosh or Video for Windows (these latter two are only required if you are planning to use animated sequences). Optional elements are a scanner, if you want to digitize any printed materials, and a microphone and cassette player, if you want to add digitized audio. I would add, however, that almost all videotape productions benefit from the addition of narration, some music, or both: They help keep the viewer's interest as well as highlight key points.

Although the rewards of multimedia production can be considerable, it will take a solid investment of time, energy, and money to master the necessary skills. If you decide to take the plunge, take it slowly. Talk to those who are making a living with this new technology (you can meet many of them in CompuServe's Multimedia Forum [GO MULTIMEDIA]). Refer to the table on page 175 for explanations of the equipment and software necessary to enter the world of multimedia. Beside each explanation is any PC- or Macintosh-specific information that you should know. For further guidance, refer to the listings of hardware and software companies, books, and magazines at the end of this appendix.

Please note that with these tools you will not be able to create Emmy Award-winning productions; they just aren't that sophisticated. But with patience and talent, you should be able to create a simple, informative videotape. The best subject for your tape is your own business, simply because you know it better than anything else. The reward for the effort you expend will be a new promotional vehicle, one that might provide your home-based business with a competitive edge. You could also make a tape to help promote a nonprofit organization in your area. Whatever your subject is, your sales tapes should last between five and seven minutes. Longer than that and you will probably lose your audience's attention.

Steps in creating a tape

Step 1: Plan

Many high-tech projects begin with low-tech tools, and our tape is no exception. Using pencil and paper, create a storyboard of your presentation. This is a simple sketch of each slide, including both the words and the pictures. If you plan to include narration or background music, indicate what they'll be and their positioning.

Step 2: Create the presentation

Scan graphics as you need them. Import clip art from a CD-ROM. Create your slides. Add transition effects. Because of the way analog video is displayed, you'll need to follow these guidelines: Center as much as you can (avoid placing items close to the edge of a slide), don't use thin lines, use large type (30 points or better), and avoid using bright colors (computers can display colors that TV can't). Play the presentation again and again and again. Edit it. Tweak it. You might get truly sick of seeing it, but that's just one of the burdens of the creative process. Play it until you can find fault with very little (you'll always find fault with something, but that's just another of the burdens of the creative process).

Step 3: Prepare the narration

With your presentation purring, write the narration. Then read the narration as the tape is playing to make sure that what you want to say is approximately the same length as the duration of the slide or slides you are talking about. A stopwatch can come in handy here. With it you can time exactly how long you have to talk. Use a measured delivery; in a sales tape you can't rattle on like you're chatting on the phone.

Step 4: Prepare placement of the background music

The simplest method of adding audio is to have no narration and just use clips of music behind your presentation. If you want to do something more interesting, take out your stopwatch, time each slide's duration, and find music to match these spaces. You won't want to use music throughout, though; it simply demands too much disk space.

Step 5: Digitize the audio

To digitize narration, you need to plug a microphone into your sound board and, using sound-digitizing software, start talking. Recording to cassette tape and digitizing this might produce better-quality audio. Experiment to see which is best for you. For the musical component, you can plug a cassette player into your sound board and digitize sound from this source, although you must be careful not to violate someone's copyright. The rule here is, if you aren't sure, find out or don't use it. Instead, try using some clip audio, which is available on CD-ROMs and floppy disks. Or ask a local musician to produce something for you; he might do it in exchange for a credit in your videotape.

Step 6: Output the presentation to videotape

Next, attach your VCR to your video adapter board. There are many video adapter boards available. What you need for this project is a board that has basic scan-converting capabilities, which means it will convert your digital computer signal to a TV signal, which is analog. Using the instructions that come with the board, output the presentation to videotape. This might be as simple as selecting a Print to Tape command from a menu.

Step 7: Play back and edit the presentation

View the first fruits of your creativity. If you find something you don't like, or notice anything that needs changing, hightail it back to your computer, change it, and output it again.

Step 8: Mix and add the audio

With the visual aspect to your liking, you now get to add the audio. First, though, if you plan to use both music and narration, you'll need to mix them with some audio-editing software. With the VCR attached to your computer and your tape inserted, switch on audio dub on the VCR, and depress the record, play, and pause buttons. Then, from within your audio-editing software, play your audio track. The pause button on the VCR will be released and audio will be added to the video track.

Step 9: Play back and edit the audio

View (and listen to) the second fruits of your creativity. If you find something you don't like, or notice anything that needs changing, hightail it back to your computer, change it, and lay down the audio again. You're almost home.

Step 10: Go forth and multiply

The final step in the process is to duplicate your videotape. Quality and price depend on many factors such as tape length and the number of copies you want. You'll need to shop around to find a duplicator. Check the back of videography magazines for leads or ask around on CompuServe or other bulletin boards. If you are working with a tight deadline, you should have duplication issues planned early in the project.

If you are excited about creating a promotional videotape but don't have the money or time to invest, don't give up. You might be able to locate someone with the equipment and expertise necessary to do it for you. While multimedia hasn't made it into the yellow pages, you should be able to find someone on CompuServe's Multimedia Forum who can help you out or point you in the right direction.

Resources

Below is a listing of multimedia products that we recommend—all provide good quality and value. Call these companies for more detailed information, or talk to people in the multimedia business and get their advice about what will work best for you.

[P] = PC, [M] = Macintosh

MPCs and Multimedia MACs

[P] Dell Computer Corp.
(800) 289-3355

[P] Compaq Computer Corp.
(800) 345-1518

[P] IBM
(800) 426-2468

[M] Apple Computer
(800) 776-2333

PC Multimedia upgrade kits

[P] Creative Labs
(800) 998-1000

[P] Media Vision
(800) 845-5870

CD-ROM drives

[P, M] NEC Technologies
(708) 860-9500

[M] Mirror Technologies
(800) 654-5294

Audio boards

[P] Turtle Beach Systems
(717) 843-6916

[M] Digidesign
(800) 333-2137

Speakers

[P, M] Bose Corp.
(800) 444-2673

[P, M] Persona Technologies Inc.
(415) 871-6000

Video adapter boards

[P] PC Video Conversion Corp.
(408) 279-2442

[M] VideoLogic Inc
(617) 494-0530

VCRs

Hi-8 VCRs:

[P, M] Sony Corp. of America
(800) 352-7669

S-VHS:

[P, M] Panasonic Broadcast & Television Systems Co.
(800) 524-0864

Color flatbed scanners

[P, M] Hewlett-Packard Co.
(800) 752-0900

[M] Mirror Technologies
(800) 654-5294

Video for Windows/QuickTime

Video for Windows:
[P] Microsoft
(800) 426-9400

QuickTime:
[M] available through Apple dealers

Presentation software

PowerPoint 3.0
[P, M] Microsoft
(800) 426-9400

Persuasion 2.1
[P, M] Aldus Corp.
(206) 622-5500

Compel
[P] Asymetrix
(800) 448-6543

Audio editing software

MasterTracks
[P, M] Passport Designs
(800) 443-3210

SoundEdit Pro
[M] Macromedia
(800) 288-4797

Books

The Desktop Multimedia Bible, by Jeff Burger, 1992, Addison-Wesley Publishing Co.; $32.95; (800) 358-4566

Multimedia: Making It Work, by Tay Vaughan, 1993, Osborne McGraw-Hill; $27.95; (800) 227-0900

	Definition	PC Specifications	Mac Specifications
CPU/monitor	Multimedia, especially on the production end, is memory intensive (10 seconds of digitized sound takes up 1MB of disk space). If you are planning to buy a new computer, get a Multimedia PC (designated by the MPC logo) or a Macintosh with built-in CD-ROM drive. Either of these machines is an excellent choice for multimedia work.	You need at least a 386SX processor, 4MB of RAM, and an 80MB hard drive to be a multimedia user. To be a successful producer, you should be equipped with at least a 486 processor, 8MB or RAM, and a 100MB to 300MB hard drive. Any color SVGA monitor will be adequate.	You need at least a 68030 processor, 4MB of RAM, and an 80MB hard drive to be a multimedia user. To be a successful producer, you should be equipped with at least 8MB of RAM and a 100MB to 300MB hard drive. Any color monitor will be adequate.
CD-ROM drive	CD-ROM drives have become a core component of any multimedia system, whether for a consumer or a producer. The best drives currently have an access time of around 200ms and a data transfer rate of 300K/sec.	All MPC systems and several non-MPC systems have built-in CD-ROMs, although as of this writing, none supports high-performance drives like the one on the Mac.	The Performa 600, and Centris 610 and 650 have optional internal CD-ROM drives. All future Macs will likely offer a CD-ROM drive as a basic option.
Audio board	An audio board connects your computer to audio components such as speakers, cassette player, and microphone. You use this equipment to get sound into your computer for inclusion in multimedia projects. 8-bit audio is fine for consumer and most production needs, but consider 16-bit audio if you are working in the high-end.	A board like the Sound Blaster Pro is fine for consumer needs, but for production purposes, you'll need something more sophisticated. Only MPC computers guarantee that 8-bit audio is included, as on the Mac. For highend multimedia, 16-bit boards can be added.	From its rollout in 1984, the Macintosh has had 8-bit audio built into the logic board. For most consumer and some simple multimedia production, this is fine. For high-end multimedia, 16-bit boards can be added.
Video adapter board	There are many kinds of video adapter boards and they perform several different functions. Essentially, they serve as a conduit between the digital world of your computer and the analog world of TVs, camcorders, VCRs, and similar video equipment. Some boards actually convert analog video to digital video, whereas others serve as a link, for example, between your computer and a VCR so you can output a multimedia presentation to videotape.	There are a full range of video adapter boards available for the PC.	There are a full range of video adapter boards available for the Macintosh.
Flatbed scanner	For the multimedia producer, a color flatbed scanner might be the most-used tool in your studio. With it you can digitize all manner of printed material for inclusion in your multi-media presentation (but beware of violating copyrights).	Almost all scanners work on the PC.	Almost all scanners work on the Macintosh.
VCR	Consumer-grade video equipment doesn't cut it when trying to produce quality multimedia. You'll need to consider a higher standard, such as Hi-8 or S-VHS. Make sure your VCR has flying erase heads and audio dub for easier editing of video and sound.	Almost all VCRs work with the PC.	Almost all VCRs work with the Macintosh.
Software	If you're a multimedia producer, you might need to get nothing more than a presentation program. On the other end of the spectrum, you might need a small library of titles for animation, illustration, video, and audio editing.	A full range of multimedia production software is available for the PC.	A full range of multimedia production software is available for the Macintosh.

Glossary

8-bit color A monitor with 8-bit color can display up to 256 colors at one time. Most PCs and Macs come with the ability to display 8-bit color on a 13" or 14" monitor.

24-bit color A monitor with 24-bit color can display up to 16,777,216 colors at one time. This level of color requires a special video card plugged into one of your computer's expansion slots. These cards are expensive, sometimes costing as much as the monitor.

active matrix vs. passive matrix Active and passive matrices are the two screen types used in notebook computers. The brightness, contrast, and refresh rate for active matrix screens is generally on par with standard monitors used on desktop computers. Passive matrix screens are harder to read and sometimes leave ghost images because of the slow refresh rate.

archive A special file format that applications and files are generally transformed into before they're uploaded to an online service. A special archiving program can take multiple files—an application and its documentation files—and combine them into one file so all the program's components can be downloaded together. Archiving is also used when compressing multiple files to free hard drive space.

ASCII (American Standard Code for Information Interchange) The international standard for assigning numbers to characters; for example, capital A is 65 and a space is 32. All computers understand ASCII.

AT command set Standard set of commands (developed by Hayes and often referred to as the Hayes command set) for controlling operation of a modem. Called the AT set because with few exceptions all commands begin with the letters AT. When a modem is "Hayes-compatible," it works with this command set.

autoanswer Either a feature or a mode of operation of a modem. A modem with autoanswer can automatically answer the phone when a call comes in.

batch command A way of executing a series of commands with a key word. (See also *macro*.)

baud A measure of the speed at which bits of information are sent and received over communication lines, like those used with a modem. Although the two don't mean the same thing, *baud* and *bps* are often used interchangeably. Baud is short for "bits audible."

BBS (bulletin board system) A BBS provides a convenient way to communicate with fellow computer enthusiasts, acquire copies of programs, and so on via modem. The programs available on BBSs are usually shareware, which means you can try a program before you buy. There are several thousand small BBSs located around the country.

bps (bits-per-second) The number of bits that can be transmitted over a communication line every second; often incorrectly confused with baud.

broadcasting Having the capability to send one document or file to numerous recipients simultaneously.

boot The process of starting up a computer.

buffer A unit of memory that temporarily stores information. A printer buffer, for example, will speed the flow of information to your printer and free your computer for other tasks.

byte A basic unit of computer memory, a byte is just large enough to store a single character. There are 1024 bytes to the kilobyte and 1024 kilobytes to the megabyte (meg or MB). If you have an 80MB hard drive, for example, it will store 83,886,080 bytes of information.

cache A special program that uses part of your computer's RAM to store the information you use most often. With a cache, when the system requests data from the disk there is a good chance the data, or part of it, will be in the cache. Since RAM access is much faster than disk access, a cache can speed up disk-intensive applications.

CCITT A United Nations organization that develops and defines the standards used by modems and other phone equipment. Any modem standard that begins with a V. is a CCITT standard, such as:

V.22	The CCITT standard for 1200 bps communications
V.22bis	The CCITT standard for 2400 bps communications
V.32	The CCITT standard for 4800 and 9600 bps communications
V.32bis	An improvement on V.32 that adds 7200, 12,000, and 14,400 bps
V.42	The CCITT standard for error-checking modems that includes LAPM and MNP error control
V.42bis	An extension of V.42 that adds on-the-fly data compression and decompression.

CD-ROM (compact disc-read-only memory) A 5-inch plastic disc that can hold as much as 680 megabytes of computer information. Although the CD-ROM's optical technology doesn't lend itself well to rewriting, its huge capacity makes it invaluable for storing large amounts of data.

CD-ROM drive A device that reads CD-ROMs. Look for drives that meet the Multimedia PC (MPC) standard to ensure the highest quality.

cell The basic unit in a spreadsheet. Cells are formed by the intersection of rows and columns and can hold data, formulas, or both.

column heading The heading placed at the top of a vertical group of spreadsheet cells. Column headings are usually labeled in A1 style (A,B,C) or R1C1 style (C1,C2,C3 or 1,2,3). (See also *row heading*.)

command line The DOS command line is the C> prompt. When you type commands at the prompt, the command interpreter executes them or tells you your syntax is incorrect.

communications software The software necessary for your computer to communicate with a modem and to access online services and other computers.

conferencing Using a special area on a BBS or commercial service where several users at a time can discuss a subject live. What you type is instantly seen by the other users in the conference area. One-on-one communication is usually referred to as *chat mode*.

connect time The amount of time you are logged on to an online service, which is also the normal basis for online service billing—usually measured in fractions of an hour.

cps (characters per second) Refers to the rate at which actual data are transmitted. Looking at cps or throughput of a transmission is more valuable than the simple bps rate.

CPU (central processing unit) The area inside the computer that houses the microprocessor and all the supporting circuitry.

DDE (dynamic data exchange) A communications link used in Windows and OS/2 that allows for two or more programs to exchange information and commands.

dialog box A special type of interactive window that allows the user to respond to a program. A dialog box typically contains controls such as check boxes or option buttons.

disk capture In a communications program, this refers to saving all data into a text file as it comes in.

docking station An external box with which you can "dock" your notebook computer, allowing it access to larger monitors and additional memory.

DOS (disk operating system) The standard operating system that comes with all PCs. DOS is a command line system, meaning that you give commands to the computer by typing them in. Other operating systems, like Windows, allow you to point to icons representing specific actions you want to perform.

dot-matrix A dot-matrix printer produces printouts by driving tiny hammers called pins against an inked cloth ribbon, leaving little dots on the paper beneath, from which graphics or text is formed on the page. Dot-matrix printers are most useful in printing multipart forms.

dot-pitch Monitors are defined by the dot-pitch, which refers to the diagonal distance between two dots of the same color. A standard dot pitch is .28mm.

download To have data transmitted from an online service or BBS to your computer.

dpi (dots-per-inch) A standard of printer resolution that measures the number of dots a printer can place along a linear inch. Most laser printers are 300 dpi, a level of output that will be sufficient for most needs. Desktop publishers will want to look at 600 dpi printers, which have become very affordable, and provide excellent graphics output.

DTP (desktop publishing) Desktop publishing software allows anyone with a computer and laser printer to output type and graphics in a professional-looking manner. For fancier work, like newsletters or magazines, some design experience is important.

e-mail (electronic mail) Written messages sent through a telecommunications medium.

emulation The ability of a printer to mimic the functions of a similar, but incompatible printer. Many printers contain the code to emulate one or more standard printers.

EPS (encapsulated PostScript) A file that contains all the necessary code to print on any PostScript printing device.

error checking Any scheme by which modem- or fax-transmitted data is verified at either the sending or receiving end.

expansion slots Places where you attach special "cards" that perform a variety of functions. Common uses include internal modems and cards that accelerate the computer's speed.

file-transfer protocol A scheme for breaking up a file into efficient blocks that can be transmitted from one computer to another and reassembled at the other end.

floppy Floppy disks are thin, round disks housed inside a 5¼" or 3½" plastic shell used for data storage.

font Technically, a font is an individual typeface in a particular style and of a particular size (for example, Roman 14-point bold). In DTP parlance, Times Roman is often referred to as a font. Due to the scalable nature of many fonts point size has become increasingly flexible, allowing for minute variations.

forums Departments of specialized interest located on online services or BBSs (such as Broadcasting or Careers) usually run by experts in that particular field. Members can exchange messages, questions, and answers; download and upload related software; and sometimes "meet" in live, electronic conferences, or chats. Also referred to as round tables, special-interest forums, and special-interest groups (SIGs).

function A spreadsheet calculation that lets you perform decision-making and value-returning operations automatically.

gateway A link between one online service and another. For example, an America Online or CompuServe user can send mail to someone on the Internet or each other via a gateway.

gray scale The progressive series of grays that a device like a printer or monitor can produce, ranging from black through white.

GUI (graphical user interface) A term usually used to describe operating systems that allow the user to control the computer using graphic symbols and menus rather than typed commands. Windows and the Macintosh System Software are GUIs.

handshaking Scheme by which two devices synchronize their operations so communication can occur.

hard-disk drive A storage device from which you load your programs and save your documents. Hard-drive capacity is also expressed in megabytes (MB). Hard-disk drive speed, called *access time* and measured in milliseconds, is important. In many cases a computer can only work as fast as the hard drive can feed it information. 28ms is the slowest acceptable speed. Something between 12-18ms will ensure good performance. Most hard drives are internal, meaning that they are contained inside your computer's case. You can buy external hard drives later to add more storage space.

icon A small on-screen image that can be manipulated in order to control a program. For example, clicking the mouse pointer on a printer icon might print the file you are working on. Icons are used extensively in GUI operating systems.

inkjet Inkjet printers spray an image on paper in tiny droplets of ink. Output is good, although not as good as lasers when it comes to graphics. Most affordable color printers are inkjet based.

interface A connection between two elements—a computer and printer, for example. In software, the manner in which a user enters commands to use the program.

Internet An international network connecting almost every computer system on the planet to every other system, including most commercial services.

key word (or jump word) Shorthand names used to quickly access forums and other services when online. For example, on CompuServe, you type Go OAG at the prompt to access to the Official Airline Guide.

laser printer A type of printer that employs the electrophotographic method used in copy machines to place images on the page. Laser printers offer both speed and very high quality.

LCD (liquid crystal display) A type of computer display that sandwiches a liquid compound between two transparent electrodes. LCD screens are found in most portable computers because they consume less power than a standard VGA monitor. (See *VGA*.)

library The department within online forums where shareware and freeware files are stored, and to and from which these files are uploaded and downloaded.

link The connection between spreadsheets, with data in one affecting data in the other.

macro A series of commands recorded and saved for future playback. Use of macros can improve the speed and accuracy of spreadsheet work. (See also *batch command.*)

MB (megabyte) A megabyte equals 1,048,576 bytes or 1024K. Memory on large systems and storage for most hard disks are measured in megabytes.

MHz (megahertz) A megahertz is 1,000,000 cycles per second. Megahertz are used as the measure of a microprocessor's speed.

microprocessor The brain of every computer, this chip determines how fast your computer runs. Each kind of chip (386, 486, etc.) has several levels of speed. This is measured by the chip's clockspeed. The higher this number is (expressed in megahertz or MHz) the faster it runs.

modem (modulator-demodulator) A modem converts digital data into signals that can be transferred over audio transmission lines, most commonly phone lines.

mouse An input device that supplements the keyboard and was first used as a pointer in graphics applications; its flexibility soon warranted its use with other applications. Most mice can be programmed for use with non-mouse applications.

MPC (multimedia personal computer) A set of standards for computers making use of multimedia technology. All PCs that meet this standard will be labeled as such. All multimedia Macs meet the standard, although they won't be labeled.

ms (milliseconds) Milliseconds are commonly used to measure the speed of hard-disk drives. Common speeds are 65ms for a 20MB drive, 28ms for a 40MB drive and 14ms for a 110MB drive. The smaller the number the faster the drive.

multimedia Some combination of graphics, sound, animation, and video in a single software program. Can also be used to describe any PC or upgrade product that conforms to MPC standards.

multitasking Running two or more programs at the same time. Macintoshes have multitasking built in to their operating systems. Windows is the most popular multitasking-capable program for the PC.

notebook computer A lighter version of the laptop weighing less than 8 pounds.

online Using a BBS or commercial online service.

operating system Software that controls how a computer functions. A well-designed operating system makes everyday computer tasks (like copying a document) natural and intuitive. The best operating systems are GUIs (graphical user interfaces). These allow you to tell the computer what to do by pointing at pictures, or icons, and selecting commands from preset menus. The Macintosh operating system and Windows for the PC are GUIs.

parallel port Parallel ports allow your computer to connect devices such as printers that use parallel interfacing. Usually parallel ports send information from the computer to an attached device, but don't receive information.

PDL (page description language) This is the "language" that your printer uses to create a page. The most popular PDLs are PostScript and PCL.

pixel A pixel or picture element is the smallest dot of color your video card can manage. Display adapters are defined by their dimensions in pixels. On a color monitor, each pixel is actually made up of three dots: one red, one green, and one blue.

PostScript A page description language from Adobe Systems. When a page is created with PostScript, it is sent to the printer as definitions of lines to be drawn, fonts to be used, and text to be printed in the specified fonts. These instructions are then interpreted by the printer and, through the hardware of a laser printer or typesetter, turned into a printed page.

print driver Software that converts a program's generic printer output into the code required by a specific printer.

RAM (random access memory) The memory your computer uses to run programs (expressed in megabytes, or MB). With enough RAM your computer may be able to run many programs at once (called multitasking). RAM will also have an impact on your computer's speed.

RAM disk A portion of memory set aside to simulate a disk drive. Though faster than a hard drive in accessing data, its contents are lost when the computer is switched off. Also known as a RAM drive, virtual disk, or electronic disk.

resolution Resolution refers to the number of pixels available to reproduce an image on the screen. Curves produced at low resolution like 320×200 have a stair-step appearance, as opposed to the smooth, even look of high-resolution curves.

row heading A heading that identifies a horizontal group of spreadsheet cells. The row heading is placed to the left of the cells. (See also *column heading*.)

script A list of instructions you can write and have a telecommunications program follow. Scripts can vary from the simple (logging on) to the complex (creating a front-end GUI).

sector Disks are divided into concentric circles called tracks, and each track is divided further into wedges called sectors. Sectors can be identified by the side of the disk they're located in, their track number, and the sector number within the track.

serial port A serial port lets you connect devices that communicate via a serial interface. Printers using an RS-232 cable are one example. Other serial devices include modems, mice, and optical recognition scanners. Unlike parallel ports, serial ports normally send and receive information.

shareware Shareware is software that you initially receive for free—if you like and use it, you send a fee to the developer—in essence, "try before you buy." Freeware is software that is free and has no fee attached. Most shareware and freeware is found on online services and can be easily downloaded.

sheet feed A mechanism that uses friction to move single sheets of paper through a printer.

shell A software program that provides the user with a means of controlling the operating system. DOS shell programs are usually add-on programs designed to make it easier to use MS-DOS.

sound board Also known as a sound card. An expansion board placed inside a PC that improves the quality of the PC's sound output. A program must support the sound board before it can benefit from the improved sound quality.

SVGA (super video graphics array) An enhancement of the standard VGA, allowing an 800 by 600 pixel screen to display 16 colors from a palette of 256. SVGA is the current standard.

TIFF (tagged interchangeable file format) A bitmapped graphics standard that is becoming the graphics equivalent of ASCII. Nearly all the high-end graphics programs will import and export TIFF files.

tractor feed A mechanism that moves continuous-form fanfold paper though a printer. The paper must have prepunched sprocket holes on the sides. Also called *pin feed.*

TSR (terminate and stay resident) This is the name of a large class of applications that remain in your PC's memory while you are working with another application. The TSR can be called up instantly by typing the appropriate key combination.

typeface A typeface refers to a similar set of characters regardless of their size. Times-Roman 12-point and Times-Roman 14-point are different fonts but the same typeface. Desktop publishers often use font and typeface interchangeably.

type style This describes the appearance of the font: bold, shadow, strikeout, underline, outline, and so on.

upload To transmit a file from your computer to an online service.

VGA (video graphics array) A monitor standard for the PC that has a maximum resolution of 640×480 pixels with 16 colors. It is being replaced by the Super VGA (SVGA) standard.

virtual memory RAM created by using free hard-drive space. Creating virtual memory allows you to run more programs or larger programs than you could otherwise, but it does cause wear and tear on the hard drive and should not be used on a consistent basis.

worksheet A spreadsheet document in which you can store, manipulate, calculate, and analyze data.

Xmodem One of the most widely supported file-transfer protocols for modems. It is also known as Xmodem Checksum, Xmodem CRC, and XModem 1K.

Ymodem An improvement over the basic Xmodem, it runs significantly faster.

Zmodem The fastest file transfer protocol, which also offers the most features.

Index

A

AbortRetryFail, 63
AccessPC, 153
accounting/bookkeeping, 98-101
  buying software, 98-99
  checkbook setup, 99-100
  checkbook vs. double-entry system, 99
  CheckFree program, 100
  double-entry system setup, 100-101
  software, 106
AccPac Simply Accounting, 107
ACT, 95
Address Book Plus, 95
address book software, 95
adhesives for mechanicals, desktop publishing, 131
Adobe Illustrator, 133
Adobe Photoshop, 134
Adobe Systems, 31, 34
Adobe Type Manager, 155
Advanced Microcomputer Systems, 45
Advantage Plus Business Master, 120
After Dark, 157
Alarming Events, 95
Aldus, 132
Aldus IntelliDraw, 133
Aldus Personal Press, 153
Aldus Photostyler, 134
alphanumeric memory, cellular phones, 37-38
Amaze Daily Planner, 157
America Online, 77-79, **77**, **78**, 80, 81, 82, 83
American Heritage Dictionary, 156
American Institute of CPAs, 113
American Power conversion, 63
Ami Pro, 138-139
amortization table, 102
Anderson, Scott R., 132
Andrew Tobias' TaxCut, 113
Annual Broadcasting Yearbook, 119
answering machines, 35-36
  electrical power requirements, **3**
  major manufacturers, 39
anti-viral software, 59
Apple, 24, 28, 34, 56, 175
Apple Adjustable Keyboard, 12, **12**
Apple Newton MessagePad, **66**
Apple PowerBook, *22*
armrests and ergonomic design, 11
Artbeats, 133
Artisoft, 73
As-Easy-As, 158
AT&T, 39, 71, 73
attic offices, 1
audio boards, multimedia presentations, 175, 176
AutoDoubler, 51, 156
Automap—The Intelligent Road Atlas, 155
automobile tax deduction, 112
Avery, 132

B

BackSaver Products, 13
backups (*see* computers troubleshooting; hard disk drives; storage devices)
Baker, Kim and Sunny, 68, 132
Bangs, David H. Jr., 107, 119
BannerMania, 156
basement office, 1
Basics of Finance, The, 107
Beale, Stephen, 56
bedrooms as offices, 2
Bennett, Steven J., 24
Bernoulli drives (*see* removable cartridge drives)
Best Power Technology, 63
Better Business Bureau, mail order/direct marketing, 18
big or oversized rooms as offices, 6
Bigelow, Stephen, 34
BiPlane, 155
Bishop, Philip, 173-176
bitmapped graphics, desktop publishing, 127-128
Bitstream, 34, 132
Bizmart, 15
BizPlan Builder, 108, 153
black-and-white scanners, 55
BlackLightning, 132
Blishak, Sylvia Ann, 120
boilerplates, 93
bookkeeping (*see* accounting/bookkeeping)
Borland International, 107
Bose Corp., 175
Boston Computer Society, 18, 25
Bowen, Charles, 86
bps rate, modems, 44
breakeven point analysis, 103
breaks from work and health, 9
Brenner, Robert C., 63
broadcast fax machines, 43, 115
  illegality of broadcast fax, 115
Broderbund, 132
brokers, buying computers, 18
Brooktrout Technology, 119
Brother International, 45
buffers
  hard disk drives, 51
  printer buffer, 32-33, **32**
bullets, desktop publishing, 129
Burger, Jeff, 175
Burke, Clifford, 133
Busch, David, 56
Business Management Toolkit, 154
Business Plan Toolkit, 108, 155
business plans, 97-98
  software, 107
Business Yellow Pages of America, 120

C

cache memory
  CD-ROM drives, 49
  hard disk drives, 51
Caddylack, 8
Caere Corp., 56
Calendar Creator, 157
calendar software, 95

Illustrations are in **boldface**

CalendarMaker, 158
call accounting, telephones/communication equipment, 71
call forwarding, telephones/communication equipment, 71
call holding, telephones/communication equipment, 71
Call Management Products, 73
call timer, cellular phones, 38
call waiting, telephones/communication equipment, 70-71
call-routing, telephones/communication equipment, 70
callback, telephones/communication equipment, 71
caller ID, telephones/communication equipment, 71
camera ready art, desktop publishing, 130-131
Canon, 54
CanOpener, 155
Captool, 108
car phones, 36
Carbon Copy for Windows, 68
card file software, 95
Carter, Donna, 25
cartridge drives (*see* removable cartridge drives)
Cash Flow Control Guide, The, 107
CashBiz, 107
catalog design makeover, 159-164, **160-164**
Cavuoto, James, 56
CCITT
  fax machines standards, 41
  modems standards, 44
CD-ROM drives, 49-50
  audio capability, audio jacks, 49
  cache memory, 49
  extended architecture (XA) drives, 49
  information/time management, 94-95
  installation, Macintosh, 49-50
  installation, PCs, 49-50
  major manufacturers, 51
  multimedia presentations, 49, 175, 176
  multisession drives, 49
  multispin technology, 49
  purchasing tips, 49
  read-only disks, 49
  sales and marketing, 120
  small computer system interface (SCSI) installation, 49-50
  speed of CD-ROM drives, 49
ceiling height vs. office design, 5-6
cellular phones, 36-38
  alphanumeric memory, 37-38
  bundling, 37
  call timer, 38
  car phones, 36
  dropped call, 38
  dual mode, 38
  dual tone multifrequency (DTMF), 38
  electronic lock, 38
  FNC, 38
  hand-helds, 36-37
  hands-free operation, 38
  major manufacturers, 39
  memory, redial memory, 38
  numeric assignment module (NAM), 38
  operation of cellular phones, 36
  options and features, 36
  problems, 37
  roaming, 38
  scratch pad, 38
  selection criteria, 37
  standby time/talk time, 38
  terminology, 37-38
  transportables, 36
  using, 37
census data on CD-ROM, 120
chairs and seating
  armrests, 11
  backs, 11
  ergonomic design, 9, 10-11, **11**
  footrests, 11
  kneeling chairs, 11
  seat material, 11
  Sensor I chair, 11, **11**
Champ Polar Filter Shields, 12
Charles Schwab, 107
CheckFree Corp., 107
checkbook accounting system, 99-100
  CheckFree program, 100
CheckFree program, 100
ClarisWorks for Windows, 151-152
ClickArt, 133
clip art, desktop publishing, 127-128, **127**, 133
  bitmapped graphics, 127-128
  commercial vendors, 128
  object-oriented drawings, 128
  online art, 128
  PostScript drawings, 128
  printed art, 128
Clip-Art Connection, 133
Cliptures, 133
Close-Up, 68
Co/Session, 68
Cobra Electronics, 39
Code-A-Phone Corp., 39
Collage Complete, 153
Color for the Electronic Age, 132
color monitors, 27
  notebook computers, 23
Color Publishing on the Macintosh, 132
color scanners, 56
Colorado Memory Systems, 51
Command Communications, 73
Commerce Clearing House, 113
communications (*see* telephones/communication equipment)
Compaq, 24, 175
Compaq DirectPlus, 18
Compel, 175
Complete Modem Reference, The, 46
Complete PC, The, 56
compression, data compression, 50, 58
CompUSA, 15
CompuServe, 76-77, 80, 81, 82, 83
  sample online session, 165-171
CompuServe Information Manager, 157
Computer Associates, 107
Computer Covers Unlimited, 12, 13
Computer Peripherals Inc., 45
Computer Power for Your Small Business, 24
computer stores, buying computers, 15
Computer Virus Handbook, The, 63
Computerland, 15
computers, 19-25
  associations and agencies, 25
  audiotapes, 25
  backup storage (*see* storage devices)
  best-buy tips, 24
  books about computers, 24
  brokers, 18
  compression, 58
  credit card purchases, 17
  delivery time, 17
  desktop computers, 19
  diagnostic programs, 59, 63
  direct manufacturers, 18
  disaster recovery checklist, 62-63
  discounts, 17
  DOS, MS-DOS, 20
  electrical power requirements, **3**
  expansion slots, 19, 20, 21, 22
  fax-modems for fax capability, 45
  file-recovery, 58
  graphical user interface (GUI), 19
  haggling for price breaks, 17
  hard disk drive (*see also* storage devices), 19-21
  IBM vs. Apple, 19

insurance, 62, 64
Macintosh, 20-21, **21**
major manufacturers, 24
microprocessors, 19-21
upgrading, 21-22
mobile (*see* mobile computing)
monitors (*see* monitors)
multimedia presentations specifications, 176
notebook computers (*see* notebook computers)
operating systems, 19, 20
OS/2, 20
PC vs. Macintosh, 19, 20, *20*, 21, **21**
PCs, 19-20
piracy and viruses, 59-60
preassembly, 17
preventive maintenance, 58
printers (*see* printers)
random access memory (RAM), 19, 20, 21
upgrading, 22
removable cartridge drives, 58
resources, 18, 24, 63
returning merchandise, 17-18
secondhand (used) computers, 16
service after the sale, 17
speed of processing, microprocessors, 19-20
storage devices (*see* storage devices)
surcharges, 17
surge suppressors, 60
tape drives, 58
troubleshooting, 57-64
backing up work, 57-58
books, 63
compression, 58
copies of essential files, 58
diagnostic programs, 59, 63
disaster recovery checklist, 62-63
dust, dust covers, 61
file recovery capability, 58
floppy disk drive cleaning, 61
hard-disk irregularities, 59
hard-disk wear, 59
insurance, 62, 64
keyboard cleaning, 61
maintenance, 61
minimizing data loss, 57
monitor cleaning, 61
monitor degaussing, 61
mouse cleaning, 61
piracy and viruses, 59-60
power failures, 58, 60
power-up switches, 61
preventive maintenance, 58
printer cleaning and maintenance, 61
removable cartridge drives, 58
resources, 63
saving work-in-progress, 57
software backup schemes, 58
spills, 61-62
surge suppressors, 60
tape drive backup, 58
temperature extremes, 61
uninterruptable power supplies (UPS), 60
viruses, 58, 59-60
uninterruptable power supplies (UPS), 60
upgrading PCs, 21
used computers, 16
user groups, 18
viruses, 59-60
warranties, 17
where to buy computers
computer stores, 15
direct sales/mail order, 16
local vendors, 15
retail stores, 15
returning merchandise, 17-18
secondhand (used), 16
service after the sale, 17
smart shopping tips, 16-17
superstores, 15-16
Windows, 20
Windows NT, 20
Conner Electronics, 51
contact list software, 95
contrast control, fax machines, 43
Copia International, 119
copiers, 53-54, **53**
automatic document feeders, 54
cost of copier ownership, 53
cost of copier use, 54
duty cycle, 54
electrical power requirements, 2, **3**
fax capability, 42
features, 53
major manufacturers, 54
moving vs. stationary copy bed, 54
paper sizes, 54
photo mode, 54
reduction/enlargement capability, 54
resources, 54
service contracts, 54
warranties, 54
cordless telephones, 35
electrical power requirements, **3**
CorelDraw, 133, 148-149
corporations (*see* incorporation)
Correct Grammar, 156
Correct Writing, 156
Country Bound, 8
CPU, 155
Crawford, Deborah E., 159-164,
catalog makeover, 159
Creating Customers, 119
Creative Labs, 175
cropping art, desktop publishing, 131
Crutchfield Personal Office Catalog, 8
cumulative trauma disorders (CTD), 9
Curtis Manufacturing, 63

D

DacEasy Instant Accounting, 154
Daily, Frederick, 113
Dashboard, 156
Data Broadcasting Corp., 108
data doublers for hard disk drives, 50
databases, 90-95
boilerplates, 93
comments, 93
entering data, 91
entering data, automatic entry, 91-92
extracting data, 92
features, 91
field limits, 91
file management, 93
FileMaker Pro, 150-151
flat files, 90
grouping data, 92
indexing, 92
mail-merge, 92
managers, database managers, 90
naming files, 93
online databases (*see* online services)
organizing data, 92
phone dialing features, 92-93
printing, 92
relational files, 91
retrieval software, 93, 95
search and select, 92, 93-94
setting up the database, 91
software, 95, 150-151
typing features, 91
viewing data, 92
Datasources, 24
Datebook Pro, 95
Davidson, Jeffrey, 120
Dead Mac Scrolls, The, 63
Debugging, 63
defragmentation of files, 50-51
degauss button, monitors, 28
delayed/timer transmission, fax machines, 43
Dell, 18, 24, 175
Delphi, 80, 81, 82, 83

Design & Layout Techniques, 133
design makeover (*see* catalog design makeover)
Design Your Own Home series, 156
Designer (Windows), 134
Designer's Club, 133
designing the home office (*see* office setup and design)
desks
  alternatives to standard desks, 7
  ergonomic design, 11-12
  height of desktop, 11
  keyboard positioning, 11-12
  mouse use, 12
  ScanCo MacTable, 11, **12**
  trackballs, 12
  wrist rests, 12, **13**
desktop computers, 19
Desktop Multimedia Bible, The, 175
Desktop Publishing, 132
desktop publishing, 121-134
  adhesives for mechanicals, 131
  advertising and marketing material, 129-130
  associations, 133
  bad breaks, 126
  bitmapped graphics, 127-128
  books and publications, 132-133
  boxing, 125
  bullets, 129
  camera ready art, 130-131
  clip art, 127-128, **127**, 133
  color, 130, 132
  consistency of type, 126
  CorelDraw, 148-149
  cropping, 131
  dam rivers, 126
  density of printout, 124
  design makeover (*see* catalog design makeover)
  design tips, 125-127
  envelope printing, 129
  fonts, 123, 124
  graphics, 132
  hardware, 121, 122
  high-end DTP, 122
  importing data, 126
  initial caps, 126
  line length, 126
  low-scale DTP, 121-122
  Mac vs. PC, 121
  mechanicals preparation, 131-132
    adhesives, 131
    board mount, 131
    communicating with shop, 131
    cropping, 131
    graphics, 132
    identifying work, 132
    pagination, 132
    paper, 131
    second color, 132
  mid-range software, 122
  nontype elements, 124
  object-oriented drawings, 128
  online art, 128
  orientation of type on sheet, 124
  overheads preparation, 128-129
  page size, 125
  pagination, 132
  paper selection, 129
  PhotoFinish, 149-150
  PostScript drawings, 128
  PostScript printers, 123
  printed art, 128
  printers, 122-123
    laser printers, 129-130
    PostScript, 123
  punctuation, 125
  resolution, 124
  resources, 132
  rule lines, 126
  scanners, 123
  shading, 125
  software, 121, 133-134, 148-150
    illustration software, 133-134
    illustration/paint/image-editing, 133
    image-editing, 134
    paint software, 134
  speed of processing, 122
  templates, 127
  testing design, 126-127
  typefaces, 123-125
    consistency of type, 126
    density, 124
    mood creation, 124, **124**
    nontype elements, 124
    orientation, 124
    resolution, 124
    serif vs. sans serif, 123, **123**
    shading, 125
    text face vs. display face, 123-124, **124**
  videotapes, 133
  white space, 125-126
diagnostic programs, 59, 63
Digidesign, 175
DigitArt, 133
dining room as office, 2
Direct Access for Windows, 155
Direct Mail Magic, 119
direct mail marketing, 118-119
direct manufacturers, buying computers, 18
Direct Marketing Association, 18
direct sales (*see* mail order, buying computers)
disaster recovery checklist for computers, 62-63
discounts, spreadsheets analysis, 104
Disinfectant, 158
DiskFit Pro, 63
DiskTop, 155
displays (*see* monitors)
docking stations, notebook computers, 23-24
Dorfler, Frank Jr., 46, 86
DOS, 19, 20
dot pitch, monitors, 28
dot-matrix printers, 29, **29**
double-entry bookkeeping (*see* accounting/bookkeeping)
Douglas, Laura C., 120
Dover Electronic Clip Art Library, The, 133
Dover Publications, 132
Dr. Macintosh's Guide to Online Services, 86
dropped call, cellular phones, 38
dual mode, cellular phones, 38
dual tone multifrequency (DTMF), cellular phones, 38
Dvorak keyboards, 12
Dvorak's Guide to PC Telecommunications, 46, 86
Dvorak, John, 25, 46, 86
Dynamic Fax, 119
Dynodex, 95

E

E Trade, 107
800 number service, telephones/communication equipment, 71
Easy PC Maintenance and Repair, 63
Easy Tax, 113
Easy Working Address Book & Label Maker, 157
Easy Working Presentation Maker, 157
Easy Working Spreadsheet for Windows, 157
economic order quantity (EOQ) inventory model, 103
Edwards, Paul and Sarah, 120
electronic lock, cellular phones, 38
electronic mail (e-mail), 83, 117
  abbreviations, 86
  character code, "smileys," 85-86
Emerson Computer Power, 63
Endrijonas, Janet, 63

engines, printers, disposable vs. modular, 31
EPE/Topaz, 63
Epson America, 34, 56
Equalizer, The, 108
ergonomics (*see* health and ergonomics)
Ericksson GE Communications, 39
Esselte Pendaflex Corporation, 8
Ethernet, 73
Excel for Windows, 108
executive summary, business plans, 98
Exide Electronics, 63
expansion slots, computers, 19, 20, 21, 22
Express Publisher, 153
extension cords, 2-3

F

fallback feature, fax machines, 43
family room as office, 2
FastBack Plus, 63
fax machines, 41-46, **41**
automatic paper cutters, 42
automatic voice/data switch, 43
books about fax machines, 46
broadcast transmission, 43, 115
computer faxing, 115
contrast control, 43
copier capability option, 42
delayed/timer transmission, 43
document feeders, 42
document size limitations, 42
electrical power requirements, **3**
fallback feature, 43
fax modems, 41
fax-on-demand, 116
fax/modems, 45
Group 3 standards, 41
halftone transmission, 43
major manufacturers, 45
modems, 43-45, **44**
modems, internal vs. external, 44
protocols, 44
transmission speed, 43-44
on- vs. off-site fax-on-demand, 116
one-call fax-on-demand, 116
paper capacity of machine, 42
paper options: plain paper vs. thermal, 42
phone-line options, 42-43
polling, 43
portable (*see* mobile computing)
printer with fax capability, 34, **41**
resolution, 41-42
resources, 45
sales and marketing use, 115-116
service bureaus for faxing, 115-116, 119
standard fax-on-demand, 116
telephones/communication equipment, 71
transmission rates, 41, 42
transmit terminal identification feature, 43
fax modems (*see* fax machines)
Fax Quest, 119
fax-on-demand, 116
FAXability Plus, 153
FAXGrabber, 153
FaxMania, 157
Fidelity's FOX service, 107
Fifth Generation Systems, 34
FileMaker Pro, 95, 150-151
filing cabinets, 6-8
finance, 97-107
accounting/bookkeeping, 98-101
buying software, 98-99
checkbook setup, 99-100
checkbook vs. double-entry, 99
CheckFree program, 100
double-entry setup, 100-101
amortization table, 102
books, 106
breakeven point, 103
business plans, 97-98
business plans, company analysis, 97
executive summary, 98
financial analysis, 98
management profile, 98
market analysis, 98
product analysis, 97-98
strategic plan, 98
cost of borrowing, PMT spreadsheets function, 101-102, **102**
discounts, 104
increasing sales, 103-104
inflation, 104-105
interest rate, APR spreadsheets function, 103
inventory control, 103
investing, 105-106
brokerless transactions, 106
fundamental analysis, 105
market information, 105-106
screening options, 105
technical analysis, 105
outstanding debt, PV spreadsheets function, 102
resources, 106
retirement planning, 104, 105
software, 145-148
Hi Finance, 146
M.Y.O.B., 148
Microsoft Profit for Windows, 145-146
QuickBooks, 146-147
QuickPay, 147-148
spreadsheets, 101-105
amortization table, 102
breakeven point, 103
cost of borrowing, PMT function, 101-102, **102**
discounts, 104
increasing sales, 103-104
inflation, 104-105
interest rate, APR function, 103
inventory control, 103
outstanding debt, PV function, 102
retirement planning, 104, 105
term of loan, 102
term of loan, 102
financial analysis, business plans, 98
Fire King International, 8
First Step Review, 108
Fisk, Ian, 165-171
Flash, 132
flat file databases, 90
flatbed scanners, 55
floppy disk drive, cleaning, 61
FontBank, 132
fonts, 33
desktop publishing, 123, 124
font library building, 124
TrueType, 34
footrests and ergonomic design, 11
form letters, 92
forums (*see* online services)
fragmentation of files, hard disk drives, 50
Freed, Les, 46, 86
Freedom of Press Light, 153
Freeman, Jeff, 62
Freierman, Richard, 24
fundamental analysis, investing, electronic, 105
furniture
chairs and seating, 10-11, **11**
ergonomic designs, 10
suppliers, 8

G

galley-type office design, 4, **5**
garage, converted garage as office, 1-2
Gateway 2000, 18, 24
GEnie, 80, 81, 82, 83
Geoworks Desktop, 155
Getting Business to Come to You, 120
Getting Organized: The Easy Way..., 8, 13

glare reduction, 5, 12
Golden Retriever, 95
Gookin, Dan, 24
Grammatik 5, 156
Graphic Impact, 153
graphical user interface (GUI), 19
grayscale monitors, 23, 28
grayscale scanners, 55-56
Grolen Inc., 8
Group 3 fax machines, 41
Guerilla Marketing Attack, 120
Guide to Modem Communications, 46, 86
Guide to Notebook and Laptop Computers, 24

H

halftone transmission, fax machines, 43
halogen lights, 3-4
Hand Scanner Handbook, The, 56
hand-held scanners, 55
hands-free operation, cellular phones, 38
hard disk drives (*see also* storage devices), 19, 20, 21
  buffers, 51
  cache memory, 51
  CD-ROM (*see* CD-ROM drives)
  compression schemes, pros and cons, 50
  data doublers, 50
  defragmentation, 50-51
  fragmentation of files, 50
  irregularities, failures, 59
  mobile computing, 66
  noncontiguous clusters, 50
  RAM disks, mobile computing, 66
  removable (*see* removable cartridge drives)
  wear and tear, 59
Hard Disk Survival Guide, 63
hardware data compression, tape drives, 48
Harwin, Ronald, 8, 13
Hayes Microcomputer Products Inc., 45
Haynes, Colin, 8, 13
Headquarters Companies, The, 8
headsets, telephones/communication equipment, 35
health and ergonomics, 9-13
  armrests, 11
  breaks, 9
  chairs and seating, 9, 10-11, **11**
  cumulative trauma disorders (CTD), 9
  desktop design, 11-12
  elbows, 9
  furniture and supplies, 10
  glare reduction, 12
  habits for health, 9
  hand-arm motion, 10
  keyboard positioning, 9, 11-12
  macro use to save time, 9
  monitor position, 9, 12
  mouse use, 9, 12
  neutral positions vs. exercise, 9
  oxygen and health, 10
  painful joints, hot and cold baths, 10
  radiation from monitors, 10
    back and side emissions, 10
    distance of radiation field, 10
    extremely low frequency (ELF), 10
    MPR II radiation emission standard, 10
    screen covers, 10
    very low frequency (VLF) radiation, 10
    walls, 10
  resources, 13
  seating position, 10
  stress, 9
  tension relief, 10
  trackballs, 12
  wrist rests, 12, **13**
Healthy Computing, 8, 13
Held, Gilbert, 46
Hello Direct, 8
Help, 63
Herman Miller Company, 13
Hewlett-Packard, 31, 34, 45, 56, 175
Hi Finance, 146
Hold Everything, 8
Home Lighting Handbook, 8
home office tax deduction, 111-112
Home Series, The, 156
Home-Office Money & Tax Guide, 113
Home-Office Tax Deductions, 113
Homebuying & Refinancing Pro, 157
Hon Company, 8
How to Get Big Results from a Small Advertising Budget, 120
How to Get the Most Out of CompuServe, 86
How to Write a Business Plan, 107
Howard, Bill, 24

I

IBM, 24, 175
IBM computers (PCs), 19-20
IBM PC Direct, 18
IBM Personal Computer Troubleshooting and Repair, 63
illustration software, 133-134
image-editing software, 133, 134
Images With Impact, 133
Improving Your Company Image, 120
incandescent lights, 3
incorporation, tax burden, 112
indexing, databases, 92
Individual Investor's Guide to Computerized Investing, 107
inflation, spreadsheets analysis, 104-105
Info Select, 95
information/time management (*see also* databases), 89-95
  CD-ROMs, 94-95
  contact managers, 90
  databases (*see* databases), 90-95
  organizing time spent searching for data, 94
  personal information managers (PIM), 89-90, **90**, 95
  research hints, 93-94
  resources, 95
  time-index tape recorders, 94
  travel tips, 94
inkjet printers, 29, **30**
Instant Artist, 156
Instant Info, 119
insurance, computers, 62, 64
integrated software, 151-152
Internal Revenue Service (IRS), 113
Internet, 83-84, 86-87
Internet Companion,The, 86
inventory control, 103
  economic order quantity (EOQ) model, 103
investing, electronic, 105-106
  brokerless transactions, 106
  fundamental analysis, 105
  market information sources, 105-106
  quote broadcasting services, 107
  screening options, 105
  software, 107
  technical analysis, 105
Investor's Accountant, 108
Iomega, 51
IRS tax publications, 113, 114

J

jacks, telephones/communication equipment, 35, 39

K

Kamoroff, Bernard, 107
Kanarek, Lisa, 8
Kane, Pamela, 86
Kensington Microware, 64
keyboards
  adjustable keyboard, 12, **12**

cleaning, 61
Dvorak keyboards, 12
ergonomic design and positioning, 9
positioning keyboards, 11-12
QWERTY keyboards, 12
Kid Pix, 156
kitchen as office, 2
Klopfer, Susan, 63
kneeling chairs, 11
Kodak, 34

L

L-shaped office design, 4, **4**
Labadie, Horace W., 34
Laplante, Phil, 63
LapLink Pro, 154
LaQuey, Tracy, 86
Laser Label Technologies, 132
laser printers, 29-30, **30**
buffers, printer buffers, 32-33, **32**
desktop publishing, 122-123, 129-130
color, 130
paper selection, 129
envelopes, 129
fonts, 33
memory upgrade, 32
PC vs. Mac printers, 33
PostScript, adding PostScript, 33-34
shared printers, 33
speed increase, 32
typefaces, 33
upgrading, 32-34
LaserJet printers, 34
LaserMaster Corporation, 34
Letraset, 132
LetterWorks, 157
Levin, Richard B, 63
Levinson, Jay, 120
LeVitus, Bob, 86
Lexmark, 34
Li'l Bits Font Packs, 156
Lichterman, Joshua, 62
lighting for the home office, 3-4
electrical power requirements, **3**
glare reduction, 5
living room as office, 2
local area networks (LAN), 72-73
advantages of LAN use, 72
cardless LAN, 73
cost of LAN startup, 72
cost of voice mail, 69
Ethernet cards, 73
installing the LAN, 73
Macintosh and LAN, 73
resources, 73
stand-alone systems, 70
starter kits, 72-73
voice-mail boards, 70
wireless LAN, 73
Logitech, 56
Looking Good in Print, 132
Lotus, 107
Lotus 1-2-3, 108, 144-145
Lotus Improv for Windows, 142-143
Lotus Organizer, 95, 154
LotusWorks, 154

M

M.Y.O.B., 107, 148
MacEKG, 63
MacInTax Personal, 113
Macintosh Bible, The, 24
Macintosh computers, 20-21, **21**
MacPaint, 134
macros, saving time, 9
Macs for Dummies, 24
MacSleuth, 63
MacTable, 11, **12**
MacTools, 51, 63
MacWrite Pro, 137-138
mail order, buying computers, 16-18
mail-merge, databases, form letters, 92
Mailboxes, Etc., 8
Makeover Book, The, 132
Mallory, Charles, 119
management profile, business plans, 98
Managing Your Money, 107, 158
Market Analyzer Plus, 108
Market Manager Plus, 108
MarketFax, 119
marketing (*see* sales and marketing)
Marketing for the Home-Based Business, 120
Marstek, 56
Masterclips, 133
MasterTracks, 175
McKeever, Mike, 107
mechanical preparation, desktop publishing, 131-132
adhesives, 131
board mount, 131
communicating with print shop, 131
cropping, 131
graphics, 132
identifying work, 132
pagination, 132
paper selection, 131
second color use, 132
Media Power, 120
Media Vision, 175
MessagePad, **66**
messaging services, 39
MicroComputer Accessories, 13
Microcomputer Market Place, 24
microprocessors, 19-20, 20-21
speed of processing, 19-20
upgrading, 21-22
Microsoft, 107, 132
Microsoft Money, 107
Microsoft Profit, 107
Microsoft Profit for Windows, 145-146
Microsoft Publisher, 133
Microsoft Word, 135-136
Microsolutions Computer Products, 51
Midwest Micro, 18
Miller, Peter G., 120
Milling, Bryan, 107
Minasi, Mark, 63
Mirror Technologies, 51, 175
Mita, 54
Mitsubishi, 39
mobile computing, 65-68, **65**, **66**
accessories, 65-66
backlight vs. power usage, 66
battery supplies, 66
books, 68
cords, 65
fax machine portable, **65**
floppy drive backup, 67
hard disk drive vs. power usage, 66
MessagePad portable, **66**
modems, 65
power management, 66
protecting your portable, 67-68
RAM disk use, 66
remote access, 67
resources, 68
speed vs. power usage, 66
storage, 65
telephone connections, 66
modems, 41, 43-45, **44**
books about modems, 46
bps-rate, 44
CCITT standards, 44
compression/decompression schemes, 44
electrical power requirements, *3*
external modems, 44
internal modems, 44
major manufacturers, 45
mobile computing modems, 65
pocket modems, 45, **45**
protocols, 44
resources, 45
software, 44-45
speed of transmission, 43-44
actual vs. data pump, 44
V.42bis data-compression standard, 44

monitors, 27-28
cleaning, 61
color, 27
controls, 28
degauss button, 28, 61
dot pitch, 28
electrical power requirements, **3**
ergonomic design and positioning, 9
glare reduction, 5, 12
grayscale, 28
major manufacturers, 28
multimedia presentations, 176
notebook computers, 23
price range, 27
radiation emissions, 10
back and side emissions, 10
distance of radiation field, 10
extremely low frequency (ELF) radiation, 10
MRP II radiation emission standards, 10
screen covers, 10
very low frequency (VLF) radiation, 10
walls, 10
refresh rate, 28
resources, 28
size of screen, 27
stands and supports for monitors, 12
Super VGA (SVGA), 27
VGA, 27
video cards, 27-28
Moore Business Forms, 8
Morgan, Sharon D., 120
Morgenstern, Steve, 133, 159-164
Moses, 73
Moss, Julien, 63
Motorola, 39
mouse, 12
cleaning, 61
saving time, 9
Mouse Systems, 56
MS-DOS, 19, 20
multimedia presentations, 173-176
audio boards, 175, 176
audio editing software, 175
books, 175
CD-ROM drives, 175, 176
computer specifications, 176
CPU, 176
digitizing audio, 174
duplicating the presentation, 174
editing audio portion, 174
editing video portion, 174
mixing audio, 174
monitor selection, 176
music for background, 174
narration creation, 174
planning, 173-174
presentation creation, 174
QuickTime, 175
resources, 174-175
scanners, 175, 176
software, 175, 176
speakers, 175
VCRs, 175, 176
video adapter boards, 175, 176
Video for Windows, 175
videotaping the presentation, 174
Multimedia: Making It Work, 175
Murata, 39
Muratec, 45
Mutual Fund Database, 108
Myriad Enterprises, 34

N

Naiman, Arthur, 24
narrow rooms as offices, 6
National Association of Desktop Publishers, 133
NEC Technologies, 28, 34, 51, 175
networking
Ethernet, 73
local area networking (LAN), 72-73
Macintosh LANs, 73
small-office communications networks, 72
New Life for Old PCs, 24
Newsletters from the Desktop, 133
No-Sweat Desktop Publishing, 133
noise control, 6
Nolo's Partnership Maker, 154
noncontiguous clusters, hard disk drives, 50
Norton Antivirus, 63
Norton Backup, 63
Norton Desktop for DOS, 139-140, 154
Norton Desktop for Windows, 154
Norton PC/Anywhere, 68
Norton Utilities, 51, 63, 154
notebook computers, 22-24, **22**
color monitors, 23
desktop computers vs., 22-23
docking stations, 23-24
features, 23
grayscale monitors, 23
PCMCIA, 23
PowerBook, *22*
screen size, 23
weight, 23
Novell, 73
Now Utilities, 63
numeric assignment module (NAM), cellular phones, 38

O

O'Sullivan Industries Inc., 8
object-oriented drawings, desktop publishing, 128
Office Depot, 8
Office on the Go, 68
office setup and design, 1-8
arranging furniture, 5
attic offices, 1
basement offices, 1
bedrooms as offices, 2
big or oversized rooms as offices, 6
bins, 7
books and publications, 8
built-in furniture, 5
catalogues, 8
desk location, 5
desks, alternatives, 7
dining room as office, 2
drawer organizers, 7
drawer space requirements, 5
family room as office, 2
filing cabinets, 6-8
flexibility of furniture, design, 5
function vs. design, 4
galley-type office design, 4, **5**
garage, converted garage as office, 1-2
glare reduction, 5
high-ceiling rooms as offices, 6
irregular walls in offices, 6
kitchen office, 2
L-shaped office design, 4, **4**
lighting, 3-4
living room offices, 2
low-ceiling rooms as offices, 5-6
narrow rooms as offices, 6
noise control, 6
office services, 8
organizing the home office, 6-8
power supplies, 2-3
problem areas and solutions, 5-6
resources listing, 8
retail suppliers, 8
shelving, 7
small or undersized rooms as offices, 6
spare-room offices, 1
strip office design, 4, **4**
supplies, list, 7-8
U-shaped office design, 4, **6**
useless furniture, 5
vertical space utilization, 7
Okidata, 34, 45
On the Air, 120
one-call fax-on-demand, 116
Online Access, 86

online services, 75-87
America Online, 77-78, **77**, **78**, 80, 81, 82, 83
booking flights, comparing major online services, 80-81
books about online services, 86
clip art, desktop publishing, 128
comparing major services, task comparison, 80-83, **85**
CompuServe, 76-77, 80, 81, 82, 83
cost of online services, 75-76, 84
databases, online databases, 84
Delphi, 80, 81, 82, 83
downloading files, comparing major online services, 81
electronic mail (e-mail), 83
abbreviations, 86
character code, "smileys," 85-86
fax transmission, comparing major online services, 82
finding information online, 84
acronyms, 84
costs, 84
selective search, 84
GEnie, 80, 81, 82, 83
Internet, 83-84, 86
Prodigy, 79-80, 80-81, 82, 83
resources, 86-87
sample session with CompuServe, 165-171
searching for forum members, comparing major online services, 83
searching for news/articles, comparing major online services, 81
stock quotations, comparing major online services, 82
support from Microsoft, comparing major online services, 82
OnTime, 95
operating systems, 19, 20
optical character recognition (OCR), scanners, 56
organizing the home office, 6-8
Organizing Your Home for Success, 8
OS/2, 20
overheads, desktop publishing, 128-129
bullets, 129
color, 128
crowding, 129
graphics, 128
line art, 128-129
print size, 129

P

Pacioll 2000, 157
PackRat, 95
Padowicz, Julian, 25
page description language (PDL), 31
PageMaker, 133
pagers, 36, 39
pagination, desktop publishing, 132
Paint Shop Pro, 158
paint software, 134
Panamax, 64
Panasonic, 34, 39, 45, 54, 175
Panorama II, 95
Paper Direct, 132
paper trays, printers, 30
Parinello, Al, 120
Parker, Roger C., 132, 133
PC Magazine's Computer Buyer's Guide, 25
PC Paintbrush, 134
PC Paintbrush 5+, 156
PC Tools, 63
PC Tools for DOS, 51
PC Tools for Windows, 140-142
PC Video Conversion Corp., 175
PC-File, 95, 153
PCFN, 107
PCs Compleat, 18
PCs for Dummies, 24
Peachtree Accounting, 108
Persona Technologies Inc., 175
Personal Computer Memory Card International Association (PCMCIA), notebook computers, 23
Personal Press, 133
Persuasion 2.1, 175
Petersen, Bill, 62
Peyton, David, 86
PFROI, 108
Phone Technologies, 39
PhotoFinish, 149-150
Picture Publisher, 134
PICTure This, 153
Pina, Larry, 63
piracy of software, 59-60
PKZip, 158
pocket modems, 45, **45**
Pogue, David, 24
polling, fax machines, 43
Poor, Alfred E., 24
Pope, Jeffrey L., 120
postage meters, electrical power requirements, **3**
Postal Inspection Service, 18
PostScript/PostScript printers, 29, 31-32
desktop publishing drawings, 123, 128
upgrading to PostScript, 33-34
power failures, computers, 60
Power Pak, 51
power supplies for the home office, 2-3
determining power needs, 2
independent circuit for office, 3
managing power wisely, 2-3
requirements of typical office equipment, **3**
surge suppressors, 3, 60
uninterruptable power supply (UPS), 60
Power Toolboxes, 157
Power Up Software Corp., 132
PowerBook, *22*
PowerPoint 3.0, 175
Practical Guide to Scanning, 56
Practical Market Research, 120
Practical Peripherals, 34, 45
Presentation Design Book, The, 133
Presentation Task Force, 133
Print Shop, 157
PrintCache, 154
Printer Control Language (PCL), 31
printers, 29-34
books about printers, 34
buffers, printer buffers, 32-33, **32**
cleaning, 61
color, 130
databases, printing form letters, 92
desktop publishing, 122-123, 129-130
dot-matrix printers, 29, *29*
electrical power requirements, **3**
engines, disposable vs. modular, 31
envelopes, 129
fax capability, 34, **41**
fonts, 33
inkjet printers, 29, **30**
laser printers (*see also* laser printers), 29-30, **30**
buffers, 32-33, **32**
fonts, 33
memory upgrade, 32
PC vs. Mac, 33
PostScript upgrade, 33-34
sharing printers, 33
speed increase, 32
typefaces, 33
upgrading, 32-3
maintenance, 61
major manufacturers, 34
memory, RAM, 30, 32
page description languages (PDL), 31
paper selection, 129
paper trays, 30
PC vs. Mac printers, 33
PostScript, 29, 31-32, 33-34, 123
Printer Control Language (PCL), 31
resolution, 30

printers, *(cont.)*
resources, 34
scanners, adding scanning capabilities, 34
shared printers, 33
smart shopping tips, 31
speed of printing, 30-31
typefaces, 33
Windows, 34
PrintSprint, 34
ProArt, 133
problem office areas and solutions, 5-6
big or oversized rooms, 6
high ceilings, 6
irregular walls in office, 6
low ceilings, 5-6
narrow rooms, 6
noise control, 6
small or undersized rooms, 6
Procomm Plus, 155
Procomm Plus for Windows, 153
Prodigy, 79-80, 80-81, 82, 83
Prodigy Made Easy, 86
Profit for Windows, 145-146
protocols, modems, 44
PSI Net, 87
Publish-It Easy, 154
Publish-It, 133

Q

QEMM-386, 155
QIC standard, tape drives, 48
QMS, 34
QuarkXPress, 132, 133
Quarterly No-Load Mutual Fund Update, 108
Quattro Pro for Windows, 108, 143-144
Queblo Images, 132
Quick & Reilly's QuickWay, 107
QuickBooks, 146-147, 153
Quicken, 107, 158
QuickPay, 147-148
QuickTime, 175
QuoteMaster, 108

R

Rabb, Margaret Y., 133
radiation from monitors, 10
back and side emissions, 10
distance of radiation field, 10
extremely low frequency (ELF) radiation, 10
MPR II radiation emission standards, 10
screen covers, 10
very low frequency (VLF) radiation, 10
walls, 10
radio advertising, 117-118
radios, electrical power requirements, **3**
Radius, 28
RAM disks, mobile computing, 66
random access memory (RAM), 19, 20, 21
printers, 30, 32
upgrading, 22
RasterOps, 28
Rathbone, Andy, 24
ReachOut Remote Control, 68
redialing, telephones/communication equipment, 38, 71
Redux, 63
refresh rate, monitors, 28
relational file databases, 91
Reliable Home Office Catalog, 8
remote access, mobile computing, 67, 68
Remotely Possible, 68
removable cartridge drives, 49, 58
Bernoulli drives, 49
capacity, 49
major manufacturers, 51
Syquest drives, 49
resolution
fax machines, 41-42
printers, 30
scanners, 56
Resource Reference Book, 25
retail stores, buying computers, 15
retirement planning, spreadsheets, 104, 105
Retrieve It, 95
Ricoh, 45, 54
Ring King Visables Inc., 8
roaming, cellular phones, 38
Ronstadt's Financials, 108
Rosch, Winn, 25
Ross, Marilyn and Tom, 8
Rothstein, Philip J., 62
RxPC: The Anti-Virus Handbook, 63

S

60 Minutes Towards Computer Literacy, audiotape, 25
SafeWare, 64
sales and marketing, 115-120
books and publications, 119
CD-ROM discs, 120
desktop publishing material, 129-130
direct mail marketing, 118-119
e-mail, 117
faxing, 115-116, 117
broadcast fax, 115
computer faxing, 115
fax-on-demand, 116
illegality of broadcast fax, 115
on- vs. off-site, 116
one-call fax-on-demand, 116
service bureaus, 115-116, 119
standard fax-on-demand, 116
follow-up actions, 116-117
letters, 116-117
market analysis, business plans, 98
radio advertising, 117-118
resources, 119
service bureaus for faxing, 115-116, 119
telephone calls, 117
telephone marketing (telemarketing), 119
Sales on the Line, 120
SAM, 63, 156
ScanCo, 13
ScanCo MacTable, 11, **12**
Scanner Book, The, 56
scanners, 55-56
black-and-white scanners, 55
books about scanners, 56
color scanners, 56
desktop publishing, 123
flatbed scanners, 55
grayscale scanners, 55-56
hand-held, 55
image-editing software, 56
major manufacturers, 56
multimedia presentations, 175, 176
optical character recognition (OCR), 56
options and features, 55
printers with scanning capabilities, 34
resolution, 56
resources, 56
software, 56
scratch pad, cellular phones, 38
searching databases, 92, 93-94
secondhand (used) computers, 16
Sensor I chair, 11, **11**
Sentry Group, 8
service bureaus, faxing, sales and marketing, 115-116, 119
setting up the home office (*see* office setup and design)
shareware, 158
Sharp, 45, 54
Simpson, Alan, 25
SkyTel, 39
Small Time Operator, 107
small-room offices, 6
"smileys," e-mail character code, 85-86
Smith, Cynthia S., 120
Snooper, 63

software, 135-158
accounting/bookkeeping, 98-101, 106
anti-viral software, 59
audio editing software, 175
backup software, 58
business plans, 107
calendars, 95
ClarisWorks for Windows, 151-152
contact list/card file, 95
contact managers, 90
database software (*see* databases)
desktop publishing, 121, 133-134, 148-150
CorelDraw 4, 148-149
PhotoFinish, 149-150
diagnostic programs, 59, 63
fax-modem software, 45
file-recovery, 58
finance, 145-148
Hi Finance, 146
M.Y.O.B, 148
Microsoft Profit for Windows, 145-146
QuickBooks, 146-147
QuickPay, 147-148
illustration software, 133-134
image-editing software, 56, 133, 134
integrated software, 151-152
ClarisWorks for Windows, 151-152
inventory control, 103
investment, 107
modems, 44-45
multimedia presentations, 175, 176
optical character recognition (OCR), 56
paint software, 134
personal information managers (PIM), 89-90, **90**, 95
piracy and viruses, 59-60
remote-access software, 67, 68
retrieval software (*see* databases)
scanners, 56
shareware, 158
spreadsheets, 101-105, 107, 142-145
Lotus 1-2-3, 144-145
Lotus Improv for Windows, 142-143
Quattro Pro for Windows, 143-144
storage devices, 51
tape drives, 47-48
tax-preparation, 109-111, 113
under-$100 programs, 152-155
under-$75, 155-156
under-$50, 156-158
utilities, 139-142
Norton Desktop for DOS, 139-140
PC Tools for Windows, 140-142
XTree for Windows, 140
viruses, 59
word processors, 135-139
Ami Pro, 138-139
MacWrite Pro, 137-138
Microsoft Word, 135-136
WordPerfect, 136-137
Sola Electric, 64
Sony, 28, 175
SoundEdit Pro, 175
spare room as home office, 1
speakers, multimedia presentations, 175
speed calling, telephones/communication equipment, 71
SpinRiteII, 63
spreadsheets, 101-105, 142-145
amortization table, 102
breakeven point, 103
cost of borrowing, PMT function, 101-102, **102**
discounts, 104
increasing sales, 103-104
inflation, 104-105
interest rate, APR function, 103
inventory control, 103
Lotus 1-2-3, 144-145
Lotus Improv for Windows, 142-143
outstanding debt, PV function, 102
Quattro Pro for Windows, 143-144
retirement planning, 104, 105
software, 107
term of loan, 102
Stacker, 154
Stacker for Macintosh, 51
Stacker for Windows and DOS, 51
Stand Up to the IRS, 113
standard fax-on-demand, 116
standby time/talk time, cellular phones, 38
Star Microtronics, 34
Steelcase, 13
Stitt, Martin, 63
storage devices, 47-51
buffers, 51
cache memory, 51
CD-ROM drives, 49-50
compression schemes, pros and cons, 50
data doublers, 50
defragmentation, 50-51
fragmentation of files, 50
hard-drive upgrade
buffers, 51
cache memory, 51
compression schemes, 50
data doublers, 50
defragmentation, 50-51
fragmentation, 50
major manufacturers, 51
removable cartridge drives, 49
resources, 51
software, 51
tape drives, 47-48
strategic plan, business plans, 98
stress, 9
strip office design, 4, **4**
StuffIt Deluxe, 63, 155
Success Inc., 108
Sullivan, Nick, 24
Sunset Publishing, 8
Super VGA (SVGA) monitors, 27
SuperMac, 28
SuperStore Pro, 51
superstores, buying computers, 15-16
suppliers and manufacturers, office furniture and supplies, 8
supplies for the home office, 7-8, 10
surge suppressors, 3, 60
Syquest, 51
System 7, Macintosh, 19
System Sleuth Professional, 63

T

3D Plan, 156
Tandy Corp., 64
tape drives, 47-48, 58
backup system capacity, 48
capacity of tape drives, 47, 48
cartridge formats, QIC vs. non-QIC, 48
format types, 48
hardware data compression, 48
internal vs. external tape drives, 48
major manufacturers, 51
mini vs. standard cartridges, 48
preformatted cartridges, 48
software for tape drives, 47-48
speed of backup, 48
task lighting, 3
taxes, 109-114
associations and agencies, 113
audits, 113
books, 113
deductions
car, 112
home office, 111-112
nonallowable deductions, 112-113
office equipment, supplies, 111-112
electronic filing, 111
expenses, business expenses, 113
Form 8829, Business Use of Home, 112
incorporation vs. taxes, 112
IRS publications, 113, 114

taxes (*cont.*)
recapturing tax dollars, 112
recordkeeping, 112
resources, 113
software, 109-111, 113
adjusting gross income, 110
auditing, 111
buyer's warning, 111
credits/taxes, 111
electronic file, 111
features, 109
forms, 110
help, 110
importing tax data, 109-110
itemized deductions, 110-111
linking schedules, 110
schedules, 110
user tips, 110-111
technical analysis, investing, electronic, 105
Telecommunications Research and Action Center, 73
Telemet America, 108
telephone marketing (telemarketing), 119
telephones/communication equipment, 35-39, 69-73
800 number service, 71
additional phone lines, 69
answering machines, 35-36
AT&T, 71
auto callback, 71
call accounting, 71
call forwarding, 71
call holding, 71
call waiting, 70-71
call-routing, 70
caller ID, 71
car phones, 36
cellular phones (*see* cellular phones)
cordless telephones, 35
databases, auto-dial feature, 92-93
electrical power requirements, *3*
fax machines options, 42-43
fax services, 71
headsets, 35
jacks, 35
local area networks (LAN), 72-73
long distance, 71, 72
major manufacturers, 39
messaging services, 39
mobile computing, 66
networks, small-office networks, 72
online service (*see* online services)
pagers, 36
repeat dialing, 71
resources, 39, 73
ring patterns, distinctive rings, 70
speed calling, 71
three-way calling, 71
voice mail, 69-70
television, electrical power requirements, **3**
templates, desktop publishing, 127
thermal paper, fax machines, 42
three-way calling, telephones/communication equipment, 71
Timbuktu/Remote, 68
Time Is Money, 158
time-index tape recorders, information/time management, 94
TimeWorks, 132
TouchBase, 153
TouchBase Pro, 95
trackballs, 12
transmission rate
fax machines, 41, 42
modems, 43-44
transmit terminal identification, fax machines, 43
travel tips, information/time management, 94
Trendlines Inc., 8
Tripplite, 64
Troubleshooting and Repairing Computer Printers, 34
troubleshooting computers (*see* computers, troubleshooting)
TrueType fonts, 34
TurboTax, 157
TurboTax Personal, 113
Turtle Beach Systems, 175
Type from the Desktop, 133
Type in Use, 133
typefaces, 33
consistency of type, 126
density, 124
desktop publishing, 123-125
display face, 123-124, **124**
mood creation, 124, **124**
nontype elements, 124
orientation of type on sheet, 124
resolution, 124
serif vs. sans serif, 123
shading, 125
text face, 123-124
typewriters, electrical power requirements, **3**

U

U-shaped office design, 4, **6**
uninterruptable power supplies (UPS), 60
United Computer Exchange, 18
Upgrade Your Computer Printer and Save a Bundle, 34
Upgrading and Maintaining & Servicing IBM PCs, 63
US Robotics, 45
used computers, 16
user groups, buying computers, 18
utility software, 139-142
Norton Desktop for DOS, 139-140
PC Tools for Windows, 140-142
XTree for Windows, 140

V

V.42bis data-compression standard, modems, 44
Valitek, 51
Value/Screen II, 108
Vaughan, Tay, 175
VCRs, multimedia presentations, 175, 176
Vector Art, 133
vendors, buying computers, 15
Ventana Press Computer Guides, 25
Ventura Software, 132
Venture, 108
Venture Horizon Corporation, 8
VGA monitors, 27
Vickman, Thomas, 113
video adapter boards, multimedia presentations, 175, 176
video cards, monitors, 27-28
video display terminals (*see* monitors)
Video for Windows, 175
VideoLogic Inc., 175
videotape production (*see* multimedia presentations)
ViewSonic, 28
Virex, 63, 154
viruses, 59-60
voice mail, 69-70
voice/data switch, fax machines, 43

W

Wall Street Journal, The, 107
WealthBuilder by Money Magazine, 155
WealthBuilder/Smart Investor, 108
WELL, The, 87
Western Telematic, 34
Wet-Paint, 133
White, Alex, 133
White, Jan, 132
Whole Earth Online Almanac, The, 86
WillMaker, 156

Windows, 19, 20
printers, 34
Windows Draw Plus OLE, 154
Windows NT, 20
WinEdit, 158
WinFax Pro Windows, 155
WinGRAB, 158
WinJet printers, 34
Winn Rosch Hardware Bible, The, 25
Winning Forms, 133
WinSleuth Gold, 63
WinSpeed, 155
Winston, Stephanie, 8, 13
Wood, Robert, 113
Word (*see* Microsoft Word)
word processor software, 135-139
Ami Pro, 138-139
MacWrite Pro, 137-138
Microsoft Word, 135-136
WordPerfect, 119, 136-137
WordPerfect, 119, 136-137
WorkAbles for Women catalog makeover, 159-164, **160-164**
World Data Delivery Service, 119
wrist rests, 12, *13*

X

Xerox, 45, 54
XTree for Windows, 63, 140, 154
XTree Gold, 63, 154

Y

Your First Computer, 25

Z

Ziff Communications Co., 24